TAKING
LIBERTIES

TAKING LIBERTIES

A DECADE OF HARD CASES, BAD LAWS, AND BUM RAPS

ALAN M. DERSHOWITZ

CONTEMPORARY
BOOKS

CHICAGO · NEW YORK

Library of Congress Cataloging-in-Publication Data

Dershowitz, Alan M.
　　Taking liberties : a decade of hard cases, bad laws, and
bum raps / Alan M. Dershowitz.
　　　　p.　　cm.
　　Includes index.
　　ISBN 0-8092-4616-3 : $19.95
　　　　1. Justice, Administration of—United States—Cases.　　2. Civil
rights—United States—Cases.　　3. Justice and politics—United
States—Cases.　　I. Title.
KF384.A7D47　　1988
342.73'085—dc19

88-2716
CIP

Published by Contemporary Books, Inc.
180 North Michigan Avenue, Chicago, Illinois 60601
Manufactured in the United States of America
Library of Congress Catalog Card Number: 88-2716
International Standard Book Number: 0-8092-4616-3

Published simultaneously in Canada by Beaverbooks, Ltd.
195 Allstate Parkway, Valleywood Business Park
Markham, Ontario L3R 4T8 Canada

To my judicial mentors Chief Judge David Bazelon and Justice Arthur Goldberg, for whom I was privileged to clerk and from whom I have learned—and continue to learn—so much about justice, liberty, compassion, and decency.

Contents

TAKING
LIBERTIES

Introduction

This book is about how the law, in the broadest sense of that word, impacts on your everyday life. It is designed to help you understand—and protect yourself against—court decisions, legislation, lawsuits and other legal and political events that affect you in big ways and in small ways. It seeks to demystify our legal system so that we, the consumers of justice and injustice, can regain control over what is rightfully ours: our constitution, our laws and our courts.

Alexis de Tocqueville, the great chronicler of 19th-century America, observed that in our country nearly every great issue eventually finds its way into the courts. If that was true in the 19th century, how much truer it has become as we begin our third century under the most enduring written Constitution in history.

The American legal establishment—judges, private lawyers, government attorneys—is the most powerful in the history of the world. There has never been a society with more lawyers per capita—one for nearly every 350 Americans. Nor has there been a nation in which judges wielded more power over the daily lives of its citizens.

No country in the history of the world has ever given more power to its lawyers, and especially to its judges—the most important of whom are appointed for life and not accountable to the electorate in any way. It is not surprising that Tocqueville saw the lawyer and judges in the new republic as the American aristocracy. Judges, with the help of lawyers—sometimes despite their hindrance—decide the most fundamental and far-reaching issues of our time: abortion, capital punishment, censorship, religion in public life, the disposal of nuclear wastes—even, on occasion, war and peace.

They also decide the most intimate and personal issues that may have profound effects on individual litigants: divorce, custody, termination of life support systems. The remarkable thing about our legal establishment is that despite its enormous power—perhaps, in part, because of it—it is essentially a secret society. Outsiders, that is, most citizens, know little about how our legal system and courts operate. We are a government of laws, but we are also a government of men and women. It makes all the difference which judge is deciding a case or issue.

Our judges reflect their personal backgrounds, idiosyncrasies and biases. A Supreme Court justice with daughters active in the pro-choice movement is more likely to strike down antiabortion laws than a justice with a fundamentalist religious upbringing. A judge who has been a private attorney for insurance companies may be less sympathetic to an injured worker than a judge with a labor union background. A judge who has lived all his life in an homogeneous small town is likely to be less understanding of those who oppose the establishment of religion.

That is why I decided to write a weekly syndicated column that would be accessible to the consumers of American justice—those most directly affected by the tangle of often incomprehensible court decisions. And that is why I decided to compile these columns into a single book which discusses in roughly chronological fashion, many of the most important legal developments of this decade—developments that have continuing importance in the day-to-day life of all Americans.

Inevitably, these columns cover the major legal controversies of our times—the Iran-contra scandal, the confirmation battles over Supreme Court nominees, the dangers to civil liberties (as well as to public health) from the AIDS epidemic, the raging debates over the death penalty, pornography, rape, abortion, homosexuality, church and state, the exclusionary rule, white-collar crime, terrorism, vigilantism, and affirmative action.

In responding to these current issues the columns also seek to address more enduring concerns such as the conflicts between privacy and public morality, between the means and the ends of justice, between liberty and security, between freedom and license, between individualism and paternalism, between equality and meritocracy, between legalism and vigilantism, and between consistency and hypocrisy.

The columns try to anticipate how our legal system is likely to respond to new challenges posed by changing technology, science, and human needs—how the law will serve or disserve our children and grandchildren.

The columns that are collected in this book appeared in newspapers throughout the country—from Boston (*Boston Herald*), to Los Angeles (*Los Angeles Times*), San Francisco (*San Francisco Chronicle*), Chicago (*Chicago Sun-Times*), Charleston (*Charleston Post-News and Courier*), Seattle (*Seattle Times*), and Washington, DC (*Washington Times*). They are presented with few changes, some updates and a small number of chronological rearrangements. Not all have appeared in every paper. The readers of this book can get an overview of the important issues of this decade through the lens of a single observer. I am, to be sure, an observer with a point of view, and that point of view comes through loud and clear—and, hopefully, with a sense of humor.

These columns present an insider's view of the most secret, but most influential, branch of government: from the Supreme Court in Washington to the local magistrate's court in your neighborhood, from the high-priced law firms to the rundown police stations. They are written from the perspective of the consumers of justice (and injustice), not the producers. They explain, expose, criticize, applaud, and occasionally even gossip about the decisions, the people, and institutions that affect our lives as consumers of the law.

This book tries to do for our legal establishment what investigative journalists such as Jack Anderson, Roger Mudd, Sam Donaldson, and Mike Wallace have done for, and to, the executive and legislative branches.

It rails against efforts by the organized bar—the private lawyers' organizations—to maintain high costs for routine legal services, such as wills, uncontested divorces, house sales, and minor injuries. It begins with the story of the Florida legal secretary who faced a jail sentence for violating a court order prohibiting her from selling inexpensive "kits"—forms and instructions—for simple legal matters. In that case, the judges who upheld her sentence were not helping the consumers; they were protecting, in the worst sense, their fellow lawyers' ability to charge professional fees for routine work that does not require a lawyer's expertise. It ends with a plea for a greater commitment to public service by the next generation of lawyers.

I try to predict the effect of current Supreme Court decisions such as the recent ruling that nativity scenes may be maintained by cities and towns as part of seasonal Christmas celebrations. Will that decision require towns to open their parks and squares to all religious symbols, even unpopular and bizarre ones? What about antireligious symbols?

I try to anticipate the effects of personnel changes on our High Court, such as the resignation of Justice Powell, the defeat of Judge Bork, and the confirmation of Justice Kennedy.

I report about developments that are important to all Americans, but are not covered in newspapers or television reports—obscure legislation or litigation that can have profound impact on consumer safety, environmental hazards and the price of services and goods.

The columns try to pose difficult dilemmas confronted by citizens caught up in the law's workings: What would you do if a judge gave you a choice between going to jail or becoming a witness against your parent, child, or lover? Should you submit to a random drug test even if you never puffed on a joint? Can you "prepare" for such a test? What are your rights as a smoker or nonsmoker? Are they different if you are a pregnant woman? Are you obliged to submit to a random road block? Should you turn on your headlights to warn oncoming traffic of a police speed trap? May you be compelled to wear a seat belt? If you don't can a driver whose car injures—or kills—you, raise your unbuckled seat belt as a defense or mitigation? Can you trust your lawyer to keep your secrets? Can the government find out which home videos you have rented? May Madonna prevent *Playboy* magazine from publishing nude pictures she once posed for? Can a professional athlete get arrested for starting a fight in the middle of a game? Should sexist or racist jokes be banned?

I try to answer these and other questions while explaining legal developments as they occur. I try to be the reader's advocate—an insider with an outsider's perspective, a producer who understands the consumer's point of view.

April 14, 1988

1
The Crime of Helping the Poor

The Florida bar's persecution of Rosemary Furman may help to explain why so many Americans hate lawyers, and why so few can afford them.

Ms. Furman used to be a legal secretary in Jacksonville, Florida. While working for several lawyers, she learned one of the deep, dark secrets of the law profession: much of the work for which lawyers charge unaffordable fees—often in excess of $100 per hour—is routine and requires no legal training, expertise, or judgment.

Simple wills, name changes, adoptions, and uncontested divorces—to mention just a few—can be accomplished by the parties themselves with the help of a few standard forms. Lawyers store these forms in word processors. Their legal secretaries retrieve them with the press of a key, then fill in the blanks by following simple instructions.

Ms. Furman had done this hundreds of times, then sent outrageous legal bills to clients for the secretarial work. She saw that many poor people couldn't afford their high-priced legal services.

When several battered wives tried to file complaints themselves, they were rebuffed by the police and court clerks because the forms were not in proper order. (Court clerks can sometimes be protective of the lawyers who practice in their courts.) Ms. Furman decided to try to help these women.

She prepared "kits"—basic forms—for a few routine legal proceedings and completed them for $50 each, a fraction of what lawyers charge for the same service. Those who couldn't afford the $50 were charged less—some nothing.

Ms. Furman's customers loved her for making their rights affordable. And she never misled them into thinking she was a lawyer, nor did she offer legal advice. She merely provided forms and instructions for self-filers and filled in the forms for those who lacked the literacy to do so.

But the Florida bar saw her as a threat to its pocketbook and decided to put her out of business. So the members of the legal club—private lawyers, prosecutors, judges, bar moguls—convened a kangaroo court. They charged Rosemary Furman with contempt of court for practicing law without a license.

By using the "contempt" vehicle, they were able to manipulate the system so that only lawyers would sit in judgment of her—rather than a jury of her peers, which might be sympathetic to her plight. (The law says that trial by jury is not required for contempt if the punishment is less than six months in jail.)

The result was that everyone involved in her persecution was a member of the legal club. Not surprisingly, she was convicted, and a sentence of four months in jail was recommended. Her crime: helping the poor to help themselves. Her real sin: challenging the monopoly that lawyers have given themselves over access to the courts.

Let there be no mistake: the legal profession *is* a monopoly. Only lawyers can represent people before the courts; only lawyers can help people prepare and file certain documents; only lawyers can give—sell—advice about legal issues. Indeed, until recently, lawyers could—and did—get together to fix prices for their services, but never maximum prices: only minimum prices. That is no longer permitted, but other monopolistic abuses contribute to the increasing price of legal services.

Most monopolies must, at the very least, attempt to provide services to a broad spectrum of consumers. But the organized bar has done precious little to assure that middle-class and working people—not to mention welfare mothers and laid-off workers—can protect their legal rights. In fact, the bulk of lawyers' time goes into representing a tiny segment of our country: the rich and superrich.

There have been some recent, small-scale improvements: walk-in law clinics that charge reasonable rates for routine services, prepaid legal-service contracts for employees, legal aid for the poor. But these have just begun to scratch the surface, and, indeed, many aspects of legal aid are being curtailed. More—much more—is needed, both for poor and working Americans.

And unless lawyers can figure out ways to provide needed legal services for all who require them, they will have no legitimate complaint against enterprising competitors like Rosemary Furman.

In the end, Ms. Furman and others who are following her path are not taking business away from lawyers. They are filling an important void left by a profession that has been unwilling to serve the poor.

Ms. Furman's four-month jail sentence was recently appealed. The Florida Supreme Court reduced it to thirty days in jail and ninety days of probation, conditioned on her going out of business.

But Ms. Furman has not given up her fight. She is taking her case—and her cause—to the U.S. Supreme Court. Perhaps the justices in Washington will understand that far more is at stake than her freedom (important as that is). The rights of all citizens—poor as well as rich—to redress their grievances in court may suffer a significant setback if Ms. Furman is sent to jail for helping people help themselves.

June 12, 1984

UPDATE
The U.S. Supreme Court denied review of Ms. Furman's case, but in November 1984, Florida governor Bob Graham granted her clemency and commuted her jail sentence. The president of the Florida Bar complained that the governor's decision was "political." The rules prohibiting non-lawyers from helping indigents are still in effect in Florida and most other states.

2
Supreme Court Ends Law Firm Discrimination

The Supreme Court's decision (May 22, 1984) outlawing discrimination in law partnerships may finally put an end to one of the worst shames of the American legal system: segregated law firms. I experienced the problem myself more than two decades ago when I was a student at Yale Law School.

I applied for jobs with several dozen prestigious law firms on Wall Street. Since my grades were good and I was an editor of the *Law Journal*, I naively assumed the firms would be eager to have me work for them. To my surprise, every one of them turned me down. To my shock, only a few tried to hide the reason: the firms were white Anglo-Saxon, and I am Jewish.

The fact that this was several years after *Brown* v. *Board of Education* had mandated desegregation of public schools seemed to have no impact on most lawyers, even those who had championed civil rights. Law firms, I was told, were different: they were more like families or social clubs, less like businesses or schools. Nor did the bar associations make any effort to integrate the firms; indeed, they implicitly accepted the reality of segregation—by religion, race, and gender—in the practice of law. And so, chastised and a bit disillusioned, I went to work for a "Jewish" law firm on Park Avenue.

Within a few years, much of that had changed—but only in relation to Jews. Many prestigious firms opened their doors to Jewish law graduates. But the principle remained the same: the firms still felt free—and were free—to discriminate against Catholics, blacks, women, and any group regarded as "different" from the mainstream.

And discriminate they did—especially in promoting associates to partners. Although 30 percent of the associates in giant law firms are now women, only 5 percent of the partners are of that gender. This reflects partly, but only partly, the recent influx of women into the law profession. The number of Italian-American, black, and Hispanic lawyers who have been made partners in large law firms is also tiny.

Indeed, several years ago, I filed a lawsuit on behalf of an Italian-American who alleged that one of the nation's most distinguished law firms—one of those which had turned me down a decade earlier—had failed to promote him from associate to partner because of his ethnic and religious background. The firm denied the charges, but argued—in "principle"—that they were entitled to discriminate in the selection of partners.

Finally, on May 22, 1984, the Supreme Court issued a landmark decision authoritatively rejecting that "principle" and holding that law partnerships—at least those with fifteen or more employees—are required by law not to discriminate in the promotion of associates to partners. The law, written by lawyers, was finally being applied to them.

The case that gave rise to this momentous decision involved a woman named Elizabeth Hishon, a graduate of Columbia University School of Law who was hired as an associate—an employee—of one of Atlanta's most prestigious firms, King & Spaulding. Among the partners in that firm was the former attorney general of the United States, Griffin Bell, who had fought for integration in schools, businesses, and other institutions of American life, but whose law firm held social events at country clubs that excluded blacks, Jews, and women.

Ms. Hishon claims that when she was hired as an associate back in 1972, she was promised she would be considered for promotion to partnership "on a fair and equal basis," without regard to her gender. Perhaps she should have been somewhat skeptical, since the firm had never promoted a woman to partnership. But the situation was changing in Atlanta, and the presence of several prominent "liberals" in the firm probably encouraged her to take the promise at face value. Six years later, she was rejected for partnership and was asked to leave the firm.

But Ms. Hishon had learned something important during her six years: a lawyer who believes she was discriminated against does not have to take "no" for an answer—she has legal remedies under the Civil Rights Act of 1964. And so Ms. Hishon, after becoming a partner in another Atlanta law firm, went to court and sued her former employers.

She lost the first two rounds: the lower federal courts ruled that a law firm was like a family and "to coerce a mismatch" would resemble "a shotgun wedding." But Ms. Hishon persisted. She asked the U.S. Supreme Court to review her case, and the high court agreed. The stage was thus set for the important decision.

In unanimously ruling in Ms. Hishon's favor, the Supreme Court did not actually find that she had been the victim of discrimination. All it said was that partnerships—as a matter of law—are not entitled to discriminate in their promotion decisions. It will now be up to a trial judge or jury to determine, as a matter of fact, whether she was turned down for partnership because she was a woman or for some other, legitimate, reason.

Although the media has widely misunderstood the Hishon decision as dealing specifically with the rights of women, that is not its major significance. It applies equally to blacks, Hispanics, Moslems, or any group protected by the Civil Rights Act. The importance of the decision is that it construes the act's antidiscrimination provision to cover promotion from employee to partner. Since the partnership form is the way in which many law, architecture, accounting, and engineering firms are organized, the Hishon case has significance both beyond women and beyond law.

It will still be an uphill fight to prove that the promotion was not denied for entirely legitimate reasons. And many more who were, in fact, passed over for discriminatory reasons will not have the resources or tenacity to challenge their employers. It takes a great deal of courage and self-assurance to open one's career and life to the public scrutiny of a trial.

June 19, 1984

UPDATE
A month after the Supreme Court's landmark ruling, Ms. Hishon and the law firm settled the case for an undisclosed amount of money. Ms. Hishon is currently a partner in another Atlanta law firm. Her former firm, King & Spaulding, now has several women partners.

3
A Requiem for the Exclusionary Rule

The Supreme Court's fifteen-year offensive against the so-called "exclusionary rule" is assuming D-Day proportions.

The exclusionary rule is a simple, though extremely controversial, doctrine. In essence, it tells the police that if they gather evidence illegally, they won't be able to use it against criminals in court. It is like a mother warning her errant child, "If I catch you stealing candy from the corner store, I'm not going to let you eat it."

But the rule is controversial precisely because it doesn't involve candy-store theft. The stakes are much higher: police violations of our Bill of Rights and the occasional freeing of guilty and dangerous criminals.

The Supreme Court recently issued two decisions undercutting the exclusionary rule, and more seem to be on the way. The cases themselves are somewhat complex, but their bottom-line message to the police is clear: the red light against constitutional violations has been changed to a yellow "caution" light, and soon it may be changed to a green light. Although the mother is still lecturing her child not to steal the candy, she is letting him eat more and more of it—and soon she may tell him he can have it all.

Before we complete the obituary for the much-maligned exclusionary rule, let us remember how it came into being and what it is supposed to do.

The U.S. Constitution doesn't tell us how to deal with illegally obtained evidence. The Fourth Amendment does prohibit the police from searching without probable cause, and the Fifth Amendment outlaws compelled self-incrimination. But the framers of our Constitution left it to future generations of lawmakers to develop fair and effective remedies for guaranteeing that these important rights are enforced in practice. For years, the courts condemned police violations of these rights, but they simultaneously opened their doors to the illegally obtained evidence. The message they sent to the police was confused and ambiguous: "Don't get evidence that way, but if you do, we will be happy to use it." The mother was yelling at her child for stealing the candy, but then she was feeding it to him.

Finally, in 1961—after decades of talking out of both sides of its judicial mouth—the Supreme Court sent one clear message to the police of every state. In the Mapp decision, written by former U.S. Attorney General Tom Clark, it ruled that keeping the courtroom door open to illegally obtained evidence "tends to destroy the entire system of constitutional restraints on which the liberties of the people rest." Pretty strong words for a man who had spent most of his life on the side of law enforcement and police! But Justice Clark understood the hypocrisy of promising liberty and denying it at the same time. He concluded that "we can no longer permit [the Bill of Rights] to remain an empty promise."

After Warren Burger replaced Earl Warren as chief justice in 1969, the entire tone of the court's approach to the Bill of Rights changed. The Burger Court has chipped away at the exclusionary rule—carving out so many exceptions that it is falling of its own weight. Policemen today figure that they might as well get the evidence by any means—legal or illegal—since the court is likely to find some exception under which it can be used.

It is against this background that the current Supreme Court decisions can be understood.

In *Nix* v. *Williams*, the defendant was arrested for murdering a ten-year-old girl. His lawyer advised him not to answer any questions, as was his right under the "privilege against self-incrimination." The police then took the defendant for a drive, promising that they would not ask him any questions without the lawyer being there. But they broke their promise and pleaded with him to locate the girl's body so that she could be given "a Christian burial." The defendant broke down and led the police to the body.

The Supreme Court concluded that the questioning violated his constitutional rights, but that the body could be introduced at the trial because it probably would have been found legally, even if the police had not engaged in their improper interrogation. This time, it is as if the kid stole the candy, then persuaded his mother to let him eat it because he could have bought it legally if he hadn't chosen to steal.

The second decision—*New York* v. *Quarles*—has even greater potential impact. A defendant was arrested by the police and frisked. The police found an empty shoulder holster. Without giving him his *Miranda* warnings—"You have the right not to answer any questions without a lawyer," etc.—they asked him where the gun was. He pointed to some empty cartons, where the gun was located. The gun, as well as the defendant's statements, were used against him.

The Supreme Court, in a far-reaching decision, ruled that the police can ask questions without first giving *Miranda* warnings when their questions are "prompted by a concern for the public safety." This vague criterion—"public safety"—creates an exception to the *Miranda* rule wide enough to drive a paddy wagon through. The police always believe that the public safety is involved when they make an arrest. Here we have the mother telling the child not to steal the candy—"unless you get really hungry."

Our twenty-five-year experiment with the exclusionary rule may well be coming to an end. We have learned precious little from it, because the exclusionary rule was never really given a chance. The public, spurred by politicians' rhetoric, closed its eyes and ears to facts like the following: that only a tiny fraction of defendants (less than half of one percent, according to a federal study) are freed because of the exclusionary rule; and that there has been a marked improvement both in police efficiency and in compliance with the Constitution since the exclusionary rule was established.

If Justice Tom Clark was right when he warned that opening the courtroom doors to illegally obtained evidence tends to destroy liberties, then we shouldn't rush to applaud the demise of the exclusionary rule.

June 24, 1984

See next column as well as columns 7, 8, 43, 50, 89, 91, 105, 109, and 140.

4
A Matter of Good Faith

A month after Richard Nixon was inaugurated as president, he invited a federal appeals court judge named Warren Burger to the White House to swear in several government officials. Never one to miss a chance, Judge Burger took with him an article he had published in *U.S. News and World Report* entitled "What to Do About Crime in U.S.—a Federal Judge Speaks." With an imminent vacancy in the chief justiceship, the article was in the nature of a platform on which Burger was running for the job. Presidential assistant John Ehrlichman is reported to have commented that if ever a man was campaigning for the chief justiceship, it was Warren Burger. And President Nixon was duly impressed with Burger's tough law-and-order views. He had copies of the article circulated among the White

House staff. Several months later—on May 21, 1969—President Nixon appointed Warren E. Burger chief justice.

Now, fifteen years later, Chief Justice Burger has lived up to many of his platform pledges.

Among Burger's planks was a promise to take a hard look at the so-called "exclusionary rule": Should we continue, he asked, to "afford the accused more procedural protections, such as the exclusion and suppression of evidence . . . than under any other system?"

The Burger Court has certainly devoted a great deal of attention to questioning the so-called "exclusionary rule." On the last day of Burger's fifteenth term, the court rendered two precedent-shattering decisions which, in the words of dissenting Justice William Brennan, mark the *pièce de résistance* of the Burger Court's complete "victory over the Fourth Amendment."

These decisions reflect the penultimate movement of a symphony carefully orchestrated by the chief justice. The finale is yet to come. But its closing crescendo has already been adumbrated by the earlier movements.

In last week's decisions, the court "modified" the seventy-year-old exclusionary rule "so as not to bar the use . . . of evidence obtained by [police] officers acting in reasonable reliance on a search warrant [that is] ultimately found to be [invalid]." In plain English, this means that if the police can talk a magistrate into issuing a questionable search warrant—which police can often do with little difficulty—they can then hide behind that fancy piece of paper, conduct illegal searches, and use the evidence.

The specific rulings in these two cases are fairly debatable, especially in the context of the facts before the court: both cases involved obviously guilty defendants and fairly "technical" violations of the warrant requirement. It is the process by which the court arrived at this long-predicted modification of the exclusionary rule that raises the most profound questions about judicial integrity. Again in the words of Justice Brennan: "It is clear that we have not been treated to an honest assessment of the merits of the exclusionary rule . . ." but instead to judicial sleight of hand under which arguments in support of the rule "are made to disappear with a mere wave of the hand."

Looking behind the facade of legal citations and precedents, this—in a nutshell—is the illusion that the Supreme Court employed to misdirect the public's attention away from the real issues surrounding the merits of the exclusionary rule.

In the beginning was the basic exclusionary rule: simple, clear, easy to explain to the police and the public. If the government obtained the evidence unconstitutionally, then the government would not be able to use that evidence in a criminal trial. Then the limitations and exceptions began: the illegally obtained evidence could be used against defendants other than the one from whom it was obtained; it could be used if the defendant took the witness stand; it could be used by the grand jury.

Having muddied the waters by a series of confusing interpretations, some of the justices began to complain that the rule was no longer clear—that the waters were indeed muddy. Since there were already so many exceptions to the exclusionary rule, they argued, it would do no further harm to add yet another one. Justice Brennan described this process as the "gradual but determined strangulation of the exclusionary rule."

The current exception—the good faith warrant exception—was a bit different from previous ones: it required an explicit overruling of nearly seventy years of precedent. For a court that claims to believe in judicial restraint—in the force of past precedent—so many years of decisional law should have constituted a formidable barrier to so sharp a change. But the court expressed little hesitation; indeed, it reached out and decided the issue with apparent relish.

It did wait, of course, for the perfect cases on which to illustrate the problems of exclusionary rule. As Oliver Wendell Holmes once said, "Hard cases . . . make bad law." And these were hard cases indeed for supporters of the exclusionary rule. The Massachusetts case involved a man suspected of multiple murders. The police had probable cause to secure a proper warrant, but the correct form was not available. So the magistrate sloppily used a drug-search form that authorized the police to look for "any controlled substances," when they were seeking evidence of murder. The California case, on the other hand, involved a drug search, but the warrant was based largely on information provided by a "confidential informant of unproven reliability."

Had the court carved out a narrow exception tailored to the specific facts of these cases, there would be some grumbling from civil libertarians, but little outcry. The court could have, for example, limited its holding—as Justice Stevens apparently would have—to situations in which the police have probable cause but use the wrong forms. This would have resulted in admission of the evidence in the Massachusetts case, but exclusion in the California case.

Instead, the court painted with a broad brush. It ruled that the exclusionary rule is generally not applicable in the wide, and potentially expandable, category of cases in which magistrates issue defective warrants. This ruling will, as Justice Brennan correctly pointed out, "convey a clear and unambiguous message to magistrates that their decisions to issue warrants are now insulated from judicial review." These magistrates, some of whom already hand out warrants as if they were candy at Christmas, may now apply even looser standards. Police have wide choices among the magistrates from whom they can request a warrant. They will shop around for the "easiest" magistrates, with the added assurance that once they have the warrant in their hot hands, the evidence will be admissible no matter how invalid the warrant may later turn out to be.

When the solicitor general of the United States was asked whether these decisions will result in more warrants being issued, his answer was, "I hope so." His logic is that even civil libertarians prefer searches conducted pursuant to warrants than searches conducted without them. But this misses the crucial point: if warrants are now issued without probable cause, then they will become meaningless wallpaper covering up massive violations of all of our rights.

If the police illegally break into your home or office (or telephone line) and rummage through your papers or medicine cabinet (or eavesdrop on personal conversations), it is small solace that they came bearing an invalid warrant received from a sympathetic magistrate. The Bill of Rights is too important—for the innocent as well as the guilty—to be left to the unbridled discretion of a hand-picked magistrate.

But even more extensive modifications may be on the way, if Justice Brennan's gloomy prophecies come to pass. The seventy-eight-year-old justice worries that "the exception unleashed" in these decisions "may well be extended" to situations in which the police have conducted a warrantless search solely on the basis of their own judgment. . . ."

If the Burger Court continues to riddle the exclusionary rule with broader and broader exceptions, a time will come when the justices may step back and look at the rule itself and declare triumphantly—if a bit cynically—that since the exceptions have left so little of the rule, there is no reason for preserving it at all. This would mark the fulfillment of Warren Burger's platform promises—and one of the most enduring, if pernicious, legacies of Richard Nixon's failed presidency.

July 6, 1984

UPDATE
To date, the exclusionary rule has managed to hang on, albeit with somewhat weakened force. For an example of its application to a criminal defendant, see column 140.

5
The Rights of Embryos

Can the law keep up with life? That is the broad question raised by recent developments in genetics and biology.

The immediate event provoking the controversy is the Australian "test-tube babies" program in which an American couple, named Rios, had enrolled during 1981. Several of Mrs. Rios's eggs were removed and put in a culture dish—"in vitro." One was then reimplanted in Mrs. Rios's womb, but she miscarried. Two remaining embryos were then frozen in liquid nitrogen and stored away for possible later implantation into another woman.

But life—and death—play unkind tricks. While the embryos remained in a state of suspended animation, the Rioses were killed in a plane crash, leaving a valuable estate.

This bizarre combination of circumstances—frozen life, violent death, and a great deal of money—could not help but fuel our collective imagination. And so the parade of pundits began. The Reverend Jerry Falwell declared that it's wrong for doctors to delve into "an area far too sacred for human beings to be involved in." Some antiabortionists—though opposed to artificial fertilization—said they would go to any lengths to protect the life of the existing embryos. (This may create a conflict for those who oppose both implanting embryos into a different carrier and permitting embryos to die.) A few pro-choice advocates wondered why so much attention was being devoted to a couple of frozen cells when real children go to bed hungry.

As with most controversial issues at the core of human existence, there are no perfect answers. Indeed, we haven't even been able to frame the questions properly. As Oliver Wendell Holmes once put it: "The life of the law has not been logic; it has been experience." And the fantastic experiences of our most innovative laboratories have been racing ahead of the capacity of our lawyers, philosophers, and theologians to apply the dry logic of traditional disciplines to developments that were unimaginable even a few years ago.

That isn't to say, however, that traditional morality and legality will have nothing to offer. They surely will, since global issues of life and death have been at the center of moral and legal discourse.

Consider the rather mundane issue of whether the existence of live embryos should affect the disposition of the Rioses' estate. This is the question—peripheral as it may seem in the large scale of things—that immediately captured the media's attention.

Some guidance is provided by traditional rules of law. What, after all, is the primary purpose of the law of estates? Quite simply, it's to see to it that, so far as possible, the wishes of those who died are carried out. Of course, that goal isn't always possible. Sometimes the desires of the dead are impossible to know. Other times, although we know them, we cannot—or should not—carry them out, because they violate important principles of public policy.

In this case, the Rioses left no will, nor did they leave any clear indications whether they wanted "their" embryos to be born and be regarded as "their children." It should be of no significance that Mrs. Rios's eggs may have been fertilized by the sperm of a donor rather than her husband. The law does not generally inquire as to whose sperm fertilized the egg, even when more conventional processes of fertilization are employed. In fact, the relevant Australian law expressly provides that a sperm donor has no parental rights or interests in his genetic offspring once he has made his "donation" to a married couple.

The major legal wrinkle in the Rios case does not, however, involve any dispute over *paternity*; the dispute—if one develops—will be over *maternity*. The frozen embryo can become a living child only if it is implanted in another woman. If the child is then born, there will have been two biological mothers: the genetic mother, whose eggs were used to begin life; and the carrying mother, whose womb was used to nurture and produce life.

It's likely that the law will declare the carrying mother to be the child's legal mother, especially if the genetic mother is dead. But what if the genetic parents sign a contract with the carrying mother, paying her to carry the embryo and to give up any legal rights of motherhood? Will such a contract be enforceable or will it be voided as against public policy? I suspect that it will be regarded as enforceable, at least under certain circumstances.

So science will continue to march on. It will boggle the imagination with increasing rapidity. The law will never be able to anticipate its progress (or regress). Nor will the law ever be able to create life. It can destroy life. It can make it difficult. Perhaps it can enhance its quality just a bit.

The best proof of the peripheral role of law is the reality that surrounds the Rios case. Oceans of ink will be spilled regarding the implications of the embryos growing into people. But the reality is that the Rioses' embryos will almost certainly die a "natural" death because of scientific inadequacies. As they die, the lawyers, theologians, and philosophers will stand by helplessly.

July 10, 1984

UPDATE
The embryos are apparently still "alive," though a committee of legal experts, philosophers, theologians, and scientists have recommended that Australian law authorize "embryo destruction." See column 22.

6
Serving "One for the Road" May Be Costly

You serve your neighbor a couple of scotches. He drives away tipsy and runs into someone. The victim sues not only the drunk driver, but you, too. To add insult to injury, your neighbor—the one to whom you served the scotches—sues you as well.

Can they collect? If this kind of liability isn't covered by your insurance, can they take away your home, your car, your children's college tuition money?

In New Jersey, at least, the answer may be yes. On June 28, 1984, in a precedent-breaking ruling, that state's highest court held that a couple who sat around for an hour or two drinking scotch with a business associate then watched him drive off, were financially liable when the drunken business associate injured a woman in a head-on collision.

Although this specific decision was unprecedented and is limited to New Jersey, it reflects a growing national trend. The trend is to stretch the law—both civil and criminal—further and further back in time to try to get to the real sources of the problem. In the context of drunken driving, the law has moved back from the driver himself to the professional bartender who should have known better than to serve him that last one for the road, to the host who serves liquor to a minor—and now to the businessman who drinks with his adult guest.

Chief Justice Robert N. Wilentz—who wrote the New Jersey decision—realized that he was expanding the law quite dramatically. But he obviously believes that this change will be acceptable to a public that is fed up with drunken driving and wants to get at the source of the problem. "This court senses," he said, "that there may be a substantial change occurring in social attitudes and customs concerning drinking, whether at home or in taverns."

What Wilentz really seems to be hoping is that decisions of this kind will help accelerate that change. The message it sends to those who serve alcohol is: you are your brothers' and sisters' keepers. You will be required to keep tabs on the number of drinks you serve those who are about to get behind the wheel of a lethal weapon. It will cost you—perhaps dearly—if you adopt the attitude that if your guest wants to get drunk, that's his problem. Now, it may also be your problem.

Wilentz's decision will certainly encourage hosts to say no, or perhaps even to offer to pay for a cab. The case itself seems to be limited to civil liability in the context of small social interactions where hosts can be expected to monitor their guests' condition and intake; however, it will not require a giant step to extend it to larger parties.

Nor is it likely that this decision will remain limited to New Jersey. If Wilentz is correct in sensing "a substantial change . . . in social attitudes," that change may soon reflect itself in the decisions of other states. Hosts throughout the nation are now on notice that serving one for the road may be costly.

Perhaps the most controversial aspect of this developing trend toward extending liability further and further backwards is the imposition of serious criminal penalties on those who serve drinks. Several states are now considering the prosecution of bartenders for manslaughter, if their customers are involved in fatal accidents after a night at the bar. And in a variation on this theme, Florida prosecutors are investigating the drug dealers who sold David Kennedy the cocaine that contributed to his death.

Such dealers are, of course, guilty of the felony of selling cocaine. But they may now be prosecuted for the far more serious crime of felony murder. Felony murder, which frequently carries the death penalty, simply means that as a result of a dangerous felony (in this case, sale of cocaine), a death resulted. It is no defense to argue that you did not intend or expect anyone to die. The fact that you sold the drugs to someone who took them and died may be enough to send you to the electric chair (or whatever newfangled method of execution your state is using).

No one has yet been sentenced to death for selling drugs or serving liquor to a customer who then kills or is killed. But the legal stage is set for even further expansion of the law. Wilentz points to "the upheaval of prior norms by a society that has finally recognized that it must change its habits and do whatever is required, whether it means a small change or a significant one, in order to stop the senseless loss inflicted by drunken drivers."

Before we make "significant" changes, we should begin a national debate on the implications of holding people responsible—both civilly and criminally—for the actions of others to whom they have provided the tools of death. The implications of such a change are mind-boggling. Already there are some feminists who would hold distributors of pornography liable for rapes committed by those who read their smut. And some advocates of gun control would prosecute weapons dealers who sell guns to customers who then use them unlawfully.

This is not a liberal-conservative debate. It is an issue that goes to the moral core of personal responsibility: should we be blamed only for our own immediate actions? Or are we responsible for what we provide to other, irresponsible, people?

It is an ancient debate, but one that has never been more relevant than it is today.

July 17, 1984

See columns 28, 69, 95, and 142.

7
Was John DeLorean Entrapped?

The highly publicized trial of John DeLorean has again introduced the word "entrapment" into our everyday vocabulary. Most Americans first heard of entrapment during the Abscam prosecutions of several congressmen and a senator, who were "tricked" into accepting bribes from a government agent disguised as an Arab sheik.

"I was entrapped" is now heard almost as often as "I was framed." But being entrapped is different from being framed, and the meaning of the entrapment defense is widely misunderstood.

A person who was framed did not commit any crime; those who framed him falsified the evidence against him.* He is innocent in every sense of that word. However, a person who was entrapped *did* commit the criminal act, but he claims that he shouldn't be convicted because the government tricked him—"scammed" him—into doing it. The difference is between the age-old cries of "I didn't do it!" and "It wasn't my fault."

Simply put, the entrapment defense means this: the government is not permitted to talk you into committing a crime that you would not otherwise have committed.

Sound pretty straightforward? It's anything but that. Let's look at the most important elements of entrapment.

Only "the government" can entrap a citizen. If your friend, boss, spouse, or enemy—any private person—talks, pressures, or tricks you into committing a crime, there is no entrapment defense available. No matter how great the pressure on you, if the government wasn't involved, there's no defense. The government may prosecute you (as well as the person who persuaded you) for the resulting crime. Thus, if James Hoffman—who proposed the drug deal to DeLorean—had been acting on his own behalf, and not as a government agent, there could have been no claim of entrapment.

What is the government not permitted to do? Surely, it may trick a criminal into committing a crime he would commit anyway—but under circumstances in which he can be caught and convicted. For example, if the police know that John Smith is a drug dealer, it is perfectly proper for an undercover "narc" to pose as a junkie and try to buy some drugs from Smith. Smith is willing to sell to a real junkie, but he doesn't want to "sell" to an undercover cop. Smith is tricked, but properly so.

But the government is not permitted to talk an innocent person into trying crime for the first time. There are, of course, some difficult gray areas. Consider the following scenario:

An undercover policeman dresses up as a drunken street bum. He places a wallet visibly stuffed with money in his back pocket. Seeing a teenage kid approaching, he decides to "test" his honesty by pretending he is asleep and having the wallet protrude visibly from his pocket. The kid passes by, noticing the wallet, but does nothing. The policeman loosens the wallet, making it easy to be lifted from his "sleeping" body. This time the kid goes for the bait and is caught.

Was he entrapped? It's a tough question. On the one hand, nobody made the kid do anything; the policeman just put the bait on the hook and waited. A completely honest kid wouldn't have bitten. On the other hand, the police did create a crime: they tempted a kid into committing a criminal act that he did not set out to commit. Would he have committed a similar crime at some other time? Who knows! If the situation were identical, he probably would have—but who can be sure there ever would have been a similar temptation? The basic question is whether it is the proper role of government to conduct periodic tests of honesty.

Nor is this merely an academic issue. Law enforcement authorities throughout the country are busy devising scams of every description. A few examples:

- New York City police ran a pornography bookstore in Times Square and even commissioned and financed the production of an obscene movie.
- The FBI established its own fencing warehouse in Washington, D.C., and bought several million dollars' worth of hot goods. They then turned around and sold the goods at prices sufficiently cheap to alert the buyers that they were stolen. (A federal prosecutor was among those arrested for buying stolen goods.)
- The Los Angeles police department dressed up two policewomen as prostitutes. They arrested ninety-one customers.

Not all scam operations go as smoothly, however. In one tragic case, an undercover policeman sold drugs to an undercover agent for a local vigilante group that was trying to rid the community of heroin. The vigilantes killed the "junkie" cop.

Sometimes the result is pure burlesque: one undercover cop pretending to be gay arrested another undercover cop pretending to be gay in a Greenwich Village bar.

Other times, a scam can produce a result that seems completely just. A dentist is suspected of making sexual advances toward his anesthetized patients. A policewoman posing as a patient allows herself to be put under anesthesia as a hidden camera records the dentist's movements. As soon as she is unconscious, the dentist begins to unbutton her blouse and is arrested.

What, then, distinguishes the "good" scam from the "bad" scam?

The boundaries are hazy, depending on value judgments and matters of degree. That's precisely why it is so dangerous to leave it up to individual policemen or prosecutors. There should be some objective guidelines instructing law enforcement officials when it is proper to employ a scam.

This view is becoming more accepted on Capitol Hill, where hearings were recently held on the issues surrounding entrapment. A bill has been drafted that would require a court order—a "scam warrant"—before a federal scam is conducted. The law enforcement officials would have to "demonstrate reasonable suspicion that [a crime] has been, is being, or is about to be committed" by the person identified as the target.

If enacted, this bill would severely limit scams that are general "fishing expeditions" or "honesty tests," but it would still permit scams to be used to detect ongoing crimes that would otherwise be difficult to prove. The bill attempts to strike a balance between the legitimate needs of law enforcement agents to prove existing crimes and the undesirability of having government agents create crimes that otherwise would not have been committed.

It is unclear how this would affect a case like that of DeLorean. The facts there are very much in dispute, precisely on the critical issue of whether the government had a reasonable basis for suspecting that DeLorean was interested in a drug deal before it assumed an active role in the scam.

What can be said with certainty is that a "scam warrant" would give the courts far more control over government agents' activities. It would make it far more difficult for the government simply, in the words of one member of Congress, "to put out the honeypot and see which flies gather round."

July 24, 1984

It is theoretically possible that a guilty person might be framed, if the prosecution manufactured evidence to help prove the truth. There is a plausible argument that this is what occurred with Julius and Ethel Rosenberg who were convicted and executed as atomic spies in the 1950s.

8
The DeLorean Verdict: Guilty but Entrapped

Millions of Americans saw John DeLorean appear to engage in a cocaine deal. Yet the jury unanimously acquitted him.

It was reminiscent of the Hinkley case, where we all saw Hinkley shoot President Reagan. Yet he too was acquitted.

What is it about the law—and the jury system in particular—that produces such verdicts?

The answer is that the American jury is more than a simple instrument for finding the facts. It is the ultimate conscience of the American community. It speaks for the common morality of the people, rather than for the dry application of the law to the facts.

In the DeLorean case, the jurors—or at least some of them—sent a message to the Justice Department which said: we don't care what the law permits you to do, this time you went too far.

They were referring, of course, to the "sting" operation mounted against DeLorean. The jurors obviously believed at least some of the defense evidence—evidence that showed a Justice Department "out to get" DeLorean, evidence that showed a sleazy undercover agent selectively recording only some conversations, evidence that showed a willingness to tamper with records.

There was also evidence that DeLorean willingly agreed to become part of a massive cocaine deal. On the basis of the facts and applicable law, the jurors could have convicted him. But they obviously chose to focus their attention on the government's conduct rather than on DeLorean's.

Indeed, the fact that they acquitted the defendant despite his unwillingness to take the witness stand and testify on his own behalf—an unusual jury response, to say the least—shows that the jurors were casting their eyes not at the defense table where DeLorean sat, but rather at the prosecution table, which represented the government and its sordid behavior.

Although the jury verdict sends an important message to prosecutors, it is a message of limited impact. One jury in one part of the country was expressing its collective outrage at the particular sting operation used against DeLorean. This verdict has no formal precedential effect on judges or other juries.

Up to now, the vast majority of juries have approved nearly every sting operation, ranging from Abscam to the New York City Police Department's operation of a pornographic bookstore.

But the DeLorean verdict will certainly send a chilling message of caution to prosecutors planning massive entrapment schemes. Jury verdicts in highly publicized cases have a way of being contagious. Jurors in other "scam" cases may become emboldened by the DeLorean verdict and its generally favorable reception. No prosecutor wants to invest millions of dollars and years of person-hours in a "scam" operation and prosecution only to see the jury nullify—indeed condemn—that effort.

Prosecutors will now begin to realize that they ignore the basic sense of morality, fair play, and outrage of the American jury at the risk of an occasional acquittal. This is a message to which cost-conscious (and publicity-conscious) prosecutors may have to pay increasing attention.

But what message does this verdict send to John DeLorean?

It certainly should not be understood as a message of praise or approval for what he did. The evidence shows DeLorean engaging in conduct that would probably have been criminal if he were "stung" by anyone but government agents. Had this sting been conducted by his private creditors or his personal enemies, he would doubtlessly have been convicted.

Indeed, he would not even have been permitted to put up an entrapment defense. That defense is available only if the government entraps. Despite statements by some of the jurors, the evidence suggests that DeLorean committed the acts and had the moral culpability necessary to commit a crime. In that respect, the verdict might well have read: "guilty, but entrapped." It is possible, of course, that some jurors simply did not believe he was guilty.

The "scam" has become one of the most frequently used prosecutorial tools in America. Every district attorney's office and police department uses variations of it. This trend will not be halted by a single jury verdict. But the American public is now more sensitive than ever to the potential abuses of entrapment.

As one juror put it: what they did to John DeLorean they could have done to someone in my family.

August 17, 1984

UPDATE
Following his acquittal in 1984, DeLorean was again indicted, this time for fraud in connection with his automobile company. Despite my somewhat unflattering comments about him, he retained me as a consultant to his defense. In 1986, he was acquitted of all charges, and in 1987 a civil suit by his creditors was settled.

9
Would You Turn in Your Own Child?

Some questions to parents:

If your own child were suspected of a crime, would you be willing to give testimony that might send your son or daughter to prison? Would it depend on whether you believed your child was guilty or innocent? On the nature of the crime? On the degree of punishment?

These are some of the questions confronting a Texas couple named Bernard and Odette Port. The Ports were sent to jail recently for refusing to give testimony before a grand jury investigating their seventeen-year-old son David's possible involvement in the murder of a twenty-three-year-old woman. They are now free on bail of $20,000, but the prospect of further imprisonment hangs over them.

The general principles of law are clear. Every man and woman—even the president of the United States—is obliged to give testimony when properly subpoenaed before a grand or petit jury. In the famous "Nixon tapes case," the Supreme Court ruled that even the president's privilege to preserve the confidentiality of state discussions must give way to the need for evidence in a criminal case.

There are a few limited exceptions to this general obligation to testify: the Fifth Amendment protects a criminal defendant from incriminating himself; and a married person cannot be forced to testify against his or her spouse. This latter exception is designed to encourage married couples to be open and frank with each other. But the courts have never extended this "marital privilege" to parents and their children, although we certainly want to encourage candor between children and parents as much as between spouses.

The issue is a wrenching emotional one for some parents. Listen to the words of Mrs. Port, who, as a young woman in Greece, hid from the Gestapo for two years in the mountains: "The Nazis forced parents to testify against children and children against parents. I simply cannot do so." And so she and her husband were willing to go to jail rather than incriminate their son.

But consider what the mother of the murder victim must be thinking:

her daughter is dead, while the alleged killer is being protected by his parents. Without their testimony, he may escape justice, and her daughter's murder may go unpunished.

This is the stuff of which melodrama is made. It is also the stuff of which landmark legal decisions are constructed.

The Ports are seeking the protection of the courts on two separate grounds. The first has already been rejected—and with good reason. The second has not yet been ruled on.

The first ground is that because the Ports are practicing Jews, they are entitled to rely on Jewish law, which, they say, forbids parents from testifying against their children. While the Jewish religious law on this subject may be more enlightened than our own secular approach, a pluralistic democracy simply cannot tolerate separate laws for members of different religions.

The fact that the Ports are being compelled to violate not only their consciences, but also their religion, may well raise a sympathetic argument for compassion in sentencing, but it cannot excuse a civic obligation that would be enforced against others who do not share the Ports' religious affiliation. We must not become a divided nation with different civil laws for Christians, Moslems, Jews, and Hindus.

If religious excuses were accepted in courts of law, matters could become exceedingly complicated. For example, in the Port case, there was a conflict of religious testimony: two rabbis were of the opinion that Jewish law forbade the Ports from testifying in a case like this, while one rabbi said that Jewish law required them to testify. Not surprisingly, the judge rejected the Ports' religious claim.

Their other claim would have universal application to mothers and fathers, regardless of their religion. It is simply that parents owe their children a moral and psychological duty of support and should not be forced by the state to become instruments in their own children's imprisonment—perhaps even execution.

This isn't the first time in which parents have faced imprisonment for refusing to testify against their children. The issue arose several times in the context of political cases, during the McCarthy and Vietnam War periods, when parents risked imprisonment for refusing to talk about their children's political views and actions. Judges have sometimes been sympathetic to the plight of fathers and mothers who simply cannot bring themselves to disclose family confidences, but the courts have not been willing to carve out a general parental privilege that applies across the board. They fear that such a broad privilege could be abused by families that engage in criminal activities together, enabling members to hide behind it to avoid giving any testimony. If a narrow privilege is to be allowed, say judges, it should be enacted by legislatures, which could draft a careful statute defining the relationships and circumstances that should come within any exception.

Without such legislation—or without a surprising court decision—parents will continue to agonize over one of the most excruciating decisions a mother or father may ever have to face: whether to testify against one's own son or daughter, or whether to go to jail to protect a possibly guilty child.

No one knows how Mr. and Mrs. Port will resolve this dilemma. Whatever they finally do, it will be unseemly for any of us to sit back from a comfortable distance and condemn them, since few of us can really know what we would do if confronted with so tragic a choice.

July 24, 1984

UPDATE
Eventually Mr. and Mrs. Port were released. Their son was convicted of killing the woman without *his parents' testimony.*

10
Court Takes Aim at Liberty

There is a sad symbolism in the fact that, by coincidence, the Supreme Court ended its 1983–1984 term the day after the Statue of Liberty's torch was removed for repair.

The high court's 1983–1984 term registered the worst score for liberty in recent memory. The state won and the individual lost most of the important judicial battles this past year. Justice William Brennan, the court's senior justice and most frequent dissenter, ended the court's work year with harsh criticism of his colleagues for undercutting freedoms, but on a note of long-term optimism: "There is hope, however, that in time this or some later court will restore these precious freedoms to their rightful place as a primary protection for our citizens against overreaching officialdom."

Brennan's hope will probably not become reality in the near future, especially if, as seems likely, President Reagan is reelected and has the opportunity to appoint a majority of justices who will serve into the twenty-first century. Even this court, with only one Reagan appointee—Justice Sandra Day O'Connor—has been solidly pro-Reagan this year. In fact, it has become so predictable that certain guidelines have been discerned by judicial handicappers.

Here are some rules that will help you to predict how any given case probably will be decided:

Rule 1: Criminal defendants and prisoners always lose. If anyone offers you a bet on the outcome of a criminal case before the Supreme Court, double the stakes and pick the prosecution. It's the closest thing to a sure winner since McEnroe vs. Connors at Wimbledon.

Among the court's pro-prosecution decisions this year were the following: even before trial, when the defendant is supposed to be presumed innocent, he may be deprived of "contact visits"—kisses and hugs—with friends and family; juveniles may be "preventively detained" on the basis of predictions of future crimes; and prisoners have no right of privacy. At trial, the "exclusionary rule"—forbidding the use of illegally obtained evidence—has been riddled with so many exceptions that government officials have little incentive to comply with the Constitution. And the death penalty may be imposed even if it is imposed disproportionately on certain groups.

Rule 2: The president almost always wins. In its most important ruling on presidential power in a decade, the court upheld Reagan's curb on travel to Cuba as part of his authority to conduct foreign policy, even though Congress had not authorized the curb.

Rule 3: Big business almost always wins. The court ruled that a large corporation may use bankruptcy laws to get around collective bargaining agreements; and that a parent company that "conspires" with one of its subsidiaries has not violated the antitrust law.

Rule 4: Women and blacks generally win in theory, but lose in practice. The court held that women and blacks may not be discriminated against in being promoted to law-firm partnerships and that states may prohibit discrimination by organizations like the Junior Chamber of Commerce. But it still makes it difficult to prove discrimination, and it has limited the right to sue of persons who would challenge certain discriminatory practices.

Rule 5: Aliens and foreigners always lose. Immigration officials may conduct unannounced raids on businesses to look for "illegals." They may conduct illegal searches without regard for an exclusionary rule.

Rule 6: Mainstream Christianity generally wins, but other religious and nonreligious groups usually lose. Nativity scenes on public property have been approved. The Reverend Moon was denied review of his conviction.

Rule 7: The established press often wins, while the offbeat media frequently lose. The court held that newspapers may not be excluded from jury selection and that public broadcast stations may air editorial opinions; and *Consumer Reports* won its right to criticize products. But *Hustler* magazine may be sued for libel in any state where it is distributed, which allows the plaintiff to pick the state most hostile to *Hustler*. Protesters may not sleep in the park across from the White House to protest administration policies regarding the poor; and a town can ban billboards and signs.

This year's scoreboard strongly suggests that the Supreme Court is quickly becoming a government court rather than a people's court. This shouldn't please conservatives, who want to get government off the back of the people—and it certainly gives little comfort to liberals. The legal director of the American Civil Liberties Union characterized the court as "statist" rather than truly conservative and said that it was becoming a "cheerleader for the government."

An important function of the Supreme Court—the only branch of government whose officials are appointed for life—is to balance the power of elected officials, who are supposed to be responsive to the short-term wishes of the electorate. In this respect, the current Supreme Court has failed: it may be a popular court, insofar as it often does what a majority of the people seem to want. But it is not serving its unique function of protecting the unpopular who cannot turn to the executive or legislative branches for help.

Nor is it a restrained court, as some of its admirers claim. Justice Stevens put it well in a recent case: "The court has acquired a voracious appetite for judicial activism . . . at least when it comes to restricting the constitutional rights of the citizen."

It is a sad time for America's most prized legacy—its Bill of Rights. While the Statue of Liberty's torch remains in the repair shop, the nation's citizens can no longer look to this Supreme Court to keep the torch of liberty aglow.

July 31, 1984

11
U.S. Legal System Is Still Number 1

GENOA, Italy—During most of the year, when at home, I write somewhat critically of the U.S. legal establishment. But nothing makes me appreciate American justice more than my periodic travels abroad.

It doesn't even take a trip to outrightly repressive countries, such as the Soviet Union or China—whose "courts" I have observed—to make me realize the uniqueness of our constitutional system. Even a visit to Western Europe points out the considerable differences between the rights of an American citizen and the rights of citizens of almost every other country.

We tend to take for granted such basic guarantees as freedom of expression, protection from arbitrary arrest, bail, and appointed lawyers for the poor. Yet even these rights are far more limited for most Europeans.

In Great Britain, for example, the media may not report about ongoing criminal investigations, nor may it publish "official secrets." Thus, the *Times* of London could not have published the results of Woodward and Bernstein's investigative reporting during the early days of Watergate, nor could it have published the Pentagon papers.

Of course, our government also tries to conceal unpleasant facts from its citizens—by "classifying" or "sealing" them. But if the press manages to get hold of the information—as if often does, by leaks—it can't be prevented from publishing it for all to see and evaluate.

This can make all the difference in the world, as shown by the publication in our country of the Watergate reports and the Pentagon papers, which helped to topple a president and end a war.

Nor does Great Britain have an "exclusionary rule"—the controversial American device that prohibits the government from using evidence it obtained unlawfully. But the British do take more seriously than we ever have the need to punish "bungling bobbies" who violate citizens' rights.

In general, British citizens' rights are less well defined than are citizens' rights in our country, because the British have no written constitution and rely more on tradition. But "tradition" is easier to define in a homogeneous country. In the United States, each region, wave of immigration, and racial group contributes some of its own traditions to our imperfect melting pot. Our Founding Fathers—themselves from differing traditions within the

Anglo-Saxon mainstream—foresaw the need for a strong written constitution binding on all Americans.

Even in European countries that have written constitutions, the courts have considerably less power to enforce their provisions than do our courts. Indeed, the legal profession in general has far less influence on the lives of Europeans than it does on ours. European lawyers rarely become as involved as ours sometimes do in momentous issues such as abortion, capital punishment, racial discrimination, and voting equality. European citizens are less aware of their rights and go to court less frequently to vindicate them.

Many Americans view the European reluctance to bring lawsuits as a positive statement about European society. But some Europeans to whom I spoke think differently: they envy Americans' willingness to stand up for their rights. Said a northern Italian man named Valerio, who has spent some time in the United States: "Here, we are afraid of courts. If you get cheated by a big store, you best shut up. If you make trouble, they make bigger trouble for you." Cynicism about corruption is apparent: "A poor person cannot obtain an advocate but, even more important, he cannot afford the bribes."

Valerio hoped that, in time, his countrymen would learn to be more like Americans. "My friends are not educated about their rights," he said. "They do not believe the courts belong to them. Someday they will learn from Americans to use the courts instead of fearing them."

Some changes already are evident in parts of Europe. Young lawyers are trying to bring law to the people. In doing so, they are borrowing heavily from the American legal services model. Understandably, there is some resistance: "The people must want the lawyers before the lawyers can come to the people," Valerio told me with a sigh of resignation.

There are a few areas in which we can learn from our Western European neighbors. There is virtually no capital punishment in Western Europe— but, of course, there is also very little violent crime. (I leave it to the criminologists to determine which is the cause and which is the effect.)

All in all, I heartily recommend a trip abroad as a remedy for the peculiar American ailment—to which I am often subject—of gleefully knocking our lawyers, our courts, and our penchant for suing each other. As I think about returning home, I offer an enthusiastic two and a half cheers for the American legal system, with all its imperfections.

August 7, 1984

12
Roadblocks to Justice

When you've been out driving on weekends, have you noticed any police roadblocks? Several cities and states are now experimenting with this device—stopping and questioning drivers at specified checkpoints—in an effort to reduce drunk driving accidents.

The patrols are out in full force during summer and holiday weekends, when the roads are crowded with vacationing revelers. While it's too early to know for sure whether these roadblocks have worked, those who use them are claiming modest gains in the war against highway mayhem.

Other changes are also being proposed as effective deterrents to drunken driving. These include a national drinking age of twenty-one, more aggressive breathalizer and blood-alcohol testing, automatic penalties for exceeding alcohol limits, and the imposition of legal liability on those who serve drinks to drivers.

But the roadblock has raised the most concern among civil libertarians. Perhaps this has something to do with the popular image of the roadblock. In the movies and on television, roadblocks are used to cordon off escaping bank robbers, murderers, and terrorists. But in real life, they're now being used to stop people like you and me who are out for a holiday drive. The sight of cars lined up on the side of a road, their drivers being questioned by uniformed state troopers, conjures up images of foreign countries and exotic crimes. But the liberal governor of my own state of Massachusetts—Michael Dukakis—has come out foursquare in favor of properly conducted roadblocks.

The key words here are "properly conducted." Improperly conducted roadblocks or spot-checks pose grave dangers to our constitutional rights, as well as to highway safety. A recent Massachusetts decision—which is likely to be followed throughout the country—focuses on the distinctions between good and bad car-stops.

Harvey McGeoghegan went out for a drive in Revere, Massachusetts, on a cold Friday night in January when he noticed a roadblock lineup of cars going back two-thirds of a mile. He was pulled over and asked some questions; since he showed some sign of having been drinking, he was escorted to a nearby van and given a breathalizer test. He failed and was arrested, and his car was towed away.

At his trial for drunken driving, McGeoghegan challenged the constitutionality of the roadblock. The police admitted that they had no "probable cause" to stop him: he was not driving erratically or visibly violating any traffic laws. He was just one of 200 or so fish picked up in the net that night. The police also admitted that all of the evidence against him was obtained as a direct result of the roadblock.

Thus the stage was set for a direct challenge to the constitutionality of roadblocks in general, and this one in particular.

The Massachusetts high court's decision has become a kind of Magna Carta for roadblocks. The court decided that properly conducted roadblocks were constitutional, but that improperly conducted ones were not. Most important, it announced guidelines for distinguishing the good from the bad. Here are some of the guidelines:

- The selection of cars to be stopped "must not be arbitrary"—that is, they may not be picked on the basis of discriminatory criteria, such as race or appearance. (A recent study found that cars sporting "Support the ACLU" bumper stickers were stopped more frequently than those with "Support Your Local Police" stickers.)
- The roadblock must assure that the safety of the drivers is maximized and that their inconvenience is minimized.
- General roadblocks involving every car passing a designated check-point are preferable to "spot-checks" of only some vehicles. When the motorist can see that other cars are being stopped, "he is much less likely to be frightened or annoyed by the intrusion."
- The procedure must follow "a plan devised by law-enforcement supervisory personnel." It should not be concocted on the spot by traffic police.
- Advance publication of the date of an intended roadblock, without giving away its precise locations, is desirable.

In applying these general guidelines, the court found the Revere roadblock to be unconstitutional for several reasons. Among them were the facts that the roadblock was devised by the local officers who carried it out; these officers used "their own discretion" in deciding who to stop or let through; the roadblock area was "poorly illuminated and unsafe for motorists"; and there were long delays and traffic congestion.

Harvey McGeoghegan went free because the Revere roadblock was unconstitutional, but the concept of the properly conducted roadblock has been vindicated. Governor Dukakis cited statistics indicating that there were fewer fatalities since he instituted the roadblocks in Massachusetts, and he made this observation following the decision:

> When we first instituted the roadblocks, we made it clear that they would be conducted following the strictest safety and constitutional guidelines. [We] will continue to adhere strictly to those guidelines. It is evident that the roadblocks and other tough enforcement measures have served as a deterrent to those who might otherwise feel they could drive drunk in Massachusetts and not get caught. We feel that the life-saving public benefit gained from the use of roadblocks outweighs the minor inconvenience to the average motorist. The court apparently agrees with us, and widespread support for the program indicates most Massachusetts citizens do, too.

We are likely to see more roadblocks throughout the country as we approach Labor Day. If they work, we may also see fewer wrecks. If these roadblocks are conducted fairly and safely, they may be a trade-off that is well worth the inconvenience and minimal intrusion on privacy.

August 14, 1984

13
Church, State, Parents, and Children

If ever a constitutional right seemed absolute, it would be parents' right to raise their minor children according to the family's religious beliefs. But if ever *another* right seemed absolute, it would be young children's right to be free from physical—indeed, life-threatening—abuse.

These "absolute" rights are coming into conflict more and more frequently as some fundamentalist religions insist on interpreting the Bible in a way that endangers children's lives.

The most recently publicized conflict is taking place in the isolated Vermont village of Island Pond. The village's 400 residents, all members of the Northern Kingdom Community Church, say they believe literally in the biblical admonition, "He who spareth the rod hateth his son" (Proverbs 13:24). Accordingly, they beat their erring children with rods and sticks. (By beating their daughters as well as their sons, they seem to be choosing a form of modern egalitarianism over traditional literalism.)

After a teenage girl complained that she had been beaten for seven hours by a church elder—allegedly leaving her body with eighty-nine marks— the Vermont authorities raided the church community and sought temporary custody for 112 church children. A judge denied the request, but several custody petitions are still before the court.

In addition, the Vermont attorney general has filed criminal charges against the elder who is accused of beating the teenage girl. But that case is also in trouble: the girl's father—who originally confirmed under oath that his daughter had been beaten—has recanted. He says that if his daughter now saw the accused elder, she would "give him a hug."

This kind of recanting isn't uncommon in religious abuse cases, due to the pressures that a church can place on its members. In fact, often there is no complaining witness at all; the children are too frightened to come forward, too isolated to complain, or aren't even aware that being severely beaten may be regarded as wrong by outsiders. (This is tragically true even in nonreligious child abuse cases.)

Nor is the problem limited to beatings. In several recent cases, fundamentalist parents refused to allow their sick young children—sometimes infants—to receive medical treatment that was necessary for their survival. The right of parents to sacrifice their children to religious absolutism raises the most profound questions about conflicting rights.

Sometimes the conflict takes a different twist: the child leaves his or her parents' religion and joins a "cult." The parents seek the aid of the state, or sometimes engage in such self-help techniques as "kidnapping" and "deprogramming" their child.

Courts are naturally reluctant to interfere in relationships involving parents, children, and religion. Generally, they will defer to parental judgment, allowing the parents enormous leeway over their children's religion and upbringing.

But parents' rights in relation to their children aren't absolute, as child-abuse laws show. Obviously, a father who sexually abused his young daughter couldn't hide behind any parental right or contrived religious claim. The state does have a duty to protect children from abusive parents, and the courts have generally applied a balancing test: weighing the importance of the religious rights of parents against the dangers to the children.

But the courts often put a heavy thumb on the side of the scale that favors the parents' rights. This is especially true when the children themselves haven't complained, but the state is suing on their behalf.

In the leading Supreme Court case, *Wisconsin* v. *Yoder*, Chief Justice Warren Burger wrote the majority opinion, ruling that members of the Amish religious community may refuse to send their children to high school. Justice William O. Douglas dissented, arguing that the children's right to an education had been ignored by the court. If a child is "harnessed to the Amish way of life by those in authority over him," said Douglas, "his entire life may be stunted and deformed." If the child is denied a basic education, he said, the child "will be forever barred from entry into [our] new and amazing world of diversity."

If that observation is true of education, then it's surely true of brutal beatings and callous deprivation of life-saving medical procedures.

We haven't heard the last of these conflicts involving church, state, parents, and children. More groups like the Northern Kingdom are seeking to isolate themselves from the "Kingdom of Satan," as they refer to organized government. The irony is that the more they seek to escape into literal and fundamentalist religious enclaves, the more the state will have to intrude to protect children who are endangered by church practices.

August 21, 1984

For other conflicts involving religion, see columns 48, 53, 72, and 119.

14
Now They're Saying, "It Ain't So, Joe"

Remember the legend of "Shoeless Joe" Jackson? Jackson was the great natural hitter of this century's second decade who was discovered playing milltown baseball without any shoes. With his homemade bat, "Black Betsy," he electrified the major leagues with his clutch slugging, bulletlike throwing, and come-from-nowhere fielding.

But then, at the height of his career, he was disgraced and thrown out of organized baseball for his alleged role in the fixing of the 1919 World

Series. The "Black Sox Scandal," as it has come to be called, involved eight members of the Chicago White Sox who were indicted for throwing the Series to the Cincinnati Reds.

The rise and fall of this great natural ballplayer—followed by his gutsy comeback as an aging minor-leaguer—provided inspiration for Bernard Malamud's novel *The Natural*, which was made into a movie starring Robert Redford.

The most famous phrase to emerge from the Black Sox Scandal was the tearful question allegedly put to Shoeless Joe by a young fan: "Say it ain't so, Joe."

But Joe did not say that it wasn't so. An illiterate naif, he gave contradictory answers about his involvement in a gambling scheme. Although he denied that he threw any games, his major league career was over.

But new information is now coming out which strongly suggests that it *wasn't* so—or at least that it wasn't as bad as the press and organized baseball made it seem at the time. A campaign is underway to clear Jackson's name and to place the primary blame for the Black Sox Scandal. where it rightfully belongs—at the door of the White Sox owner and president, Charles Comiskey, who actively conspired with others to cover up his own knowledge of the scandal.

Spearheading the campaign is Donald Gropman, author of a recent book that is aptly titled *Say It Ain't So, Joe.*

Gropman's convincing account of the scandal—based on interviews, grand jury minutes, diaries, and other new information—makes the 1919–1920 White Sox seem like the 1972–1974 White House. The White Sox cover-up was intended to protect club president Comiskey, much like the White House cover-up was intended to protect President Nixon. The big difference is that the White Sox cover-up worked. And therein lies an interesting story about how much our legal system has changed for the better over the intervening half-century.

The facts, as they now have emerged, seem to be as follows: Jackson was approached by a teammate and offered $10,000 to throw the series. He declined the offer and informed Comiskey that to avoid any suspicion, he wanted to be benched for the World Series. Comiskey refused and went on with business as usual. The White Sox lost the series five games to three, but Jackson led all batters on both teams with 12 hits and a .357 average. He made no errors.

After the series, he was given an envelope containing $5,000. He took the money to Comiskey's office, but the president refused to see him.

Comiskey then arranged for his own lawyer to meet with Jackson and pressure him into taking the rap and "forgetting" about his communications with Comiskey. Jackson believed that the lawyer was acting for him, when in fact he was trying to make him a scapegoat for Comiskey. The lawyer made all kinds of promises of support from the club for his cooperation. Jackson went along and told the story that Comiskey wanted to hear.

Eventually, after obtaining his own lawyer, Jackson retracted his earlier statement. Two juries believed his retraction and his innocence. He was acquitted of all criminal charges.

But the baseball higher-ups ignored the jury verdicts and banned him from the major leagues for life.

Today this would not have happened. A modern-day Jackson would have his own lawyer from the very beginning. Nor would the shenanigans employed by Comiskey's lawyer be tolerated by the bar today. Most important, an honest prosecutor today generally seeks to follow the criminal trail to the top of the mountain. Convicting the Watergate burglars was not enough. The special prosecutor followed the trail to the attorney general, and eventually to the president.

But in post-World War I Chicago, corruption tainted more than the White Sox: the entire city—judiciary and all—reeked with influence-peddling and power-brokering, and among the most influential brokers was Charles Comiskey.

It's therefore no surprise that Comiskey now holds an honored place in the Baseball Hall of Fame, while Shoeless Joe Jackson remains a scapegoat. Though both are now long dead, the true story deserves to be known. Former baseball commissioner A. B. "Happy" Chandler has now gotten behind the efforts to clear Jackson's name: "I never in my life believed him to be guilty of a single thing," said the man who was privy to the secret files of the major leagues.

Baseball is a game of legends. Memories play as important a role as current events. If it "ain't so"—or even if it wasn't as bad as legend has it—big-league baseball should be big enough to admit it made a mistake about Shoeless Joe.

August 28, 1984

UPDATE

A committee has recently been formed to reopen the Jackson case. It includes former major league commissioner Happy Chandler.

15
Grim Views of a Future Justice

The man who may well be appointed to the next Supreme Court vacancy has just written an opinion that previews his philosophy as a justice.

That man is Robert Bork, whom you may remember as the official who implemented President Nixon's infamous "Saturday Night Massacre." When the attorney general and deputy attorney general refused Nixon's order to fire Watergate special prosecutor Archibald Cox, Bork—then the third ranking official at the Justice Department—did the dirty work.

Bork was recently appointed to the U.S. Court of Appeals for the District of Columbia Circuit—the nation's second most important constitutional court. Some observers believe that President Reagan appointed Bork as a tryout for the Supreme Court. If so, Bork's opinion in *Dronenberg* v. *Zech* passes any Reagan test.

The case grew out of the United States Navy's discharge of petty officer James L. Dronenberg, who according to Bork had "an unblemished service record and earned many citations praising his job performance" as a code breaker. But the navy discharged Dronenberg when he admitted to engaging in homosexual acts.

Navy policy mandates the discharge of practicing homosexuals. Although Dronenberg's acts took place in a barracks, the policy applies equally to acts in the privacy of one's home. In contrast, the navy does not automatically dismiss sailors who are guilty of other forms of misconduct, such as heterosexual abuses, but considers such acts on a case-by-case basis.

Dronenberg sued the navy, arguing that its automatic discharge policy for homosexuals violates the constitutional rights of privacy and equal protection.

Judge Bork ruled that the right of privacy does not encompass "private, consensual, homosexual conduct" among adults. He observed that most Americans condemn homosexuality on moral grounds and concluded that "legislation may implement morality."

It is surely not convincing, however, to argue that a state may always enforce the public morality of the majority against a minority's private practices that hurt no one. A majority of Connecticut voters favored criminalizing birth control when the Supreme Court struck down that prohibition. And most Virginians regarded interracial sex and marriage as immoral when the court held that the state had no business in telling its citizens that they could not marry across racial lines.

Why, then, may the navy single out private homosexuality for automatic discharge?

Bork's answer reveals his troubling philosophy: he argued that "common sense demonstrate[s]" that, given military superiors' powers over their subordinates, allowing homosexuals to remain in the navy would "enhance the possibility of homosexual seduction."

Bork's logic may sound somewhat convincing on first reading: if the commanding officer is gay, he may use his power to seduce sailors who fear him. But think about the implications of that argument for other aspects of life!

The day of the all-male business or government office is gone. More women are now in positions of power over men; more women work, many or most of them for male bosses. Gender integration of the work force—even, to a limited degree, of the armed forces—has become a welcome fact of life. And heterosexual bosses can, and too often do, misuse their power to seduce employees of the opposite sex.

The remedy for this evil is not automatic discharge of all heterosexuals or all homosexuals. It is the selective discharge of *individuals* who abuse their authority by sexual exploitation of any kind.

If Dronenberg abused his power to seduce younger male sailors (as a congressman was recently charged with seducing a male congressional page), then he should be punished. But so should heterosexual officers who misuse their authority (just as another congressman was recently charged with seducing a young female employee).

The implications of Bork's opinion are not limited to homosexuals or to the military. They threaten to return us to those not-so-wonderful days when courts condoned the imposition of the majority's often immoral morality on the private lives of all citizens. In the name of popular "morality," we have practiced discrimination against Catholics, Mormons, Asian-Americans, atheists, women, blacks, and trade unionists—to name just a few.

Bork's opinion is a bill of rights for bigotry. Whatever one may think of homosexuality—or other private "deviations" from some majority norm—it is simply wrong to generalize about gays. Yet that is precisely what Bork encourages by implying that all homosexuals will use their power to seduce male subordinates.

Bork's arguments—which are a blend of moral majority philosophy, armchair psychology, and selective judicial restraint—are sure to place him high on any list of potential Reagan nominees to the Supreme Court.

September 4, 1984

UPDATE
On July 18, 1987, President Reagan did nominate Judge Bork to be an Associate Justice of the Supreme Court. This precipitated one of the most divisive confirmation controversies in history. For my views on the matter see columns 122–128. For further developments on the issue of homosexuality under the Constitution, see columns 84 and 85.

16
Common-Sense Verdict on "Name-Calling"

Should a name-calling scientist be entitled to sue and collect from a journalist who calls *him* names?

That was the intriguing issue presented to an Atlanta jury in a million-dollar libel suit brought by Nobel Prize-winning physicist William Shockley against journalist Roger Witherspoon and his employer, the *Atlanta Constitution*. The jury found that Shockley had been libeled, but gave him only one dollar in damages.

After helping to invent the transistor, Shockley turned his attention to genetic research on alleged differences among the "races." He concluded—on the basis of data largely discredited by other scientists—that blacks as a group are intellectually inferior to whites.

Nor did Shockley stop there: he has advocated putting his racial theories into action, proposing that genetically "inferior" people be offered cash for voluntary sterilization. Shockley readily acknowledges that, under his plan, 85 percent of American blacks would be offered financial inducements to end their contribution to the human gene pool. If a substantial number bought into the sterilization program, it would be a national disaster. Many of the world's great geniuses, leaders, and just ordinary people have been produced by families with genetic backgrounds that Shockley would regard as inferior.

Shockley's outrageous plan led science reporter Witherspoon, who is black, to write an article titled "Designer Genes by Shockley." The article itself is nearly as stupid as the plan. It compares Shockley's suggestion for paid voluntary sterilization to Hitler's actual program of enforced sterilization: "The Shockley program was tried out in Germany during World War II," writes Witherspoon, "when scientists, under the direction of the government, experimented on Jews and defectives in an effort to study genetic developments."

Read quite literally, the above statement is false: the "Shockley program" of voluntary sterilization in exchange for cash was never tried in Nazi Germany. Had it been, very few would have volunteered. And the many who died at the hands of Nazi butchers would be alive today (as would their children and grandchildren).

It could perhaps be argued that adoption of the Shockley program might possibly lead to a situation similar to involuntary Nazi sterilization, or that since unemployed blacks might be forced to "choose" quick cash, the effect would be a kind of cultural genocide. But this is still a far cry from saying that the "Shockley program was tried" by the Nazis.

In sum, the Witherspoon article was bad journalism, and the *Atlanta Constitution*—a distinguished newspaper—showed poor judgment in publishing it without change.

But should poor name-calling journalism be a basis for winning a million-dollar libel suit? Consider what that would do to freedom of the press. It would make it virtually impossible for any newspaper concerned about its balance sheet—and few are not—to publish negative opinions about controversial figures.

Journalists, politicians, and average people often use exaggerated comparisons to express strong opinions. We often hear conservatives described as "fascists" or "McCarthyites," liberals as "communists," opponents of affirmative-action quotas as "racists," and critics of school prayer as persons "intolerant of religion." Hyperbole has become the currency of modern polemics, and most people have learned to discount the inflated dollars of debate to arrive at their truthful worth.

It's important not to confuse the limited role of courts in regulating political discourse with the appropriate role of newspaper editors. The courtroom can't become a substitute for the editing desk. It isn't the proper function of government to determine the nature of the rhetoric to be used in debating important public issues. As Justice John Harlan—who had a diehard conservative lifestyle—once said in striking down the conviction of a draft opponent who came into court wearing a jacket emblazoned with a four letter description of what he thought of the draft: "Surely the state has no right to cleanse public debate to the point where it is grammatically palatable to the most squeamish among us."

The irony of Shockley's assault on freedom of speech is that many Americans would like to prevent Shockley from expressing his obnoxious opinions. Indeed, several years ago I came to Shockley's defense when students at Stanford tried to stop him from lecturing on his genetic theories. Now Shockley is trying to prevent journalists from expressing their ill-informed opinions about his ill-informed opinions.

The jury's verdict—that Shockley was libeled, but that he should only collect a single dollar—seems to reflect a common-sense criticism of both sides: Witherspoon did make false statements about Shockley, but Shockley had so destroyed his own reputation by his nasty theories that it wasn't worth much more than a buck.

Let the debate go on. Let Shockley falsely call blacks "inferior." Let Witherspoon falsely call Shockley a Nazi. Let us—the readers, listeners, and viewers—use our own good sense to decide where the truth lies. But for freedom's sake, let us not give President Reagan, Chief Justice Warren Burger, or any other government official the power to limit what we can hear or read.

September 18, 1984

For some additional comments on name-calling see the following column, which was written several years before the previous one.

17
The Childish Political Name-Callers

When Ralph Nader recently leveled a serious charge against the Justice Department's antitrust policies, Attorney General Mitchell responded by declaring that Nader was having "hallucinations." This followed on the heels of a similar Justice Department retort to charges leveled against J.

Edgar Hoover by Congressman Hale Boggs. Boggs, according to the Deputy Attorney General, was "either sick or not in possession of his faculties." That this kind of psychiatric name-calling is not limited to national politics is evidenced by Governor Rockefeller's recent diagnosis that Mayor Lindsey is "not responsible for what he's saying. He's emotionally upset."

Declaring one's political opponents insane has a long and unfortunate history. The Soviet Union's use of "insanity" as a euphemism for political deviance is well known. (Witness the recent case of the Jewish Red Army General who, after returning his medals in protest over his country's treatment of his coreligionists, was committed to a mental hospital on the ground that no sane man would do such a thing.)

Our own government has never employed mental hospitalization against political radicals on a large scale. We do, however, have a tradition of attempting to explain extreme political behavior in psychiatric terms. We find it comfortable to believe, for example, that assassins like Oswald and Sirhan were crazy. Indeed, a recent report to the National Commission on the Causes and Prevention of Violence concluded that "All those who have assassinated or attempted to assassinate presidents of the United States (with the possible exception of the Puerto Rican nationalist attempt upon President Truman) have been mentally disturbed persons who did not kill to advance any rational political plan." In England, as well, most attempts on the life of the king or prime minister have been attributed to insanity. (The famous McNaughten and Hadfield cases both grew out of such crimes.) And the recent abortive assassination attempt on Pope John Paul was also seen as the act of a madman.

There is little doubt that some of these criminals were suffering from diagnosable mental illness, but the point is that we are far more willing to accept a nonpolitical (and nonconspiratorial) explanation for an attempt on the life of a popular leader, than to lend any degree of legitimacy to the crime by ascribing rational motives. (The truth probably is that some of the assassins—for example, John Wilkes Booth and Sirhan Sirhan—were mentally ill *and* pursuing a rational political plan.)

The undue emphasis we have placed on mental illness as a cause of assassinations may help to explain why almost half—eighty-five out of 179—of the people who demanded to see President Nixon without a prior appointment last year were immediately shipped off to the local mental hospital.

Nor is our desire to "make mad the guilty" (as Shakespeare put it) limited to assassination. It is much easier for us to accept the "diagnosis" that Ezra Pound's pro-fascist radio broadcasts during World War II were the product of a disturbed mind than to believe that this great native American poet really understood what he was saying.

Similarly, General Edwin Walker's extreme right-wing utterances were substantially discredited when the Federal government ordered him committed to a mental hospital for observation.

That this phenomenon is still with us was brought home to me when I was recently invited to address a conference on judges on the subject of unruly defendants and lawyers. I was selected because I teach courses in the legal aspects of mental illness—the assumption being that the disrupters were behaving in an insane rather than in a political manner. (I declined the invitation.)

Perhaps the high—or low—point in this psychiatric name-calling was reached during the 1964 campaign when thousands of psychiatrists were polled on whether they regarded Barry Goldwater as psychologically fit to be president. A significant number concluded that he was suffering from a disabling mental illness. Goldwater recently collected a libel judgment against the magazine that conducted the poll and published the results, but generally there is no legal recourse against those who call their political enemies crazy.

Nor is there any effective political response that can be made to such an accusation. Public figures cannot call press conferences to announce that they are sane.

I do not believe that we are on the road to mass hospitalization of political deviants. Nor do I expect the current administration to adopt psychiatric name-calling as a general technique for discrediting its opponents. We should, however, be alert to any spread of this childish—but potentially dangerous—phenomenon. It is far too easy to become the kind of society that Emily Dickinson once wrote about.

> Assent, and you are sane;
> Demur—you're straightaway dangerous
> And handled with a chain.

June 27, 1971

18
Is Heckling Really Free Speech?

Amidst growing speculation that organized heckling campaigns may have been directed against various political candidates, the question has once again been posed: is heckling a legitimate form of free speech?

Heckling has long been part of the political tradition in Great Britain, as well as in some other countries. But it has taken a very different form in its recent American incarnation. I have observed British hecklers, both on the streets and in the House of Commons. They tend to be clever individuals who throw brief wisecracks or rapier-witted questions at the speaker, and the speaker is challenged to respond with an even wittier or sharper put-down. Heckling and responding have achieved the status of a high art form in Great Britain; the net effect is to encourage interchanges and focus the debate. British hecklers rarely attempt to drown the speaker out—as a group at the University of Southern California recently tried to do to Walter Mondale, or as some antiabortionists tried to do to Geraldine Ferraro.

The problem of heckling speakers isn't limited to the current presidential election or to the radical right. Indeed, its most abusive practitioners have been persons identified with the radical left. Since the days of the Vietnam conflict, left-wing college students have repeatedly tried to—and often succeeded in—shouting down speakers with whom they disagree. Ambassador Jeane Kirkpatrick and Secretary Caspar Weinberger have been recent victims of attempted censorship by heckling.

But the real victims are those who want to hear what the speaker has to say—whether they agree or not. I'm proud to report what happened just a few weeks ago when the Reverend Jerry Falwell came to my own school, Harvard Law. Several groups held protest meetings outside, while some members of the audience planned to heckle him into silence. But the vast majority of students wanted to listen—and to learn. I'd say that all but a handful of people in that audience of 500 fundamentally disagreed with everything Falwell stands for, and some seemed ready to boo and laugh at the slightest provocation. But Falwell maintained control by being substantive enough so that the students remained interested in listening to his message.

Only once was there an outburst—and that was Falwell's fault. He made a nasty retort to a lesbian questioner who asked about abortion rights. Falwell's absurdly parochial quip—"Why do you, as a lesbian, care about abortion?"—was greeted with prolonged booing and hissing. But eventually the audience quieted down and the woman won the day by pointing out that as a white, she cared about blacks, and as a lesbian woman, she cared about her sisters whose sexual preference made them more likely to become pregnant. Someone else in the audience reminded Falwell that rapists do not always distinguish between lesbian and heterosexual victims.

The point of this vignette is that there is an appropriate place for *certain kinds* of heckling, but *not for others*. The difference has nothing to do with conservatives or liberals. It has to do with whether the purpose and effect of the heckling is to facilitate the expression of all points of view or to prevent a speaker from making his or her point.

In response to several disturbing episodes of abusive heckling at Harvard University, its president, Derek Bok, recently issued some guidelines for appropriate heckling within the academic community. They include the following important distinctions: "the latitude given to expressions of audience disapproval usually varies from one setting to another—less latitude is given in a religious service than in the classroom and less latitude in the classroom than in a public speech or open meeting. Expressions of disapproval begin to infringe on free speech when they have the effect either of preventing the speakers from communicating their ideas effectively or of keeping the audience from hearing what is being said."

Bok acknowledges that drawing such lines in the context of highly emotional discussions will be difficult, but he suggests that "temporary booing or cheering at a public speech is not considered an infringement of free speech. Sustained noise does represent an interference if it lasts long enough or is repeated often enough to interfere with the orderly expression of ideas or to prevent a significant segment of the audience from hearing the speaker."

These are wise guidelines and should become part of the emerging American tradition of heckling. We must recognize that heckling itself is an important form of free expression, as long as it does not prevent the equally important free expression of others. As the maxim goes: "Your freedom to swing your fist stops at the point of my nose."

October 9, 1984

19
Who Gets Credit for Reducing Crime?

Both President Reagan and Vice President Bush have claimed partisan credit for the welcome reduction in crime that the United States has experienced over the past two years. The most recent FBI report documents an overall reduction of 7 percent in serious crimes and 5 percent in violent crimes in 1983. These statistics reflect only crimes actually reported to the police, and are subject—as are most statistics—to a degree of political manipulation. Another government report has shown an increase in the same year the FBI report shows a decrease.

Even if the decrease is as substantial as the Republicans claim, it's doubtful that the Reagan administration deserves much credit for it. Well before Reagan was even a candidate for the presidency, criminologists were predicting that the advent of the 1980s would bring a reduction in violent crime. No, these criminologists weren't prophesying the election of a conservative Republican president in 1980: they were just looking at the birth records for the 1960s and observing that the post–World War II baby boom was coming to an end. It didn't take a Jeanne Dixon to figure out that if fewer babies were born in the late sixties and early seventies than in the fifties and early sixties, the ratio of teenagers to adults would go down in the 1980s.

This is where the criminologists' expertise comes in. They know, through extensive cross-cultural and cross-national experience, that there's an important relationship between the rate of violent crime and the percentage of males aged fourteen to twenty-four. A vast disproportion of violent crimes is committed by males in that troublesome age period.

For example, although fourteen- to twenty-four-year-olds accounted for only 15 percent of the population in 1960, they were responsible for nearly 70 percent of all arrests for serious crime. Therefore, criminologists could confidently predict back in the mid-sixties that the violent-crime rate would begin to drop in the early eighties—regardless of who was president and what his criminal justice policies might be.

Even if California's liberal former Governor Jerry Brown had been elected president in 1980 and had appointed the entire board of the American Civil Liberties Union to the Supreme Court and the lower federal courts, we would still have the current decrease in violent crime.

Naturally, the Reagan administration wants to claim credit for this decrease in crime. The administration claims the decrease results from more arrests, harsher sentences, and more crowded prisons. Criminologists dispute whether such factors have any impact on crime rates; even if they do, the effect is tiny.

The truth is that courts and legal rules have very little to do with the crime rate. The vast majority of violent crime never comes before any court. Most criminals are simply not apprehended; most of those who are apprehended are not brought to trial; most of those who are brought to trial are not sentenced to prison; and most of those who are sentenced to prison get out after a brief stay.

This is true under the Reagan crime program, just as it was under the Carter program. Nor should that be at all surprising, since the federal government—which is the only government directly influenced by a president's crime program—has almost no authority over or responsibility for violent crime. Murders, rapes, assaults, and the like are investigated by local police and prosecuted by state governments. There is little evidence at all, and none in the FBI report, suggesting any significant decrease in the kinds of crimes that *are* the responsibility of the federal government—felonies such as the importation of heroin and cocaine, interstate racketeering, and corporate crime.

The irony surrounding the Reagan-Bush grab for credit is that many of the very cities and states that have experienced the most significant reductions in violent crime in the past few years have been governed by Democrats—often liberal Democrats, such as Governor Mario Cuomo of New York, Governor Michael Dukakis of Massachusetts, Governor Joe Frank Harris of Georgia, Mayor Andrew Young of Atlanta, Mayor Marion Barry of the District of Columbia, and Mayor Edward Koch of New York.

The reality is that politicians—whether they be conservative Republicans or liberal Democrats—deserve almost no credit for the recent decreases in crime. Ironically, some of the credit should go to that archenemy of the moral majority, Margaret Sanger, who introduced the birth control clinics that contribute to slowing down the baby boom.

The issue of crime is emotional enough without the addition of simpleminded political slogans. Let candidates avoid trying to pin blame or claim credit for one of the most complex social phenomena faced by any society.

October 23, 1984

20
Sex Abuse: The Child as Witness

It's difficult to imagine a crime more heinous than the sexual abuse of helpless children. For that very reason, we must be certain that those defendants accused of so horrible a crime are truly guilty. A false accusation of sexually abusing a child may destroy an innocent life.

Yet sometimes the only evidence of sexual abuse comes from the uncorroborated word of a three-year-old child. In these sex abuse cases, the children are usually between ages three and seven.

Should the law authorize the criminal conviction of an accused child abuser on the basis of such evidence? That is the emotional question facing prosecutors in Jordan, Minnesota, and in other cities and towns around the country.

In Jordan, the stakes are even higher. The prosecutor has dropped charges against twenty-one adults accused of sexually abusing children in order to avoid compromising "sensitive documents" that point to an even bigger story: that some of the abused children might have been murdered. The children, who have been telling local authorities stories about rape, incest, and sodomy for more than a year, have now begun to mention murders. However, no bodies have been found; no children have been reported missing; and Jordan is a small town of 2,700 people.

Have the children who said they knew of such murders been fibbing? Are they confused? How can we know whether their statements about the sexual abuse itself are reliable?

These questions are very tough, if unpopular, ones to ask these days as stories about suspected sexual abuse of children at day-care centers circulate nationwide and attract the attention of parents and professionals. New therapies aimed at encouraging children to discuss possible abuse are being developed, using dolls and pictures. Medical journal articles have discussed the detection of physical evidence of sexual abuse.

In juvenile courts, children's testimony is generally admitted. In ordinary courts, children's testimony requires corroboration from another source.

In cases where there is independent verification of what the child says— such as physical evidence of sexual abuse, or the child's description of a place or act he or she couldn't have otherwise known about, or the independent testimony of another child—the testimony is generally deemed admissible, as it should be.

But often the alleged victim is the only witness. Should we accept what the child has to say at face value? Some psychologists and children's therapists say we must—that children don't often lie, that their lies can usually be detected, and that the story they tell is generally detailed and explicit enough to make what they say believable. Many defense attorneys say we shouldn't—that children are known to lie, that it's too easy for a prosecutor to put words in a child's mouth, and that children aren't aware of the serious consequences of the accusations they may be making in an effort to please the friendly questioner. In Jordan, children have said they were forced to eat gerbils and tomcats (the animals had names, according to the children). Their stories have changed and expanded over time.

This nationwide outbreak of suspected sexual abuses at day-care centers is quite sudden. Skeptics are wondering whether some parents, terrified about the stories they hear on television, have been prompted to question their own children persistently enough to encourage them to tell similar stories, or to tell stories with vague details about which the parents assume the worst. Other observers believe it may reflect a phenomenon like rape, which was heard about so much more only after media exposure made it safer and more comfortable for the victims to speak out.

The conflict between the right of a child to be safe from sexual abuse and the right of a defendant not to be falsely accused is most dramatic in the context of a criminal prosecution carrying a long prison term. But there are other ways—short of criminal prosecutions—to protect the child: removing the child from the home or center; educating the child at a very early age about the wrongness of anyone's fondling his or her genitals; restructuring or reorganizing the staff at centers. Many of these approaches are already being tried. They, too, carry the risk of false accusation, but with somewhat less serious consequences.

Our understandable desire to assure the highest degree of safety for the most vulnerable among us—young children—tests the constitutional principle that no person should be convicted except upon proof of guilt beyond a reasonable doubt. We should not compromise that important principle, even for the protection of our children. Remember that your loved ones could become victims of a false accusation, just as they could become victims of a sexual assault.

October 30, 1984

UPDATE
In 1987, the Supreme Court ruled that a defendant could be excluded from a pretrial hearing at which the competency of a child witness was determined.

21
Rehnquist Errs on Court Packing

Now that the elections are over, William Rehnquist, associate justice of the U.S. Supreme Court, should take some time off and go back to law school to learn something about our American constitutional system. In a speech during the presidential election campaign, Rehnquist offered the opinion that "there is no reason in the world" why a president should not try to "pack" the Supreme Court with justices who agree with him.

But there are at least three good reasons that Rehnquist is wrong. The first is that a justice of the Supreme Court had no business interjecting himself into the politics of a presidential campaign. Rehnquist, a Republican, sided with President Reagan on a controversial issue on which the president disagreed with his opponent. During the campaign, Walter Mondale argued that it would be wrong for a president to pack the court with appointees who met the ideological test set out in the Republican platform. Indeed, Mondale expressly condemned Rehnquist's remarks, thus injecting the justice even further into the campaign. Supreme Court justices aren't supposed to take sides publicly in political campaigns.

The second reason Rehnquist is wrong is that the Supreme Court is an important part of our system of checks and balances. It isn't the proper role of the nine justices, who are appointed for life, to promote the incumbent administration's political programs. Their job is to ensure that the political trends of the day don't overwhelm the enduring values of liberty, equality, and due process that distinguish our country from most others. The fact that Supreme Court justices don't run for election or reelection—as they do in some states—gives them powers and responsibilities that differ from those of elected presidents, senators, and congressmen. They should not be appointed because of their party affiliation, their loyalty to the administration, or their willingness to overrule particular decisions on a president's "hit list."

The Supreme Court's most important function is to provide an independent review of important governmental actions that affect citizens' constitutional liberties. If the justices become political clones of the incumbent executive and legislative majorities, they will provide a less effective "check" on the excesses of the current majority. The delicate "balance" among our branches will then tilt heavily in favor of government and against the individual, and in favor of the majority and against minorities.

Our very best presidents appointed a diverse array of justices who reflected differing philosophies and ensured a relatively balanced court. Franklin Roosevelt—the last president who sought to pack the court— ended up appointing the great conservative leader Felix Frankfurter, the great liberal William Douglas, and the great iconoclast Hugo Black. With that kind of diversity, there was little danger that the Supreme Court would become a rubber stamp for the policies of any administration.

The third reason Rehnquist is wrong is that his message—that there is no reason for a president not to try to pack the court—sends out a political challenge to the senators of the opposition party.

After all, the Constitution does not vest the process of Supreme Court appointments solely in the president. Article II, Section 2 provides that the president shall have power, "by and with the advice and consent of the Senate," to appoint Supreme Court justices. Nor are justices like Cabinet members. The president is entitled to have *his* Cabinet—unless a particular nominee is unqualified. But the Supreme Court is not supposed to work *with* or *for* the president. If the president decides simply to assert his power to pack the court to his political liking, senators from the opposing party could try to use their constitutional power to defeat him. An early commenter on the U.S. Constitution put it this way: "A party nomination may be justly met by party opposition." The Federalist Papers looked upon the senate as "an excellent check upon the spirit of favoritism in the president" that might otherwise produce nominees who were selected "from a view to popularity." Rehnquist offers no response to these cogent historical claims.

The appointment of justices should be more than an exercise of naked power. It is among the most important and enduring decisions any president and senator must make. Appointments made in the 1980s will continue to affect our children and grandchildren well into the twenty-first century.

Let us hear no more ill-considered talk of court packing—especially from a sitting justice. Let us instead insist that the president appoint thoughtful and independent men and women who will ensure that our system of checks and balances remains the vigorous safeguard of liberty that was intended by the framers of our Constitution.

November 6, 1984

UPDATE
President Reagan's attempt to pack the court with ideological soulmates has met some resistance. Although Justices O'Connor and Scalia were confirmed without real opposition, Rehnquist himself received some tough questioning when he was promoted to Chief Justice. See columns 92, 93, and 98. Robert Bork's nomination was defeated and Judge Douglas Ginsberg withdrew, before Judge Anthony Kennedy was finally confirmed.

22
Abortions, Transplants, and the Courts

"That's like saying she's just a little pregnant—or a bit dead." This quip used to be a real conversation-stopper. But it now makes all the difference in the world whether a woman is a "little" pregnant or a "lot" pregnant. If she's a "little" pregnant, she can choose abortion; but if she's a "lot" pregnant, she can't.

Even death, that most absolute of absolutes, has become somewhat relative as courts define death as occurring when one principal organ—the brain—dies, although another major organ—the heart—is still beating. And Wordsworth's immortal words extolling the unique virtues of "the human heart by which we live," and that is home to the "soul" may lose some of their poetic force as baboon and other animal hearts are transplanted into human bodies.

Changing technology, biology, and law require that we develop new vocabularies, new aphorisms, new analogies—even new poetry.

There are those who are troubled by any "tampering" with the "natural order." Theologians worry about the religious implications of implanting the heart of a soulless animal into the body of a human "made in God's image." Fundamentalists fear that successful cross-species transplants may undercut the "scientific truth" of creationism and strengthen the claims of heathens who believe that baboons and humans are on an evolutionary continuum. Antivivisectionists rail against using animal organs for experimentation; and some ordinary folks still feel queasy about humans borrowing organs from lower species. (There was, after all, even racist opposition from some white South Africans when Dr. Christiaan Barnard—the heart transplant pioneer—mentioned the possibility of transplanting the heart of a dead black person into the body of a live white person.)

Despite these concerns, the clock won't be turned back on scientific efforts that might extend human life. The question of whether to transplant baboon hearts into babies' bodies won't be answered by clerics, lawyers, or philosophers: it will be answered by the results of ongoing experiments. If the transplants work, they will continue. They will continue because preserving the lives of human beings will inevitably take precedence over the claims of animal lovers, religious critics, and politicians.

As long as there are humans who want to live and doctors who want to help them live, no laws or rules will be able to keep the medical profession from preferring human life over animal life. Parents will not be denied the right to choose experiments with animal organs in order to extend their children's lives. In the end, a species that eats other species primarily for the pleasure of taste won't tolerate a ban on transplants that would extend human life by sacrificing baboons.

Nor will the clock be turned back on abortions, even if the Supreme Court were to reverse its pro-choice decisions. Women who choose to terminate their pregnancies will find ways to secure abortions. Some— especially the poor—might be forced to endanger their lives by resorting to medically unsafe procedures, but the net result probably would not be a substantial decrease in abortions.

These life-and-death decisions involve issues of conflicting morality, but there are also issues of naked power. Humans have the power to prefer their own lives and welfare to the lives of lower species—regardless of what antivivisectionists may prefer. Women generally have the power to prefer their own lives and welfare to the potential life of a fetus—even if some regard abortion as murder.

One of the law's main functions is to impose a degree of morality on the exercise of power. However, the law can't ignore the realities of power and the limitations of imposing one particular set of moral standards on a diverse array of people. When the stakes are as high and personal as they are in the areas of heart transplants and abortions, individuals will insist on making their *own* moral decisions. They won't accept having their choices restricted in the name of someone else's morality.

As science and technology make it increasingly possible for humans to enhance both the quality and quantity of life, the law will have to find its proper role in regulating these exciting—if somewhat frightening—developments. When it comes to life and death, personal and family decisions, the law should neither eschew all morality nor attempt to impose the morality of one group on the equally moral choices of other groups. This will not be an easy balance to strike.

November 13, 1984

23
Would TV Really Wreck the Court?

A legal "Trivial Pursuit" question: guess what Chief Justice Warren Burger considers to be the "most destructive thing in the world"?

If you guessed nuclear weapons, you lose. You also lose if your response was poverty, crime, hunger, or even disease: Chief Justice Warren Burger recently told a Tampa audience that he thinks that the "most destructive thing in the world" is television in the courtroom.

Although Burger's hyperbole obviously wasn't intended to be taken literally, it does reflect his obsessive hatred of the media—and especially of television news. He has shouted at, walked out on, and shoved TV reporters. Once he even pulled a gun on reporters. And now he has announced that "there will be no cameras in the Supreme Court of the United States while I sit there."

The decision, of course, isn't his to make. It's up to Congress and the nine justices of the Supreme Court to determine whether the public should have the right to observe *their* Supreme Court in action. Warren Burger is apparently the only justice who opposes all televising of Supreme Court proceedings.

The issue of televising *jury trials*—involving witnesses and jurors—is controversial. Forty states now permit some coverage. But no persuasive arguments have been offered in favor of a total ban on permitting a TV camera to record and broadcast arguments before the Supreme Court.

There are no witnesses or jurors in the high court—only experienced lawyers, the justices, the press, and the few citizens who can fit into the small courtroom. Modern technology also makes it possible to televise an argument without visible cameras or lights: all that's needed is a small hole in the wall.

I can testify from my own experience that appellate lawyers simply forget that they're being televised. I argued the appeal of Claus von Bulow and the appeals of two young death row inmates before television cameras. Those experiences were no different for me than the dozens of other appeals I have argued. However, the judges in televised proceedings seemed better prepared, asked more intelligent questions, and listened to the arguments more carefully.

The sad truth is that some appellate judges—even Supreme Court justices—are often woefully unprepared. Many haven't read the briefs or the trial record. A few ask silly questions; others seem bored. Justice William Douglas used to write books and articles while lawyers were arguing. Burger has a penchant for asking irrelevant questions and straying from the real issues. I can fully understand why some judges may not want TV cameras to record their performances for posterity.

Most judges, of course, do their jobs admirably. Televising important Supreme Court arguments would help ensure that all members of the least accountable, least supervised, and least reported on branch of our government are doing their homework.

Allowing TV in the Supreme Court also would help inform the public about important issues decided by the justices, such as capital punishment, abortion, affirmative action, and religion. Network television would only carry snippets of some arguments, but educational or cable stations could provide fuller coverage of major cases with wide public interest. Even the kind of capsule coverage the networks might provide would supplement the somewhat unrealistic views presented by popular TV courtroom shows like "The People's Court."

Finally, television could provide an archival and educational function, since videotapes of arguments would be preserved. Law school students could learn a great deal by watching tapes of great Supreme Court arguments. It's tragic that there are no visual records of such classic legal confrontations as the "Nixon tapes" case, the school desegregation case, and the abortion arguments.

Balanced against these considerations is Burger's obsessive stance against cameras in the courtroom and the current absolute prohibition against televising *any* federal proceedings. I know of no thoughtful public judicial discussion of the pros and cons of permitting unobtrusive televising of some Supreme Court arguments.

I challenge Chief Justice Burger to offer some valid reasons that the absolute ban on televising Supreme Court arguments should not be amended. It is not responsible of him simply to impose his bias on the American public, nor should he hide behind the facade of judicial silence. He already has spoken publicly on the subject—but he has not spoken persuasively. Judges are supposed to offer reasoned arguments for their conclusions. Burger already appeared once on "Nightline" to discuss his views on the prison system—a subject of frequent litigation. Ted Koppel has invited him back to discuss other issues. I can hardly imagine a subject more suited for television discussion than Burger's ukase that "there will be no cameras in the Supreme Court while I sit there."

November 20, 1984

UPDATE
Although Burger is no longer chief justice, there is still no TV or radio coverage of federal courts, but that is likely to change. For further discussion of the media and criminal justice, see columns 44, 55, and 77.

24
If Westmoreland Wins, We All Lose

What would happen to freedom of the press if Generals William Westmoreland and Ariel Sharon won their respective libel suits against CBS and *Time* Magazine?

Westmoreland, claiming that he was libeled in a TV program about the Vietnam War, is suing for $120 million in damages. Sharon, alleging that he was libeled by a *Time* article about the Phalangist massacre of Palestinians in Lebanon, is trying to collect $50 million.

Though it's unlikely that either general will get anything close to what he's seeking, juries have a way of showing their dislike for the press by socking it to them with gargantuan verdicts. Remember the jury that awarded a former Miss Wyoming $26 million on the basis of her claim that she resembled a character in a story published by *Penthouse* magazine, which she said insulted her? The jury's disdain for *Penthouse*, rather than the actual damage suffered by Miss Wyoming, probably explains the excessiveness of the verdict—which was eventually reversed on appeal.

Even when excessive verdicts are reversed on appeal, much of the damage has been done. Legal fees in these big libel cases are astronomical— often in the millions! The prospect of expensive libel trials, appeals, and verdicts is already having an impact on the kind of investigative reporting that brought us Watergate.

Picture the following scene: a small newsweekly has learned from a reliable source that the mayor is about to abscond with money from the pension fund. An emergency editorial meeting is convened to decide whether to run the story. The publishing deadline is that afternoon.

REPORTER: "I'm convinced it's true. My source has never burned me."

EDITOR: "But we really have to have more than your own conviction. You hate the mayor. I'm worried that you may be applying a softer standard of certainty to him."

PUBLISHER: "Look, it's a great story if it's true, but I don't want to go with it unless we're pretty well convinced. Where do you think we are on a scale of one to ten?"

REPORTER: "I'd put it up around eight or nine."

EDITOR: "Maybe it's my age, but I'm a bit more skeptical. I'll say six or seven."

PUBLISHER: "So you're both telling me it's more likely to be true than false. If we don't go with it, there's a better-than-even chance that the mayor will get away with it. But if we do go with it, there's a significant possibility—but not a probability—that we may be falsely accusing the mayor of a serious crime."

Up to now, the conversation sounds the way it should in a responsible news office—but suddenly the publisher calls in the paper's lawyer. The publisher briefs her on the prior discussion, and the conversation continues:

PUBLISHER: "What if, despite our best efforts, we turn out to be wrong? What's our libel liability? How much could a mistake cost us?"

LAWYER: "Well, you've got a real problem here. A jury could find that the reporter acted out of malice."

REPORTER: "I don't like him, but that doesn't mean I didn't try my best to find out the truth. Sure, I get a kick out of exposing bad people. What's wrong with that?"

LAWYER: "Nothing, as far as I'm concerned. But the law says that if you make a mistake about someone you don't like—even if that person is a public figure like the mayor—you may owe him a bundle."

PUBLISHER: "What's a bundle?"

LAWYER: "It could be in the millions."

PUBLISHER: "That's it. Kill the story. I can't afford that kind of gamble. Let some other newspaper stick its neck out."

The same conclusion might not be reached in the more affluent offices of the *Washington Post*, CBS, or *Time*, but even those media giants are becoming increasingly concerned about having to pay large libel verdicts for their honest mistakes. During Watergate itself—one of our finest examples of investigative reporting—Woodward and Bernstein made a mistake in reporting an uncorroborated tip about a grand jury proceeding. If they had been sued for a staggering sum, who knows whether they would have been permitted to pursue the rest of the story as aggressively as they did?

Juries and judges also make honest mistakes about people. Not only do they occasionally convict an innocent defendant, but the effect is worse than that of libel: the innocent person goes to prison or to the electric chair.

Yet our system of justice couldn't survive if we punished judges and juries for their honest mistakes. Accordingly, the judges have given themselves (and the juries) a near-absolute immunity for their mistakes. At the very least, the same rules that apply to those who make mistakes in the name of government should apply to those who err in the process of reporting on public figures.

Thomas Jefferson reminded us that the healthy survival of an inquiring press is no less important to democracy than government itself: "Were it left to me to decide whether we should have a government without newspapers, or newspapers without a government," he said, "I should not hesitate a moment to prefer the latter."

November 27, 1984

UPDATE
General Westmoreland withdrew his suit before it was submitted to a jury.

25
Time v. *Sharon*:
The Right to Be Wrong

The jury's verdict in General Ariel Sharon's libel suit against *Time* magazine represents a major victory for both the freedom and the accountability of the American press. The three-tier verdict also reflects the genius and uniqueness of our First Amendment.

The jury made three findings. The first was that *Time* magazine had defamed Sharon to an "aggravated" degree by reporting that just before the Phalangist massacres in Beirut, Sharon had discussed "the need for the Phalangists to take revenge for the assassination" of their leader. The second jury finding was that the *Time* report was false. These two findings constituted a "moral victory," according to Sharon. But the jury's third finding—that *Time* magazine's false reporting was not malicious—denied Sharon any financial remuneration for his defamation.

The jury concluded that *Time* had not acted with "actual malice"—that is, the editors did not know the offending paragraph was false, nor did they print it with reckless disregard for the truth. The jurors added—almost as a consolation prize for Sharon—that they believed the *Time* reporter responsible for the false information had "acted negligently and carelessly in reporting and verifying the information which ultimately found its way into the published paragraph. . . ." But under the unique libel laws of the United States, even that is not enough: the media may negligently print a lie defaming a public person without fear of a libel verdict, so long as it did not have "actual malice."

The United States is the only country in the world whose law requires "actual malice" before a public person can win a libel suit. In other civilized and law-abiding nations, it would be enough to prove defamation and falsehood. The reason we require a public plaintiff to overcome the "actual malice" barrier is rooted in our First Amendment protection of freedom of the press.

The Supreme Court has said that the media needs breathing space in order to flourish. If the press can be exposed to a bankrupting libel verdict every time it makes an honest mistake, it will tend to err on the side of caution and silence. A vigorous investigative press will necessarily make some mistakes in the course of breaking controversial and important stories.

The most significant difference between freedom of the press in the United States and elsewhere is that our media have a constitutional right to make honest mistakes. The American press has the right to be wrong! And there can be no more important safeguard for the freedom of the American public to obtain information necessary to the functioning of a democracy. If the press were protected only when it turned out to be right, it would be unduly risky to publish timely accounts of controversial, fast-breaking events. In the real world of competitive, deadline journalism, a daily or weekly newspaper, magazine, television, or radio reporter cannot wait until he or she is absolutely certain of the truth. The reporter—and, ultimately, the editor—must weigh the costs of nondisclosure (or delay in disclosure), against the costs of false disclosure. And the media should bear the moral consequences of their mistakes.

Time magazine has certainly suffered the moral consequences of publishing its false paragraph about Sharon. The American reading public—indeed, the international reading public—now has a far better understanding of the fallibility of the *Time* reporting, fact-checking, and editing process. The reporter responsible, David Halevy, has certainly had his own journalistic reputation tarnished.

Nor has *Time* escaped all financial costs. When it receives the final bill from its legal team, it will have to be reminded that—at least in a technical sense—it won the monetary portion of this lawsuit. Its out-of-pocket costs will be in the millions, without even counting the loss of prestige it will suffer from the jury verdict.

But that is as it should be in a free and open society. *Time* magazine can hardly be heard to complain that the truth has emerged about the carelessness of its reporting. The beauty of the American system is that if *Time* doesn't agree with the jury's assessment, it is free to try to persuade its readers that the jury was wrong. It may continue to complain that it did not have complete access to all the Israeli information. And the public can draw its own conclusions about whether this sounds like a legitimate grievance or sour grapes. As long as no one is prevented—either by government or by private bankrupting libel verdicts—from continuing the conversation, we the public are the ultimate beneficiaries.

And once again, the common sense of the American jury has shown itself. The *Sharon-Time* verdict was just about right on every score.

January 25, 1985

26
Libel Wins Aren't "Vindication"

Another libel defendant—this time the *Boston Globe*—has boasted that it was "vindicated" by successfully defending itself against a libel suit brought by a public figure.

Recently a judge ruled that the *Globe* had not libeled John Lakian—an unsuccessful candidate for the Massachusetts Republican nomination for governor—even though a jury had found that several paragraphs in a story about Lakian's background had been false, defamatory, and published with "knowing or reckless disregard" as to their falsity. The jury had also found that the "gist" of the entire story had been true and that Lakian had not suffered actual damages.

In claiming vindication, the *Globe* has echoed *Time* magazine and CBS, which also staved off megabuck judgments over this past year, despite some questions about the quality of their reporting.

But any suggestion that winning a libel suit constitutes vindication for journalists reflects a profound misunderstanding of U.S. libel law.

For a public figure to beat the press in the libel game, he or she must prove four independent facts:

1. That the statement made about him or her was *false*
2. That the false statement *defamed* the plaintiff
3. That the false statement was made *maliciously* or with a reckless disregard for whether it was false and
4. That the person defamed has suffered *damages* measurable in dollars

If *any one* of these four factors is not proved by the public figure, the press wins the libel suit.

To understand why a legal victory in a libel suit does not constitute vindication, imagine the following case: a newspaper negligently prints a false statement that Candidate Jones was convicted of business fraud several years ago. Jones is defamed by the false story and loses the election, which he otherwise would have won. He then sues the paper and the reporter. The court finds that the newspaper made an honest—but stupid—mistake: it was the candidate's father, not the candidate himself, who had been convicted. Since father and son had the same name—John Jones—the story somehow got by.

In such a case, the press would probably "win" the libel suit because the candidate could not show malice or recklessness. But surely the newspaper and its reporter would in no way be "vindicated." They still would be guilty of very bad journalism.

This isn't to say that the *Globe*, CBS, or *Time* were, in fact, guilty of bad journalism in their reporting on John Lakian, General William Westmoreland, or General Ariel Sharon. The point is that a libel trial is not supposed to make that kind of judgment. Neither a judge nor a jury is competent to distinguish good journalism from bad journalism. "Vindication" must come from journalistic peers, who have the background and expertise to judge the quality of the reporting that is being challenged.

The Pulitzer Committee and others like it are involved in an ongoing process of judging excellence. As far as I know, there is no analogous peer-group review of incompetence, other than ombudsmen at a few newspapers. More and more, therefore, the courts have been resorted to in the form of libel suits.

The U.S. law of libel has quickly become a high-stakes roulette wheel. If the public figure wins, he wins so big that he can virtually bankrupt all but the largest media corporations. Seven- and eight-figure demands are commonly attached to the lawsuits. Lakian sued for $50 million; Westmoreland for $20 million; Sharon for $50 million. Senator Paul Laxalt (Republican-Nevada)—not one to be outdone in setting a price on his reputation—is suing a newspaper chain for $250 million.

If the public figure loses—for whatever reasons—the media defendant claims vindication, and the public figure gets nothing. In the Lakian and Sharon cases, the juries decided that the *Globe* and *Time* had, in fact, made false statements—yet neither plaintiff won a nickel.

The time has come for a sensible middle ground. There should be a forum in which an aggrieved public figure can establish that a false, defamatory statement has been published about him—a forum for quickly correcting the record when the press has made a mistake, honest or otherwise.

It would be best if this forum were nongovernmental, since there are grave dangers in granting any branch of government the power to "correct" the press. The press should clean its own house, both to be fair to those unjustly defamed and to stave off governmental incursions into its freedom of expression. A private review board—comprised of reporters, editors, publishers, and readers—should be established. Its sole function would be to "vindicate" either the aggrieved citizen or the press by issuing reports on well-grounded complaints. It would have no power to award monetary damages.

The press must recall that when it wins a libel suit, it is the First Amendment that is vindicated. That amendment gives the press the most fundamental right of expression known to a democracy—the right to be wrong in order to be bold. And the ultimate beneficiaries of that right are supposed to be the informed citizens.

August 20, 1985

27
Political Life vs. Human Death

It makes King Solomon's decision about the baby seem like an easy choice—but Governor James Hunt of North Carolina can't split the difference in the case of Mrs. Velma Barfield. If the moderate governor refuses to commute Mrs. Barfield's death sentence and lets her execution go forward, he may win his Senate race against incumbent ultra-conservative Senator Jesse Helms. If he spares her life, he probably will lose the election and see Helms return to the Senate.

The story is as simple as it is poignant. Mrs. Barfield was convicted of poisoning her boyfriend. There were arguments for and against sentencing her to death. On the one hand, she confessed to poisoning three other people, including her own mother. On the other hand, there was evidence that she was mentally ill and the product of a perverted father who raped her, an alcoholic husband who beat her, and an exploitative doctor who addicted her to drugs when she was ten. The sentencing judge decided that the aggravating factors outweighed the mitigating factors and imposed the death penalty.

All of this sounds familiar. Other than the fact that Mrs. Barfield is a woman, there is little to distinguish her from the hundreds of other inmates on death row—or, indeed, from the thousands of murderers who are sentenced to life imprisonment every year.

But Mrs. Barfield's situation is unique in another critical respect: the only person who stands between her and the gas chamber (or possibly a lethal injection) is James Hunt, the governor of North Carolina. Under North Carolina law, only the governor has the power of commutation, and he can't delegate that life-and-death decision to anyone else. And Hunt is involved in what is perhaps the tightest Senate race in the country: polls have him neck-and-neck with Helms. To make things even more dramatic, a state superior court judge has set the execution date for November 2, 1984—just four days before the election.

Hunt's political supporters are telling him that if he commutes Mrs. Barfield's sentence—or even if he postpones the clemency decision—it may cost him enough pro-capital punishment votes to make the difference between victory and defeat. The overwhelming majority of North Carolinians—even those who now support the moderate Hunt—favor execution in general, and Mrs. Barfield's execution in particular.

The situation has posed a dilemma of Faustian proportions for those of Hunt's advisors who are opposed to the death penalty, but see Helms as the devil incarnate. Some are urging the governor to sacrifice Mrs. Barfield's life to the higher need of defeating Helms. Others are urging him to act on principle and—at the very least—to postpone the decision until he can pass on her clemency petition without concern for his own electoral fortunes.

Hunt has said that he will make the decision without regard to political considerations, but few people in North Carolina believe that is possible. At this time, it is difficult to predict what he will do.

What is absolutely clear is that Mrs. Barfield has been placed in an untenable—and, in my view, unconstitutional—situation as a result of the timing. The superior court judge who set the execution date could have set it after the election, but he chose not to do so. Whether or not the judge did this deliberately in order to put pressure on Hunt, the reality is that Hunt simply cannot act as he is mandated to—without concern for his *own* interests.

The critical constitutional issue is not whether Mrs. Barfield deserves to live or die. Reasonable people—and reasonable governors—can disagree about this. Friends and relatives of the victims are urging Hunt to permit the execution; supporters of Mrs. Barfield—including Billy Graham's wife—are pleading for her life on the ground that she has become a model prisoner who has devoted her prison time to helping other inmates. The real issue is whether Mrs. Barfield is entitled to have the clemency decision made by a governor who does not have to weigh his political life against her actual life.

The courts must intervene and postpone the scheduled execution until after the election. If the state courts will not, then the federal courts should. The constitutional right to an impartial and disinterested decision-maker demands no less.

Whichever side one may be on in the capital punishment debate, surely most Americans will agree that the decision to let Mrs. Barfield live or to let her die should not be made on the basis of an impending election.

September 25, 1984

UPDATE
Governor Hunt allowed the execution to go forward and Mrs. Barfield was executed on November 2, 1984. A few days later, Governor Hunt lost the election to Jesse Helms.

28
Arresting the Good Samaritan

You're driving down the highway at 65 mph—just a bit above the speed limit. Out of the corner of your eye, you spot the top of a police car that's hiding behind a distant knoll. Realizing that you're about to enter a speed-trap zone, you slow down—not so quickly as to be obvious, but just enough to get you down to 55 mph before you come within range of the radar.

You nervously pass the police car, pretending not to notice it, and you begin to smile as you realize that you've gotten away with it. For the next several minutes, you watch your speedometer as you reflect on your close encounter with the law.

You're feeling lucky and happy, and you want to share your good fortune with a stranger, so you blink your lights at several approaching cars that are about to enter the radar zone from the opposite direction. They blink back appreciatively, recognizing the universal highway warning signal of an impending speed trap.

The motorists slow down and escape the trap. No harm has been done. You've been a double good Samaritan—saving a fellow motorist from an expensive ticket, while simultaneously reminding him to slow down.

Suddenly you hear a siren. You look behind you: it's the police car, and it's signaling you to pull over. Have you been caught after all? As the policeman approaches your car, you open the window and—mustering your most respectfully subservient tone—you mutter, "But Officer, I was only going a wee bit over 55."

"I know that," he says, looking you straight in the eye. "I'm not stopping you for speeding." You express relief—but he continues, "You're in much more trouble than that. I'm arresting you for obstructing justice.

"I saw you signaling those cars," he says, as you go into a panic. "You were interfering with a lawful traffic-enforcement operation."

No, this isn't just a fantasy: it's a real nightmare that's now being experienced by Massachusetts motorists. Instead of being praised as good Samaritans, blinking motorists are in danger of being ticketed as impeders of justice.

One motorist, Reinhard Bartelmann, thirty-four, has decided to fight back. He insists that his citation on charges of "impeding operation" of a speed trap constitutes "an infringement of my civil rights." His warning to other motorists was, he says, "an expression of free speech." The American Civil Liberties Union is looking into the matter.

Whether or not blinking a warning is "free speech," it's certainly not a crime—at least not yet. Even the Massachusetts public safety commissioner acknowledges that there's no specific state law prohibiting the widespread practice of flashing warnings about speed traps.

That should end the matter—at least for now. The U.S. Constitution forbids the creation of "common-law crimes" by the police or the courts. Only the legislature is authorized to enact legislation creating new crimes—and it can only enact it for the future. So Bartelmann will win his case, because he had no "fair warning" that what he was doing was regarded as illegal by law enforcement authorities.

But what if the legislature were now to make it a crime to flash warnings? Could future flashers be convicted?

The prospect of legislation that would make it a crime to warn others of police traps has broad implications that go well beyond radar zones. Law enforcement authorities throughout the nation are relying increasingly on "stings," "scams," and other traps analogous to the radar zone. These include governmentally run fencing operations, prostitution rings, bribery offers, decoys, and drug networks. To be effective, all of these operations require that potential law violators not be informed that the government is observing their actions. If the congressmen who took money from the Abscam "sheik" had been told that the sheik was really an FBI agent, they obviously would have turned down the bribes.

Cynics might ask: what harm would have been done if the congressmen had been warned? They would then not have committed the crimes! Those who support scams would respond that the crooked congressmen—like the speeding motorists warned about the trap—would have avoided being caught this time, and would simply be more careful in their future corruption.

The narrow debate over criminalizing speed-trap warnings is thus really part of a broader debate over the fairness and effectiveness of scams and traps.

As a constitutional matter, a legislature could possibly pass a lawful statute prohibiting one citizen from warning another about a police trap—if the law were clear and unambiguous. Some state laws prohibiting the use of radar detectors have been upheld.

Bartelmann's claim of free speech will almost certainly be rejected by the courts. A law prohibiting highway warnings might be foolish, but the police do have the constitutional power to conduct their speed traps, unimpeded by good Samaritans.

December 4, 1984

For other discussions of stings, see columns 7 and 8.

29
The Extent of Corporate Liability

As he stepped off the plane in Bhopal, India, Warren Anderson—chairman of Union Carbide—was "detained" by Indian authorities and charged with several crimes in connection with the chemical leak that killed more than 2,000 men, women, and children.

Although Anderson was released on bail six hours later, the charges raise anew several sticky legal questions concerning the scope of a multinational corporation's criminal liability for the negligent acts of its subsidiaries around the world.

The questions include the following:

- Can an American corporation be held criminally responsible for crimes committed by a foreign subsidiary?
- What does it mean to say a corporation has committed a crime?
- Can a corporation be punished in any way other than by a fine?
- Can the officers of a corporation—board members or even

stockholders—be held "personally" responsible for the crimes of their corporation?

- Can a foreign government haul American citizens before its local courts to stand trial and face punishment for crimes committed by local subsidiaries?
- Would American courts authorize the extradition—forceable sending abroad—of American citizens to stand trial under foreign rules of justice that did not meet American standards?
- How will the financial liability of Union Carbide be measured?

These and other difficult questions may well be mooted by the political and economic realities surrounding the Union Carbide tragedy. If the Indian government wants to see its citizens receive medical assistance and financial compensation when they are most critically needed, the matter will probably have to be settled.

Indeed, immediately after Anderson's detention, signs of a settlement atmosphere were already evident. The detention was described not as an "arrest," but rather as a protective measure designed to allay the anger of the gathering crowds (who were holding signs reading "Hang Anderson").

It was also seen by some as a show of strength by frustrated local officials. Indian prosecutors urged Anderson to leave the country lest he "provoke strong passions against him."

If the Indian authorities do decide to prosecute American officers of Union Carbide, it will not be an easy task. The first step would be to get the American citizens into the physical custody of Indian courts. Without their physical presence, any trial would be an exercise in futility. Even if they were convicted "in absentia," no American court would recognize such a bogus conviction.

So unless the Americans voluntarily go to India, the Indian authorities would have to appeal to American authorities for their extradition.

But American law does not encourage the extradition of American citizens for trial in foreign countries. The alleged criminal act would have to be covered by an extradition treaty and be a crime in both countries. The laws of the extraditing country—India in this case—would have to permit the extradition of Indian citizens to the United States in a comparable situation. And the legal protections accorded defendants in Indian courts would have to meet certain standards.

It is unlikely that these conditions would be satisfied in the Union Carbide case.

The American law on holding corporate officers guilty of crimes for the acts of their subordinates is far from clear. It is even more obscure when the acts are committed by foreign subsidiaries. Generally, our law requires that the particular corporate official charged have the specific knowledge and intent necessary to commit the crime.

Thus, unless it could be proved that Anderson was personally aware of the hazardous conditions prevalent in the Bhopal plant, he would probably not be held criminally responsible for the crimes.

That is not to say that his corporation could not be held liable, both criminally and civilly. Under American law, a corporation—inanimate as it is—may be found guilty of crimes. Corporations have been convicted of fraud, theft, conspiracy—even manslaughter. The punishment, of course, is economic.

Union Carbide can also be held civilly liable for the damages caused by the negligence of its employees and agents. Already, multi-billion-dollar lawsuits have been commenced by American and Indian lawyers. Where these suits will end up—in American or Indian courts, or most likely both—is not yet certain. Nor is it clear which law will apply or what the measure of damages will be.

Three conclusions are, however, clear: the first is that these complex issues will increase in importance as more multinational corporations spread their hazardous enterprises throughout the world; the second is that this chemical leak will end up costing Union Carbide a fortune; and the third is that however much Union Carbide ends up paying, it will not come close to compensating the dead and maimed of Bhopal for their incomprehensible suffering.

December 11, 1984

For further discussion of corporate crime, see columns 56 and 106.

30
Private Tastes, Public Knowledge

You check *TV Guide*. Nothing good is on. Just to make sure, you flip the channels. Still nothing. Reruns! Movies you've already seen! Insipid sitcoms.

"Come on," you suggest to your wife, "let's go rent a movie." The two of you browse through the cassette boxes as your eye lights on the new James Bond movie. You notice your wife casting a nervous glance at the top shelf—the one with all the "adult" titles.

"I've never seen one of these," she says. "I'm curious. But I'd never go into one of those seedy movie houses that show them."

"Well, I saw one or two in my fraternity days," you assure her, "and you're not missing anything."

She persists. "I really would like to see what everybody's talking about, and besides it might be fun—just the two of us alone watching a good dirty movie."

"All right," you give in. "Let's rent *Debbi Does Dallas*."

You take the cassette home and watch it together. Your wife's curiosity has been satisfied, but you were both upset at the sexism of the film. You decide you're not going to rent from the top shelf again.

Several weeks later you see an article in the local newspaper reporting that a subpoena has been issued against the video store you rent from. The subpoena demands that the store produce the names of every customer who rented obscene films. Included on the list is *Debbi Does Dallas*.

Suddenly your private act of renting a film for home use has become the subject of a public court proceeding. If the subpoena is complied with, your name will become part of the court files. The newspapers will be free to print the list of people who rented dirty movies. And your friends, relatives, and business associates will learn what you and your wife were watching that night.

No, this isn't an Orwellian fantasy celebrating the close of 1984. It's based on a real case now pending before the courts in Cincinnati.

In that case, the subpoenas listed the titles of five cassettes (ranging from *Tapestry of Passion* to *Exhausted*). It demanded the names of all rental-club members as well as all rental and sales receipts. The subpoenas were served on video shops, convenience stores, and newsstands that sell magazines advertising mail-order, X-rated videos.

Although no names have been given to the government, the subpoenas have already sent a quiet shockwave through the community of video dealers and consumers. But there has been little public outcry—for obvious reasons.

Video dealers don't want to alert their renters to the prospect that their names might have to be disclosed. And citizens who rent "dirty" cassettes certainly don't want to bring themselves to the attention of the public.

The issue *should*, however, provoke public outcry. It has grave implications beyond dirty movies. If the government can subpoena lists of customers, then it can learn what books we buy or borrow, what magazines and newspapers we order, what films we see, what concert or theater series we subscribe to.

And as more and more financial transactions are done by credit card, more and more of our private lives will be permanently recorded and made subject to subpoena.

I'm reminded of a Soviet dissident whom I helped to emigrate. After his first week in the United States, I asked what he saw as the biggest difference between his homeland and his new home. Without hesitation he pointed to the fact that in America there were "open shelves" in the libraries.

"You can read books here without the government keeping a record of what you've checked out," he said with amazement.

It's an important difference that may be difficult to appreciate unless you've lived in a country where records are kept on everything you read.

It is the responsibility of the courts to set limits on the power of government to subpoena records of citizens who rent or purchase material protected by rights of privacy or expression. Unless some precise limits are imposed, citizens will understandably be frightened away from exercizing their constitutional rights. They will be "chilled" by the fear that their names will be publicly associated with controversial material.

Even if the subpoenaed names of consumers were to be kept under government wrap and not disclosed to the press, there would still be concerns about "government files" that contained the names of citizens who exercized their rights in a controversial manner.

One Cincinnati lawyer has related the specific subpoenas to the more general mood of his city: "We're the new 'banned in Boston' community."

But the old "banned in Boston" mood seems to be spreading to other cities and towns. And if the Cincinnati subpoena is upheld, you can be sure that prosecutors throughout the country will welcome this new tool in the war against smut—a war that could easily spread to other unpopular forms of expression.

December 18, 1984

UPDATE
Following press disclosures of video rental records of Lt. Col. Oliver North and Robert Bork—neither of whom has shown much respect for the privacy of others in their professional lives—legislation was introduced mandating the confidentiality of video rental records.

31
Laughing with the Law

Charles Dickens once had one of his characters, Mr. Bumble, declare, "If the law supposes that . . . then the law is an ass—a idiot." Every so often, cases come along that seem designed to confirm Mr. Bumble's assessment. Here are a few from recent news accounts.

First, here's one in the true spirit of the season: a *New York Times* story headlined "Man Jailed For Alleging Santa Doesn't Exist." The story concerns Brian Pearl, a fundamentalist Christian who thinks that Santa is too commercial and has no Biblical basis. He was apparently yelling "no such thing" at children who were waiting in line to see Santa at a shopping mall.

A compassionate judge offered to put Pearl on probation if he promised to desist from his dastardly deeds. But Pearl said that his religious principles require him to tell the truth. So the judge had no choice but to sentence him to jail.

Score one for Santa and against Scrooge.

Pearl will have some high-class company in jail, as the quality of inmates seems to be improving.

One Constance Moore was sent to jail as a result of having thirteen overdue library books in her possession. A Woody Allen joke comes to mind: police cordon off his house and shout through a bullhorn, "We know you're in there; throw out your library books, and come out with your hands up!"

I wonder if Ms. Moore was allowed to bring any of the overdue books with her to help pass the time? Actually, she only had to spend a few hours being "booked" (if ever a judge made the punishment fit the crime!). The remainder of her one week sentence was served in the library itself, performing community service.

Imagine Pearl and Ms. Moore trying to convince their hardened cellmates that they're doing time because of Santa Claus and overdue books.

This brings to mind Aleksandr Solzhenitsyn's story of the Gulag guard who asked the Soviet political prisoner what crime he had committed to deserve his ten-year sentence. "Absolutely nothing," answered the prisoner. "I don't believe you," shouted the guard, "for absolutely nothing they give only five years."

On a more serious note, I wonder how many muggers and other violent criminals are given probation because the jail cells are filled with these kinds of criminals—those sent to jail just to make a point.

Pity the criminals who may have to serve time with Daniel Moody, Linda Ryder, and Perley Ryder. This trio is facing charges of having "argued a man to death." The complaint is that they started an argument with their landlord, knowing that he had a weak heart, and intended to aggravate him to death. It will be one of the rare occasions where defendants will be allowed to bring their deadly weapons—their mouths—with them to prison. Maybe they'll be able to argue their way out.

(My mother will surely be vindicated by the knowledge that it is actually possible to aggravate somebody to death.)

Perhaps the deadly debaters can get help from a Vermont jury that recently acquitted twenty-six protesters of trespassing in the office of a United States senator. Their defense was "necessity." Simply put, they said they had "no choice" but to trespass in order to save the United States from an even greater danger: "Our alleged criminal act was necessary to bring to light the illegal wars being waged in El Salvador and Nicaragua."

There's an old legal principle that when a person's life is directly at stake—for example, when he is in danger of drowning—he may swim to any port, even if he must trespass. That principle is summarized in the pithy phrase "necessity knows no law." The judge who instructed the Vermont jury that it could apply that principle to the trespass into the senator's office should change his own name to "necessity," because he too seems to "know no law."

And speaking of foolish juries, we have the case of the *Reverend Jerry Falwell* v. *Larry Flynt*. The fundamentalist preacher sued the publisher of *Hustler* magazine for $45 million, claiming he was libeled by an ad parody that portrayed him as an incestuous drunkard.

The jury rejected the libel claim, on the ground that anyone—even the "readers" of *Hustler*—could realize the ad was a parody. But it gave Falwell a $200,000 consolation prize for the "emotional distress" he suffered as a result of the experience.

Falwell's emotional distress has paved a road all the way to the bank: he sent the parody to supporters who, outraged by *Hustler*, sent him nearly $1 million in contributions.

These cases prove the wisdom of an old British adage: "It is a common error to suppose that our law has no sense of humor, just because the judges who expound it have none."

The law can be humorous—as long as you're not the butt of the joke.

December 20, 1984

See column 137.

32
The Reality of Terrorism

At about the same time that President Reagan was demanding that Iran extradite or try the hijackers who murdered two Americans, a federal judge in New York was making it impossible for Great Britain to bring to justice a member of the Provisional Wing of the Irish Republican Army who escaped while on trial for murdering a British soldier.

The case that gave rise to Judge Sprizzo's controversial decision had all the drama of a John LeCarré novel. Joseph Patrick Doherty, a twenty-nine-year-old member of the radical group, was captured in Belfast in 1980 after participating in an ambush of a British army patrol in which a British captain was killed. He was brought to trial on murder charges in 1981. Two days before the close of the trial, Doherty and eight others shot their way out of Crumlin Road Prison.

Doherty was convicted in absentia for murder, but managed to sneak into the United States, where he adopted a false name and a new life as a Manhattan bartender. In 1983, he was taken into custody by U.S. Immigration agents. The British authorities requested that he be extradited back to Great Britain to serve his prison sentence for murder and to stand trial for escaping from prison.

Doherty resisted extradition on the ground that his crimes were political, pointing to the terms in the extradition treaty between Britain and the United States that forbid extradition for crimes of "a political character." The British authorities insisted that Doherty's crime was simple murder.

The issue was thus starkly presented: is the killing of a British soldier during an ambush conducted by members of the outlawed IRA a crime "of a political character" or an ordinary murder?

Sprizzo, in his opinion, referred to the "centuries-old hatreds" between the Irish and English and concluded that "the offenses which gave rise to this proceeding are but the latest chapter in that unending epic." There would be "little doubt," therefore, he said, that if the killing had occurred "during the course of more traditional military hostilities," it would fall within the political offense exception to the extradition treaty.

He also found that if the killing had been an isolated act of terrorism against a civilian committed by a small amorphous group, it probably would not qualify for the political-offense exception. The only real issue, in the judge's view, was whether the political-offense exception is as applicable to the kind of "more sporadic and informal mode of warfare" engaged in by the IRA, as it is to conventional warfare.

After reviewing the evidence, Sprizzo concluded that the Provisional Wing of the IRA, though a "radical offshoot of the traditional Irish Republican Army," is more like a real army than it is like a group of terrorists. It has "an organization, discipline, and command structure that distinguishes it from more amorphous groups such as the Black Liberation Army or the Red Brigade."

The court rejected the British government's claim that "the political-offense exception is limited to actual armed insurrection," noting that "political struggles have been commenced and effectively carried out by armed guerrillas long before they were able to mount armies in the field."

Putting all these conclusions together, Sprizzo held that the death of the British officer, while a most tragic event, was a political offense "in its most classic form" and that extradition would be denied.

In an effort to provide guidance for future cases, Sprizzo listed several types of crimes that, in his view, would not qualify as political under the many treaties that contain an exception for crimes of "a political character." He included:

- Crimes that violate international law
- Crimes that are "inconsistent with international standards of civilized conduct"
- Crimes that cause indiscriminate killing of innocent civilians
- Crimes that involve the killing of hostages

Sprizzo's decision still leaves its many questions unresolved. Why are small amorphous terrorist groups any less "political" than disciplined paramilitary organizations? Crimes directed against innocent civilians are certainly more heinous than attacks on soldiers, but are they really less political?

There is an even more basic and profound question raised by the current British-American extradition treaty and many clones: why should extradition be denied for *any* crimes of violence, whether or not of a political character? In his opinion, Sprizzo correctly observed that the political-crimes exception "was in its inception an outgrowth of the notion that a person should not be persecuted for political *beliefs*."

At a time when political terrorism and violence have become the bane of civilized society, it is appropriate for nations like the United States and

Great Britain to reassess their extradition treaties. Perhaps the time has come to limit the political-crimes exception to speech, advocacy, and peaceful demonstrations.

The United States should take the lead in condemning terrorist violence of all kinds, regardless of its political character and motivation. Changing our extradition treaties to reflect the new reality of increasing international terrorism might be a good beginning.

December 25, 1984

UPDATE
For an update on the problem of extradition and terrorism, see next column.

33
Can We Extradite Political Fugitives Fairly?

One of the most divisive issues currently being debated in Washington is whether, and under what circumstances, the United States should extradite alleged terrorists. To extradite a person is to return him (or her) forcibly to a country charging him with a crime so that he can stand 'trial there.

Most civilized countries have treaties with other civilized countries mandating reciprocal obligations to extradite certain categories of fugitives. Ordinary murderers, common robbers, and other criminals are traditionally subject to mutual extradition. But every treaty carries exceptions.

For centuries, extradition treaties have exempted crimes of "a political character." The precise language of our treaties has varied, but the point has been generally clear: activists whose crimes were motivated by political considerations—for example, revolutionary or insurrectionary leaders—could find asylum within our borders. Our own national origins as a revolutionary republic whose founding fathers were regarded as traitors by Great Britain certainly have played a role in our sympathetic attitude toward political crimes.

But now that we have become the number one potential target of international terrorism, our attitude is undergoing some reevaluation. And the current debate over the new Anglo-American extradition treaty seems to reflect our growing ambivalence toward what some people call political activism and others characterize as brutal terrorism.

The case that has captured the imagination of both sides of the controversy involves Joseph Patrick Doherty [see previous column for facts]. Great Britain demanded his extradition, but Doherty resisted on the ground that his crimes were of "a political character."

A U.S. judge agreed with Doherty, likening his actions to the inflicting of casualties "during the course of more traditional military hostilities." Not surprisingly, the British authorities were furious and proposed that our treaty be amended to permit the extradition of what they consider "I.R.A. terrorists."

After the Thatcher government aided the American bombing raid on Libya, President Reagan began to put some real political muscle behind the movement to change the treaty. Under the administration's proposal, the "political character" exception would be considerably narrowed. It would not encompass most crimes of violence, such as murder, hostage-taking, bombings, and manslaughter.

Some senators have objected, not so much to the types of crimes that could lead to extradition, but rather to the quality of justice the extradited fugitive would face back home. Massive complaints have been made against the manner in which Catholic activists—violent and otherwise— have been brought to "justice" in Northern Ireland. And these complaints, if true, are legitimately the concern of the U.S. government, since its courts are being used to return fugitives for trial.

A compromise has now apparently emerged, in which U.S. courts will— for the first time in history—be empowered to inquire into the kind of justice awaiting the fugitive. As Senator John Kerry, whose role in the compromise has drawn widespread praise, put it: "We opened up an important right of inquiry [by U.S. courts at extradition hearings] into the ability of defendants to get a fair trial in Northern Ireland courts."

The issue, of course, goes beyond Northern Ireland and the IRA. With the increasing use of terrorism as a tool for political change, fugitives of many backgrounds and ideologies from numerous countries will become the subjects of extradition proceedings. They will claim that their crimes were of a political character and that they will be subjected to unfair trials.

A set of objective standards is now needed to evaluate the many situations that inevitably will confront our courts. It is frequently argued that one person's terrorist is another's freedom fighter, and that one nation's due process is another's kangaroo court. But there are some standards to which all civilized people subscribe.

In the area of purely political activism, there is a general consensus that physical violence is unacceptable except in self-defense. Even when military or paramilitary action is deemed justifiable, we distinguish among targets: civilian targets are less acceptable than military ones, and destroying property is less heinous than taking lives. Objective standards of due process and judicial fairness are more difficult to agree upon, but even there we understand the difference between a rigged trial and a fundamentally fair one.

The compromise over the British extradition treaty marks a new beginning, rather than a completely satisfying resolution, to the debate over how we should deal with foreign requests to render political criminals. The world will be watching how our courts decide these delicate issues. The key will be for them to apply a single standard of justice to our friends and enemies alike, rather than the double standard so familiar to most governments.

June 17, 1986

34
Marital Rape: Court-Created Crime

One of the most widely heralded criminal-law opinions in recent years may prove to be among the most dangerous precedents of our age. New York's highest court has just ruled unanimously that it is unconstitutional for the state legislature to exempt coerced sex by the victim's husband from the prohibition against rape.

"A marriage license," said the court, "should not be viewed as a license for a husband to forcibly rape his wife with impunity."

So far, so good. All reasonable people should applaud a decision that equates the right of married and single women to control their bodies from unwanted sexual attack. But the loud cheers are drowning out the quiet concerns of some civil libertarians about the *method* used by the court to reach its result.

Instead of declaring the New York law unconstitutionally discriminatory, it rewrote the statute and *created a new crime.* Prior to its decision, it was not a crime in New York for a married man who lived with his wife to rape her. Following the decision—and without any new legislation—that act has now become a crime in New York.

You might ask, "What's wrong with that?" A gaping loophole has been plugged. Now married women are protected, whereas before they were not. What earthly difference should it make whether the loophole was plugged by the courts or by the legislature?

It makes all the difference in the world! In one of the foundation cases of our Union, the Supreme Court held that courts may not create or expand crimes: "The legislative authority of the Union must first make an act a crime. . . ."

The Supreme Court has always followed that rule. In 1964, for example, the South Carolina Supreme Court plugged up a loophole in its trespass statute, which made it a crime to enter "upon the lands of another . . . after notice . . . prohibiting such entry." The defendants in that case had not been given notice *before* entering, but were told to leave as soon as they began their sit-in at a segregated lunch counter. The South Carolina Supreme Court interpreted the statute—quite logically—as covering not only the act of entering the premises of another after receiving a warning, but also of "remaining on the premises of another after receiving notice to leave." It affirmed the defendant's trespass conviction.

The U.S. Supreme Court reversed on the grounds that "judicial enlargement of a criminal act by interpretation is at war with a fundamental concept" of American justice. It cited the "fundamental principle" that "the required criminal law must have existed when the conduct in issue occurred" and freed the defendants because they "did not violate the statute *as it was written.*" The principle of that case transcends segregation and applies to any legislative creation of new crimes, regardless of how desirable the law may be.

The decision to make a noncriminal act criminal should always come from the legislative branch, after full opportunity for public debate and input. This is fundamental to our democratic principles for several reasons. Among them is that the decision to use the powerful weapon of the criminal law should never be made unless the legislature—representing the popular will—votes for it.

On a more practical level, the promulgation of new crimes requires more elaboration than a court can provide. For example, Professor Yale Kamisar has suggested that legislatures enacting a marital rape law may wish to impose time limits within which a wife who continues to live with her husband must file a rape complaint—as the Pennsylvania Senate recently provided. This would protect against the misuse of rape accusations as leverage in subsequent divorce cases. Some states provide different penalties for different kinds of rape. The point is that legislatures have the flexibility that courts lack in tailoring crimes to specific situations.

The New York Court of Appeals recognized that a "court should be reluctant to expand criminal statutes, due to the danger of usurping the role of the legislature," but it concluded that "in this case [there were] overriding policy concerns [that] dictate following such a course."

Judge Sol Wachtler, writing for the court, argued that the "only alternative" to expanding the rape statute to cover marital rape would have been to "invalidate the rape [statute] in [its] entirety"—which would have been catastrophic.

Wachtler is correct in pointing out the difficulties facing the court, but he exaggerates the dilemma. The court did have other alternatives—none simple, but all more protective of civil liberties than the dangerous path of judicially created crime. The court seems to have taken the most dangerous path in order to earn credit from feminists for doing what the legislature should have—and clearly would have—done, had the court directed the issue back to the legislative branch.

The American Civil Liberties Union should be concerned. I predict, however, that we will hear nary a peep from that organization about this important, but subtle, violation of civil liberties engaged in by the New York court in the name of a "good cause."

January 1, 1985

For additional discussion of rape see columns 20, 45, 46, and 54.

35
Vigilantism and Self-Defense

Every so often a crime captures the public imagination because it reflects our collective frustrations. The shooting of four teenage punks on a New York subway train three days before Christmas seems to be such an event.

The punks allegedly clustered around a man in wire-rim glasses and asked for five dollars. The man responded, "I have five dollars for each of you," reached into his pocket for a gun, and shot all four—critically wounding two of them. He then helped a frightened woman to her feet before escaping into the subway tunnel.

The teens all had arrest records and three were carrying sharpened screwdrivers in their jackets.

Even before the alleged assailant was identified, he became something of a folk hero. Dubbed by tabloids the "Death Wish Vigilante"—after the Charles Bronson character—he was offered sympathy, praise, and legal assistance by hundreds of citizens who called a police hot line. Some even suggested that he run against New York Mayor Ed Koch, who had condemned the gunman's act, stating, "Vigilantism will not be tolerated in the city."

Now that a thirty-seven-year-old businessman named Bernhard Hugo Goetz has surrendered himself as the subway shooter, a jury will decide whether his actions constitute lawful self-defense or unlawful vigilantism. The jurors will have to decide such fuzzy questions as whether the teenagers were threatening Goetz, whether Goetz reasonably feared for his safety, whether he overreacted, whether the threat had abated by the time of the shooting, and whether he responded in defense or revenge.

(Goetz, who foolishly talked to interrogators without requesting counsel, has apparently boasted that he was not in fear when he fired the shots.)

Even if the jury decides these questions against Goetz, it could still acquit him. The jury, after all, acts as the conscience of the community. If the jurors identify with Goetz and decide that he did "the right thing," there is little a judge can do to make them render a guilty verdict.

New York law—which is fairly tough on self-defense claims—allows a crime victim to shoot in self-defense only if he "reasonably believes that [his attackers are] about to use deadly physical force," and if he cannot safely resist or escape without shooting.

(The law is somewhat more permissive if the defendant shoots someone who is robbing him—but it may be difficult to show robbery here.)

Juries sometimes acquit defendants even if their actions do not fit neatly into this rigorous legal definition. The bottom line questions seem to be: "What would I have done in similar circumstances?" and "Did the victims get what was coming to them?"

For that reason, the teenage shooting victims will probably be as much on trial as the defendant. The defense lawyer will try to portray the teenagers as larger-than-life killers. He or she will parade the sharpened screwdrivers in front of the jurors' noses—if the judge allows the screwdrivers into evidence. That may depend on whether Goetz was actually aware that they were carrying these lethal weapons.

If Goetz didn't know, then the fact that the sharpened screwdrivers were later discovered in their jackets would not be relevant to Goetz's state of mind at the time he fired the shots. Nor would the teenagers' arrest records—which were obviously unknown to Goetz—be relevant. The defense will also try to show the inadequacy of the police in responding to subway assaults.

The prosecutor may portray Goetz as a racist with a chip on his shoulder and an illegally owned gun in his pocket. According to neighbors, Goetz had expressed anti-black sentiments, especially since he was mugged in 1981 by three youths.

He had apparently sworn revenge against black street thugs. "Sooner or later, I'm going to get them," friends quoted him as saying.

All four teenagers shot were black. Ironically, one of the groups offering legal assistance to Goetz is the Congress of Racial Equality, a black civil-rights organization whose Harlem-based director compared Goetz to "many blacks who face that situation every day—mugged before, assailed by criminals, harassed on the subway."

In their rush to praise Goetz, many New Yorkers are forgetting that he repeatedly discharged his pistol in a crowded subway car. Would the reaction to Goetz have been the same if one of his bullets ricocheted and killed another passenger?

In the end, the jurors—speaking for the community—will have to decide whether the dangers of allowing frustrated individuals to take the law into their own hands outweigh the dangers of unchecked subway crime.

If their message is that our society is willing to glorify vigilantism, then we will be abdicating control of our collective destiny and placing it in the hands of individuals answerable to no authority.

Punks with screwdrivers are surely dangerous. But shootouts on the subway may be even more so.

January 7, 1985

36
Vigilante Prosecutor?

Most of the media accounts of the New York grand jury's refusal to indict Bernhard Goetz for attempted murder misunderstand the actual relation-ship between the prosecutor and the grand jury. These accounts suggest that an independent group of twenty-three citizens decided on their own that Goetz was justified in shooting his four teenage harassers. However, every experienced criminal lawyer understands that grand jurors rarely act on their own: they generally do the bidding of the prosecutor "in charge" of the grand jury. A grand jury meets in secret, hears only the evidence presented by the prosecutor, is instructed on the law by the prosecutor, and receives implicit "recommendations" from the prosecutor. It hears nothing from the defense attorney, and in the Goetz case, it heard no testimony from the defendant, other than his videotaped admission.

I have been told many times by prosecutors that unless a suspect cooper-ates, "I [the prosecutor] will have my grand jury indict him in five min-utes." It's almost unheard of for a grand jury to refuse to follow the "recom-mendations" of its prosecutor. Indeed, the rare grand jury that defies a prosecutorial recommendation is labeled a "runaway grand jury."

The prosecutor controls the grand jury in subtle as well as overt ways. The evidence presented, the tone of voice, the nature of the legal instruc-tions—these may be more important than any overt recommendation.

In the Goetz case, for example, District Attorney Robert Morganthau refused to call any of the four victims as witnesses. His rationale was that if he called them, he would, under New York law, have had to give them im-munity from prosecution—a free ride.

However, this is a half-truth, at best. First, it's unlikely that all four will be prosecuted for their activities in the subway on the day they were shot; Morganthau himself said, "There is no evidence against them." Second, Morganthau would only have had to give immunity to one of the four. Had he done so, his case probably would have been strengthened not only against Goetz, but also against the other three alleged robbers.

But lawyers who know Morganthau widely perceive him as an extremely political district attorney. He saw which way the political winds were blowing, and he expressed satisfaction with the grand jury's decision. In a classic bit of hypocrisy, Morganthau later declared at a press conference: "Anybody who shoots another person in the subway or anywhere will have the case presented to the grand jury, and [they will have to establish justification]."

But Goetz did not have to establish anything! He never testified, nor did his excellent lawyers present any evidence of justification. Goetz didn't know that the punks carried screwdrivers; he didn't know of their prior records. All he knew was that one kid asked him for five dollars. He then pulled his illegally possessed pistol from his fast-draw holster and emptied its dum-dum bullets into the bodies of his harassers. He shot two of the them in the back while they were fleeing, and later boasted that he was not frightened. This is not legal justification under New York law. It is attempted murder. Imagine the outcry if a policeman shot fleeing kids in the back!

If a petit jury—a trial jury—had acquitted Goetz after hearing all of the evidence, there would be little cause for concern. Petit juries are expected to act independently—as a reflection of the community's conscience. They are neutral arbitrators. Neither side has exclusive access to the petit jury. No one can "whisper" secretly to a petit jury.

A grand jury is different. It hears only the prosecutor's side and indicts if the (prosecutor's) evidence—without considering the defendant's possible defenses—shows that a crime may have been committed. Following a petit jury acquittal at trial, at least the public has some assurance that the whole story has come out. It has no such assurance here.

The citizens of New York should demand to see a transcript of the legal portions of the Goetz grand jury proceedings, especially the prosecutor's instructions about the law. Morganthau has declared publicly that he didn't try to "push" the grand jury either for or against an attempted murder indictment. However, he then added that "we don't ever push a grand jury to return an indictment." Since it's well known that his office often places considerable pressure on grand juries to indict, it seems likely that Morganthau is using the word "push" in a rather unusual way. There is little argument for secrecy in a case like this, where the evidence and legal maneuvers have been so extensively described at politically opportune press conferences.

There is one phenomenon even more dangerous than a vigilante subway shooter—and that is a vigilante prosecutor who takes the law into his own political hands, while pretending that the decision was made exclusively by an independent grand jury. The public is entitled to know exactly what role the prosecutor actually played in the grand jury's decision not to indict Bernhard Goetz for attempted murder.

January 29, 1985

UPDATE

A second grand jury later indicted Goetz.

37
The Bernhard Goetz in Us All

An American jury has once again disregarded the law of self-defense and rendered a verdict based on its own sense of right and wrong. The acquittal of Bernhard Goetz on all charges of attempted murder was completely unjustified as a matter of New York law—and indeed the law of most states and civilized nations.

Putting legal jargon aside, the principle is clear: any person who is in immediate danger of death or serious bodily harm may use any means necessary to prevent the assault, but once the danger has passed, the person who was assaulted may not exact revenge.

The difficult question, of course, is how to decide precisely when the danger has passed. It may be easy to draw such lines in the classroom and in textbooks. But when you're in a crowded subway and four young punks come up to you with evil designs, it is difficult to remember—or to act on—the pristine principles of law.

The Goetz jury verdict seems to reflect an understanding of the terror that must go through the mind of the urban victim when he or she looks into the barrel of a pistol or sees the gleam of a switchblade or feels the dull pain of a screwdriver against his or her neck.

The jurors' verdict convicting Goetz of possession of an unregistered firearm may be as significant as their verdict acquitting him of the attempted murder charges. Goetz's decision to carry the gun was premeditated and in clear violation of the law. In that respect, it was not unlike the decision of the punks who surrounded him to carry screwdrivers and to threaten subway riders. The jurors were prepared to pass judgments of condemnation on both such acts of calculated law breaking.

But once the encounter began, the jurors were not prepared to second-guess the spontaneous actions of the party with whom they most closely identified—Bernhard Goetz. In acquitting Goetz of the most serious charges, the jurors disregarded the judge's instructions, which would have required them to convict on at least some of the attempted murder charges. After all, Goetz continued to shoot into the body of at least one of the punks after he was prone and completely disabled. Goetz's own words made it plain that he would have continued to fire if only he had had more ammunition. No civilized law tolerates such vigilantism—at least not in theory.

But law is not a theory; it is a process. And that process gives the final say to twelve representatives of society. In this case, several of them were subway riders, and some had been crime victims. They might not have agreed with what Goetz did, but they understood. Our system of trial by jury allows—at least implicitly—for such understanding to nullify the rigors of the law.

But jury nullification is a double-edged sword, especially in self-defense cases where it is frequently found. There is a little bit of Bernhard Goetz in nearly everybody, and it is the job of the law to keep that spirit of vengeance in check. But the law cannot stray too far from the passions of the people, or else occasional nullification will become the rule of lawlessness.

For centuries, legal philosophers have sought to strike a balance between preventive self-defense and after-the-fact vigilantism. They have never done much better than to propose rules to be obeyed and processes for finding exceptions.

It would be a mistake to see the Goetz verdict as a precedent-setting innovation. It is still a serious crime to shoot a prone assailant in the back after he has been subdued. But some people will misunderstand the Goetz verdict as an invitation to imitate Dirty Harry. The next jury may not be as understanding, especially if the characters in the drama are somewhat different in race, background, or appeal. It is useful to remember that Goetz's bullets barely missed innocent bystanders. I doubt the jury verdict would have been the same if one of Goetz's fellow train riders had been seriously injured or killed by his bullets.

That is the great danger of jury nullification—it is ad hoc, unprincipled, and not subject to review. When we approve of the outcome, we applaud the process. But when the result is the acquittal of, say, a racist lynch mob in the Jim Crow South, we deplore the process. In this case, many Americans will probably feel an uncomfortable sense of vindication coupled with an uneasy sense of fear. There were no heroes on that subway train in New York two-and-a-half years ago.

Bernhard Goetz took the law into his own hands. The jury that rendered its compromise verdict also took the law into its own hands. Neither our subways nor our rights will be any safer for this double lawlessness. But that is the worthwhile price we pay for trial by jury.

June 17, 1987

UPDATE
In October of 1987, Goetz was sentenced to six months in jail and probationary supervision on the gun possession charge.

38
Arresting Johns *Isn't* "Equal"

I wonder if certain feminists will be cheering loudly as Olympic Gold Medal hurdler Edwin Moses faces charges of soliciting a policewoman posing as a prostitute during a sting operation designed to nab "johns" along Sunset Boulevard. "It's about time they started arresting the johns instead of the prostitutes," I've heard some of my feminist friends say. "After all, without the customers, there would be no market for the product."

It has become part of the rhetoric of certain feminists that johns must be arrested in the name of equality and feminism. Indeed, the recent spate of sting operations designed to sweep up johns is partly attributable to the pressures of this feminist fringe, which has demanded equal enforcement of the prostitution laws.

This equality argument has even received the benediction of some high-ranking officials of the American Civil Liberties Union. "There is no possible basis for arresting or prosecuting only the women who sell the service and not the men who buy it," argues the associate director of the ACLU's Women's Rights Project.

That's a strange argument coming from the lips of a civil libertarian. It has long been recognized that there is a legitimate—indeed, a compelling—basis for distinguishing between the full-time professional purveyor of an illegal commodity and its occasional consumer. Thus, civil libertarians have long supported laws that decriminalize the purchase of small amounts of marijuana, even if the sale of large amounts is still punishable. The same is true of gambling, pornography, and other consensual crimes. The fact that the operators of big-time gambling rings and pornography distribution networks are arrested isn't a very good argument for prosecuting every two dollar bettor and every occasional purchaser or renter of a hard-core videocassette. Many civil libertarians would like to see all consensual crimes taken off the books. But they welcome laws—such as the one enacted in Ann Arbor, Michigan—under which users of small amounts of marijuana aren't criminally punished, while professional suppliers are still sent to jail.

You don't have to be a card-carrying member of the ACLU to see the virtue of not using our limited police resources to arrest every unhappily married accountant who takes a bimonthly trip to his local Fantasy Street to get his jollies—even if the police decide to go after the pimps and prostitutes. Every policeman and policewoman who patrols these neighborhoods in quest of an errant customer is a cop who could otherwise be used to prevent rapes, muggings, and burglaries.

Some feminists argue that the only way prostitution will ever be made legal is by throwing the book at the male johns: then the pressures will increase to take the crime of soliciting sex off the books. Without the arrest of the middle- and upper-class male clientele, there will be no effective constituency for helping the prostitute. There probably is something to that argument, but not enough to justify the kind of offensive sting operations that led to Edwin Moses's arrest on Sunset Boulevard.

There really is an enormous difference in impact between the arrest of a professional prostitute and the arrest of an otherwise law-abiding citizen who occasionally seeks to taste the forbidden fruit of sex for hire. For the prostitute, an occasional arrest is an expected occupational hazard. The quick arraignment, bail, and fine are regarded as a cost of doing business. She is back on the street hustling her next john within hours. Certainly there is little stigma or embarrassment in being arrested; the streetwalker publicly advertises what she's doing every time she puts on her "uniform" and takes to the sidewalks.

For the john, the public arrest can be a catastrophic event. It can ruin a marriage, destroy a reputation, sear his children, terminate a career. For a man like Moses, it can undo years of positive achievements—even if he's eventually exonerated.

It isn't sexist to speak honestly about the different impact an arrest can have on the professional prostitute and the occasional john. The same argument would apply to a professional male gigolo and the occasional female "jane," or to the professional gay male hustler and his occasional customer. These are the facts of life and should be taken into account when deciding whether to conduct sting operations that target johns for arrest and prosecution.

Moses may well beat his rap. The police will have to prove that he solicited the ersatz prostitute, or at least that he firmly accepted her offer. If there's a reasonable possibility that he was just kidding around or testing the waters, he should be acquitted. Cases like this are generally plea-bargained quietly, but Moses's high visibility makes that path unlikely.

Perhaps Moses's troubles will awaken us to the foolishness—even immorality—of uncritically accepting the vindictive argument of those feminists who demand the prosecution of johns. That policy, in the name of a false equality, engenders the most thoughtless of inequality.

January 22, 1985

UPDATE
Moses was acquitted of soliciting a prostitute.

39
Vanessa Redgrave:
Blacklisted Blacklister

I've been preaching about the First Amendment for most of my adult life. A couple of weeks ago, I went out on the street and practiced what I'd been preaching. There I stood, at the entrance of the Boston Shakespeare Company, handing out leaflets I had printed up. The event was a fund-raiser for an organization called the Anti-Blacklisting Defense Fund.

Now why in the world would I be leafletting an antiblacklisting fund-raiser? My own views on blacklisting have always been unequivocal: I'm against it. The reason I was there is that the event was a thinly disguised fund-raiser for Vanessa Redgrave—who is suing the Boston Symphony for blacklisting her, but who is herself in favor of blacklisting and has proposed her own blacklist of certain artists. I thought it was important for the public to know the facts about Redgrave's attitude toward blacklisting artists whose politics differ from her own.

The facts are as follows: In 1978, Redgrave offered a resolution demanding that the British Actors Union blacklist Israeli artists and boycott Israeli audiences. The resolution included a "demand" that "all members working in Israel terminate their contacts and refuse all work in Israel." (So much for the sanctity of contracts!) Several years later, she justified as "entirely correct" the blacklisting of Zionist speakers at British universities. And she has praised the ultimate form of censorship: the political assassination of Israeli artists, because they "may well have been enlisted . . . to do the work" of the Zionists.

Redgrave herself has used her art "to do the work" of the Palestine Liberation Organization. In 1977, she made a film calling for the destruction of the Jewish state by armed struggle. She has personally received training in terrorism at PLO camps from which terrorist raids were staged. She advocated the assassination of Nobel Peace Prize winner Anwar Sadat. After playing her controversial role as concentration camp survivor in Arthur Miller's 1980 teledrama "Playing for Time," she traveled around the world arguing that her selection for the role constituted a propaganda victory for the PLO against Israel.

In 1982, the Boston Symphony Orchestra hired Redgrave to narrate several performances of Stravinsky's opera-oratorio "Oedipus Rex." There is some dispute over whether she was hired entirely because of her unquestionable acting ability or also because of her political "courage." There is no dispute that as soon as the decision was announced, there was outrage among some of the orchestra's musicians, subscribers and board members.

Some musicians suggested that they would exercise their own freedom of association by refusing to perform with a PLO collaborator who justified the assassination of artists. Board members feared that the controversy might reduce contributions to the financially shaky orchestra. There was some concern about disruptions of the performances by protestors. And Seiji Ozawa—the orchestra's principal conductor—feared that Redgrave might turn the artistic program into a political event by making speeches in response to booing.

In the end, the orchestra decided—wrongly, in my view—to cancel the performances of "Oedipus Rex." They offered to pay Redgrave the $31,000 she would have received if the show had gone on. Redgrave declined the offer and sued the orchestra for breach of contract, seeking $5 million in damages. She claims that the effect of the cancellation was that she was "blacklisted" by the Boston Symphony Orchestra and can no longer find appropriate work.

The orchestra board responds that Redgrave has earned more money since the cancellation than before it, and that if anyone has refused to hire her, it is because she has used her art to serve the political ends of terrorism. The board has also proved that Redgrave has turned down roles—such as that of Andrei Sakharov's wife in a recent HBO production—because she believed the film might be seen as "anti-Communist propaganda."

My leaflet provided these facts to those attending the antiblacklisting fund-raiser and urged them to ask Redgrave "to explain her hypocrisy." Several members of the audience were surprised to learn of her views on blacklisting Israeli artists. Others said they knew of Redgrave's selective condemnation of blacklisting but didn't care, because—as one woman put it—"anything is fair in the war against Zionism."

If Vanessa Redgrave had not practiced the hateful brand of blacklisting she is now preaching against, I would not have had to go out on the street to practice the First Amendment leafletting I preach about. Let Redgrave have her day in court. But let the public know what a hypocrite she is about artistic freedom.

November 11, 1985

40
Look Who's Blacklisting Now

One of the greatest evils of the notorious McCarthy era in the United States was the emergence of blacklists.

A blacklist was literally a published listing of individuals who—because of their political beliefs, associations, or actions—should not be hired. Among the most frequent victims of blacklisting were performers, writers, and others in the entertainment industry.

During the early 1950s, the major Hollywood film studios blacklisted actors, screenwriters, and directors who were suspected of communist affiliations or activities. Red Channels blacklisted television talent in much the same way. Civil libertarians, liberals, and ordinary decent folks objected to blacklisting. More recently, Woody Allen starred in a film called *The Front*, which poignantly explored the human tragedies generated by the entertainment blacklists.

Over the past thirty years "blacklisting" has become a dirty word among most decent people. The movie and TV studios that participated in this odious practice don't even try to defend their past indiscretions. Most Americans surely believe that this shameful episode in our history is behind us.

But a recent news story has disclosed the existence of an international blacklist published in New York. And this time, blacklisting is being practiced in the name of a progressive cause—the antiapartheid movement.

It turns out that the Register of Entertainers to be shunned is officially published by the United Nations Special Committee Against Apartheid "as a means to promote the cultural boycott of South Africa." It included the names of entertainers and actors who have performed in South Africa since 1981. Anyone whose name appears on the list is prohibited from performing at any function sponsored by the United Nations. Other organizations also use the U.N. blacklist to screen politically unacceptable artists.

The introduction to the U.N. blacklist boasts that "a number of city counsels and other local authorities have decided to deny use of their facilities for entertainers" whose names appear on the blacklist. It also urges "organizations and the media to give it widest publicity."

This official blacklist of artists has been in existence since 1983, yet there has been no outcry from those whose voices are always heard condemning right-wing blacklists. The *end* sought to be achieved by the U.N. blacklist—the demise of South Africa's disgraceful policy of apartheid—is laudable. But the *means* it has selected is difficult to distinguish from McCarthyism.

Surely the fact that this blacklist is part of an official U.N. boycott does not diminish the civil liberties violation implicit in the enterprise. If anything, it makes it worse.

Consider an artist who is against apartheid, but who decides to perform to a black audience in Soweto. Reasonable people may agree or disagree with that decision, but surely the artist shouldn't be punished for his or her political decision. Even the artist who supports apartheid, or who simply doesn't care about it, should have the right to harbor such despicable views without endangering his or her artistic career.

Moreover, the procedures for being placed on the U.N. blacklist appear to be as arbitrary and political as those used by McCarthy.

The introduction to the Register of Entertainers acknowledges that the list was prepared "mainly on the basis of press reports" and invites "additional information by organizations and individuals." No advance notice is given to persons who are to be blacklisted, and the list includes some performers who "were not aware of the cultural boycott."

The assistant secretary general for the Center Against Apartheid—which prepares and administers the list—has acknowledged that "often people don't even know they're on the list and if they say they're sorry and won't go anymore, they are taken off." The blacklist compilers admit there are mistakes and apologize: "Any embarrassment to them is regretted."

Among those currently on the blacklist are Ray Charles, Linda Ronstadt, Frank Sinatra, the Beach Boys, Cher, Goldie Hawn, Sha Na Na, Ernest Borgnine, and the British rock group Queen.

The recent flap that publicized the existence of the U.N. blacklist involved a proposed concert to raise money for African famine relief. Among those volunteering to perform was the rock group Chicago. But Chicago was on the blacklist. And because of the absolute prohibition against using blacklisted artists at U.N.-sponsored events, plans for the concert had to be postponed. It is ironic that some black African children may die of hunger because of the U.N. blacklist.

The American Civil Liberties Union recently complained loudly when the Boston Symphony Orchestra canceled a concert with Vanessa Redgrave because of her support for and complicity with PLO terrorists. Though no blacklist was published, the American Civil Liberties Union decried the "blacklisting" of Ms. Redgrave because of her politics as a violation of her civil liberties.

I am waiting to hear from the American Civil Liberties Union on the U.N. blacklist. I doubt we will hear much, because the ACLU is growing increasingly timid in the face of civil liberties violations committed in the name of liberal causes.

February 19, 1985

For another blacklisting case in which the ACLU did become involved, see Column 86.

41
Jury's Word Isn't the Last

Several cases in the news recently have raised questions about the jury system. What exactly is the function of the twelve—sometimes six—citizens who are asked to decide such complex and controversial issues as those involved in the Westmoreland and Sharon libel cases, and the Edwin Moses solicitation case?

We often hear the phrase "the jury decided that"—as if a verdict by a particular jury settles, for all time, the factual issues in a case. But a jury is not a scientific fact-finding mechanism. Its function is not to determine—for all time and for all purposes—the "Truth."

Consider the jury that recently acquitted Edwin Moses of soliciting an undercover policewoman who was posing as a prostitute. The jury didn't necessarily conclude that Moses hadn't solicited her. Some of the jurors may have believed that he did, but that he was unfairly picked on because of who he is. Others may have been expressing disagreement with the use of undercover cops to "sting" occasional "johns." The jury verdict in that case didn't establish the *factual* certainty that Moses hadn't offered to pay for sex; it decided that Moses was legally innocent of the crime for which he was charged.

Nor did the jury verdict in General Ariel Sharon's libel suit against *Time* magazine establish any historical facts about the massacres in Lebanon. These are for historians to debate over the years. Judge Laval was correct when he said, after dismissing the jury in General William Westmoreland's suit against CBS, that the verdict on troop counts during the Vietnam War is best left to history. But he was wrong in implying that if the jury had been allowed to decide that case, its verdict somehow would have usurped the role of historians.

The jury isn't in a position to resolve large disputed issues of fact. It rarely hears all of the evidence; it generally lacks the expertise to evaluate the evidence it does hear, and it is never instructed to decide the issues before it on a scientific or historical basis.

It's the judge's job to exclude a great deal of material that a scientist or historian would want to consider. Hearsay testimony, items obtained illegally by the government, privileged information, highly prejudicial evidence—all of these may be kept from the jury.

Jurors are selected precisely because they *lack* expertise about the issues in dispute. Accountants are kicked off of tax juries; structural engineers aren't permitted to serve on juries that decide cases involving building collapses.

Most importantly, juries are deliberately instructed to skew their findings in one particular direction. A proper instruction in a criminal case would sound something like this:

"Even if you decide that the evidence that the defendant did it is stronger and more convincing than the evidence that he didn't do it, you must still acquit, unless you find that the evidence that he did it satisfies you beyond a reasonable doubt."

This, of course, isn't the standard for scientific or historical truth-finding. Scientists and historians aren't supposed to skew the evidence in either direction. But our legal system proudly proclaims that it's better to make the kind of mistake that frees several guilty defendants than to make a mistake that convicts even one innocent defendant. (Although the standard isn't as demanding in civil cases—such as libel suits—the plaintiff still has the "burden of proof.")

A remarkable case now being litigated in Canada illustrates the incapacity of a jury to determine historical facts. The Crown—which is what Canada calls the prosecution in a criminal case—is prosecuting a crank historian who claims that the Nazi Holocaust never occurred. Under Canadian law, it's a crime to willfully publish news that a defendant knows to be false and that is likely to cause injury or mischief to public interest.

The defense being offered is "truth." Accordingly, the Crown must prove, beyond a reasonable doubt, that the Holocaust actually occurred. What if the jury were to acquit the defendant? Would that establish the historical "fact" that the Holocaust never occurred? Would it bring life back to the millions of bodies brutally slaughtered by the Nazis?

Of course not. It would merely demonstrate that—for one reason or another—the Crown hadn't been able to prove its case. The reason might well be that the Holocaust was so thorough that it left few eyewitnesses capable of giving direct evidence forty years later. Or the reason might be that a Canadian jury didn't believe that criminal punishment is the appropriate response to a lying historian. The important point is that whatever the jury decides in the pending case will be irrelevant to the verdict of history.

Juries play a crucial role in preserving our liberties, in helping to achieve justice, and in resolving particular cases. But we should not make the mistake of believing that juries have the last word on truth. That, in the end, is a verdict we must all render.

February 26, 1985

42
The Right to a Free Psychiatrist

The Supreme Court has just decided that an indigent criminal defendant has the right to an appointed psychiatrist in certain situations.

The case involved a death row inmate named Glen Ake, who was convicted of murdering his wife and minister. His behavior at arraignment was so "bizarre" that he was found incompetent to stand trial. After taking numerous doses of a powerful tranquilizer, he was found competent to be tried.

Despite his obvious mental illness, Ake was unable to support his defense of insanity, because he could not afford to hire a psychiatrist. After being convicted, he was sentenced to death, in part on the basis of a prediction that he would continue to be dangerous if not executed—a prediction that he could not rebut because of his inability to retain a psychiatrist.

The *Ake* case has been hailed as "the first Supreme Court ruling in years to extend an important new constitutional right to criminal defendants," and as "a direct descendant of the court's landmark 1963 ruling, *Gideon* v. *Wainwright*, which held that an indigent defendant was entitled to the assistance of counsel at trial."

In practice, however, this new ruling is not likely to help many poor defendants. First, few criminal defendants will be able to "demonstrate . . . to the trial judge that [their] sanity at the time of the offense is to be a significant factor at trial." The defendant must "demonstrate" this without the initial assistance of a psychiatrist. Thus, only the most visibly psychotic defendants—or those with documented psychiatric histories—will qualify for the free aid.

Second, many defense attorneys will be unwilling to take advantage of this "free" assistance because of the terms on which it is offered. The Supreme Court went out of its way to point out that a poor defendant—as distinguished from a wealthy one—has no right "to choose a psychiatrist of his personal liking or to receive funds to hire his own." The state will decide how to pick the defendant's free expert. This little-noted aspect of the decision makes the new right practically worthless, and certainly not a worthy offspring of *Gideon*'s right to counsel.

Under *Gideon*, the state also picks the indigent defendant's lawyer, but there is an enormous difference between a *lawyer* selected by the state to represent an indigent defendant and a *psychiatrist* selected by the state to assure that the defendant has "access to a competent psychiatrist."

A lawyer—whether paid privately or publicly—knows precisely what his or her role is supposed to be: to defend the client whether innocent or guilty. The role of the state-appointed psychiatrist is anything but clear. Is the psychiatrist supposed to be an advocate for the defendant's contentions? An explainer of psychiatric facts? Or a medical judge?

As a defense attorney with experience in psychiatric defenses, I would not allow a state-appointed psychiatrist to interview my client unless I was assured either that the psychiatrist was on our side, or—at the very least— that he could not use the information he learned in the interview to *hurt* my client.

The last thing I would want a "free" psychiatrist to do is to examine my client, conclude that he is guilty and sane, and then turn around and testify for the prosecution. Even if the psychiatrist decided to testify "neutrally"— or not at all—the information secured from the client could be used to bolster the prosecution's case.

I suspect that many defense lawyers will not take the risk of accepting a "shrink-in-the-poke" situation in which a client's life or liberty may depend on the attitudes of a state-picked psychiatrist.

The basic question avoided by the *Ake* case is whether the indigent criminal defendant should be entitled to do what a wealthy defendant and the prosecution can do: select a psychiatrist who will present his or her side of the case in an adversary manner. Unless the indigent defendant is given the right to select—within appropriate limits—a psychiatrist of his choice, the right to a *free* psychiatrist may turn out to be illusory.

A reasonable solution to this dilemma would be for the state to provide a sum of money for the defense lawyer to retain an expert of the defendant's choice. The amount could vary with the seriousness of the charge (for example, $1,000 in noncapital cases and $2,500 in capital cases). This would at least give the indigent defendant the right to counter a prosecution expert with a defense expert.

Perhaps in an ideal world, all experts would be neutral advocates for the "truth." But in the adversary process of justice—as it presently works— even experts work one side of the street.

As Judge David Bazelon—the world's most influential jurist on the issue of law and psychiatry—likes to say: "The role of the courts is to open issues by raising hard questions, not to close issues by providing easy answers." The *Ake* case raises fundamental questions about inequalities in our criminal justice system.

March 5, 1985

43
Putting the Cat Back in the Bag

You might not be able to get the cat back in the bag or the toothpaste back in the tube—but the Supreme Court recently decided that if a suspect confesses to a crime illegally, the illegal confession can be put back in the bag; and if the police can get him to repeat the confession legally, everything will be perfectly OK.

The case involved an eighteen-year-old youth named Elstad who was suspected of burglary. The police went to his house with an arrest warrant. Without giving him his *Miranda* warnings ("You have the right to remain silent; you are entitled to a lawyer"; etc.) the police asked him if he was involved in the burglary. He said, "Yes, I was there."

Under the *Miranda* ruling, the police could not use that confession because Elstad had not been informed of his right to remain silent or to obtain a lawyer. But an hour later—at the stationhouse—the police gave Elstad his *Miranda* warnings and he repeated the confession.

The Oregon Court of Appeals ruled that the second confession also could not be admitted into evidence. It concluded that the first confession—the one that was clearly illegal—had a "coercive impact" on the defendant and contributed to his making of the second confession. In the young man's mind, the court reasoned, "The cat was out of the bag." The Oregon court reversed Elstad's burglary conviction and sent it back for a new trial.

At this point, there was little reason for the U.S. Supreme Court to become involved in this state case. The state court of appeals had made a ruling against the state prosecutor, based on illegal actions by the state police. To be sure, the U.S. Constitution had allegedly been violated, but the state courts are empowered to interpret and apply that Constitution.

If the people of Oregon were dissatisfied with the way their state judges interpreted the Constitution, they have plenty of recourse within the state. No person's constitutional rights had been violated by the state court's decision, because the court had ruled in favor of the person and against the state. But the Oregon prosecutor's office was dissatisfied with its own state court's decision, so it sought review in the U.S. Supreme Court.

One would think that a busy Supreme Court—which constantly complains of its heavy workload—would have better things to do than review yet another complaint brought by a state prosecutor against his own court. One might equally expect that those justices who claim that they practice "judicial restraint" might restrain themselves from interceding into this intrastate family quarrel.

"But *noooo*," as the late John Belushi used to say. The conservative wing of the court reached out, took the case—a case they were entirely free not to review—and reversed the Oregon Court of Appeals.

Justice Sandra Day O'Connor—who is emerging as one of the court's most reactionary members in criminal cases—ruled that the illegality of the police's action in not giving a Miranda warning before the first confession could be "cured" by a subsequent warning. Although the suspect already had admitted to the police that he was guilty, his second confession, said Justice O'Connor, should "be viewed as an act of free will." Believing that a later warning can "cure" the effects of an earlier illegality is a little like believing that an inoculation administered after the patient had displayed the symptoms can cure the disease.

In a stinging forty-six-page dissent—more than twice as long as the majority opinion—Justice William Brennan called the six-to-three ruling "a potentially crippling blow to *Miranda*" and the culmination of "a studied campaign to strip the *Miranda* decision piecemeal."

In practical terms, the new decision will encourage police to obtain initial confessions without giving *Miranda* warnings. Experienced interrogators all know that once a suspect has admitted his guilt, it is far easier to get him to repeat his admission—even after a *Miranda* warning—than to get him to undo the admission in the first place. Once you've rung the bell, it's very difficult to un-ring it.

Imagine the following scenario: the clever cop or prosecutor has a young suspect in custody. The suspect is denying any involvement in the crime. The cop begins to ask tricky questions. The prosecutor calls him aside and tells him that he'd better administer the *Miranda* warnings. "Why should I?" asks the cop. "If he gets a lawyer, he'll never talk. But if I can get him to incriminate himself now, we can always *Mirandize* him later. Then he'll be easy pickings, having already told us everything."

Even more significant than the trend toward crippling the *Miranda* ruling is the Supreme Court's seemingly voracious appetite to review and reverse state court rulings that favor individual citizens over the state. The Supreme Court is quickly becoming a court of last resort for state prosecutors, rather than a court of last resort for individual citizens.

This is not the vision of the Supreme Court contained in our Constitution.

March 12, 1985

For further discussions of the exclusionary rule, see columns 3, 4, 50, 89, 91, 105, 109, and 140.

44
Indictments That Talk

The code of professional responsibility—the rules governing how lawyers are supposed to behave—prohibits a prosecutor from giving any information to the press about "the character, reputation, or prior criminal record of the accused." It also forbids the prosecutor from expressing any opinion as to the guilt or innocence of the accused or the merits of the case.

These rules are designed to prevent the prosecutor from convicting the defendant in a "trial by the media." This fear grows, in part, out of the notorious murder trial of Dr. Sam Sheppard some twenty years ago. In that case, the Supreme Court reversed Sheppard's conviction because the adverse publicity generated by the prosecutor had denied the defendant a fair trial. Sheppard was subsequently acquitted after a trial by jury, uninfluenced by leaks to the media.

But the recent indictment of nine organized crime figures in New York demonstrates that the rules haven't solved the problem. The indictment in that case was announced at an elaborately orchestrated news conference convened by seventeen law enforcement officials, including the director of the FBI and the U.S. attorney in Manhattan. The prosecutor noted, in dramatic terms, that the indictment "covered the Mafia's ruling council" and that the case "charges more Mafia bosses in one indictment than ever before."

Now that potential jurors have been authoritatively assured by the nation's highest law enforcement officials that the defendants on trial in this case are "Mafia bosses" and members of the "Mafia ruling council," it will be difficult—to say the least—to select a jury that can fairly weigh the actual evidence to be presented at trial.

How could these law enforcement officials make such statements without running afoul of the rules prohibiting trial by the media? It's rather easy. The rules contain a loophole so gaping that one could drive the entire Justice Department through it. The prosecutor is permitted to describe the "indictment." That sounds reasonable enough; after all, the indictment is the public accusation against the accused.

But in recent years, prosecutors have developed creative new techniques for circumventing the protections of the rules prohibiting trial by the media. They've simply used the indictment as an excuse for a full-blown press conference and discussion of the case. There's even a name for this new development. It's called the "talking indictment."

Instead of being a bare-bones recitation of the statutory charges against the defendant, the "talking indictment" tells the prosecutor's whole story in vivid terms more suitable to a lurid novel than to a dry legal document.

For example, in the recent organized crime case, the indictment reads like an early script for the movie *The Godfather*. It says that in 1931, the various heads of organized crime families formed themselves into a commission. The powers of the commission, according to the indictment, include establishing rules for organized crime, deciding which illegal businesses to run, and extending formal recognition to newly elected family bosses.

According to the prosecutors, the commission has been responsible for authorizing murders, distributing narcotics, and controlling various business enterprises, such as concrete pouring and shipping. The "talking indictment" describes, in gory detail, execution-style murders and other crimes committed years ago by people who aren't now being charged. One can almost hear the soundtrack in the background as these sordid historical events are recounted.

"It is a great day for law enforcement, probably the worst day for the Mafia," said the U.S. attorney whose office will prosecute the case.

Someone listening to all of this hoopla might imagine that the trial is already over and the defendants have been convicted. However, an indictment is no more than a grand jury's judgment that there's enough evidence to bring the defendants to trial. The prosecutor already has announced that his office has a 95 percent conviction rate, so that the trial itself is viewed as little more than a predictable detail.

There's something rather dangerous about this conviction by indictment mentality. It's reminiscent of that line in *Alice's Adventures in Wonderland*: "Sentence first—verdict afterwards."

The defense attorney has no effective way to respond to these "talking indictments." He's prohibited from doing any more than stating "that the accused denies the charges made against him." This kind of pat response is no match for the vivid detail contained in the "talking indictment."

Why should anyone care about what the government does to convict these "bad" members of organized crime? It's plainly because of this widespread feeling that prosecutors regard themselves as having a license to do almost anything to "get" alleged members of the Mafia. However, it takes a fair trial to determine who is guilty and who is innocent—and even if the defendants are both bad and guilty, it's still important to treat them lawfully.

As H. L. Mencken used to say: "The trouble with fighting for human freedom is that you have to spend so much of your life defending S.O.B.s; for oppressive laws [and practices] are always aimed at them originally."

March 19, 1985

45
False Accusations of Rape

A woman named Cathy Crowell Webb recently admitted that her accusation of rape, which sent an innocent man to prison for six years, was false. This recantation raises profound questions that go beyond the injustice done to Gary Dotson. The horrible crime of rape poses extraordinary dilemmas for our criminal justice system. There probably is no serious crime for which more guilty criminals remain unprosecuted. Recent studies suggest that only half of all rapes are even reported, and fewer than that are prosecuted.

But the crime of rape—like other crimes—occasionally is the subject of a false accusation. Sometimes the entire story is fabricated; at other times the degree of force or persuasion employed to obtain "consent" is exaggerated. The point is that there is a substantial risk that an innocent defendant will spend years in prison, as Dotson did.

Perhaps because so few guilty defendants are prosecuted, when a rape suspect is brought to trial, the "need" to convict him sometimes seems to outweigh the obligation to ensure that justice is done. The rules of evidence have been changed to make it easier to convict defendants of rape and harder to cross-examine the alleged rape victims. This is understandable, since one reason so few rapes are prosecuted is the trauma to which a complaining witness is often subjected at trial. However, these legal changes have not been without substantial costs: each change makes it *both* easier to convict the guilty rapist *and* more difficult to acquit the innocent.

For example, it used to be the law that before a defendant could be convicted of rape, the victim's story had to be "corroborated." This meant that the alleged victim's story alone wouldn't be enough. The law was changed to permit conviction on the basis of the victim's word alone. In general, that has been a positive change, since it no longer places alleged rape victims in the unique category of being distrusted without "real" proof. However, it also makes it somewhat easier for a woman to lie and make up the entire story.

The law used to state that the defendant's lawyer could cross-examine the alleged victim by asking her about her "prior sexual history." This invasion of privacy not only deterred many victims from bringing rapists to trial, but also led some jurors to disbelieve that a woman who had been sexually active—"promiscuous," as some put it—could be raped. Now the defense attorney may not cross-examine the complaining witness about her prior sexual activity unless it is specifically relevant to the issues in the case.

Some newspapers used to publish the names of both the alleged rapist and the alleged victim before the trial. Now many newspapers no longer publish the names of the alleged victims, on the grounds that it would be unduly embarrassing to a rape victim. This presumes the conclusion sought to be reached at the trial: that the alleged victim was, in fact, raped by the defendant. It also denies the defendant the opportunity to obtain relevant negative information about the complaining witness—for example, a prior history of false accusations.

It used to be common for judges to be uniquely insensitive to complaining witnesses in rape cases. Now—as a result of court-watching programs by antirape groups—some judges seem fearful of making legal rulings in favor of rape defendants.

These and other changes reflect a healthy realization that more must be done to prevent and combat the scourge of rape in our society—but they also reflect a diminishing concern for the defendant, who may have been falsely accused.

As one civil liberties lawyer, who is concerned about the sometimes vigilante attitude toward accused rapists, puts it: "Some people regard rape as so heinous an offense that they would not even regard *innocence* as a defense." In our rush to put guilty rapists behind bars, we must never forget that under Anglo-American principles of justice, it's better for ten guilty to go free than for even one innocent to be wrongly convicted. This salutary approach applies just as much to rape as to other vicious crimes.

Although the whole story has not yet emerged, Dotson spent six years in prison because a sixteen-year-old girl apparently preferred to cry rape rather than admit her own sexual experimentation. The legal system that convicted Dotson—despite his corroborated alibi and weaknesses in the state's case—failed us all.

There will be time to assess blame and learn lessons after Dotson has been freed. However, this travesty should serve as a constant reminder that injustice is a two-way street: it's unjust for a guilty rapist to go free, and it's also unjust for an innocent defendant to be wrongly convicted.

Our legal system must strike a balance to ensure that in our understandable ardor to convict the guilty, we do not sacrifice the rights of the innocent, even—perhaps especially—when they are charged with horrible crimes such as rape.

April 2, 1985

46
Dotson Case: Who Has the Burden of Proof?

The specter of a convicted rapist being returned to prison in the face of his accuser's sworn recantation has perplexed many observers. In 1979, Cathleen Crowell Webb swore under pains and penalties of perjury that Gary Dotson had brutally and violently raped her two years earlier, when she was sixteen.

Now—eight years after the alleged rape and six years after her testimony sent the defendant to prison—Mrs. Webb has sworn under pains and penalties of perjury that she had made up her earlier story. After a perfunctory hearing—with little new in the way of hard investigation—the original trial judge ruled that Dotson would have to remain in prison.

This is clearly not the end of the road for Dotson. He can still pursue further legal remedies or seek a gubernatorial pardon. But Judge Richard Samuels's refusal to free Dotson as soon as Mrs. Webb recanted her testimony has raised confusing questions about how "recanted testimony" should be evaluated.

In ruling against Dotson, Samuels applied the usual rule that recanted testimony should be viewed with suspicion—but this isn't the "usual" case. In the usual case, the defendant's accomplice has testified against the defendant in exchange for a "bargain" from the government. After the accomplice has received the benefit of the bargain—usually a reduced charge or sentence—he turns around, recants his incriminating testimony, and tries to help his friend. In that case—or others like it—it's wise to view recanted testimony with suspicion.

Here, however, the victim herself, who apparently had had no contact with the defendant over the years, came forward on her own and recanted. Some rape counselors have opined that nearly all recantations by the victim are false and "part of the rape trauma syndrome." But there are reasons to doubt that conclusion, especially in the context of a recantation that occurs so many years after the alleged rape and testimony.

The only conclusion that has emerged with absolute certainty from Mrs. Webb's flip-flop is that she is a witness who is capable of lying under oath in a convincing manner. No one can know for sure whether she was lying when she persuaded a judge and jury that Dotson had raped her, or whether she's lying now, when she has persuaded many courtroom and television observers that she was not raped.

The jury that convicted Dotson saw a frightened young girl with no history of dishonesty. If the case went to trial now, the jurors would see a more mature woman who is an admitted perjurer. They still would have to decide *which time* she committed perjury. Or they might decide—as I suspect they would—that since she admittedly perjured herself once; *neither* account can be credited beyond a reasonable doubt.

Because of this inherent uncertainty, the question comes down to: which side must shoulder the burden of proof? If Dotson must prove that he is innocent, then he'll lose. If the prosecutor must prove that Dotson is guilty, then the prosecution will lose. Neither side can shoulder the burden—prove its side—by relying on the testimony of an admitted perjurer. And without Mrs. Webb's testimony, the remaining evidence—scientific and alibi—cuts both ways.

We've all been taught that the prosecution has the burden of proving the defendant's guilt beyond a reasonable doubt. Many people—knowing of that truism—must have been startled to read Samuels's conclusion that Dotson "has failed to sustain his burden." But the prosecution has the burden of proof only *before* the defendant is tried and found guilty. Once the defendant has been convicted, the burden shifts. To secure a reverse of his conviction, or even a new trial, the defendant must shoulder the burden of proving that he is innocent (or that there are legal reasons why his conviction was improperly secured)—and the defendant's burden is a heavy one.

This shifting burden creates a confusing paradox. Even if an imprisoned defendant can cast substantial doubt on his guilt, he still may be required to serve his entire sentence. Even if he can show that he's "probably" innocent, the law—according to Samuels and many other judges—forbids his early release. This is because the "law loves finality." Once a defendant has been convicted, it's extremely difficult to get the law to admit that it may have erred.

But if we believe the age-old aphorism that it's better for ten (some say a hundred) guilty to go free than for even one innocent to be wrongly imprisoned, then the law should always be open to reconsider questionable convictions.

These are the tensions that are operating in the Dotson-Webb case: The law's love of finality argues in favor of keeping a possibly innocent man in prison, while the law's abhorrence of convicting the innocent argues for Dotson's release.

The irony is that the legal system's rigidities may keep the courts from doing justice here. Instead, the flexibility of the governor's pardoning power may have to be called upon.

April 16, 1985

UPDATE
The governor did commute the sentence to the six years that Dotson had

already served, because that was more time than the "average rapist" serves. The governor also expressed skepticism about Webb's recantation. Dotson was returned to prison in 1987 on battery charges brought by his wife. Shortly thereafter he was again released and quickly rearrested after getting drunk in a bar.

47
Police Dilemma: Shoot or Don't Shoot?

The policeman, having been informed of a burglary in progress, sees a young man running from the house. He shouts, "Stop! Police!" The suspect begins to climb a fence. The policeman knows that if he makes it over the fence, he'll almost certainly escape. He also knows that the suspect isn't holding a gun, since he's using both hands to scale the fence.

In a split second, the policeman must make a life-or-death decision: should he shoot the suspect and risk killing him? Or should he hold his fire and risk the suspect's escape?

Variations of this dilemma have confronted countless police officers in every city and town throughout the world. Most recently, a Soviet sentry resolved a similar dilemma—to the outrage of most civilized people—by shooting U.S. Major Arthur D. Nicholson, Jr., who was apparently fleeing after being spotted photographing military secrets in East Germany.

Some ten years earlier, Memphis police officer E. R. Hymon had resolved the dilemma by shooting and killing a fifteen-year-old Edward Garner, who was climbing the fence after having burglarized ten dollars and a purse.

The father of the boy brought suit against Hymon and various Memphis officials for violating his son's civil rights. After a ten-year ping-pong match through the lower courts, the case eventually reached the U.S. Supreme Court.

The High Court decided—in a six-to-three vote—that it was unconstitutional for Hymon to have employed "deadly force" to effectuate the arrest of Garner. Justice Byron White—the former football player whose nick-name was "Whizzer"—wrote the majority decision, which concluded that: "The use of deadly force to prevent the escape of all felony suspects, whatever the circumstances, is constitutionally unreasonable."

White directly confronted the argument that unless deadly force is per-mitted, some fleeing felons will evade justice: "It is not better that all felony suspects die than that they escape."

The court's majority went out of its way to emphasize that the *Garner* decision isn't intended to deprive the police of their power to protect themselves and other innocent citizens from dangerous suspects. The police may shoot to kill "if the suspect threatens the officer with a weapon or if there is probable cause to believe that he has committed a crime involving the infliction or threatened infliction of serious physical harm." The lower courts surely will resolve doubts in favor of police officers who must make split-second decisions in ambiguous situations, where they can't be sure whether the fleeing felon is toting a gun.

Despite the cautious nature of the *Garner* decision, it has provoked outrage in some quarters. Coming as it did on the same day that Bernhard Goetz—the so-called "subway vigilante"—was indicted for attempting to murder his alleged assailants, the Supreme Court's ruling has been accused of "tying the hands" of our police forces and "sending a message" to criminals that they might as well try to escape rather than submit to the lawful orders of the police. As one critic put it: "The Goetz indictment tells us that we can't protect ourselves and the Garner case tells us that the po-lice can't protect us. What's left?"

But these criticisms surely overstate the effect of the Supreme Court's ruling on the ability of the police to do their jobs. In fact, most urban police departments have had regulations in effect for years that restrict the power of the police to use deadly force against unarmed fleeing felons. The International Association of Chiefs of Police—representing some 15,000 high-ranking police officials—applauded the *Garner* decision.

There is no evidence that in states that have authorized deadly force against all fleeing suspected felons, the police or the citizenship are any safer than in states where the police are directed to hold their fire against unarmed nonviolent suspects. Any time a pistol is discharged, there is a risk that an innocent victim may be killed by a ricocheting bullet.

Several years ago, the Supreme Court ruled that it would be unconstitu-tional to execute a defendant convicted of rape, armed robbery, or kidnapping. Only the deliberate taking of human life, the court reasoned, could justify the terrible punishment of state-inflicted death.*

There are differences, of course, between execution after conviction and the use of deadly force to effectuate an arrest. But these differences cut both ways. On the one hand, the fleeing felon may escape entirely from all punishment, whereas if the convicted defendant avoids execution, he will at least be subjected to imprisonment. On the other hand, the convicted defendant has been found guilty and the sentence carried out only after a trial and appeal, whereas the police officer who shoots the fleeing felon serves as instantaneous prosecutor, judge, jury, and executioner.

A balance must be struck between the needs of the police to bring suspects to justice and the rights of suspects not to be gunned down if they panic and fail to heed an order to "halt."

In the United States, we pride ourselves in respecting life more than property. The Supreme Court struck the appropriate balance when it resolved the police officer's dilemma with a decision in favor of life.

April 9, 1985

The Supreme Court subsequently changed that ruling. Now a defendant convicted of participating in a crime that resulted in death can be executed if his actions showed a "reckless disregard for life." See column 100.

48
Suing Churches for Malpractice?

Do U.S. courts have the power to decide whether the Bible holds the key to human emotional difficulties? This issue is now coming before our courts with increasing frequency.

The specific case now being tried before a California jury is based on a heart-rending situation that is certain to test the limits of our First Amendment's mandate of religious freedom.

Kenneth Nally was a UCLA student who converted from Catholicism and joined the Grace Community Church, the largest nondenominational evangelical congregation in Los Angeles County.

Nally established a relationship with a woman who was active in the church, and he began to work in the church while pursuing a divinity degree. Eventually the relationship with the woman dissolved, and Nally became quite depressed. Rather than seeking medical or psychological help, the young man turned to his church for counseling.

The pastors, consistent with the principles of their church, told Nally that the Scriptures would be used as the basis of their counseling. The Bible, they assured him, was the "best resource" for curing emotional illness. Indeed, the church was so certain of the curative powers of the Bible that it allegedly "advertised" that it could successfully counsel believers who suffered from such severe mental illnesses as schizophrenia.

The religious prescription did not work for Kenneth Nally. After being counseled about the relationship between depression and sin, the young man put a shotgun to his head and killed himself. He was twenty-four when he died.

Now his distraught and angry parents are suing the church for $1 million. In effect, they are charging "religious malpractice." Their lawyer is arguing that "the church undertook to treat and provide medical care to a very seriously disturbed and depressed young man and they did a very inadequate job of it." The church, relying on the First Amendment, is claiming that "religious malpractice" is an oxymoron—a contradiction in terms. Religions, the lawyer for the church contends, can't be judged by medical standards of malpractice: "There is no way, according to the pastors, that you can unscramble the soul and the mind."

Although the complex issues of this case will be decided initially by a jury, the eventual ruling will almost certainly be made by a high court, perhaps the Supreme Court. The factual issues include the claim made by the parents' lawyer that "Ken would be alive today if he had gotten the proper treatment." But even if the parents can establish that difficult contention by introducing psychiatric or psychological expert testimony, that won't end the constitutional dispute.

Under our First Amendment, religions are free to propose solutions to life's problems that are alternatives to those accepted by science. As long as the person choosing the religious way is a competent adult, the state— through its courts—may not ordinarily second-guess the choice. There can be no official consumer watchdog agencies for religion. Competent adults must be free to choose any brand of religious salvation, no matter how irrational it may seem to others. To entrust the government to monitor the religious choices of its citizens would mean that civil judges, legislators, or executives would be empowered to "prefer" some religions over others—

and that's exactly what the "establishment clause" of the First Amendment is supposed to prohibit.

Fraudulent quacks may not, of course, use the pretext of religion to sell a phony brand of salvation that they themselves don't believe in. The law is empowered to test the bona fide of alleged religious hucksters. However, the only issue courts may inquire into is whether the person claiming religious protection is acting in good faith.

Thus, Christian Scientists may elect prayer over prescriptions; Jehovah's Witnesses may choose trust over transfusions; and other believers may opt for salvation over surgery—as long as they are competent adults.

And there, of course, is the rub when it comes to mental illness. Is a seriously depressed young man "competent" to choose religious counseling over the tested—if not always successful—techniques of psychotherapy? Was Kenneth Nally in a position, mentally and emotionally, to make the decision that may have cost him his life? These difficult questions must be decided before the church can comfortably fit under the umbrella of the First Amendment.

Mental illness poses another complex factual question. The claims of "scientific" psychotherapy are very difficult to prove by objective methodology. Some studies purport to show that nonintervention—doing nothing—may be as good or better than some forms of psychiatric intervention. Surely prayers—even placebos—will help some. In an area as shrouded in uncertainty as psychotherapy, it would be especially inappropriate for a court to "declare" that there is a right and a wrong way to deal with depression—a problem that has plagued humankind from Biblical times.

About all that can be done is to urge consumers to be wary of what they are being offered in the name of religion: "*Caveat Congregant.*"

April 30, 1985

See column 119.

49
There's No "Right to Risk Death"

Recent statistics seem to confirm what most of us already knew: seat belts save lives. The motor vehicle commissioner of New York state announced that automobile deaths declined by a whopping 27 percent in the first three months since the state has been requiring all drivers, front-seat passengers, and children under ten to buckle up.

If these data prove accurate over time, it will mean that enactment of the mandatory seat-belt law may save more than 250 lives a year in New York state alone. Extrapolated over the rest of the United States, a national law could save as many as 4,000 lives each year.

Yet despite its potential for saving lives, many Americans are fundamentally opposed to a law that would punish people for not taking an action designed to protect them from themselves. This opposition is led by libertarians who react passionately to any governmental compulsion whose goal is to make people help themselves. They quote the great philosopher John Stuart Mill, whose influential essay "On Liberty" has become a nearly biblical prohibition against governmental "paternalism." Mill warned that "the only purpose for which power can be rightfully exercised against any member of a civilized community, against his will, is to prevent harm to others. He cannot rightfully be compelled to do or forbear because it will be better for him to do so."

But the equally eloquent John Donne presented an opposing view in this age-old philosophical dispute when he reminded us that: "No man is an island, entire of itself . . . any man's death diminishes me, because I am involved in mankind; and therefore never send to know for whom the bell tolls; it tolls for thee."

The debate over paternalism will continue into the next millennium. But we don't need to wait for its ultimate resolution to realize that mandatory seat-belt laws should be enacted *now*. No one is suggesting that violators be imprisoned or whipped. The New York statute authorizes fines of no more than fifty dollars for failure to comply with its simple and minimal compulsion. In a society that already mandates Social Security payments, minimum wages, drug and sexual prohibitions, and many other significant paternalistic intrusions on our liberty, a fifty dollar "death-tax" is a small price to pay for violating a law that could save thousands of lives and millions of dollars.

Moreover, this is one law that really seems to work, and with little cost. It's estimated that before the New York statute was enacted, only about 16 percent of drivers and front-seat passengers wore seat belts. However, during the first month of enforcement, compliance was estimated at 69 percent. Although that figure settled down to about 60 percent after a couple of months—a slippage common in other parts of the world that have experimented with similar laws—the expectation is that so long as the law is enforced, compliance will remain well above the rate prior to enactment and lives will continue to be saved.

Nor does the seat-belt law—as distinguished from some victimless crime laws—divert substantial resources away from other, more pressing, needs. Ninety percent of the 7,000 summonses issued in New York were given to motorists who had already been stopped for other traffic infractions.

How much are human lives worth in the currency of inconvenience? That's the question contemporary philosophers should ask in the debate over mandatory seat-belt laws. If people really are determined to risk their lives or kill themselves, there is very little a society can do to stop them. However, a humane society should try its darnedest to prevent *unintentional* deaths caused by the carelessness and laziness of people *who want to live*, but who need a financial reminder that seat belts save lives.

It may seem preposterous that a fifty dollar fine will have more deterrent effect than the real punishment for failing to buckle up—a measurably increased risk of death—but the data seem to support that conclusion.

Let's temper our abstract philosophies with pragmatic and life-giving realities. People often need the help of gently paternalistic laws to get them where they want to go. It's no victory for liberty when a parent or child who wanted to live is killed because of avoidable forgetfulness.

Laws aren't written to protect only the rights of rationally calculating philosophers. They're designed to protect the rest of us as well—even from our own weaknesses. I, for one, want the law to keep reminding me—and all those I love—that we should care enough about life to warrant the minimal inconvenience of buckling up.

Even if I'm deprived of a tiny portion of one liberty—my inherent right to be foolish—I'll have plenty of time to exercise more important and fulfilling liberties. But if, in the name of a trivial liberty, my life is sacrificed, it will be the last liberty I'll ever enjoy.

My question to libertarians is: do you really want your epitaph to read, "He died exercising his fundamental right not to wear a seat belt"?

May 7, 1985

50
When a Home Is Not a House . . .

There's no question that Charles Carney was using his Dodge Mini Motor Home as a pad that afternoon in the Horton Plaza area of downtown San Diego.

While the police were observing the motor home, a young boy entered it and the curtains were drawn. When the boy emerged an hour and fifteen minutes later, he told the police that he had engaged in sex with the man in the motor home. In exchange for oral copulation, the man had given the boy some marijuana.

At that point, the police could easily have obtained a warrant to arrest the man and search the van. They had what is known as "probable cause" to believe that a crime had occurred. Trading sex for dope is a felony.

Indeed, a warrant could have been obtained in a very short time, since the motor home was parked in an off-the-street lot only a few blocks from the courthouse. One of the several police officers who had the motor home under surveillance could have gone to the court and obtained a warrant from one of the numerous magistrates on duty at the time. Nor was there any basis for concluding that Carney was about to drive away: he had been parked there for a while, and there was every indication he was staying put.

But instead of sending a policeman to secure a warrant, the officers decided to take a shortcut. They requested that the young boy who had just left the motor home return, knock on the door, and ask Carney to come out. As he did, the police entered the motor home, searched it, found marijuana, arrested Carney, and drove him and the van to the police station.

Carney challenged the search in the state courts. The Supreme Court of California ruled in his favor, concluding that his motor home—equipped with a much-used bed, refrigerator, table, chairs, and other facilities—"is more properly treated as a residence than a mere automobile." This conclusion was crucial, since the Constitution—for reasons that have never been entirely convincing—gives far more protection to a residence than it does to a car. Specifically, the police generally don't need a warrant to search a car, whereas they generally do need a warrant to search a residence.

The California Supreme Court cited William Pitt's famous exhortation about the sanctity of the home: "The poorest man may in his cottage bid defiance to all the force of the Crown. It may be frail; its roof may shake;

the wind may blow through it; the storms may enter; but the King of England cannot enter—all his force dares not cross the threshold of the ruined tenement!"

A rundown American motor home, the court concluded, "is entitled to a degree of protection similar to that accorded an Englishman's cottage or ruined tenement."

The case might well have ended there. The highest court of a sovereign state had ruled—on the basis of both federal and Californian court precedents—that Carney's constitutional rights had been violated by the California police. But the conservatives on the U.S. Supreme Court—who proclaim their adherence to judicial restraint—reached out and voted to reconsider the issue.

Moderate Justice John Paul Stevens lashed out at the voracious judicial appetite of his brethren and sister: in recent times, he said, "the court had displayed little confidence in state and lower federal court decisions that purport to enforce the Fourth Amendment. . . . Much of the court's 'burdensome' workload is a product of its own aggressiveness in this area."

He added that "this is not a case in which an American citizen has been deprived of a right. . . . Rather . . . a state court has upheld a citizen's assertion of a right, finding the citizen to be protected under both federal and state law."

But the Supreme Court, which is quickly becoming a court of last resort for governments rather than citizens, decided to hear arguments—perhaps because they thought the case would be entertaining, as their questions to counsel suggest.

Justice Sandra Day O'Connor asked about a mobile "tent," and then answered her own question: "It doesn't have wheels, right?" That led Justice Thurgood Marshall to inquire about the constitutional status of a houseboat without a motor. "There may be oars," answered the resourceful prosecutor. Even a large house can be moved, persisted Marshall. That's true, acknowledged the prosecutor: "I've passed a few of them on the beltway." Although no one has passed an old covered wagon in recent years, Justice William Brennan invoked that historic frontier symbol. Even the prosecutor had to acknowledge that the wagon, which "functioned as a . . . temporary residence while [the pioneers] were making the trek across the country," should be given some of the dignity of the home.

But when it came time to decide the case, Chief Justice Warren Burger wrote a turgid, unenlightening, and doctrinaire opinion which simply declared that six justices believe that a mobile home is constitutionally analogous to a car, not a home.

In a footnote, Burger left unresolved the legal status of movable homes that are temporarily immobilized because they are "elevated on blocks" or "connected to utilities."

The basic message, however, is clear: if it's mobile, it's a car, not a home, regardless of what's inside.

May 21, 1985

For another example of an illegal use of a van, see the next column.

51
When Consensual Sex Is a Crime

It was two o'clock in the afternoon when the police first observed the suspected criminals preparing to commit the heinous felony. They saw one of them get into a suspicious looking van, driven by an unsavory character. Two armed policemen followed the van, making sure to remain out of sight as the unsuspecting criminals led the police to their secret destination in a secluded area near a factory. The two policemen waited anxiously, giving the felons an opportunity to commence their foul deed before arresting them. Then, suddenly, without any warning, the two enforcers of the law burst onto the scene of the crime and caught the criminals in the act of committing the felony.

No, they were not planning a bank robbery. They weren't even dealing drugs. They were making love. Two consenting adults—one male, the other female—making love in the privacy of a van in a secluded area!

The arrested felons immediately confessed that they were married—but not to each other. That makes both of them guilty of adultery—a felony under Massachusetts law. Nor is the punishment merely the wearing of a scarlet A or a few hours of public humiliation in the stocks, as it was in colonial times. The current Massachusetts statute—most recently amended in 1978—punishes adultery by imprisonment for up to three years "in the state prison." (Imagine an adultery "con" having to explain to his hardened cellmates what he was in for: "Come on, you gotta be kidding. They got you for what?")

You might well wonder what two armed Worcester policemen were doing following the loving couple. There must be *some* violent crime in Worcester more deserving of their investigative talents than an illicit rendezvous. And how did they find out what the couple was up to? Maybe there's a special adultery unit of the Worcester Police Department, which keeps records, relies on undercover bartenders, and plants electronic listening devices in bedrooms!

But there is no need to worry, you are surely saying. The courts would never uphold such an archaic relic of our puritanical past. The only reason the adultery law is still on the books is that is hasn't come before the courts in recent years. Wrong! Just a few weeks ago, the Worcester adultery bust did come before the Supreme Judicial Court, Massachusetts' highest court, and generally a bastion of liberty. That Court ruled *unanimously* that the adultery statute was perfectly constitutional, and that it can be freely applied "to consensual acts between adults in private."

Several years ago, Saturday Night Live did a hilarious sketch of a couple in the privacy of their bedroom. They were about to begin making love, when suddenly, nine black-robed old men appeared in the room and started checking on the marital status, sexual positions and birth control. The sketch was intended as satire. In Massachusetts it has become reality. Big Brother has entered our bedrooms and vans one year *before* 1984.

The reasoning employed by the Supreme Judicial Court is even more frightening than its conclusion. Judge James P. Lynch, Jr., opined that since "adultery is a ground for divorce," it should follow that it can also be made a crime. But "impotence," "intoxication," "desertion," "failure to provide suitable support," and "irretrievable breakdown of the marriage" are also grounds for divorce in Massachusetts. Should they be made crimes as well?

Moreover, the Supreme Judicial Court took judicial notice of the fact that "adultery frequently has a destructive impact on marital relationship." But so do Sunday afternoon football, *Playboy* magazine, and children growing up. In any event, the adultery laws apply to marriages that have already been irreparably destroyed. During the separations or the six months after a decree of divorce, the parties still remain technically married, for purposes of the adultery laws.

Telling adults what they can and cannot do in private is both wrong and ineffective. It promotes cynicism and disrespect for the law. By branding millions of otherwise law-abiding citizens as felons, it makes it easier for some to take the next step and commit a real crime.

No criminal law should remain on the books if we are unwilling to have it enforced. Giving the police and the courts the power to enforce a law selectively against a tiny percentage of those who violate it is an invitation to abuse. There are surely some who would encourage across-the-board enforcement of the adultery statute—and perhaps the fornication, cohabitation, and sodomy laws as well. If that were done the remaining police, prosecutors and judges—those who are not themselves imprisoned for committing these crimes—would have no time to enforce any other criminal statutes.

May 25, 1983

See Column 84.

52
An A-1 Cure for an X-Rated Problem

While the debate over censoring pornography rages, a group of New York state legislators has come up with what seems to be a sensible compromise. The proposed law will make extremists on neither side happy, but it promises to eliminate one of the major evils of pornography without imposing censorship.

The bill, which was passed by the New York Legislature last week, is quite simple: it requires all stores that are generally accessible to the public—such as drugstores, supermarkets, and newsstands—to cover up the sexually explicit covers of magazines or books that are kept in plain view of patrons.

The statute doesn't ban or censor any books or magazines, but it's intended to protect citizens from being forcibly exposed to what they might regard as "offensive sexual material" when they go to pick up the family newspaper or magazine.

It also protects children—even those who don't necessarily want any protection—from sexually titillating material on the covers. As the assemblyman who sponsored the measure put it: "The passage of this bill marks a victory for those citizens who object to these materials and those who are concerned with maintaining the basic principles of the First Amendment."

Of course, this approach isn't problem-free. Someone will have to define the operative terms of the law—"offensive sexual material." Do the current covers of *Playboy* and *Penthouse*—which are certainly suggestive, but generally not explicit—meet the test? Will the book jackets of risqué novels have to be covered up? What about the "swimsuit issue" of *Sports Illustrated*? If "offensiveness" is in the eye of the beholder—as it surely is—then whose "eyes" will decide which covers to wrap in brown paper?

Even if these problems can be solved, some civil libertarians will protest the state-imposed covering-up of *any* part of a book or magazine: "Today the cover; tomorrow the foldout; next week the stories." That cry can't be ignored by any of us who oppose government censorship—but there's also a right not to be forcibly exposed to sexual material. Nude beaches, for example, may have their place—so long as the sun worshipers select isolated locations and forbear from cavorting naked along main streets or the most populated public beaches.

In the context of books and magazines exhibited in general-access stores, there's a real difference between what's exposed on the cover and what's discreetly tucked within.

Some civil libertarians may be unhappy with this compromise, but the extremists on the side of book-burning—whether they be moral majoritarians or censorial feminists—will be even more outraged. They don't want people to voluntarily open the "offensive" books or magazines and read or view their contents. The contents are precisely what they want to ban, since they believe that reading the words or viewing the pictures will cause a degradation of values and a change in behavior. That, of course, is censorship personified, whether the censor is a fundamentalist or a feminist.

The New York bill is part of a more general middle ground that should be taken seriously in the search for a practical compromise that's consistent with First Amendment values. The middle ground approach focuses on what I call the "externalities" of pornography. By "externalities," I mean that part of the pornography problem that's outside—exposed to public view, rather than limited to what the consenting adult consumer has chosen to encounter. Included in such externalities are movie theater marquees, bookstore windows, and the covers of books and magazines. The externalities can be regulated by the state without substantially curtailing the willing adult consumer's freedom to open the pages or enter the theater.

The need for such an approach is becoming more evident as pornography moves from public places—such as movie theaters—into the privacy of the home. The home video-cassette recorder is quickly overtaking the theater as the primary vehicle for pornographic films. These films are being discreetly rented by the millions in video stores around the country. Instead of regulating the *externalities* of such establishments—for example, the manner in which the cassette boxes are exhibited and the prohibition on rentals to children—prosecutors in several cities have begun to arrest legitimate video-store owners because of the *content* of the cassettes they rent. That's censorship, pure and simple.

Recently, while in Washington, D.C., I drove past an establishment that is several blocks from the White House, the Capitol, and the Supreme Court. It's a bookstore called—quite aptly—The Plain Brown Wrapper. Nothing is exposed to public view other than the name, a façade that looks like a brown wrapper, and a small subtitle designed to ensure that only those adults who are willing consumers will walk past the closed door. The subtitle reads: Purveyors of Fine Smut Since 1976. I chose not to enter. Others choose to enter. All of our rights are protected. That's how it should be in a free and open democracy that prizes both freedom of speech and freedom from offensiveness.

June 4, 1985

53
School Prayer: Silence Isn't Golden

The Supreme Court has ruled that silence isn't constitutionally golden—if its purpose is to encourage religious prayer by public school students. The case was a rather simple one for the high court.

The state of Alabama used to have a statute that authorized a moment of silence at the beginning of the school day "for meditation." But in 1981, State Senator Donald Holmes introduced a bill that amended the law by adding the words "or voluntary prayer." In proposing the change, Holmes said it was an "effort to return voluntary prayer" to the public schools.

When asked if the law had any purpose other than putting prayer back in schools, he responded: "No. I did not have no other [sic] purpose in mind."

A forty-year-old black lawyer named Ismael Jaffree brought a lawsuit that challenged the exposure of his children to "religious prayer services" in the public schools. W. Brevard Hand, a federal district court judge, acknowledged that the Alabama law encouraged prayer, but ruled that it was perfectly permissible for Alabama to establish an official state religion. According to Hand's decision, it would be all right for each state to pick one religion—just as it picks a bird or flower—as its own particular favorite. It could pay for the churches and ministers of that established religion, and it could discriminate against members of other religions. In reversing Hand's decision, the Supreme Court characterized his views as "remarkable"—a judicial euphemism for ridiculous.

When Hand's bizarre decision was first delivered, I included it in my "judicial dishonor roll" and explored its implications.

> In Massachusetts, there would be a religious struggle between Catholics and Protestants for official recognition. In New York, the Jews would get into the act. . . . In Utah, Mormonism would win. In California, perhaps the various cults and fringe religions would unite and present a common political front. Even if a state settles on Protestantism, there would—of course—be the question of *which* Protestant denomination would become the official one? The Ayatollah Khomeini award for Attempting to Divide a Country Along Religious Lines goes to Judge W. Brevard Hand.

The Supreme Court has made it clear that neither a state nor the federal government may "establish" a particular religion, nor may any governmental entity prefer religion over nonreligion. In the United States, an atheist or agnostic isn't any lower in the hierarchy of good citizenship than a religious believer. This country, unlike most other countries, doesn't have second-class citizens.

As Justice Stephens, writing for the Supreme Court's six-person majority, declared: "The court has unambiguously concluded that the individual freedom of conscience protected by the First Amendment embraces the right to select any religious faith or none at all." And all state functionaries—from presidents to public school teachers—"must pursue a course of complete neutrality toward religion." The state of Alabama thus violated its obligation to remain neutral when it passed an amendment that was intended "to characterize prayer as a favored practice."

The court went out of its way to suggest that it would approve state laws authorizing neutral moments of silence during which the students were free to think whatever thoughts they wished—religious or otherwise.

Of course, the dry words of a statute tell only part of the story. Even if the law says nothing about prayer, particular teachers will urge students to pray. Some will probably even criticize students who refuse to bow their heads in reverential devotion.

It will be impossible, of course, to monitor every public classroom in America, and few parents will want to bring lawsuits to enforce the constitutional prohibitions. As Jaffree—the lawyer who won the most recent Supreme Court case—bemoaned: "I'm still sorry for my children. They have told me that they wish I'd never filed the suit. They said they have lost friends over it." Nor has Jaffree himself been immune from criticism. He says he has become "sort of persona non grata in the black community now." No American should have to pay that price for standing up for the rights of his children.

Recent trends in Supreme Court decisions dealing with the establishment of religion are confusing at best. Last year the Supreme Court ruled that the public sponsorship of a Christian nativity scene had a secular purpose and that the state didn't violate its obligation of neutrality by promoting it. Now it has ruled that the Alabama moment of silence for "meditation or voluntary prayer" has no secular purpose and violates the rule of neutrality. Although the nativity scene would appear to be far more religious and less neutral than the moment of silence, the former was approved and the latter disapproved by a majority of justices. The difference may be that the moment of silence is for young and impressionable students, while the nativity scene is for general consumption.

The message sent out by the Supreme Court in the moment-of-silence case is that the justices will continue to keep a watchful eye on the relationship between the state, religion, and the public schools.

June 7, 1985

54
Rape: Sexism Is No Excuse

A bizarre case in Fresno, California, highlights an unresolved conundrum in the law of rape.

The case involved members of the Hmong community—a primitive mountain tribe from Laos—about 30,000 of whom have settled in Fresno. The traditional marriage ritual among these people is called "marriage by capture." The courtship begins with the man engaging in ritualized flirtation; the woman follows by giving the man a token signifying acceptance of the courtship. So far, there's no problem under American law.

But then the man is required to take the woman to his family's house in order to "consummate" the union. Here's where the trouble begins. Under Hmong tradition the woman is supposed to protest: "No, no, no, I'm not ready." If she doesn't pretend reluctance by weeping and moaning, the Hmong woman is regarded as insufficiently virtuous, and hence undesirable. The Hmong man—understanding the tradition—is required to ignore her mock protestations and firmly lead her into the bedroom, where the union is consummated. If the man isn't "brave enough" to take the initiative, he's regarded as too weak to be her husband.

Most of these marriages seem to work out according to tradition and with no complaint, just as my great-grandparents' "arranged" marriages seemed to work out better than many in our generation. But in at least one case, a Hmong woman's family filed rape charges against a man. In that case, the woman claimed her protests were real and that the union was "consummated" against her will.

The prosecutors and the judge apparently believed both the man and the woman. Thus, the man genuinely thought that the woman wanted to have the union consummated—despite her verbal protests. The woman, however, didn't consent. The legal system resolved this failure of communications by allowing the man to plea-bargain to the misdemeanor of "false imprisonment" and sentenced him to ninety days in jail. But in refusing to face up to the difficulties inherent in the rape charge, it left open some important questions that transcend the unique cultural aspects of the Hmong case.

A considerable number of mainstream U.S. rape cases also involve tragic failures of communication, and the law hasn't yet figured out how to deal with this recurring problem. Consider the following scenario:

A young man with a macho, sexist upbringing has dated young women whose backgrounds endorse this role. Part of his dating ritual has been for the male to be the aggressor and for the female to resist—at least in the beginning. The young man has learned to understand that for many of the women he has dated, "no" means "maybe," "maybe" means "yes," and that to really say no, a woman must slap him firmly in the face. (Of course, by describing this warped, sexist world—a world that tragically persists among certain subcultures—I don't mean to condone it.)

One evening, the man meets a woman in a local bar. He erroneously believes that she is part of his subculture. They flirt and she goes back to his apartment. They begin to kiss and neck. He aggressively pursues further sexual contact. She politely whispers "no." He persists. She says that she's not ready for "that" yet, maybe next time. He misunderstands this response as an invitation to further aggression and he climbs on top of her. She becomes petrified, believing that she's being raped and that further protest will endanger her life. The episode ends with the man believing that he has aggressively seduced the woman, and with the woman believing that she has been raped.

The woman presses rape charges. How should the judge instruct the jurors to decide the case if they believe *both* the man and the woman—if they conclude that the man genuinely *but erroneously* believed that the woman was going along with his aggressive seduction?

This would be an easier question if we were deciding how to legislate for the future. Men should be required to take a woman's verbal refusal at face value. "No" must be understood to mean precisely that. Old cultural patterns—no matter how entrenched—must adapt to developing concepts of equality.

However, a criminal rape trial isn't intended to create law for the future. Its purpose is to determine the past culpability of the defendant, and the defendant's state of mind is an important component of his culpability— hence the complexity of the problem.

Perhaps one solution is to "staircase" the crime of rape—to break it down into several categories. It would thus be a less serious crime, but a crime nonetheless, to act on a mistaken belief that the woman has consented. And it would be a far more serious crime to force sex upon a woman with full knowledge that she hasn't consented.

Eventually, even the American Hmongs will have to change their culture to conform with American concepts of sexual equality. Surely the rest of us should understand that sexist stereotypes of "no" meaning "yes" can't justify aggression against women.

June 11, 1985

55
The von Bulow Case:
A Personal Look

Three years ago, I was awakened by a phone call at 6:45 A.M. from a man with a pronounced British accent. He said his name was Claus von Bulow and that he had just been found guilty of twice trying to murder his wife. Would I prepare and argue his appeal? he asked.

I hadn't followed the soap-opera first trial of Claus von Bulow very closely, but I did remember that he was Danish by background. I concluded, therefore, that my early-morning British caller was an imposter—one of many cranks who manage to get through to me. The fact that it was April 1—a day that brings out more fools than usual—confirmed my suspicion. And so I told this Mr. "von Bulow" what I thought of his pre-dawn sense of humor.

But it *was* Claus von Bulow—and I did argue the appeal that led to his retrial, and I consulted on the second trial that led to his acquittal. My involvement over the past three years in one of the most highly publicized criminal cases in American history has prompted me to reflect on the interaction between the U.S. criminal justice system and the U.S. media.

The media—television, radio, daily newspapers, magazines—have a profound impact on criminal justice. Everyone within the system understands that fact of life and attempts to manipulate the media to serve the interests of his or her side of the case. (The media, of course, also try to use the case to serve their interests.) Yet nearly all of the participants in a criminal case go through the charade of pretending that they aren't playing to the press.

In the von Bulow case, each side fought hard to convince the Fourth Estate of the righteousness of its cause.

The prosecution convened press conferences, leaked stories, and timed its news for maximum coverage.

Claus von Bulow's stepchildren—who initiated the investigation against him—made the rounds of national television magazines and talk shows, telling the world that they believed he was guilty.

The defense also, of course, tried to generate a media atmosphere favorable to von Bulow.

Although the jurors who sat in judgment of—and ultimately acquitted—von Bulow were sequestered during the entire trial, most of them came to their task with some knowledge of the case. They obtained that knowledge from the media. Had the defense not counterattacked, the second jury would have known only that von Bulow had been unanimously convicted by one jury, that his conviction had been reversed on legal grounds, and that the Rhode Island attorney general believed there was enough evidence for a second jury to convict him.

Therefore, it was important for the defense to respond to that perception by presenting the other side of the story to the public through the media.

Trial by the press is, of course, no substitute for trial by jury. The jury eventually hears all the relevant and admissible evidence and is instructed to decide the case on that basis alone. But students of psychology understand that people—even people who take the solemn oath of jurors—perceive evidence in light of their predispositions. A juror who is predisposed against a defendant will hear and see the very same evidence differently from a juror who is predisposed in favor of that defendant. That's why no vigorous defense lawyer can afford to ignore the prosecutor's efforts to manipulate the media.

In light of recent media cases—such as von Bulow, DeLorean, and some others—critics have proposed that the United States adopt the English rule, which prohibits the press from reporting about ongoing criminal cases. However, such a rule wouldn't suit our national style—or our Constitution. An English-style press ban would have made Watergate and other triumphs of U.S. investigative reporting impossible—or at least far more difficult.

The press performs a critical function in monitoring and exposing all three branches of our government. And the criminal justice system is an important—and frequently abused—part of our government. In fact, the judiciary is the government's least thoroughly examined and investigated branch. We need more, rather than less, reporting about criminal cases.

Moreover, the public is entitled to know about interesting cases—even if the public wants more titillation than information. Censorship of any kind requires a higher degree of justification than the English offer to defend their restrictions of the press.

We pay a price for our freedom of the press. However, that price shouldn't be paid entirely by those accused of crime, as it would be if prosecutors were permitted to announce their accusations in the press with no opportunity for a full response by the defense. We should acknowledge the important role that the press plays in our criminal justice system and recognize that the adversary system isn't limited to the courtroom alone, but extends to the courthouse steps.

The media played a role in Claus von Bulow's first conviction. They also played a role in his acquittal. They did their job, and we—the lawyers—did ours.

June 12, 1985

For additional discussion of the media and criminal justice, see columns 23 and 44.

56
Murder by Corporation

Judge Ronald J. P. Banks of Cook County, Illinois, solemnly pronounced his verdict: the three defendants were guilty of murder. They faced sentences of between twenty and forty years in prison. Banks immediately revoked the defendants' bail, meaning that they would have to be in prison during their expected appeals.

All very appropriate for criminals convicted of murder—the most heinous crime known to humankind, the *only* crime for which an American can be executed under current interpretations of the Constitution.

What was it that these three defendants had done to warrant the full panoply of the law's vengeance? Had they pulled off a gangland contract killing? Had it been a crime of passion? A felony-murder carried out during a bank robbery?

No. The defendants were executives of a company called Film Recovery Systems, and one of their employees—Stefan Golab—had died after falling ill while working in a plant that reclaimed silver from old film.

The defendants claimed that Golab had died of a heart attack. The prosecutors set out to prove that Golab had died of exposure to hydrogen cyanide fumes emitted from the bubbling vats of hazardous chemicals at the plant. Prosecutors also alleged that the three executives—the former president, plant supervisor, and foreman—knew about the hazardous conditions and failed to take appropriate actions to warn the employees. Indeed, there were even allegations that skull-and-crossbones warnings had been scraped off drums of cyanide. The safety problem was compounded because many of the plant's employees did not read English and could not understand warning posters, if indeed there were any.

Banks agreed with the prosecution and found that the "conditions under which workers performed their duties were totally unsafe," and that the defendants were "totally knowledgeable" of the hazardous conditions.

He found the corporation guilty of involuntary manslaughter—a crime punishable by a fine of up to $10,000. That slap on the wrist against the company was typical of the law's response to death resulting from corporate greed.

The verdict that sent shock waves through the business community, however, was Banks's unprecedented conclusion that the worker's death was "no accident, but murder," and that the individual executives would serve murder sentences.

The crime of murder conjures up images of shootings, stabbings, and deliberate poisonings. We imagine murderers as brutal street thugs, hit men, or fanatical terrorists. The image of a well-dressed executive as a murderer is a difficult one for many Americans to comprehend. But Banks had no difficulty seeing—and treating—the three Film Recovery executives as heinous murderers.

The defendants' lawyers were, understandably, "very disturbed" and are planning to appeal the murder conviction. Both sides agree that a murder verdict in this kind of case is unprecedented. As the prosecutor put it: "It's the first case we know of where executives have been found guilty of murder in an industrially related death."

It is surely not the first time, however, that corporate executives have deliberately tolerated conditions that have led to the deaths of workers. Nor will it be the last.

The question that criminal law experts are asking is whether this murder conviction will—on balance—increase the effectiveness of criminal sanctions. On first blush, the answer would seem to be yes. The common view is that the harsher the punishment, the greater the deterrent.

But some experts are doubting that simplistic symmetry. Dean Norval Morris, one of the world's leading authorities on the subject, has opined that a manslaughter conviction might have had a more broadly felt impact than the murder verdict. Pointing out that murder implies a deliberate intent to kill, while manslaughter connotes a "willingness to risk killing," Morris concludes that corporate officials are more likely to "identify with . . . a manslaughter conviction than a murder conviction."

Corporate executives do not think of themselves as potential murderers who plot the deaths of others. They are more likely to be influenced by the threat of punishments imposed on greedy officials who take money-saving shortcuts with safety.

There is also the risk that convicting reckless corporate officials of the most heinous crime will dilute the impact of "real" murder charges. The crime of murder, according to this view, should be reserved only for the most heinous and premeditated killings. These corporate executives— whatever else one can say about them—did not *want* their employee to die. They would have preferred the employee to live—so long as they did not have to spend undue corporate funds on his safety.

Perhaps the solution lies in creating a new crime that is specifically directed against employers who deliberately refuse to spend the money necessary to assure acceptable minimal standards of safety. The new crime should be a very serious one indeed, carrying significant imprisonment. But it should not be the same as premeditated murder.

Back in the eighteenth century, Pennsylvania became the first state to recognize that there are degrees of homicide. Illinois may have taken a step forward by holding corporate executives guilty of a serious crime for endangering the lives of their workers. But it may have taken a step back by not recognizing that homicide is very much a matter of degree.

June 18, 1985

For further discussion of white-collar crime, see columns 29 and 106.

57
Can the Court Define Lust?

History has certainly vindicated the nineteenth-century observation of Alexis de Tocqueville that in the United States, virtually every important issue eventually is decided by the courts.

Indeed, now the Supreme Court has even gotten into the thicket of deciding what constitutes "good old-fashioned, healthy lust," as distinguished from morbid "lasciviousness." This time it has certainly bitten off more than it can chew.

The case arose out of a Washington state statute, enacted in 1982, that declared it to be a "moral nuisance" to sell or exhibit any film or book "which incites lasciviousness or lust."

The Court of Appeals had declared the statute unconstitutional. It ruled that although a state is empowered to censor sexually explicit material that incites "lasciviousness," it is *not* empowered to censor sexually explicit material that merely incites "lust." Reminding us that even President Jimmy Carter had admitted looking "on a lot of women with lust," the court concluded that to most Americans, the word "lust" suggests "a healthy, wholesome human reaction common to millions of well-adjusted persons." To qualify as obscene—and therefore constitutionally bannable—the material must appeal to "a shameful or morbid interest in . . . sex."

In fact, the Court of Appeals observed that "if the arousal of good old-fashioned, healthy lust" can be made illegal, "it might be necessary to haul into court our leading couturiers, perfumers and manufacturers of soft drinks, soap suds, and automobiles . . . as well as mainstream stage, movie and television producers, directors, and performers." The court insisted that to protect the boundary around potential First Amendment expression, we must distinguish between "the arousal of sexual instincts and the perversion of those instincts to morbidity."

The U.S. Supreme Court agreed with the Court of Appeals's conclusion that books or films couldn't be banned if they simply "aroused any sexual responses, whether normal or morbid." It interpreted its precedent-setting cases on censorship as requiring "sexual responses over and beyond those that would be characterized as normal."

In the end, the Supreme Court reversed the Court of Appeals decision and upheld the constitutionality of the Washington statute. However, it did so on the grounds that the statute referred to lasciviousness as well as to lust, and that, since it's perfectly permissible for a state to prohibit material that incites lasciviousness, the Court of Appeals should simply "have excised the word [lust] from the statute entirely."

This may seem complex, but the bottom line is quite simple: from now on, the courts must decide whether sexually explicit material incites (a) "lasciviousness" or (b) "lust." If the former, the material can be banned. If the latter, it cannot.

This distinction, it seems, turns on whether the aroused sexual feeling is "good," "old-fashioned," and "healthy" or "shameful," "morbid," and "unhealthy."

How, in the name of Sigmund Freud, can the courts ever begin to make this kind of subjective value judgment? Which "experts" will be summoned before the august tribunals to pontificate on the "health" or "un-health" of particular sexual feelings? Will Dr. Ruth Westheimer become a courtroom regular debating the Reverend Jerry Falwell on the virtues of old-fashioned vs. new-fangled sex?

This entire attempt to differentiate between lust and lasciviousness would be laughable—except for the fact that real people will go to prison on the basis of such preposterous distinctions. Nearly every state now has a law making it a crime to sell or purchase obscene material. The typical definition of obscene follows the Supreme Court test that allows the states to censor any books, films, or videotapes that "taken as a whole, appeal to the prurient interest, must contain patently offensive depictions or descriptions of specified sexual conduct, and on the whole have no serious literary, artistic, political, or scientific value."

It doesn't matter whether the material is intended for private home use by consenting adults. Both the seller and the customer are at the risk that what seemed normal and healthy eroticism to them may later be determined to be "lascivious," "prurient," or offensive to other people wearing black robes.

Alexis de Tocqueville would be mightily distressed to know that American judges have now become arbiters of taste in sexuality, literature, and art. It isn't a role to which most judges are particularly suited by background or experience.

It's one thing for the issue of healthy vs. unhealthy sexual feelings to be debated on talk shows, in church meetings, and among sex therapists. But it demeans the law—and endangers our freedom—when courts pretend that they can give definite answers to eternal questions about the varieties of human sexuality that have divided and intrigued humankind from the beginning of history.

June 25, 1985

58
When Is Conduct "Unbecoming"?

Writing indignant letters to public officials is as American as booing the umpire at baseball games. Indeed, the First Amendment specifically protects the right of all citizens "to petition the government for a redress of grievances." Nor does the Bill of Rights require that the letter or petition must be written in respectful terms. American history is replete with examples of disrespectful petitions by some of our most respected citizens.

The Declaration of Independence itself is full of disrespect for King George. Every citizen in this free country of ours has the right to tell any public official what he or she thinks of him or her without mincing words.

In a recent case, however, a panel of three federal judges ruled that this inalienable right to send disrespectful letters to public officials is not so inalienable when the letter writer is a *lawyer* and the public official is—you guessed it!—an official of the *courts*.

The case arose out of a dispute between a young North Dakota lawyer named Robert Snyder and the chief judge of the U.S. Court of Appeals for the Eighth Circuit, Donald Lay. Snyder was appointed to represent an indigent criminal defendant. He did a competent job and submitted a bill for his services in the amount of $1,898.55. Because the bill exceeded $1,000, it had to be approved by the chief judge.

Lay "returned" the request for technical reasons. Snyder then exercised his right to gripe. And gripe he did. He sent off an angry letter complaining about the "puny amounts" paid to lawyers who represent indigent defendants and the "extreme gymnastics" required of lawyers in completing the paperwork. "We have sent you everything we have concerning our representation, and I am not sending you anything else," he wrote. "You can take it or leave it."

Snyder concluded his letter by saying that he was "extremely disgusted" and had "simply had it."

Anyone reviewing this letter would have the right to be upset at its tone. But only a judge has the "power" to take action against what he regards as a "disrespectful" letter. Accordingly, Lay responded to Snyder by threatening to suspend him from the practice of law in the federal courts unless he apologized "by return mail."

Snyder responded by return mail, but his response was anything but an apology. "I cannot, and will never, in justice to my conscience, apologize for what I consider to be telling the truth, albeit in harsh terms," he wrote. "[I]f one stands on principle, one must be willing to accept the consequences."

The consequences were swift and savage: suspension from the practice of law in the federal courts for six months, after which he would have to apply for readmission.

A three-judge panel of the Court of Appeals upheld Snyder's suspension. The opinion was written by—you guessed it again!—Chief Judge Donald Lay.

Snyder then appealed to all nine judges of the court, who upheld Lay's decision by a seven-to-two vote. The majority first ruled that there was nothing wrong with having Lay rule on the propriety of his own actions, since he "possessed no personal bias against Snyder." In response to Snyder's invocation of the First Amendment, the court said that disrespectful remarks by a lawyer against the judiciary "do not fall within the ambit of protected speech," because lawyers are held to a higher standard of respect than "ordinary citizens."

Put another way, lawyers who show disrespect for judges will soon *become* "ordinary citizens." The message is that lawyers should keep their true feelings about judges to themselves (as Mae West tried in *My Little Chickadee*, when the judge asked her if she was trying to show contempt for the court, and she responded, "No—I'm trying my best to hide it.").

With the aid of the seven largest law firms in Bismarck, Snyder sought review of his suspension by the U.S. Supreme Court. The Supreme Court unanimously reversed Lay's suspension of Snyder—a rare display of cohesiveness in a normally divided court. Most surprisingly, the opinion was written by Chief Justice Warren Burger, who had frequently chastised lawyers as well as journalists for their incivility.

Burger found that although the tone of the letter exhibited "unlawyerlike rudeness," it did not "rise to the level of 'conduct unbecoming a member of the bar.' "

The villain of the piece, Lay, did not appear to feel chastised by his unanimous rebuff. "The decision doesn't bother me," he said. "It's just another case among many." But for Robert Snyder, it was not just another case. Lay's overreaction might have cost the young attorney his chosen profession.

The bottom line is that if a lawyer oversteps the bounds of propriety, he may place his entire career in jeopardy. But if a judge oversteps the bounds of his power, he risks little but a mild rebuke from a higher court.

It is unlikely that Lay realizes how profoundly wrong—and dangerous—his action was. The real question is whether Lay's judicial temper tantrum was itself "conduct unbecoming" a federal judge.

July 25, 1985

For another example of conduct unbecoming a federal judge, see columns 117 and 137.

59
It's the Silly Season for the Law

Summer seems to bring out the looniest laws. A few summers ago, I received a panicked phone call from a friend vacationing on Fire Island.

"You won't believe what I got busted for," he said. Images of the most culpable crimes ran wildly through my mind. "Eating a cookie in public."

It seems the Town Parents had gotten upset about summer revelers promenading along the streets eating fast food. So they enacted the anti-cookie, anti-ice cream, anti-popcorn ordinance, prohibiting people from eating and walking at the same time. Angry residents called it "The Gerald Ford Law."

A few weeks ago, I nearly got arrested for walking—without even chewing gum or eating a cookie. I had apparently run afoul of an equally bizarre law. There I was on July 4, contemplating the state of our liberties during a long walk on a Martha's Vineyard beach. Suddenly, an officious young beach patrol officer ran up to me and announced, "You can't walk there." I had no idea what the "there" referred to, since there were no obvious boundaries marked on the expanse of open beach.

"You're about to cross from the town beach to a beach owned by a private association." At the time, I happened to be wading knee deep in the ocean surf, which I thought I was allowed to do.

"Can private associations own the ocean?" I inquired. "In Massachusetts, they can," replied the guard. "Except that hunters, fishermen, and mariners can walk along any beach."

So the next time I want to take a long walk down a Massachusetts-ocean beach, I have to remember to bring along some rods and reels.

Someone once called to ask me about the constitutionality of a Palm Beach ordinance that required men as well as women to wear "tops" while jogging. Just last month, a woman on Cape Cod took off her top at a beach, demanding equality of exposure with men. She was told that the Bill of Rights guarantees the "right to bare arms," but no other part of the anatomy. (I hope the Cape Cod cops don't respond by invoking the Palm Beach equality principle, requiring men to don those old-fashioned bathing suits with shirts.)

Speaking of "separate-but-equal" clothing requirements, one town has an ordinance prohibiting anyone from hanging male and female undergarments on the same clothesline. I suppose the jockey shorts might get the wrong idea and attack a provocative pair of panties. I wonder how this law would apply to the new Calvin Klein unisex undies.

There is not even a pretense of equality in the Tennessee law that requires all "bitches" to be confined for twenty-four days "during the time [they are] proud." Pride may be a virtue in males, but in females it can get you locked up.

Massachusetts has another strange law which—if it were ever enforced—would require a stadium as large as Fenway Park to imprison all violators. Most of the violations, in fact, occur right in Fenway Park. The statute makes it a misdemeanor for any sports fan to direct "any profane, obscene, or impure language or slanderous statement" at any umpire. "Get yourself a pair of glasses, you blind . . ." can get you in real trouble in Beantown.

If you go to the horse races for recreation this summer, you can be sure you're being well protected in Ohio, which has a law prohibiting the owner of a racing horse from "painting" or "disguising" it. So if you spot a painted pony wearing one of those nose-mustache-and-glasses masks, call the cops.

And if your pet frogs are planning to get married this summer, it may cost you five bucks. That's the price under North Dakota law for "a resident husband and wife frog license."

In certain parts of California it's perfectly OK to skinnydip, but it's a misdemeanor to "willfully and lewdly counsel" another person "to expose himself." There may be trouble brewing for that woman from the old shaving cream commercial who used to whisper suggestively: "Take it off. Take it all off."

But if you're driving around New York state this summer, you'd better "take off" any false insignias attached to your windshield. Among the insignias you are specifically prohibited from displaying—unless, of course, you're a bona fide member—are those of the International Veterans' Boxers Association, the United Scottish Clans of New Jersey, and the Chapeaux de la Société des Quarante Hommes et Huit Chevaux.

You can count on it, fellas, I'm not going to exhibit any of those insignias on my car.

Loony laws are always good for a laugh, except when you're the butt. Several summers ago, a couple was out frolicking in the back of a van in Worcester, Massachusetts. The police checked their licenses. No, not their drivers' licenses, their marriage licenses. They were married. But not to each other. The police hauled them in for adultery and the court said that the old adultery statute—not so different from the one that mandated a scarlet letter—was perfectly constitutional.

It's about time we took some of these loony laws off the books and put them where they belong—in loony bins.

July 23, 1985

60
ACLU Takes a Wrong Turn

A few years ago I was asked by the Massachusetts affiliate of the American Civil Liberties Union to assist in the representation of a twelve-year-old girl who wanted to live with her mother rather than her father.

The divorce court had ordered her to live with her father in Chicago after her mother had moved to Massachusetts. You see, her mother was a lesbian who had taken up residence with her lover, and the court didn't think the mother would provide an appropriate environment for the young girl.

We were not asked to represent the mother; she had a lawyer. We were asked to argue that the young girl had her own right to decide, within reason, who she wanted to live with. In the end we won, and the girl chose to live with her mother. The last I heard, she was getting along fine. It was a great victory for the civil liberties of children.

Then a few years later, the ACLU went to court to champion the rights of young girls to obtain abortions over the objections of their parents. Again, the ACLU was not arguing that abortions were desirable, but rather that pregnant young girls should have the right to choose whether or not to give birth. The young girls won, and the ACLU again declared it a great victory for the rights of children to decide matters important to their futures.

More recently, a young man named Walter Polovchak wanted to make an important decision about his life. Walter did not want to spend the rest of his life in the Soviet Union.

His parents had moved to the United States with their children, but decided to go back to the Soviet Union when Walter was twelve. Both he and his older sister, Natalie, resisted. They liked the United States—for both its freedom and its comforts—and they wanted to make their lives here. The parents did not resist Natalie's wishes, because she was a bit older, but they went to court to try to get an order requiring Walter to go back to the Soviet Union with them.

Walter fought back, knowing full well that a trip back to the Soviet Union was a one-way ticket. The door to that vast prison swings only in one direction. There is no "right" to leave the Soviet Union, especially for someone who has already embarrassed his motherland by expressing a preference for another homeland.

It won't surprise you to learn that the ACLU jumped into the case. It should shock you—as it did me—to learn which side it was on: this time it championed the rights of the Soviet parents to force their son—now nearly eighteen—to spend the rest of his life in a country he hates.

The ACLU resisted Walter's efforts to remain in this country until he turns eighteen and is legally able to apply for citizenship. Walter had argued—quite logically—that if he turned eighteen in the Soviet Union and decided to live here, he wouldn't be able to act on that decision; whereas if he turned eighteen here and then decided to return to the Soviet Union, nothing would stand in his way.

In mid-July, Walter Polovchak lost his case. A federal judge has ordered him to go back to the Soviet Union—never to return. His lawyers are now trying to stall the effect of the decision until Walter's eighteenth birthday. I hope, for the sake of liberty, that they succeed. The ACLU has applauded the federal court's paternalistic decision, which states that "a minor child of tender years does not have the right to control his own destiny."

But what about a girl's right to control *her* own destiny in the abortion or custody context? How can the ACLU justify its double standard in supporting the right of a girl to choose abortion over both parents' objections, while denying the right of a boy—a somewhat older boy, at that—to decide where to spend the rest of his life?

Is the right to choose which parent to live with for a few years more fundamental than the right to choose where, and with whom, to spend the rest of one's life?

My grandparents and many of their contemporaries left their parents and made their way to this land of opportunity as teenagers. They would have been shocked at the ACLU's lack of confidence in children's ability to determine their destinies.

This double standard is due, in part, to the fact that the ACLU and many of its local affiliates have increasingly become the captive of feminists and leftists in recent years. Women's issues—particularly the right to have an abortion—have dominated the agenda.

If the issue involved in these three cases—the lesbian mother, the child's abortion, and the Polovchak matter—were viewed as a teenager's civil liberty *to choose*, then the ACLU would have come out the same way in each. The ACLU's different positions can be understood only if the issues are defined *politically*—a preference for abortion, an alliance with lesbianism, and an unwillingness to criticize communism.

The end result of this politicization of the ACLU is an increasing hypocrisy in the positions it takes and a tragic decrease in its credibility.

July 30, 1985

61
A Birthday to Remember

Happy eighteenth birthday, Walter Polovchak! And congratulations on applying for U.S. citizenship.

Now you can spend the rest of your adult years wherever you please. You can exercise your freedoms—of religion, speech, movement, and political affiliation—without fear of imprisonment or confinement in a mental hospital.

It was a long, hard battle, and you almost lost. The American Civil Liberties Union went to court in support of your parents' right to make you return to the Soviet Union. If they had prevailed, you might have been spending your eighteenth birthday behind steel bars and an Iron Curtain. If you had turned eighteen in that country, instead of in this country, you wouldn't have been able to choose to emigrate, as you are now free to do.

I know that you must be wondering why the ACLU—our nation's leading defender of civil liberties—opposed your efforts to choose freedom in the United States rather than be forced to return to a life of oppression in the Soviet Union. I wondered also, and I have been an active member of that fine organization for nearly two decades.

In a recent column, I wondered aloud about the ACLU's inconsistency in defending the rights of young girls to choose to defy their parents by having abortions, while siding with your parents' efforts to make you return to the

Soviet Union. As soon as my column appeared in print, the ACLU—which encourages dissent within other organizations far better than it tolerates it within its own ranks—sent out a directive to all board members urging them to plant the ACLU's official answer in local papers that had run my "attack."

Part of that official answer—drafted by the lawyer who tried to prevent you from remaining in this country—was that every court had sided with the ACLU. (Quite a remarkable defense for the ACLU, which rarely defines liberty by referring to how the courts—especially these days—decide cases.)

Several weeks after the ACLU circulated its official answer, your case, Walter, was decided by the U.S. Court of Appeals for the Seventh Circuit—the highest court to which it has been submitted. That court's decision constituted a firm rebuke to the ACLU.

The judges ruled that your parents did have a "very strong interest" in your destiny—a view that I'm sure you share. But it also ruled that the lower court had wrongly decided the case in your parents' favor "without apparently giving any but the most perfunctory attention to [your] interests." And then, in words that seemed to be directed just as much to the ACLU, the appellate judges criticized the trial judge for "failing to make any provision for the protection of Walter's rights. The subject of his order was a human being who, though a minor, has a constitutionally protected right of personal liberty that is as important as a parent's right to custody of minor children."

The appellate judges also disagreed with the contention—implicitly advanced by the ACLU—that "the 'private interest of . . . Walter . . . is by its very nature considerably less than that of his parents,' particularly at his present age of seventeen." Judges need not "blind" themselves, the Court of Appeals reasoned, to "the commonly recognized fact that Soviet citizens who refuse to return to the Soviet Union and who publicly derogate that country are at risk of seriously adverse governmental action if they return involuntarily to the Soviet Union. In this connection, it would seem patently inequitable to force a seventeen-year-old against his will to return to a country where he faced threat of persecution."

It is a tragedy that the ACLU has to be reminded by a court that a young person's right to choose where to spend the rest of his life is at least "as important" as a parent's right to custody of that child.

Although you probably regard the ACLU as the Grinch that tried to steal your Christmas, I hope that you won't be too angry at that organization.

Over the past half-century, the ACLU has been a bulwark of liberty for all Americans. It made a tragic mistake in your case by focusing exclusively on your parents' procedural rights, without considering your substantive rights.

The ACLU is paying a price for its mistake. Conservatives like George Will are having a picnic criticizing the ACLU for failing to "take cognizance of children's rights." Will, of course, is selective in defending children's rights as well: he'd never defend a young girl's right to choose an abortion over her parents' objections. He's on your side because you're against the Soviet Union on this one. Civil liberties, like politics, make strange bedfellows.

Well, enough talk about politics and civil liberties. This is a personal triumph for your determination and willpower. You've earned the right to be free, Walter. Now exercise your liberty wisely. And don't forget those you left behind in the Soviet Union: they aren't as fortunate as you.

October 1, 1985

62
Who Owns Madonna's Image?

The recent publication of old photographs of Madonna in the nude by *Penthouse* and *Playboy* magazines has once again raised a legal storm about who owns the rights to a person's photographic image.

The issue is a recurring one. It generally begins with an obscure model seeking to earn some extra cash by posing in the buff for an equally obscure photographer. Then several years later, the model makes it big—with her clothes on—and achieves celebrity status. Suddenly the photographer sees an opportunity to cash in on his small investment by selling the old photos for big bucks. (Occasionally, the photographer will "offer" to sell the photographs—with all negatives—back to the celebrity, so that she can destroy them.)

The Madonna case is a perfect example of the general phenomenon at work.

When she was an eighteen-year-old dance student at the University of Michigan, Madonna Louise Ciccone began posing nude for ten dollars an hour. During the next few years, she sat for portrait sessions with three New York photographers. For several years, the "artsy" black-and-white shots remained tucked away in the photographers' files.

Then last spring, one of the photographers just happened to go to the movies to catch a showing of *Desperately Seeking Susan*. He thought he recognized the movie's star as the woman who had once posed for him. Shortly thereafter, Madonna's picture appeared on the cover of *Time* magazine as one of the superstars of rock. And the bidding war was on.

One photographer sold his pictures to *Playboy* for six figures. Another sold his pictures to *Penthouse* for a percentage of the magazine sales. Madonna was not consulted, nor did she receive any of the profits, since she had signed an absolute release, selling all her rights to her own image to the photographers.

Other celebrities have sold their rights and later come to regret it, including the former Miss America, Vanessa Williams, TV star Suzanne Somers, and, of course, the most famous of all—Marilyn Monroe. The market for old nude pictures of current celebrities—both male and female—has now become a stock in trade for some photographers. They photograph young models, actresses, students, and dancers—often for no charge—for purposes of "speculation." Most of their "investments" remain tucked in their files. But every so often, they hit paydirt and receive a bonanza for their few hours of work and several rolls of film.

Inevitably there are lawsuits. Madonna is now seeking to prevent her name from being used in connection with a soft-core film entitled *A Certain Sacrifice*, which she acted in before she became famous. Madonna claims she was paid nothing for her role; the producer said she got $100. This is how Madonna put it in an affidavit: "While I may have consented to the use of my voice and pictures of my physical likeness from the movie, I did not consent to the use of my name."

Miss Williams also has filed lawsuits for damages. And various photographers are suing each other and the magazines over the rights to what has come to be known as "roulette-wheel celebrity skin."

A few years ago, I participated in a lawsuit that presented an interesting variation on this theme. I assisted in the representation of Brooke Shields—whose mother had allowed her to be photographed in the nude, and who had signed a release for her when she was ten years old. The pictures were by no means pornographic, or even particularly revealing. But Miss Shields was entering Princeton University at the time and she did not want posters of her taking a bath being displayed throughout the dorms. "They are not me now," she complained.

She argued, in essence, that since she was a child when she had posed, she was legally incapable of signing away her rights, and she should not now—as an adult—be bound by her mother's earlier decision.

We lost the suit. The court ruled that a contract was a contract and Brooke Shields had, through her mother, relinquished all rights to her image. When it comes to being photographed in the nude, there is—it seems—no right to change one's mind.

If even a child can't get out of a release, it's unlikely that adult plaintiffs like Madonna or Vanessa Williams will fare any better. Nor does the answer lie in suggesting that the obscure models should demand more rights when they sign their original releases, as some courts have said. These often starving, starry-eyed, and inexperienced models have virtually no bargaining power in relation to the photographers.

Perhaps one solution may lie in legislation affording some degree of protection from the worst forms of exploitation. The interests of photographers are legitimate, but so are those of the models. The right to limit the use of one's image is an important one, worthy of a somewhat greater protection than it is now generally afforded.

August 6, 1985

63
Seers' Futures Are Under Siege

Fortunetellers in California and elsewhere are worried about the future. The nay-sayers among them predict that they may be put out of business by a case now pending before the California courts.

Several cities have enacted ordinances banning the "foretelling of the future," either for a fee or for free. Fearing that such ordinances may shut down the hundreds of fortunetellers who read palms, tea leaves, and cards in nearly every city, a Gypsy couple, John and Fatima Stevens, have challenged an ordinance banning fortunetelling. Their lawyer is arguing that the ordinance is unconstitutional on several grounds:

- It violates the First Amendment by prohibiting free expression and freedom of religion
- It's so vague and broad that it could be applied to biblical prophecies, newspaper horoscopes, and weather forecasting

- It discriminates against Gypsies, a specific ethnic group to which many fortunetellers belong

If the lawsuit succeeds and the ordinance is declared unconstitutional, "the floodgate will open," says a detective who specializes in preventing fortunetelling ripoffs. In an interview with the *Los Angeles Times*, Detective Jose Alcantaro—one of the officers assigned to the Los Angeles "Gypsy detail"—predicted that without the anti-fortunetelling law on the books, "California will be crawling with fortunetellers looking for people susceptible to the con games." He believes that there's no such thing as an honest Gypsy fortuneteller, and he can tell horror story after horror story of how people have been "gypped" (the term is an ethnic slur) during the sixteen years in which he has conducted his open campaign to close down the fortunetelling parlors.

Even if the ordinance is ultimately upheld—and a long court fight that may end up in the Supreme Court is foreseen—it won't be easy to control the flourishing trade in fortunetelling. The relationship between fortuneteller and fortuneseeker is consensual and generates few complaints. As with all such prohibited consensual relationships—gambling and prostitution are other examples—the authorities must send undercover cops to pose as gullible customers in quest of the future.

In a recent case, a member of the "Gypsy detail" went into a fortunetelling parlor, complained about a backache and told the fortuneteller that he had recently come into $2,000 that might be "cursed." The Gypsy suggested that he bring in some of the money—$200—for a blessing. Suddenly the fortuneteller realized that this might be a setup: the "customer" was practically throwing his money at her. She touched his leg, felt a recorder, and changed her tune, urging him to seek medical advice. The case was dropped.

"We're the poor man's psychiatrist," one Gypsy said. "People who can't afford $100 an hour come here to talk about their problems . . . and we do help a lot of people." Those who enacted and enforce the anti-fortunetelling ordinance obviously disagree.

The issues raised by the challenge to the anti-fortunetelling law transcend Gypsies and fortunetelling parlors. They involve the constitutional right of every individual to reject "rational" solutions to the existential problems of life and to seek solace in the irrational, supernatural, or parapsychological world—a world whose premises are not subject to empirical validation.

The First Amendment surely cannot be interpreted to limit "religious" freedom to conventional, accepted, and established religions. The "establishment clause"—which has been construed to prohibit any state preference for a particular type of religious experience—requires equal treatment for any set of "beliefs" that "occupies in the life of its possessor a place parallel" to that filled for others by traditional religions.

No state may declare that a Gypsy who sincerely believes that he can prophesy is being any less rational than were biblical prophets or current religious leaders who fill the airwaves every Sunday morning. Recent attempts to prohibit religious groups from administering biblical therapy have failed.

The state does have the power to combat religious "fraud," but it must prove that the practitioner doesn't sincerely believe in the doctrine he's selling. It's obviously quite difficult for the courts to determine who is sincere and who is exploitative, since these two characteristics aren't always mutually exclusive. A great danger to religious freedom inheres in the likelihood that jurors will be more ready to find that nontraditional and unpopular beliefs—like those espoused and practiced by Gypsies—lack sincerity.

In the end, our national commitment to religious freedom requires us to tolerate a certain degree of hypocrisy, and even exploitation, that cloaks itself in the mantle of religion. An even greater danger than the occasional defrauding of a fortune- or salvation-seeker would be granting the government the power to pick and choose among alleged religions, saviors, and prophets. Let's leave it to the consumers of salvation to be wary, lest we find the police confiscating our astrological charts, our horoscopes, and even our fortune cookies.

I predict that the courts will strike down the ban on fortune-telling. Go ahead, arrest me!

August 27, 1985

UPDATE
The California Supreme Court did strike down the ban on fortunetelling. It ruled that the statute was far too broad and could be applied to economists, political scientists, and members of the clergy—all of whom predict the future.

64
AIDS Presents a Legal Challenge

As the fear of the dreaded disease AIDS reaches epidemic proportions, it isn't surprising that difficult legal questions have arisen. For example, the Colorado Board of Health had decided to begin keeping a list of people who have been exposed to the virus that causes acquired immunodeficiency syndrome. The local American Civil Liberties Union chapter is protesting on the grounds that such a list will foster discrimination against gay men, the group most closely associated with the disease.

This fear is understandable, especially since right-wing politicians and moral majoritarians have taken up the issue of AIDS as part of their campaign against the "sin" of homosexuality. Patrick Buchanan, now a presidential aide, once wrote, "The poor homosexuals. They have declared war on nature and now nature is exacting an awful retribution." Reverend Jerry Falwell, invoking the biblical concept of exclusion, is calling for the "quarantine" or imprisonment of homosexuals who continue sexual activity after catching AIDS. A federal appeals court has just upheld the constitutionality of a Texas law criminalizing homosexual activity, thus lending credibility to the Falwell threat.

Several AIDS victims have contemplated lawsuits against those whom they believe transmitted the virus to them. The argument is that a person who knows he is a contagious carrier of the deadly virus has both a moral *and a legal* obligation to disclose his condition to any sexual partners. Actress Linda Evans was reportedly furious that Rock Hudson had not advised her that he had AIDS prior to a kissing scene in "Dynasty."

Some AIDS sufferers and those exposed to the virus argue that if they— or the state—make public disclosure of their condition, they will be branded as "Typhoid Marys" or worse: "It's like wearing the Scarlet Letter," says a lawyer who lost his job when AIDS was diagnosed.

Some gay men who haven't been exposed are on the other side of the disclosure issue. As the group most at risk, they have an obvious interest in knowing who has AIDS or has been exposed to the virus. Some also feel that unless the public can distinguish among people who have AIDS and those who don't, *all* gay men will become suspect and thus victims of increased discrimination. In some cities, gay men are even putting on pounds to avoid being mistaken for AIDS sufferers who generally lose weight: "In Los Angeles, it is almost a sign of health among gays to be too fat," reports an art director.

But all gay men are suspect in the eyes of some. Already there are reports of actresses declining to work with gay actors, of patrons shying away from restaurants run by gay men, and of police and fire personnel refusing to administer mouth-to-mouth resuscitation to "gay-looking" men.

Perhaps the most poignant cases are those involving youngsters who got AIDS from blood transfusions, or even from their mothers during pregnancy. Several children have been denied permission to attend school for fear that they might infect others. As one school superintendent put it: "What are you going to do about someone chewing pencils or sneezing or swimming in the pool?"

Other potential battlegrounds have already been staked out:

- Doctors who treat AIDS patients are being evicted from their offices
- Job applicants are being asked to submit to blood tests for the virus
- Patients who have contracted AIDS from blood transfusions are bringing malpractice suits
- Doctors, nurses, and ambulance drivers are refusing to handle suspected AIDS sufferers
- Health officials are threatening to close down gay bathhouses

These and other legal issues will soon reach the courts for resolution. But the courts will find few guidelines in the old cases, because of the uniqueness of AIDS and its devastating potential.

One of the most difficult policy choices will be whether—and to whom—to disclose information about the identities of AIDS victims and virus carriers. The more disclosure is authorized, the less likely it is that potential sufferers will seek testing. California has already enacted a law assuring the confidentiality of AIDS tests and protecting sufferers from some forms of discrimination.

But few governmental lists are ever completely confidential. If and when a person who caught AIDS from a sexual partner sues that partner, he or she will probably seek to subpoena health records in order to prove that the partner knew he or she had AIDS and failed to provide appropriate disclosure. Insurance companies will also seek disclosure in contesting claims.

There remain a great many unanswered medical questions about the communicability of AIDS. While the disease itself is doubling every month, the fear of AIDS is multiplying even more quickly.

Epidemic fear is a fertile breeding ground for massive deprivation of civil liberties. Some of Europe's most enduring repressive measures were enacted during the great plagues. Our legal system is likely to be confronted with enormous pressures from a frightened populace and demagogic leaders. It can prove its mettle by striking an appropriate balance between legitimate public health concern and the rights of AIDS sufferers.

September 3, 1985

For additional discussion of AIDS, see columns 65, 66, 115, and 136.

65
AIDS Crisis: A Rational Approach

Law cases often serve as a metaphor for society's most pressing concerns and fears. Recent news reports covered the arrest of an AIDS carrier named John Richards, who was charged with deliberately spitting at a police officer who had stopped him after a traffic accident.

Normally, "man spits at cop" would deserve slightly less coverage than the perennial "man bites dog" item. But our society has become inflicted with a serious case of AIDS-phobia.

This isn't to say that the fear isn't justified. Just as paranoids have real enemies, AIDS-phobics have something real to be frightened about. A recent editorial in the *Journal of the American Medical Association* concluded that "not since syphilis among the Spaniards, the plague among the French, tuberculosis among the Eskimos, and smallpox among the American Indians has there been the threat of such a scourge. Yet the Acquired Immune Deficiency Syndrome is different from any disease seen clinically or epidemiologically."

In general, our legal system is prepared to deal with new problems of the kind posed by the AIDS-spitter. If he and his intended victim both believed that AIDS could be transmitted by spitting, there is a basis for criminal prosecution, even if those beliefs turned out to be unfounded. Legal precedent establishes that if "A" points a gun at "B," and both erroneously believe that the gun is loaded, "A" can be prosecuted for assault even if the gun turns out to be empty.

But other questions of public health policy won't be so easy to answer by analogy to established legal precedent.

Some of those questions were recently the subject of a televised debate between William F. Buckley, Jr.—among our country's most thoughtful conservatives—and me. We argued over the broad civil liberties issues surrounding various responses to the spread of AIDS, including closing down gay bars, quarantining AIDS sufferers, and requiring that AIDS carriers be tattooed with the equivalent of a discreet scarlet letter on an appropriate part of their anatomy.

Our disagreements centered on the relationship between moralistic condemnation of homosexuality and public health approaches to checking the spread of a potentially devastating epidemic. Buckley condemns homosexuality on religious and moralistic grounds. He believes that it's unnatural and wrong, regardless of medical consequences. He believed that before AIDS became prevalent among gays, and he will continue to believe it even if a definite cure for AIDS is discovered tomorrow.

My private preference also runs against homosexuality, but I have no religious or moralistic views about the subject, any more than I do on other matters of taste and lifestyle among consenting adults. (A literal interpretation of my religion, like most others, condemns homosexuality but, like many people, I don't follow the most conservative interpretations of my religion on all contemporary moral issues.)

It's imperative that the debate about AIDS remain a public health debate and not be permitted to degenerate into moralistic name-calling about sexual lifestyles. If an equally dreaded disease were caused by some activity that most citizens regarded with neutrality or approval—in the way that polio was believed, when I was a child, to be caused by swimming in cold water—we could focus our exclusive attention on the medical and civil liberties issues.

But many right-wing moralists are too busy gloating about how the etiology of AIDS confirms their religious or natural-law bias against homosexuality. Some religious zealots have called AIDS "God's revenge."

People with strong moralistic opinions about homosexuality—either pro or con—should keep their biases out of the public health debate about how to check the spread of the disease; they have too great a stake in using this important issue to validate a priori views.

We must insist on getting the facts, unvarnished by moralistic prejudgments. We must learn more about how the virus is transmitted, the risks posed by carriers, the accuracy of testing methods, and the consequences of being labeled a carrier.

But we must also act now, before all the facts are known. In so acting, we are sure to make mistakes. Normally, before we confine or stigmatize anyone, we demand near certainty about our judgments. Our usual credo is, "Better for ten guilty to go free than for even one innocent to be wrongly punished." It's unlikely that we will be so cautious in our attitude toward people suspected of carrying the AIDS virus.

But it's essential that we understand the costs of making *both* kinds of mistakes: of failing to take necessary actions to prevent the spread of AIDS; and of taking unnecessary actions motivated by our prejudices against gays and others who pose the threat of transmitting the disease.

For once, let's get together and confront a grave danger rationally, without allowing extremists on both sides to exploit human tragedy for political and other ends.

December 31, 1985

66
AIDS Threatens Our Freedom As Well As Our Lives

Over the next four years, we will celebrate the bicentennial of our Constitution and our Bill of Rights. During this period, these great documents are likely to experience some of the most grueling tests they have been asked to endure during their history. Our founding fathers protected us well from the dangers of political tyranny and oppressive government. But they could not have anticipated the dangers to liberty posed by the current AIDS epidemic and the fears it has aroused.

The challenge to our legal system is how to assure that a public health crisis does not turn into a civil liberties crisis as well. Whenever there is fear of the unknown, the dangers to liberty increase.

Sometimes the fears are exaggerated—for example, the fears generated by Senator Joseph McCarthy in the early 1950s of a communist subversive takeover of America, or the fears directed against immigrants, stimulated by know-nothing chauvinists in the post–World War I period. But when the fear is of something real, as it is with AIDS, the dangers are even greater. And the dangers are greatest when the fear is directed against groups of people who already are despised or feared by many, such as gay men and intravenous drug users.

Though the framers of our Constitution knew of past plagues and epidemics that had ravaged Europe—such as the Black Death—they had never experienced anything quite like AIDS. The Bill of Rights does not speak directly to such issues as mandatory testing, quarantine, and discrimination against AIDS sufferers. Resort to the "original intent" of the framers will not answer the difficult public health and policy questions raised by AIDS. This is a twentieth-century problem that must be addressed by twentieth century interpretations of our fundamental principles of liberty.

As the AIDS issue moves from the laboratories and public health offices to the center of political debate—and it may indeed become a major campaign issue during the next presidential election—the rhetoric is likely to become shriller, and the muscle flexing more pronounced. Already, we see political considerations at work. It is no coincidence that the first groups selected for mandatory testing are those with little political power or electoral influence: prisoners, immigrants, prostitutes, and soldiers.

It will entail a greater political risk for politicians to advocate wider mandatory testing of mainstream Americans, such as insurance applicants, government employees, and those seeking marriage licenses. But some politician probably will grab this issue and run with it in an effort to capitalize on the fear. If that happens, other politicians may be forced into reactive political positions that are far less cautious than the ones they would like to support.

The wisest position a politician can take is to recognize the AIDS crisis for what it is—the major public health issue of the day—and to try to keep partisan politics out of it. Is it really too much to expect that the war on AIDS become a bipartisan issue, as so many other crises have become during our nation's history?

President Reagan could perform a historic act if he were to declare that he is removing the AIDS issue from the political arena and appointing a nonpolitical panel of public health experts to advise him on policy. Such a panel could also perform an enormously useful—and currently missing— public service by giving the American public absolutely straight information on how AIDS is transmitted and what the risks really are for various groups. Much of the information we are now receiving, from all sides, sounds suspiciously partisan and designed to serve agendas other than that of disseminating the truth. The president, in particular, seems to be trying to score political points with his get-tough attitude toward AIDS testing and his equation of the disease with the plagues of old.

The need to depoliticize is far greater with AIDS than it's been with any other disease. When I was a kid, the great plague was polio—a dreaded disease, but not one that you contracted through unpopular activities. President Franklin D. Roosevelt was said to have contracted it by the all-American act of swimming in a lake and not changing out of his wet bathing suit. No one can condemn a polio victim because of the source of his disease. But you don't contract AIDS from swimming; you get it from sex and drugs. And sex and drugs are controversial and invite moralizing and politicizing—which is precisely what must be eliminated from the response to AIDS.

Taking the politics out of AIDS is our best assurance that this grave public health hazard will not become the civil liberties crisis that breaks the back of our Bill of Rights even before its two-hundredth birthday.

June 23, 1987

67
Meese Misspeaks on Civil Rights

Let's play a little game of political trivia: which American public figure has declared himself to be "in the forefront of the civil rights movement in the country today," the "champion of minorities, and of all citizens, for that matter," and the most adamant—"no one is more adamant"—supporter of civil rights?

No, it isn't the head of the National Association for the Advancement of Colored People or the American Civil Liberties Union. It's the head of the Reagan Justice Department—Attorney General Edwin Meese III.

These are verbatim quotes from our blunt-spoken attorney general in a recent television interview.

Now, Ed Meese is a very nice man—but no one would ever mistake him for a civil rights advocate, a defender of the Bill of Rights, or a protector of minorities. If he were all of those things, he wouldn't be President Reagan's attorney general and chief adviser on these issues.

The Ed Meese I know is the attorney general who has asked the Supreme

Court to overrule its 1973 decision recognizing women's right to choose whether to terminate pregnancy. Are pregnant women not a part of "all citizens"?

The Ed Meese I know is the attorney general who just declared that the Supreme Court's *Miranda* decision—requiring the police to advise arrested suspects of their rights—was not only wrong, it was "infamous." Are indigent and ignorant suspects, who may not be aware of their rights, not part of "all citizens"?

The Ed Meese I know is the attorney general who describes the coalition of civil rights organizations that helped defeat William Bradford Reynolds, the nominee for associate attorney general, as a "pernicious lobby," and who once referred to the ACLU as the "criminals' lobby." Does Meese deny that these organizations—whose members have devoted lifetimes to defending the rights of minorities and supporting civil liberties—are *also* "in the forefront" of "the civil rights movement in the country"? Does he really claim that mantle for himself alone?

The Ed Meese I know is a strong advocate of the death penalty, despite hard evidence that it's imposed far more frequently on blacks who kill whites than on whites who kill blacks.

The Ed Meese I know is trying, by every means possible, to pack our judiciary with judges who are willing to submit to a political litmus test of conservatism and opposition to civil rights. He wouldn't tolerate the nomination of any judge who was truly "in the forefront of the civil rights movement."

The Ed Meese I know vigorously supports only one of the first ten amendments to the Constitution, which constitute the Bill of Rights—the right to bear arms—and he misunderstands that one as prohibiting effective gun control.

The Ed Meese I know is the "champion" of only one minority: the white minority government of South Africa, which fosters apartheid.

The Ed Meese I know would scuttle the First Amendment's protection against the establishment of religion by authorizing religious prayers and meetings in public schools.

The Ed Meese I know would considerably weaken the Voting Rights Act by making it far more difficult to challenge discriminatory practices. This isn't the approach of a "champion" of minorities, who are still the subject of discrimination in voter registration in some parts of our nation today.

By describing himself as a champion of minorities when he opposes many aspirations of blacks and Hispanics, Meese engages in the kind of "newspeak" parodied by George Orwell in *1984*. By declaring himself as being in the "forefront" of the civil rights movement, Meese seeks to turn the concept of civil rights on its head and to co-opt its symbol for his own partisan political purposes.

The power of words and symbols isn't lost on this very smart attorney general and his clever advisers, nor is this the first time in recent years that this kind of newspeak has been tried. Radical feminists who are seeking to enact legislation that would ban material which they deem sexist or offensive call their model censorship law a "civil rights" act as well.

It's both easy and cheap to invoke the name of civil rights in the cause of censorship, repression, and discrimination—whether by the left or the right. Claimants to the mantle of civil rights can always concoct a rationalization for why they are really supporting *someone's* rights: even slaveholders claimed a civil right to keep their property.

The essence of civil rights—the essence for which true civil rights advocates have struggled and died—is freedom and choice. There is room for debate, of course, in such areas as abortion, where the choice of the woman to terminate her pregnancy may be said to deny the fetus its "choice" to live or die. But it is sophistry to invoke civil rights in support of censorship, barriers to voting, and the opportunity to secure legal counsel.

Truth in advertising requires that the attorney general tell the public what he really is: a very smart, very personable, and very competent lawyer who is the champion of majorities and who is in the forefront of trying to roll back many of the gains made by the civil rights movement over the past quarter-century.

September 10, 1985

68
The Danger of Record-Rating

As popular music becomes raunchier and more explicit, efforts are underway to assure that parents are provided some warning about the nature of the lyrics their children are listening to.

Recently, a congressional committee heard testimony—some itself raunchy and explicit—on all sides of this controversial issue.

The Parents' Music Resource Center—which includes the wives of some prominent Washington politicians—has been pressing for the labeling of all records. Those that "contain explicit language, sexual references, and inferences to situations not commonly recommended for all age groups" would have to carry an "R" on their outer jacket. This would presumably warn concerned parents about the words their children would hear if they bought an R-rated recording.

The center is now calling only for the recording industry *voluntarily* to provide warnings, as the movie industry does. But several congressmen would go further: they would legislate mandatory warning labels unless the industry acts quickly and decisively on its own.

The Recording Industry Association of America is running scared of this threat of regulation. A spokesman has announced that all new recordings released by members of the RIA—who comprise 80 percent to 85 percent of the industry—will provide the following warning on the jackets of records that contain "questionable" material: "Parental Guidance—Explicit Lyrics." But the decision about which lyrics warrant the warning label would be left to each individual company.

This compromise seems to please no one. The proponents of more stringent warnings want—at the very least—enforceable industrywide standards for deciding whether lyrics are sufficiently explicit or sexual to warrant the warning label. They point to the uniform rating system established and enforced by the Motion Picture Association of America, which determines whether a movie receives a G, PG, PG-13, R, or X rating.

Opponents of warning labels feel that the RIA has already caved in and established a dangerous precedent. Many of those who record and play the music are vehemently opposed to labeling, whether voluntary or mandatory. Such labeling "would approach censorship," said John Denver. Pointing to his own hit song, "Rocky Mountain High," Denver argued that labeling agencies might misinterpret the meaning of lyrics—just as many had misinterpreted his song to refer to drugs, when it was intended to extol the virtues of the outdoors.

Rock star Frank Zappa, whose music is widely censored by radio stations, cited the First Amendment as expressing a "preference for the least restrictive alternative" and characterized the demand for warning labels as "the equivalent of treating dandruff by decapitation." He would prefer that record companies print the lyrics of songs on the record jackets, without making judgments as to their suitability. He predicted that if mandatory ratings—which he characterized as this "ill-conceived piece of nonsense"—were ever enacted into law, it would keep the courts busy for years.

Whatever one thinks of Zappa's other comments—and some of the senators thought very little of them—he is clearly correct in predicting that courts would have great difficulty defining such vague criteria as "explicit language," "sexual references," and "inferences to situations not commonly recommended for all age groups." Many jazz classics and show tunes would fit comfortably into these accordion-like categories. Cole Porter's "Love for Sale," as well as several Billy Holiday, Alberta Hunter, and Bessie Smith tunes, come immediately to mind.

It's unlikely that industrywide standards would be as effective in the record industry as they have proven to be in the movie business. The movie business is dominated by a handful of major film distributors that make up the MPAA and a relatively discrete number of theater chains that belong to the National Association of Theater Owners. An unrated movie has little chance of being exhibited by a major chain. But records and tapes can be produced independently and sold nearly anywhere. It would be difficult, if not impossible, to administer a voluntary rating system within the recording industry.

Thus, the issue of governmentally mandated warnings is certain to be pressed by the watchdog groups that now clamor for some change. In 1967, the U.S. Supreme Court struck down as unconstitutionally vague a Dallas, Texas, ordinance that mandated a rating system specifying whether or not a given film was "suitable for young persons." The criteria included open-ended language similar to that now being proposed for records. The court warned that the "vice of vagueness is particularly pronounced where expression is sought to be subject to licensing." Although no one has yet proposed that records be officially licensed, a ratings system can lead to pressures on retail stores not to sell recordings that carry undesirable ratings. This may, in turn, cause recording companies to refuse to produce and distribute "questionable" items.

Every step on the road to censorship—especially when taken at the urging of the government—should be considered with care and skepticism. Parents should play a more active role, and government a less active role, in determining what is suitable for our children to hear.

September 24, 1985

69
Suing Those Who Make Guns That Kill

Olin J. Kelly is one of many Americans who has been shot during a holdup. But he was lucky in two ways. First, he recovered from his 1981 chest and shoulder wounds. Second, the Maryland Court of Appeals just ruled that he can sue the company that designed and marketed the "Saturday night special" that nearly killed him.

In so ruling, Maryland's highest court became the first court in the nation to rule that those responsible for the easy availability of cheap weapons used in committing crimes will be held financially liable for criminal injuries caused by such guns.

This remarkable decision promises to have enormous impact on the availability of Saturday night specials, especially if other states follow Maryland's lead. It will almost certainly drive manufacturers and sellers of such guns out of Maryland, for fear that they will have to pay whopping damages to gunshot victims. Nearly every victim who can trace his or her wound to a specific manufacturer or seller of Saturday night specials will probably sue.

Even before this decision, victims could sue their assailants—those who fired the guns. But few such defendants have enough money to make it worthwhile for a lawyer to go to court. Now there's a "deep pocket" to which they can turn: the manufacturers and sellers of weapons are generally solvent and will be easy targets for lawsuits.

Under the Maryland decision, all the victim must show is that he was shot during the commission of a crime by a weapon that can be categorized as a Saturday night special. The manufacturer, distributor, or retailer of the gun is then automatically liable. The victim must, of course, be able to trace the gun back to its source, which could be difficult in some cases. But if it can be traced to a particular manufacturer or retailer, there will be little difficulty in collecting.

The Maryland court's seven-to-zero opinion found that Saturday night specials, because of their "cheap-quality materials, poor manufacture, inaccuracy and availability" are "virtually useless for the legitimate purposes of law enforcement, sport and protection of persons, property and businesses." It concluded that "the manufacturer or marketer of a Saturday night special knows, or ought to know, that he is making or selling a product principally to be used in criminal activity."

The Maryland decision is part of a growing trend toward holding those who profit from the sale of an item responsible for the ultimate harm it causes. Thus several states have made saloon owners responsible for automobile accidents caused by drunken drivers they have served. One state court, in New Jersey, went so far as to allow a victim of a drunk driver to sue the neighbor who had served him one for the road during a party.

This trend can get out of hand, as evidenced by a proposed statute now before the voters in Cambridge, Massachusetts. If that law were enacted, the publisher of an adult magazine could be held liable if one of its readers attacked a woman after leering at the centerfold.

Under our Constitution, there is, of course, an enormous difference between suing those who exercise their right of free speech and those who sell guns or liquor.

Free speech is supposed to be dangerous. As Oliver Wendell Holmes, Jr., once put it: "Every idea is an incitement." Our Bill of Rights protects all ideas, whether they take the form of a Marxist pamphlet advocating revolution, a feminist leaflet urging women to "take back the night," or a sexist magazine that "turns on" some of its readers. Idea control isn't permitted under the Bill of Rights.

But our Bill of Rights doesn't protect those who sell cheap guns to criminals. The Second Amendment provides that "a well-regulated militia, being necessary to the security of a free state, the right of the people to keep and bear arms, shall not be abridged." This amendment has been interpreted by the courts as permitting effective gun control, especially of cheap weapons that are designed for crime rather than security.

Advocates of gun control have hailed the Maryland decision as a milestone of progressive jurisprudence. Gun dealers see it as a millstone around their collective necks. Gun-control lobbyists claim that guns kill; gun lobbyists argue that people kill. But the average American, who legitimately fears the easy availability of the Saturday night special, should applaud the Maryland court's recognition that it is people with easy access to cheap handguns who kill and wound.

The powerful gun lobby in this country has made it virtually impossible for legislatures to enact effective gun control—even gun control limited to holdup weapons. State courts, especially those whose judges don't run for reelection, may impose their own compromise on gun control by following

Maryland's lead in imposing financial responsibility on those who profit from the sale of murder weapons. Victims' rights groups should be pleased that at least one holdup victim, Olin J. Kelly, will be compensated for his wounds.

October 8, 1985

70
Trying the Hijackers

Now that the hijackers of the *Achille Lauro* have been captured, the question still remains whether they can be brought to justice. Several complex and potentially troubling legal issues swirl around the case.

- Was the U.S. action in forcing an Egyptian plane out of international airspace itself an act of air piracy in violation of international law?

International law, in this question, as in many others, is murky at best. When Israel diverted an airplane into its territory several years ago in an unsuccessful effort to capture terrorist leaders thought to be aboard, there was widespread condemnation of the act as a violation of international law. But condemnation of Israel is hardly a precedent, since Israel is often singled out for criticism on political grounds. Moreover, the U.S. action here seems more justified, since the United States had evidence that the killers themselves were in the process of evading justice.

In any event, the law is clear that neither U.S. nor Italian courts will free a defendant on the grounds that he was brought into the country illegally. Put another way, the "exclusionary rule"—requiring the exclusion of illegally seized evidence—doesn't apply to the seizure of the defendants themselves. So Italy and/or the United States can try the hijackers and deal separately with any complaints that they may have violated international law, just as Israel tried Adolph Eichmann after "kidnapping" him from Argentina.

- Do the U.S. courts have "jurisdiction"—legal authority—to try foreigners for a crime that occurred on foreign territory because Americans were among the victims?

This issue isn't as simple as it sounds. U.S. law generally doesn't extend beyond the geographic confines of the United States. Even if a U.S. citizen murders another citizen in a foreign country, the United States has no power to try the case; it must be tried where the crime physically occurred.

In a 1962 case, *Robinson vs. California*, the Supreme Court ruled that American states are generally confined to punishing acts committed within their territories. But recent federal statutes have given the federal courts the power to try a limited number of "extraterritorial" cases, especially those involving international terrorism. The head of the Justice Department's Criminal Division, citing a recent prosecution of Colombians who attacked federal agents in Colombia, has assured the administration that "we do have jurisdiction that extends way beyond the territories of the United States; that's been carefully spelled out by Congress."

- Can the United States extradite the hijackers and have them
  brought physically into the United States?

The answer is almost certainly yes. Under a new extradition treaty between Italy and the United States, each country can demand the extradition of criminals in the other's territory. But there are limitations: Italy won't send anyone to the United States who faces the death penalty, since capital punishment is prohibited under Italian law; nor will Italy permit extradition for a "political crime."

The terrorists are sure to claim that their crime was political, and they'll find some support in a recent federal case out of New York. In that case, the federal court ruled that the ambush-murder of a British Army captain by members of the Provisional Wing of the Irish Revolutionary Army was a crime of "a political character" and thus not subject to extradition. However, the court went out of its way to distinguish the killing "of innocent civilians" from the murder of police. Therefore, it seems likely that the hijackers' crimes won't be deemed "political" for purposes of extradition.

- Can the terrorists be tried both in Italy and in the United States?

The answer is almost certainly yes. Our Constitution's prohibition of double jeopardy doesn't apply when the first trial was conducted abroad, especially if the crime charged is a different one.

For example, if the terrorists are first tried in Italy for crimes against the Italian ship and crew, and then tried in the United States for crimes against the Americans, there can be two separate punishments. This ensures that the Italians can't get away with imposing light sentences and then freeing the hijackers—or capitulating to further terrorist demands by freeing them outright. The United States, by seeking the terrorists' extradition, now has a valid claim over their destinies.

- Finally, and perhaps most difficult of all: can terrorists of this kind receive a fair trial in Italy or in the United States, in light of the extraordinary emotions generated by the recent events?

The answer is that a defendant is entitled to the fairest trial possible under the circumstances. Both Italy and the United States have proved they are capable of providing fair trials in highly charged atmospheres. According to Farouk Kaddoumi, the head of the Palestine Liberation Organization's political department, the allegation that the terrorists killed an American is "a big lie fabricated by the intelligence service of the United States." That claim will surely be tested in a real court of law—not in the kind of kangaroo court that would have been convened if the PLO had been permitted to "try" the hijackers.

In the end, more is at stake than the punishment of four accused terrorists. Western justice itself is on trial.

October 11, 1985

71
Banned in Cambridge?

I recently visited the beautiful Renoir retrospective now being exhibited at the Boston Museum of Fine Arts. As I stood in front of *The Bathers*, admiring Renoir's gorgeous use of color and form, my thoughts suddenly turned to a particularly ugly piece of legislation about to be voted on by the citizens of my hometown, Cambridge, Massachusetts.

The proposed law—placed on the ballot by a group of radical feminists—would allow any woman who was offended by art like Renoir's to try to close the exhibition.

This referendum, disguised as a "human rights" law, is simply another attempt at censorship. Its definition of pornography—broader than any now on the books in this country—covers any pictures or words that are "sexually explicit" and that describe "subordination of women." It includes within this accordion-like definition the display of any "woman's body parts" in "postures of sexual submission, servility, or display."

I thought about these words as I looked at Renoir's depiction of nude women with their arms raised over their heads so as to accentuate their full breasts. As if to allay any doubt about the sensuality of the painting, the tour guide recording went on about Renoir's rendition of "great vulcanized women loll[ing] in the searing landscape, their pneumatic flesh aglow with health and fecundity."

Renoir was, in fact, a sexist. He disliked "women who thought and . . . who aspire to a profession." He insisted that his models be submissive and that women never lose their most important talent: "to make love well." The "best exercise" for women, according to Renoir, was "to kneel down and scrub the floor" because "their bellies need movement of that sort." Many of Renoir's paintings reflected his sexist subordination of women and display of their body parts. But sexist expression—like racist, anti-Jewish, and other forms of bigoted expressions—is free speech, protected by the First Amendment.

Andrea Dworkin, the radical feminist who travels around the country trying to get cities to enact her "model human rights" censorship statute, assured me during a TV debate that she would not want to shut down the Renoir exhibit. But her statute would authorize "any woman" who feels she has been subordinated by any sexually explicit "exhibit" that displays women's body parts to bring "a claim." Nor could a museum defend itself on the grounds that it "did not know or intend that the materials were pornography or sex discrimination."

Of course, the major purpose of the proposed law isn't to shut down museum exhibits of fine art. But its language is so open-ended that it could be applied to nearly anything containing partial nudity or sexually explicit language. *Lady Chatterley's Lover*, R-rated movies and videocassettes, photography magazines—even dirty jokes—can fit comfortably under its umbrella.

The drafters of the law readily acknowledge—indeed, boast—that it isn't limited to hard-core porn of the peep-show or X-rated variety. (Much of that has already been banned by existing laws approved by the Supreme Court.) Rather, the new law is intended to get at mainstream and Main Street media that offend women. *Playboy* magazine is among its specific targets.

Another part of the proposed law would make any store that sold adult magazines financially responsible if anyone injured or assaulted any woman because of what he read or saw in those publications. The implications of this approach are frightening: bookstores could become responsible if a reader of Karl Marx engaged in a revolutionary act, if a reader of Andrea Dworkin's diatribes against men were to assault a particularly obnoxious sexist, or if a black reader of Malcolm X were to bomb a Klan meeting.

Of course, speech is dangerous. As Oliver Wendell Holmes, Jr., once put it: "Every idea is an incitement." It is the essence of free speech that we must tolerate expression that is obnoxious, offensive, and even capable of causing injury.

Holmes also cautioned that free speech doesn't allow anyone to falsely shout "fire!" in a crowded theater. And most groups believe that offending *them* is like shouting fire. Many Jews believed that having Nazis march through Skokie, Illinois, was like shouting "fire." Some blacks feel that allowing schoolchildren to read *Huckleberry Finn* is dangerous. And many feminists think that dirty books, magazines, and films cause rape. Pornography may indeed contribute to sexist violence by some, but it probably also provides an outlet or substitute for violence by others. No one knows whether the net result is that pornography—however defined—causes or prevents more violence against women.

But that isn't the issue. The issue is censorship and choice. If the censors of the right and left get their way, there will be little left to read or view, except the blandest and least controversial. It would be particularly ironic if this repressive law were to be enacted in Cambridge, Massachusetts, a center of learning, scholarship, and diversity. "Banned in Cambridge" would replace the old slogan, "Banned in Boston." If this referendum wins in Cambridge, no city will be safe from the scourge of censorship.

October 29, 1985

UPDATE
The Cambridge referendum was defeated 13,031 to 9,419. The "model" statute, as enacted in Indianapolis, was declared unconstitutional in an opinion written by a conservative Reagan appointee, and the U.S. Supreme Court declined review. For further comment on banning items or activities which may cause harm, see columns 72, 83, 87, 94, 96, and 142.

72
First Amendment Is the Winner

My taste in movies runs more along the lines of Woody Allen and Alfred Hitchcock than Jean-Luc Godard. But last weekend I found myself walking past a picket line to see Godard's pretentious and confusing movie, *Hail Mary*.

I didn't like very much of what I saw on the screen inside the movie theater. But I loved what I saw on the street outside. It was the U.S. First Amendment in action, and it was a beautiful picture.

On one side of the theater there were dozens of Catholic protesters exercising their First Amendment right to condemn the film, to assert the sanctity of their religious symbols, and to try to persuade potential viewers not to enter the theater. On the other side there were a few lonely picketers opposing censorship and urging bystanders to see the film and decide for themselves. Between the two groups were the Finest of Cambridge, Massachusetts, keeping the peace and making certain that the signs were used solely to inform and not to batter.

Then there was the fact that the Orson Welles Theater was making a controversial film available to those who elected to see it. And finally, there were the ordinary citizens—entirely free to join either side of the picketers, to enter the theater, or to stay home, as they wished.

As I observed this wonderfully cacophonous and somewhat disorderly scene, I reflected on the sad reality that in 90 percent of this planet's nations, *either* the film would be banned *or* the picketers would be banned. But in our great country, neither is outlawed or preferred. Our governments—local, state, and national—can take no position on religious "truth" or blasphemy; they must remain entirely neutral on the substance of the debate, limiting their role to keepers of the peace.

There are those, of course, who demand that the government censor in the name of religion. "God censors immortality, we merely obey," read one sign. Another picketer presented his audience with the following false choice: "First Amendment or First Commandment"—conveniently forgetting that without the First Amendment, the First Commandment would be in great jeopardy, as it is in many communist countries. And one sign declared, "Freedom for religion, not blasphemy." One person's blasphemy, however, *is* another's religion. If pornography is in the eyes of the beholder, then blasphemy is in the soul of the believer or disbeliever—and government must keep its distance from our souls.

To its credit, the Boston Archdiocese, under the enlightened leadership of Cardinal Bernard F. Law, did not demand governmental intervention. It simply advised its parishioners "to refrain" from seeing the film and it cautioned that "other ways of expressing disapproval are often counterproductive."

But some of the angry faithful did not listen. They threatened to stop the film from being shown even if violence was required. The giant Sack theater chain, which was originally scheduled to show the film, canceled the booking because of "the intensity of the reaction," acknowledging regretfully that it had "capitulated." The *Boston Globe* wrote a somewhat schizophrenic editorial characterizing the chain's decision as "a compassionate response" and denying it was censorship, and then acknowledging that the cancellation had created a questionable precedent. It was as if the first part of the editorial was written by the newspaper advertising director (the chain is among the *Globe*'s biggest advertisers) and the second part by its editorial writer.

After the giant chain capitulated and a tiny Cambridge theater, the Orson Welles, decided to stand up to the pressures and show *Hail Mary*, the threats of violence increased. The city manager of Cambridge urged the Orson Welles not to show the film, ostensibly on "the basis of public safety." The small movie house persisted. The city of Cambridge then demanded that the theater pay for additional police protection.

Eventually, a compromise was arranged in which the city would provide some of the protection and the theater would pay for the rest. Naturally, the theater's cost was passed on to the patrons who had to pay an additional twenty-five cents to see the controversial film. Although a quarter is a small price, any "First Amendment Tax" for controversial speech establishes a dangerous precedent. Protecting the public's right to see a film or picket it is the government's obligation, and the general treasury should pay for it. Imagine charging the protesters a twenty-five cents picketing fee for the additional police required to protect them.

The result of this controversy is that many more people will go to see *Hail Mary*. "Banned in Boston"—whether by government or private censorship—is one of the best ways to generate interest in a film. But the protests have also succeeded in sensitizing people to what many Catholics perceive as a blasphemous attack on an important religious symbol. Thus, in one important respect, both the First Amendment and the First Commandment have emerged victorious from the *Hail Mary* controversy.

The big loser will be the Sack Cinema chain, which will now find it far more difficult to stand up to the inevitable barrage of protests that will accompany every film deemed offensive by any group: "You gave in to them. How can you do any less for us?" It will be a hard argument to answer.

November 26, 1985

73
Seat Belts and Civil Liberties

"A conservative is a liberal who's been mugged," says an old cliché. Wherever I hear that one, I respond, "And a liberal is a conservative who's been indicted." Most people shift ideologies as quickly as chameleons change colors—and for the same basic reason: they adapt their ideological "color" to what they feel is necessary at the moment.

The ongoing debate over mandatory seat-belt laws is a case in point. Many "macho men" who never before espoused any belief in civil liberties—except, perhaps, the right to own guns—have suddenly discovered that they're really closet followers of John Stuart Mill. They go around quoting the great author of *On Liberty* and other modern libertarians in defense of their unwillingness to comply with misdemeanor statutes requiring them to buckle up. Mill's famous dictum is that "the only purpose for which power can be rightfully exercised against any member of a civilized community, against his will, is to prevent harm to others. He cannot rightfully be compelled to do or forbear because it will be better for him to do so. . . ."

But many of the strongest opponents of mandatory seat-belt laws just happen to be among the most pigheaded proponents of "mandatory" prohibitions against adult pornography, drugs, prostitution, homosexuality, and other victimless crimes. They conveniently forget about Mill when the prohibition is against something they find personally disgusting. They selectively invoke their own freedom to choose to act self-destructively, but deny others the freedom to choose to act "immorally" in relation to their own bodies. (Some opponents of seat-belt laws also oppose a woman's right to choose whether to have an abortion, but that's a somewhat more complex issue—especially if you believe that the fetus is an independent person.)

However, the fact that many of those who support a particular position are hypocritical about liberty doesn't necessarily mean that they're wrong about that position. Some consistent civil libertarians also oppose mandatory seat-belt laws. They're entitled to a justification from civil libertarians who favor such a mandatory deprivation of liberty.

I am a civil libertarian supporter of mandatory seat-belt laws. I generally agree with Mill and I oppose most laws that require adults to take action to protect themselves. I agree that adults should be entitled to take risks that endanger only themselves. I wouldn't ban skydiving, motorcycle riding, or even taking a vacation in Beirut.

But seat-belt laws are different. They aren't addressed primarily to the relatively few people who have made a calculated decision to refuse to wear seat belts. Mandatory seat-belt laws are designed for the typically lazy, negligent, forgetful drivers who simply don't bother to buckle up. The law tells such people that they're no longer entitled to be lethargic. If people want to obey the law, they must buckle up. If they choose not to, they're violating the law and are subject to a relatively trivial fine.

The vast majority of people choose to obey—and they're thankful for it. There are many stories of people who, before the law was enacted, never wore belts—but, later, their lives were saved by seat belts, and they thanked the authorities for "making them" wear the belts.

This "thank-you theory" of paternalism can be overextended—but it makes sense in the case of the ordinary driver who really doesn't care either way and will do whatever the law says. (Other examples of paternalistic laws that make sense are those that require airline passengers to wear seat belts and boat owners to carry lifejackets.)

Those who have conscientious objections are—in practice—free to not buckle up. They certainly can't complain about a fifteen or twenty dollar fine. That's surely less than their fair contribution to the state treasury, which must spend millions of dollars on health and welfare services for those who are injured as a result of not wearing seat belts. The "nonwearers" would have no legitimate complaint if insurance companies required that drivers check a box if they refused to wear seat belts, then imposed a surcharge proportional to the added risks. People may have the right to take risks, but they have no right to pass the costs of those risks onto other, more prudent people.

Of course, criminal statutes aren't like insurance surcharges. A surcharge may exceed a fine in dollar terms, but it doesn't involve a formal governmental sanction. A fifteen or twenty dollar fine is hardly a major condemnation. However, it's just enough to nudge the lethargic into doing what they'd probably want to do if they really thought about it—without requiring that the civilly disobedient act against conscience or face the government's wrath.

As these laws continue to prove their ability to save lives, there will be fewer and fewer protesters. If we wait long enough, the survival of the "fittest"—which, in the age of weapons on wheels, means those who opt for safety over macho—may eliminate the problem of civil disobedience against sensible seat-belt laws.

March 25, 1986

74
Prostitution Can't Be "Buckled Up"

A new argument in favor of mandatory seat-belt laws has just been developed by the ingenious officers of New York City's Tenth Precinct. The Tenth Precinct—which includes New York City's mid-town convention area—is among the prostitution capitals of the world. Hundreds of hookers promenade along the avenues and streets each night, approaching the cars stopped for traffic lights. When a "john" agrees to a proposition, the woman gets into the car, and they drive to their agreed place of assignation.

Although police officers in patrol cars observe these transactions, it is difficult for them to make arrests unless they actually see cash changing hands. And so the clever cops have come up with a new weapon in their war against vice.

When a policeman observes a prostitute getting into a john's car, he rushes over to the car and checks to see whether the driver-john is wearing his seat belt. Generally he is not—so the police give him a fifty dollar ticket for not being buckled up.

"You have to be as ingenious as the prostitutes are in devising legal means to deal with the problem," boasted the commander of the Tenth Precinct. The commander explains that this novel approach is both simple and effective: "To tell the truth, they probably get a heavier fine for seat belts than for the crime of prostitution." Few johns would ever challenge the ticket in court, for fear that the circumstances surrounding the arrest would be made public.

During one recent month, fully one-third of the seat-belt tickets issued in Manhattan were in the Tenth Precinct, and most of those were given to johns. The professionals who work the area are "aware of the enforcement," says one sergeant. "The pimps are all wearing their seat belts now."

There is no evidence, of course, that this new weapon has had any impact on reducing the number of prostitutes or johns. Its primary impact seems to be an increase in the price of the transaction. For those johns who are caught with their belts unbuckled, the Tenth Precinct has—in effect— added a tax of fifty dollars to the prostitute's price.

The police acknowledge that current laws have no real deterrent effect on the prostitutes. Most judges don't even bother to fine them; they just sentence them to prison for the few minutes they have already been waiting for trial, and then release them. The pimps are rarely caught. If the dangers of disease, disgrace, or mugging are not enough to discourage the desperate john, there is little likelihood that a fifty dollar seat-belt fine will make the difference.

Sooner or later, the wives of these johns probably will get wise to what those seat-belt tickets are all about. I can imagine the following conversation:

Wife: "Dear, this is the third seat-belt ticket you've gotten this month. What's going on?"

Husband: "Well, you know how much traffic there is up around Columbus Circle. I get restless and take my belt off."

However, unless the wives can manage to keep their husbands at home, the business of "turning tricks" will continue as usual along Seventh Avenue, as well as along the hundreds of streets and avenues in almost every city and town in the world where prostitution flourishes. The "oldest profession" has not changed much over the past several thousand years. The cat-and-mouse game between police, who really don't care about arresting the women, and prostitutes, who really don't worry much about being arrested, will continue to operate in the shadows of the law.

Every so often, a new weapon will be developed. Yesterday it was publishing the photographs of johns. Today it's the seat-belt law. Tomorrow it may be some new-fangled, high-tech surveillance method—but nothing really works.

The most frightening deterrent to prostitution—both from the prostitute's and the john's point of view—are the extra-legal ones: horrible venereal diseases and the ever-present danger of violence. Yet even with the epidemic proportions that herpes, AIDS, and violent crime have assumed, there is no evidence of any substantial reduction in the prostitution business.

Nor are our feeble efforts at enforcing these victimless crime laws without cost. For every policeman on the prostitution beat, there is one policeman less out there preventing crimes against victims. A very high proportion of our local law enforcement budgets are devoted to victimless crimes like prostitution, gambling, and homosexuality.

The time has come for a serious reevaluation of our approach to sex for hire. There must be a better way to protect the prostitute from her pimp and john, the john from his prostitute, and the general public from a wasteful misallocation of law enforcement resources.

March 26, 1985

75
Politicizing the Courts

The U.S. judicial system is once again at the center of a firestorm. Not since the days of President Franklin Roosevelt's court packing plan has so much political attention been focused on the courts.

The executive branch has promised to appoint judges who are ideologically committed to the administration's programs. These programs include rolling back women's constitutional right to choose to terminate unwanted or unhealthy pregnancies; the rights of blacks and other minorities to have effective access to education, work, and essential services; criminal defendants' right to the tools necessary to defend themselves against false charges and overreaching government; and the rights of all citizens to be free from the establishment and enhanced influence of religion in public life.

The Reagan administration has established a judicial screening procedure that is designed to assure that no mistakes are made. The president himself is involved in the process. Every Thursday, a small group that includes the attorney general, the White House chief-of-staff, the president's counsel, and seven other high-ranking political operatives meets to approve and disapprove judicial nominees. Never before in history, says an expert on judicial appointments, has the senior White House staff played such an active role in the appointment process.

The early returns are already showing effective results. Preliminary studies show that President Reagan's 231 appointees—80 percent of whom are white males, most with a net worth of more than $400,000, and only sixteen of whom are black or Hispanic—are twice as likely to rule against constitutional claims in criminal cases than Carter appointees; five times as likely to rule against women's rights; and considerably more likely to deny pretrial bail and impose harsher sentences.

Of course, numbers don't tell the whole story. The Washington Legal Foundation recently reported that three out of four Reagan appointees exercised judicial restraint in all or nearly all of their decisions in 1981–83. The foundation concluded that "the critical difference between the Reagan judges and their predecessors is . . . what they *don't* do." And it's awfully hard to quantify inaction.

Difficult as it is to quantify, the emerging picture seems clear: the White House is showing some success in its attempt to use the judiciary to implement its political program. As a former Reagan Justice Department official put it in a moment of candor: "It became evident after the first term that there was no way to make legislative gains in many areas of social and civil rights, [so] the president has to do it by changing the jurisprudence."

Put another way, it seems that an administration that preaches judicial restraint is attempting to use the judicial process to achieve political goals that it has failed to achieve through the political process. Never before in recent history has an administration seen the judiciary as so affirmative a part of its political program.

The use of questionnaires and other devices for probing judicial candidates about their views on particular issues, and even cases, didn't begin in the last few years. Special-interest groups on the left and right have always tried to get their agendas achieved through the courts. But never before has it been so systematic, pervasive, and apparently successful.

Among the greatest dangers of judicial politicization is the farm-league approach this administration seems to be taking to court of appeals appointments. The word has gone out that several appeals court appointees are being groomed—really being watched over—for possible elevation to the Supreme Court. And the people who are doing the watching aren't necessarily looking for qualities of fairness, open-mindedness, craftsman-ship, or intellectual integrity: they seem to be looking for bottom-line results, ideology, and politics. This can't help but influence particular cases before these judges.

Nor is it honest to invoke the concept of judicial restraint when what's really wanted are particular political results. "Arrogance cloaked as humil-ity" is the way Justice William Brennen characterized the view that "feigns self-effacing deference" only when it serves specific political ends. This administration isn't looking for neutral practitioners of judicial restraint, who would defer *even* to legislators and state courts with which they fundamentally disagreed.

One example in point: more and more *state* courts are interpreting their own constitutions to give greater protection to defendants than the U.S. Constitution does. Therefore, several justices who claim to be practitioners of judicial restraint have been actively reaching out to bring these cases before the Supreme Court. That isn't judicial restraint under any interpreta-tion, as Justice John Paul Stevens pointed out when he referred to his conservative colleagues' "voracious appetites" for deciding cases that have no business being before the Supreme Court.

However one feels about these recent developments, one prediction seems incontestable: more political and media attention is going to be focused on the judicial process. In a democracy, increased public aware-ness of how any branch of government operates is desirable. But the judi-ciary should be the branch that is most insulated from pressure to conform with what the current majority demands. We should keep a watchful eye on this emerging constitutional crisis.

November 12, 1985

76
The Right to Trust Your Lawyer

In *Henry VI, Part II*, Shakespeare has one of his villains boast that when the revolt succeeds, "the first thing we do, let's kill all the lawyers." The modern equivalent of killing lawyers seems to be subpoenaing them to testify against their own clients.

The net result of turning lawyer against client is often to destroy the confidentiality and confidence upon which the lawyer-client relationship is built. There is no surer way to "kill" the Sixth Amendment's right to counsel.

Until the middle 1970s, it was almost unheard of for prosecutors to subpoena lawyers to testify about their dealings with clients. There were few formal prohibitions, but there seemed to be an unwritten rule that the confidential communications entrusted to a lawyer by his or her client were out of bounds for prosecutorial inquiry.

Not that prosecutors were uninterested in these secrets. Obviously, most district attorneys would give a great deal to know what the defendant secretly told his lawyer about the crime. But to defend a client properly, the lawyer must promise to keep the client's confidences. Without such a promise, the client is unlikely to tell the lawyer his deep, dark secrets—and without knowing these secrets, the lawyer can't perform properly. The same is thought to be true of doctors, priests, and other care-givers who rely on full disclosure to perform their important jobs.

Not everything a client tells or shows a lawyer is covered by the "lawyer-client privilege." The lawyer-client privilege doesn't cover future crimes. If a client tells a lawyer that he's about to go out and rob a bank, the lawyer can report that to the police. But what if a criminal defendant tells his lawyer that he really committed the murder with which he has been charged, and now plans to take the witness stand and deny, under oath, that he committed it? Is the lawyer then free to disclose both the past crime (the murder) and the future crime (the perjury about the murder)?

This question has divided lawyers over the years and is now pending before the U.S. Supreme Court. Nor is there any easy answer, as some of the court's justices seem to believe, judging from the questions they asked of lawyers during the recent argument. If the court rules—as it seems likely to—that lawyers should disclose a client's intention to lie about past crimes, criminal defendants will surely learn about this rule and act accordingly: they will either lie to their lawyers or refuse to confide in them.

The current slew of subpoenas directed against lawyers focuses primarily on the fees paid to secure legal representation. They direct the lawyers to disclose how much they were paid and by whom. This information can be very useful to prosecutors, especially in drug and organized crime cases. If an unemployed twenty-five-year-old suspected of dealing cocaine paid a six-figure legal fee, that fact would be quite interesting to the Drug Enforcement Administration, as well as to the Internal Revenue Service. If the legal fees for a lower-level drug courier were paid by a person suspected of being the Mister Big of a drug importation ring or an organized crime family, that fact would certainly corroborate suspicions.

Admission to the bar isn't a license to join one's clients in committing crimes. Lawyers aren't, and shouldn't be, immune from responding to valid subpoenas. But lawyers also shouldn't become the star witnesses against their own clients as a result of the confidential information given to them as part of their sacred trust. An appropriate balance must be struck between the legitimate needs of law enforcement and criminal defendants' constitutional right to effective counsel. There is the question not only of where that balance should be struck, but of who should strike it.

Today, the power to issue subpoenas against lawyers lies in the hands of prosecutors. Advocates often lose perspective and become overzealous in the quest for victory. This surely has happened in several recent cases involving subpoenas directed against lawyers, and the practice seems to be spreading.

Past and potential abuses have led one court—the Supreme Judicial Court of Massachusetts—to promulgate a new rule that requires prior judicial approval before a prosecutor can issue a subpoena against a lawyer for information about a client. Under this rule, which goes into effect in 1986, all prosecutors would be required to obtain a ruling from a judge indicating that the information they seek isn't privileged and is necessary to the investigation. In short, issuing a subpoena to a lawyer without prior judicial approval will become an unethical practice in Massachusetts after the New Year.

It remains to be seen whether this rule will help to strike the proper balance and whether it will be emulated in other states. What is clear is that something must be done to check overzealous prosecutors from interfering with entirely proper confidential relationships between clients and lawyers.

December 3, 1985

UPDATE
The Supreme Court decided that a lawyer may disclose his client's perjury. See column 82.

77
Art Spurs Action—
And Truth-Seeking

Two recent legal developments dramatically illustrate how art can have a profound impact on life and law. Rubin "Hurricane" Carter—whose 1966 murder conviction became a national cause célèbre as a result of Bob Dylan's hit record, "Hurricane"—was granted a writ of habeas corpus and freed from prison. A federal judge in New Jersey essentially agreed with what Bob Dylan had written in his 1970s ballad: that the case against the black boxer and a codefendant on charges of killing three whites in a bar was based on "an appeal to racism rather than reason, concealment rather than disclosure." Dylan, of course, put it more lyrically than the judge did:

> Here comes the story of the Hurricane,
> The man the authorities came to blame
> For something that he never done . . .
> It won't be long before they clear his name.

There's little doubt that the Dylan song had a major impact on the Carter case. The song helped to raise more than a half-million dollars for a defense fund and planted the seeds of doubt in the minds of many people who would otherwise never have heard of the case.

Naturally, the judge's decision to overturn Carter's conviction wasn't directly influenced by Dylan's ballad: it was based on a reading of the trial records and an application of the governing case law. Many people now in prisons around the country have equally compelling legal claims. However, no one is writing songs about them, raising funds for their defense, or even providing them with minimal legal assistance. On our nation's death rows alone, there are more than 500 inmates who don't even have a lawyer who can confer with them or file petitions on their behalf.

When a man has spent nearly twenty years in prison for a crime he may not have committed, it's hard to characterize him as "lucky." However, compared to some other prisoners, Rubin Carter *is* a lucky man. Someone wrote a song about him, and that stirring ballad eventually evoked a responsive chord among lawyers, the public, and a judge.

At about the same time that Carter received his good news, I was meeting with another black prisoner. His name is Wayne Williams. The crimes he is believed to be guilty of committing are among the most heinous in history. The authorities in Georgia believe that he is the infamous Atlanta Child Killer, the man responsible for dozens of murders in the Atlanta black community. Although Williams was actually convicted of two murders—of black adults—the book has been closed on the other twenty-seven deaths, since the Atlanta child killings apparently stopped after Williams's arrest in 1981.

But new questions have been raised about the evidence used to convict Williams. Prosecutors in that case relied heavily on circumstantial evidence of a pattern of killings. They were allowed to argue to the jury that Williams may have been responsible for ten other murders that seemed to fit into a particular pattern. They also argued that fibers found on the victims were "consistent" with fibers that came from Williams's home.

New evidence has now come to light which suggests that the state may have withheld evidence tending to show that others may have been responsible for some of the killings thought to be part of the alleged pattern. Doubts have also been cast on the state's fiber theory, as well as on the claim that all of the killings stopped after Williams's arrest.

These issues must be resolved by the courts after a thorough review of all the evidence, both old and new. It's too early to speculate as to how the case will come out, but it certainly is in a new posture, and Williams has a new hope—as do several of the mothers of the dead children, who believe that the real killer or killers have not been brought to justice.

I was in Williams's prison cell in Bucks County, Georgia, not because of a song, but because of a television docudrama written by Abby Mann. Watching that docudrama and listening to discussions about it raised considerable doubts in my mind about the fairness of Williams's trial, and, indeed, about his guilt. It stimulated me to read the legal record in the case and to agree to serve as one of his new lawyers in an effort to reopen the case.

The docudrama, titled "The Atlanta Child Murders," was roundly criticized by Atlanta officials and by the press for taking liberties with the facts. Bob Dylan's song also indulged in poetic license. But that is in the nature of art. The song, like the docudrama, stimulated some listeners and viewers into action. That action, to be effective, requires a scrupulous review of the cold records of these highly controversial cases.

Neither songs nor docudramas win legal cases. However, the lesson of the *Carter* and *Williams* cases is that art may play an important role in provoking doubts, raising questions, and generating change.

November 19, 1985

UPDATE
Following the CBS broadcast, I was asked to help Williams reopen his case. I met with Williams in prison, and I also met with several of the murdered children's mothers. They also support a reopening of the case. That issue is now before the Georgia courts.

78
Pornography and Abortion: Let Citizens Choose

Last week I testified before the U.S. Attorney General's Committee on Pornography—the so-called "Meese Commission," named in honor of Edwin Meese, the great American who appointed eleven people to recommend whether the country needs more censorship.

The commission has been traveling around the various states hearing testimony from an assortment of experts, religious leaders, kooks, fanatics, and others with an interest in pornography, free speech, and crime.

I testified during the last day of hearings in "the smut capital of the world," New York City. The day of the hearing fell on the thirteenth anniversary of *Roe* v. *Wade*, the Supreme Court decision that recognized a woman's right to control her body and to choose whether or not to have an abortion. Throughout the nation, women and men were celebrating this great victory of personal choice over governmentally dictated conformity to religious and moral doctrine. But inside the commission hearing room, woman after woman demanded that American citizens be denied personal choice in what they read, watch, and hear.

The leader of the pack was Andrea Dworkin, who claims to speak on behalf of feminists. Invoking images of women being tortured, mutilated, and even killed for the profit of pornographers, Ms. Dworkin repeatedly insisted that the commissioners "listen to women" and censor what men (and women) read. "The issue is simple, not complex," she explained. "Either you're on the side of the women or on the side of the pornographers."

But issues of censorship are simple only for the simple-minded and the single-minded. Ms. Dworkin reminded me of those polemicists—her archenemies on most issues—who regard the abortion issue as "simple": "Either you're on the side of the innocent fetuses or on the side of the murdering abortionist."

These issues are anything but simple. Whenever one group of citizens purports to tell another group how to use their bodies, their minds, their sexuality, and their freedoms, the issues are complex and go to the heart of minority rights in a democratic society.

The issues are particularly troublesome when the government seeks to regulate ideas, propaganda, advocacy, and expression. And if the commission's hearings have made anything clear, it's that one of the principal reasons that many people want to increase the censorship of sexually explicit material is precisely because of the "ideas" it promotes or represents.

Ms. Dworkin characterizes pornography as "genocidal pornography" and claims that America (which she spells "Amerika") is "approach[ing] the atrocity of Nazi Germany." Putting aside that hysterical comparison, which demeans the slaughter of millions, Ms. Dworkin seems to forget that all "propaganda" is protected by the First Amendment. The Reverend Bruce Ritter, a Franciscan priest who is a member of the commission, made the same argument as Ms. Dworkin, but from the right flank: "If attitudes toward marriage are being affected by pornography, which says that extramarital and premarital sex is [all right], then we have there a major attack on the . . . family."

But the Constitution forbids censorship that is designed to affect attitudes. As the Supreme Court said in striking down New York's attempt to ban the film version of *Lady Chatterley's Lover*: "What New York has done, therefore, is to prevent the exhibition of a motion picture because that picture advocates an idea—that adultery under certain circumstances may be proper behavior. Yet the First Amendment's basic guarantee is of freedom to advocate ideas. The state, quite simply, has thus struck at the very heart of constitutionally protected liberty."

The entire operation of the Meese Commission—the manner by which its members were selected, its list of witnesses, the censorial attitudes of several of the commissioners—strikes at the very heart of constitutionally protected liberty.

The social science methodology apparently being employed by a majority of the commissioners is replete with error. Witness after witness has been testifying that pornography is the devil that turns normal men into rapists, child molesters, and wife beaters. One witness solemnly declared pornography to be an addiction.

The fact that millions of law-abiding Americans enjoy X-rated films, dirty books, and *Playboy* magazine (all of which qualify as pornography, under the commission's loose working definition) doesn't seem relevant. Nor do some of the commissioners seem to want to hear about possible distinctions between violent, sexist pornography and adult erotica. One witness said that to build "an artificial wall of separation" between child pornography and adult erotica would be as ridiculous as distinguishing between heroin and marijuana.

(I don't think he understood the irony of his own point. We *should* make precisely those kinds of distinctions, both with smut and with drugs.)

Fortunately, there were a few rational voices—some by women who were against pornography, but even more against censorship. They made it clear that neither Andrea Dworkin nor Edwin Meese speaks for them.

Let us not join the more than two hundred countries throughout the world that practice massive censorship. American adults are wise and mature enough to choose for themselves what to read, see, and hear. We don't need a censorship czar or commission to tell us what's best for us.

January 28, 1986

79
Getting Tough on Car Crimes

While the Justice Department rails against the evils of pornography, abortion, and drugs, the nation's most serious crime goes virtually unpunished. No, I'm not talking about murder, rape, or burglary: I'm referring to drunken driving and other crimes of the road.

Many more people are killed by cars every year than by the combination of guns, knives, beatings, and poison. And most auto victims are crime victims, since most auto-related deaths are associated with drunken driving, speeding, and other car crimes.

Yet we see far too little attention being paid to this form of criminality. Drunken drivers and speeders are generally given a slap on the wrist, even when they've barely missed killing or maiming. Since few drunken drivers or speeders set out deliberately to hurt anyone, these menaces to mankind assume that they will get away with their crimes. It's therefore no surprise that so many drivers who do eventually kill have long records of prior convictions for drunken driving and speeding. Our current punishments not only fail to deter car crime, but they actually encourage it by creating an atmosphere of tolerance and acceptability.

Part of the reason for the problem is that our legal system focuses too heavily on fortuitous results. Consider two drivers—let's call the first Miller and the second Killer—who both drink the same excessive amount and drive in the same reckless manner down the same busy street. Miller makes it home, barely missing a child who darted out from between parked cars. Killer hits and kills a child.

From a moral perspective, both Miller and Killer are equally culpable: they each took the same actions under the same circumstances. But the roulette wheel of fate turned up the red of life for Miller and the black of death for Killer. Under prevailing approaches, Miller probably would be fined the cost of a few drinks. Killer, however, might well be imprisoned for manslaughter. Since almost all drinking and speeding drivers believe that they will turn out to be "Millers" rather than "Killers," the current roulette wheel approach to punishment minimizes the deterrent impact of the law.

It would be more effective—and fairer—to narrow the gap between equally culpable car criminals who fortuitously cause unequal results. Thus, Miller should be punished as if he was the potential killer he surely is. If luck was the only factor that kept Miller from becoming a killer, then Miller belongs in jail along with Killer.

The law has difficulty treating Miller like a potential killer because the blindfold of justice covers a cross-eyed and confused face. The law always looks in two diametrically opposed directions. It looks to the past in order to do justice to the specific individuals involved in the case—the driver and the victim. It also looks to the future as it may affect potential defendants and victims.

Although Miller's past actions did not actually kill anyone, treating him like a potential killer will save lives in the future. But judges and juries are reluctant to imprison drunken drivers who didn't kill. Drunken drivers and speeding are so common that almost everyone has friends or children who fit into these categories—"There but for the grace of God go I," is the common refrain.

We seem to require a dead or maimed body—preferably of an upstanding, socially "useful" citizen—to generate the kind of moral indignation necessary to imprison one of "our kind." Drunken drivers and speeders aren't unemployed muggers, drug fiends, or perverts. They're respectable citizens, just like the judges, jurors, and prosecutors who have to make the difficult decision to treat them like the criminals they are.

The Scandinavian countries have learned how to deal with this conundrum. They impose short but mandatory imprisonment on potential killers who are caught driving while drunk. I visited a work camp for drunken drivers in Sweden and met several prominent citizen inmates. Their imprisonment, while a major inconvenience and disruption in their lives, isn't regarded as so serious a punishment that it has to be reserved only for the dregs of society. But it surely makes the point. Every driver in Sweden knows that if he or she is caught drinking while driving, imprisonment is virtually certain.

This realization—coupled with other tough approaches to car crime—has contributed to a significantly lower automobile homicide rate in those countries that treat Millers like potential Killers. We owe it to our pedestrians and drivers to try a similar approach here.

We all identify with the mugging or burglary victim who is killed—but it's far more likely that we and our children will become victims of a recidivist drunken driver who got away with his previous crimes. Instead of thinking "There but for the grace of God go I" when a friend is given a ticket for drunken driving, we should recall that expression every time one of the tens of thousands of law-abiding citizens is killed by a car criminal. Let's get tough on the crimes that really endanger human lives.

February 4, 1986

80
"Go to Your Room!"

The courts are getting tougher on crime, meting out more and longer prison sentences. This toughness has come at a time when nearly all categories of violent crime are down, primarily due to the increasing average age of the U.S. population.*

Violent crime is primarily a function of youth and gender: the higher the proportion of young men to the general population, the higher the violent crime rate. Since the baby boom ended in the 1960s, the percentage of men now between the high-crime ages of fifteen to twenty-five has gone down—and so has violent crime. Criminologists predicted this trend nearly twenty years ago, but current politicians are, of course, claiming the credit for curbing crime.

But fear of crime is up, due largely to the rhetoric of these same politicians who pander to our understandable terror of becoming victimized. Any judge who has aspirations for promotion must learn to throw the book—hard, often, and without compassion—at convicted criminals, without much selectivity.

The result is that our prisons are being filled beyond capacity. However, since violent crime is down, more and more nonviolent offenders are being sentenced to prison. Since the prisons are overcrowded, this means that for every nonviolent offender sent to prison, there may be a violent offender for whom there is no room. (Despite the reduction in violent crimes, there are still more than enough violent criminals filling every available prison cell.)

These new developments have led some judges and correctional officials to experiment with new techniques for confining nonviolent offenders without taking up valuable prison space.

For example, in suburban Westchester County, north of New York City, a judge has been sentencing certain types of criminals to a form of house arrest. These offenders include people convicted of drunken driving and other crimes that require serious punishment, but that involve people who aren't generally dangerous—at least when they're not behind the wheel of a car. The "house arrest" sentence requires that the "inmate" stay inside of his home except for specified trips: to church, to doctors, and, in some instances, to job interviews. This house arrest is enforced by periodic phone checks, house visits, or surveillance. Inevitably, however, there is some slippage in enforcement and some abuse of the privilege of serving the sentence at home.

To ensure greater compliance with house arrest, some correctional officials have begun to rely on a Buck Rodgers piece of futuristic technology. Several years ago, a Harvard Law School student developed an electronic device that transmits a signal which enables the police to follow the wearer's whereabouts. If the bracelet or ankle cuff is removed, an emergency signal is transmitted. If the wearer leaves a predetermined location, the violation shows up on a central monitoring screen. Thus far, the electronic monitor has been made available only on a "voluntary" basis. (I put "voluntary" in quotes, since the choice of wearing a bracelet or going to prison is an offer that's hard to refuse.)

Some civil libertarians are concerned about the potential abuses inherent in this electronic monitoring. One suggested variant of the bracelet would "gently remind" the wearer that he has left the approved zone by transmitting a small electric shock back to the bracelet. This shock technology is currently being used to train dogs not to leave the family yard. Variations on this *Clockwork Orange* behavior modification aren't difficult to imagine.

Despite these concerns, the electronic monitor experiment is about to be tried in a number of jurisdictions around the country. This will surely lead to an increase in house arrest as an alternative to imprisonment. It will also lead to the increased use of house arrest as an alternative to probation and other forms of nonincarcerative punishment and supervision. Judges who today would sentence a defendant "to the street" will tomorrow sentence him to "go to your room and stay there." Since house arrest is far less expensive than imprisonment and can be imposed without regard to available cell space, it could create a revolution in punishment and supervision. The result may well be an increase in the total amount of confinement.

House arrest is inherently discriminatory. Confinement to one's twelve-room mansion—with Jacuzzi, videotape machine, and gourmet cook—is a lot easier to take than confinement to a crowded, roach-infested slum apartment. Nor would it be feasible for the judge to enforce an order to "go to your room without TV or snacks," although some such restrictions could at least be tried.

Despite this inherent inequality, house arrest provides an inexpensive supplement to our current limited alternatives and may be a wave of the future. (Another variant might reduce the discriminatory impact: a "time-sharing" arrangement under which everyone sentenced to house arrest would have to spend two days of each week in jail.)

A man's home may be his castle—but for some, it will soon become a castle with electronic bars.

February 11, 1986

See column 19.

81
End of Affirmative Action?

The U.S. Supreme Court has just heard legal arguments in a pair of cases that could determine the future of racial equality in this country. At stake is a concept that is loosely called "affirmative action." But behind this vague label lie a variety of remedial devices designed to help minorities overcome this nation's history of racial discrimination.

Those who favor most forms of affirmative action—such as the National Association for the Advancement of Colored People, the American Civil Liberties Union, and other liberal groups and individuals—see them as necessary to redress past patterns of discrimination that prevented blacks and other minorities from entering the workforce and other areas of opportunity.

Those who oppose most affirmative action—such as the Reagan administration, many old-line unions, and conservatives—characterize it as "reverse discrimination," "a form of racism," and just plain "not fair."

In order to understand the raging debate over affirmative action, it's important to break that multifaceted concept down into its component parts. Some forms of affirmative action are far more controversial than others. Here are some of the most frequently used devices, beginning with the least controversial:

- *Affirmative search programs.* Many employers and educational institutions, realizing that many potential minority candidates aren't aware of available opportunities, have shifted their recruitment priorities and now spend more time and money actively recruiting qualified minority applicants.

  Universities, for example, send recruitment officials into ghetto and barrio high schools instead of limiting their efforts to prep schools and wealthy suburban public schools. Corporations also try to recruit—especially for entry-level jobs—in minority neighborhoods and in newspaper and radio ads aimed at minorities. Hardly anyone, other than a certified bigot, can complain about such affirmative-action efforts.

- *Affirmative training programs.* A variant on affirmative search programs is to offer training to help those minority candidates who have suffered educational deprivations develop skills that will let them compete with those who come from more advantaged backgrounds.

Again, there is little controversy about the availability of such training, but some complaints are heard about the criteria for admission into the programs. If individual whites who are as disadvantaged as eligible blacks are excluded from such programs, the specter of discrimination is raised. The Supreme Court did, in 1979, uphold the constitutionality of a training program that set aside half the places for blacks in an industry with a history of discrimination.

- *Affirmative entry criteria.* This is where the real battleground begins for many. Under this device, a decision is made to hire or admit members of specific minority groups by using lower criteria than those used for applicants who aren't members of such groups. This may mean that a university that generally admits students with B+ averages and scores of 600 out of 800 on nationwide competitive tests will admit blacks with B— averages and scores of 500. In employment decisions, it may mean that job applicants with less experience may be given preference because of their race.

The rationale behind these differences in criteria may vary—the need for diversity, the fear that certain tests may be discriminatory—but the bottom line is that race is taken into account in selection decisions. The Supreme Court has authorized this in the context of a university's desire to diversify, but not yet in other contexts.

- *Affirmative set-asides, goals, and quotas.* Under these, a certain number or percentage of places—sometimes exact, sometimes rough—are reserved for minority applicants. Generally these are in industries or locations with a history of racial discrimination against minorities, but the specific individuals affected generally were neither the victims nor the perpetrators of the past discrimination.

These devices are designed as affirmative aids—as floors—for specified minorities, but they are often perceived by rejected non-minority candidates as negative barriers, or ceilings—especially where the size of the employment or educational pie is fixed or shrinking.

- *Affirmative protection against dismissal.* In the context of a shrinking employment pie, decisions must necessarily be made to fire certain employees. Ordinarily this is done on the basis of seniority—last in, first out. But if the last in were minority employees, some courts have refused to allow them to be fired first. Thus, affirmative action has come into conflict with seniority. In a 1984 case, the Supreme Court ruled in favor of seniority.

The cases just argued before the Supreme Court involve a decree entered against the Cleveland Fire Department and a New York City union. In the Cleveland case, black and Hispanic firefighters were promoted ahead of whites who made higher scores on promotion tests. In the New York case, a court required the union to meet a "goal"—really a quota—of 29 percent nonwhite membership.

The Reagan administration is foursquare against these kinds of affirmative action devices. The lower courts, in general, have favored them. The ball is now in the Supreme Court. By July, we'll have at least some guidance in this controversial, and often confusing, area of law and social policy.

February 25, 1986

82
Must Lawyers Warn Their Clients?

What should an ethical criminal lawyer do when his client tells him he's going to lie on the witness stand?

Sounds easy: make him tell the truth, of course. But what if he insists on lying? Should the lawyer inform the judge about his own client's planned perjury? Wouldn't such a tattletale lawyer be violating his promise to keep secret everything his client told him in confidence?

These are some of the questions the Supreme Court recently addressed in the important case of *Nix* v. *Whiteside.*

Whiteside had been convicted of second-degree murder for the stabbing of a marijuana dealer, Calvin Love. Love and his lover were in bed when Whiteside and two companions arrived at Love's apartment seeking to purchase some pot. An argument ensued. Love told his girlfriend to get his "piece." The room was dark. Love started to reach under his pillow.

Whiteside, believing that Love was going for his gun, pulled his knife and stabbed Love in the chest, killing him.

The police conducted a cursory search and found no gun. Shortly thereafter, Love's family removed everything from the apartment.

Since Whiteside had no money, a lawyer was appointed for him. In their initial interviews, Whiteside told his lawyer that he believed that Love was pulling a gun on him, but he said that he hadn't actually seen the gun. About a week before trial, Whiteside changed his story: he told his lawyer that he had seen "something metallic" in Love's hand.

The lawyer didn't believe this new variation and warned Whiteside not to lie. Whiteside persisted in claiming that he had seen a metallic object. The lawyer threatened that if Whiteside testified about any metallic object, he would inform the judge that his client was lying.

As a result of that threat, Whiteside testified at the trial that although he believed Love had a gun, he had never actually seen it. Whiteside was convicted and sentenced to forty years in prison.

After his conviction, Whiteside appealed on the grounds that his lawyer's threats had deprived him of his Sixth Amendment right to effective counsel. After losing several rounds, he won in the U.S. Court of Appeals. That court ruled that his lawyer's threat to inform the judge violated Whiteside's right to have his lawyer keep secret what his client told him in confidence, even if he told him two different stories.

The U.S. Supreme Court reversed the Court of Appeals ruling and reinstated Whiteside's conviction. Although the Supreme Court's decision was unanimous, there were four separate opinions, each taking a somewhat different view. All the justices railed against the evils of perjury, as if anyone would defend or support a defendant's "right" to lie. Much of the chief justice's majority opinion was dedicated to a windy attack on this straw man. But none of the opinions addressed the really hard conflict between the lawyer's dual obligations to preserve his client's confidences *and* to prevent perjury.

The only reason Whiteside's lawyer knew that his client was going to commit perjury was that the lawyer had assured Whiteside—either explicitly or implicitly—that whatever Whiteside told him would remain secret. On the basis of that assurance, Whiteside had leveled with his lawyer. Then his lawyer turned around and threatened to expose him—and the Supreme Court has now commended that lawyer.*

The end result of *Nix* v. *Whiteside* will, in my view, be *more*, not less, perjury. From now on, ethical lawyers will have to begin their interviews with their own clients by giving them "Whiteside warnings"—somewhat akin to the *Miranda* warnings that police officers are now required to give. For example, criminal lawyers may have to warn their clients: "Now look, you may believe that anything you tell me will remain confidential, but that isn't so. If you tell me anything different from what you intend to say on the witness stand, I may have to turn you in—so be really careful about what you say to me."

The street-smart client will get the point. He'll make up his whole story before he even tells it to his lawyer. He'll become a *better* and more consistent liar than Whiteside. He'll treat his lawyer as a potential adversary, rather than as his advocate. This will create a considerable number of problems both for the lawyer and for our system of justice.

It's important for a defense lawyer to learn the truth from his client. Most good lawyers will do everything—short of turning in their clients—to persuade them not to commit perjury. Perjury is generally a bad tactic as well as bad ethics.

But now more clients will lie to their own lawyers, and they'll lie more effectively. The net result will be less trust between lawyers and clients and more perjury in the courtrooms.

The Supreme Court may feel better about its simplistic condemnation of perjury—but it has created at least as many problems as it has solved.

March 4, 1986

*See Column 76.

83
The Right to High School Humor

The Supreme Court recently heard a case that brings back memories of my own high school days. The case involved a seventeen-year-old Washington state high school student named Matthew who was disciplined—suspended for three days and denied the right to be a graduation speaker—because of a speech he made at a school assembly. The offending speech was in support of his friend Jeff, who was running for vice president of the student body.

Matthew's speech was full of adolescent sexual innuendo. There were no four-letter words, but there were plenty of allusions to macho phallic prowess: Jeff is "a man who is firm . . . who takes his point and pounds it in . . . he drives hard . . . Jeff is a man who will go to [the] climax. . . ."

The reaction was just what one might expect. A few students in the audience joined in the juvenile fun, hooting, cheering, and making sexual motions. Some teachers found it offensive. There was even a claim that "the speech was sexually harassing to female students," although it contained no references to women. Jeff won the election, and Matthew was called into the principal's office and disciplined.

But Matthew refused simply to sit in the corner wearing a dunce cap. He went to federal court, sued the school, and won. The school fought back and took the case to the U.S. Supreme Court, whose decision, expected this spring, may well redefine the free-speech rights of public high school students.

My own interest in this problem is nostalgic as well as academic: "I was a teenage high school discipline problem" (soon to be a minor motion picture, starring Frankie Avalon as the principal and Annette Funicello as my mother). Like Matthew, I was suspended for making a speech at a high school assembly. Unlike Matthew's, my speech was not sexual. I accused some of my teachers of closing their eyes to rampant cheating.

My principal's response was swift. Instead of investigating my charges, he suspended me for making "disrespectful" remarks. (I wasn't disqualified from delivering a graduation speech only because my C average never qualified me for any such honor in the first place.) I didn't sue. I simply accepted the suspension and improved my bowling game at Freddie Fitzsimmon's nearby alley. My parents were mortified, but I was happy.

So, although I don't particularly care for his speech, I can clearly identify with Matthew. He's my kind of kid. I suspect that he'll become my kind of grownup—a bit "disrespectful" of his elders and challenging to authority. He exercised his freedom of speech to the limit—or, if you agree with the school authorities, beyond the limit.

In 1969, the Supreme Court ruled that public high school students do have some freedom. That case—*Tinker* v. *Des Moines Independent School District*—involved a group of high school students who defied a teacher's order not to wear black armbands to protest the Vietnam war. They were disciplined and the Supreme Court ruled in their favor, holding that high school students don't "shed their constitutional rights to freedom of speech or expression at the schoolhouse gate."

The Supreme Court also noted that school boards must retain authority to discipline where the expression has a disruptive effect on the educational process. Thus a delicate balance must be struck between freedom and disruption in the context of high school education.

In this case, the school board's claims seem spurious. There were no literal disruptions, either of the assembly or of classes. Indeed, there was evidence that many of the students at the assembly weren't paying much attention to the speakers (remember how boring high school campaign speeches can be?) until Matthew caught their attention with his gimmick.

The only evidence of disruption was a teacher's testimony that some students expressed so much interest in the speech that she devoted approximately ten minutes of valuable home economics class time to discuss freedom of speech. Any teacher who didn't take advantage of the educational opportunity generated by Matthew's speech should be called down to the principal's office and made to sit in the corner. There's plenty of time to discuss the virtues of one-step detergents.

What must be remembered is that a high school education is supposed to prepare young men and women to participate in an adult democratic society that is diverse in its tastes. We tolerate a wider variety of free expression than any other society in history. The process of tolerance must begin in school. Students should be taught to discuss controversial ideas, formulations, and lifestyles, rather than to try to close down disagreeable stalls in the marketplace of ideas.

Matthew may well lose his case before this Supreme Court, which seems more concerned these days with authority than with freedom. That would be unfortunate for Matthew. But it would be even more of a tragedy for our high school students, who would be deprived of one of the most important facets of real education—namely, controversy.

March 18, 1986

UPDATE
Matthew did lose his case before the Supreme Court, which ruled that school principals have broad power to regulate student speech.

84
Big Brother in the Bedroom

The Supreme Court recently heard oral arguments in a case that raises the most fundamental conflict between individual liberty and public morality. At stake is the right of adult homosexuals to engage in private sexual conduct.

A Georgia statute makes it a felony for anyone to commit "sodomy"—a polite legal euphemism for oral or anal intercourse. Michael Hardwick and his boyfriend were violating that law in the privacy of their bedroom when Big Brother—in this case, the Atlanta police—knocked on the door and arrested them. Although the criminal charges were eventually dropped, Hardwick decided to bring a lawsuit challenging the constitutionality of the Georgia sodomy law (and others like it in about half our states).

Not surprisingly, civil liberties and gay-rights groups are urging the Supreme Court to strike down these intrusive laws on the grounds that they violate privacy rights, while several fundamentalist religious groups are demanding that sodomy laws be upheld in the name of traditional morality. The Supreme Court's decision is expected late this spring.

Whatever the justices decide in the Georgia case will have wide implications, both beyond Georgia and beyond the homosexual community. What's really at stake is the right of all U.S. adults to conduct their private sex lives—whether homosexual, heterosexual, or anything else—free of governmental intrusion. The Georgia statute, as written, would literally apply to *all* couples, married or single, gay or straight. It outlaws several types of consensual sexual activity that are widely practiced throughout our society. Although the Georgia authorities would never seek to enforce the law's broad prohibitory language against married couples, the statute does reflect a claim that the state has the power to regulate all sexual encounters on moral grounds.

Because of the current composition of the Supreme Court, the *Hardwick* case had to be argued narrowly. A broad-based attack on a state's power to regulate all private sexual activity between consenting adults probably would fail. This Supreme Court simply isn't going to strike down the laws of nearly every state that prohibit adultery, prostitution, polygamy, and adult incest. Each of these prohibitions involves the preservation and sanctity of the traditional marital or family unit. Although some might argue that maintaining the felony status of homosexual conduct would encourage a few bisexuals to give up their same-sex lovers and try heterosexual marriage, that argument is far-fetched, at best, and isn't supported by any empirical research.

Thus, the court might well deny the states the power to intrude on private adult sexual conduct that doesn't have a direct impact on marriage and family, while continuing to grant states the power to criminalize adultery, prostitution, and adult incest. Such a ruling would decriminalize both private homosexual and private heterosexual activities between unmarried adults.

This would follow trends already in evidence: twenty-six states have legalized private homosexual activities, and even more have eliminated prohibitions against "fornication" (the law's polite way of describing sex between an unmarried male and female, which is still prohibited in several states, including my home "liberal" state of Massachusetts).

In the end, all laws that seek to punish private "victimless" conduct constitute a danger to a free society. The legalized imposition of public morality—whatever that may mean in a heterogenous society with no established religion—should remain limited to public places, children, and unconsenting victims. If an individual adult, either alone or together with other adults, wishes to engage in a private act that has no perceptible impact on unconsenting others, Big Brother should keep his distance. Puritanical public morality is neither good morality nor good law. As H. L. Mencken once defined it, puritanism is "the haunting fear that someone, somewhere, may be happy." If individuals can make themselves happy without hurting others, the state has no business interfering.

For now, it would be a great triumph for liberty if the Supreme Court ruled that the states lacked the power to criminalize private adult homosexual conduct. Such a ruling would constitute a Magna Carta for the rights of a beleaguered minority.

It would also come at a time in which much of the progress that gays have made over the past few years has been endangered by shrill cries for repressive legislation growing out of the fear of AIDS (which some are calling "afr-AIDS"). There is much that our society can and should do to control the AIDS epidemic. But the continued criminalization of private homosexual conduct—by statutes that draw no distinctions between safe sex and contagious practices—is not a proper response. AIDS is an appropriate subject for public *health* legislation, not for public *morality* legislation.

By striking down the felonizing of private homosexual acts, the Supreme Court would not—as some fear—legitimize what many consider an "abnormal" or "unnatural" sexual orientation. It isn't the office of our courts to legitimate or delegitimate private activities. It's very much the function of our courts to tell Big Brother to stay out of our collective bedrooms unless the state has a compelling interest in preventing conduct that harms children or nonconsenting adults.

April 8, 1986

For the Supreme Court decision see next column.

85
Supreme Court Throws Out Our Unwritten Rights

The Supreme Court's decision on gay sex marks the end of an era and seems to signal a dramatic shift in the court's approach to interpreting the Constitution.

The court's holding in *Bowers* v. *Hardwick*—that consensual homosexual acts between adults in their bedrooms are not protected by any constitutional right of privacy—could not have surprised any astute court-watchers. There has been a discernible trend away from supporting the claims of individual citizens against big government. But the language employed by Justice Byron White in announcing why the majority reached its result was plainly intended to convey an unmistakable message to the lower courts and to the bar.

Justice White acknowledged that in the past, the Supreme Court had recognized "rights that have little or no textual support in the constitutional language." Primary among such rights is "privacy." The great Justice Louis Brandeis spoke of "the most comprehensive of rights and the right most valued by civilized men," namely "the right to be let alone." Justice White himself—a Kennedy appointee—had voted in favor of privacy rights in numerous cases. But now he, and the court's majority, are apparently having second thoughts.

White seemed to be reacting to the Reagan administration's criticism that the justices have expanded their influence too much by creating new rights. We are no longer "inclined," announced the majority, "to take a more expansive view of our authority to discover new fundamental rights." The ruling continues, "The court . . . comes nearest to illegitimacy when it deals with judge-made constitutional law leaving little or no cognizable roots in the language or design of the Constitution." These lines could have come from a speech by Edwin Meese. Their implications for our nation are momentous.

To understand how much of a shift this language suggests, consider some of the most important Supreme Court decisions since the end of World War II. Desegregation of Southern schools is not required by the "language or design of the Constitution." Indeed "separate but equal" facilities—as well as legalized apartheid in marriage and other areas of public and private life—were expressly contemplated by those who enacted our Fourteenth Amendment. "One man, one vote" is nowhere to be found in our Constitution. Legislatures controlled by a few rural landowners had been the practice in many states since the founding of the nation.

The list of other rights now taken for granted by Americans, but not found in our Constitution, is legion: the right to choose an abortion; to use birth control; to refuse medical intervention for noncontagious illness; to send one's children to private school; to travel within and without the country; to prevent the government from listening to our phone calls; to dress and wear one's hair as one wishes; to live in the same house as one's grandchildren in violation of local zoning laws; and to engage in a business or occupation of one's choice.

These fundamental rights—some of which are supported by political conservatives—have come to be taken for granted by nearly all Americans in the twentieth century, though they were not contemplated by those who framed our eighteenth-century Constitution and its post–Civil War amendments.

The Constitution was supposed to be a living document, capable of reflecting changing times. Supreme Court Justice Joseph Story—who declared himself to be "the last of the old race of judges"—taught us in 1816 that "The Constitution unavoidably deals in general language. . . . The instrument was not intended to provide merely for the exigencies of a few years, but was to endure through a long lapse of ages, the events of which were locked up in the inscrutable purposes of Providence."

"Judge-made constitutional law" will always be with us. So long as words do not interpret themselves, human beings will have to interpret them. And interpretation of a living document necessarily requires that the reality of progress be taken into account. The dead hand of the past should not be allowed to dictate the future, especially in a country that has changed so dramatically over the past century.

We just celebrated the 100th anniversary of the Statue of Liberty and will soon commemorate the 200th anniversary of our Constitution. The mass immigration symbolized by the statue near Ellis Island changed the face of our country. That change is an ongoing process. The Constitution can endure and protect our citizens only if its custodians—the justices of the Supreme Court—continue to apply its eighteenth-century language to twentieth- and twenty-first-century issues in a creative and responsible manner.

The far-sighted framers of our Constitution would be disappointed by the narrow-minded constructions accorded the rights of gay citizens. All Americans are the poorer for the decision in *Bowers* v. *Hardwick*.

July 8, 1986

86
A New Government Blacklist

Last week I became one of many victims of a threatened government blacklist. It began innocently enough. All company-operated 7-Eleven convenience stores—more than 4,500 across the country—decided to stop selling future copies of *Playboy* and *Penthouse* magazines. The 7-Eleven chain accounts for a significant percentage of newsstand sales of these magazines.

The reason the chain gave is that the Attorney General's Commission on Pornography, the so-called Meese Commission, had elicited testimony suggesting "a possible connection between adult magazines and crime, violence and child abuse." This was a particularly lame excuse, since no scientifically valid evidence heard by the commission suggested any such link to mainstream adult magazines like *Playboy* and *Penthouse*.

One of my articles is scheduled for publication in the July issue of *Penthouse*; ironically, it's a criticism of the Meese Commission. I'll have fewer readers because of the 7-Eleven decision. Thousands of potential readers of *Penthouse* and *Playboy* will have to shop elsewhere, and some simply won't be able to find their favorite magazines in any store in their vicinity.

But how does that make us—writers and readers—victims of *government* blacklisting? The Reverend Jerry Falwell, whose organization has been boycotting and picketing the 7-Eleven stores, claims the credit for pressuring the chain into complying with his "morality." What, then, does the government have to do with this "private" dispute between a censorship group and a chain of convenience stores?

The answer requires a look at a letter sent by the executive director of the Meese Commission to 7-Eleven stores (and other chains that sell *Playboy* and *Penthouse*) just a few weeks before 7-Eleven made its decision to terminate the sale of these magazines.

The letter, which was written on official Justice Department stationery, carried an ominous warning. It advised these convenience stores that "the commission received testimony alleging that your company is involved in the sale or distribution of pornography." That's a fairly serious charge to direct at a respectable chain of stores, especially when it arrived on the stationery of the prosecutorial arm of the federal government.

But the next sentence of the letter was even more frightening: it disclosed, for the first time, that the Meese Commission was intending to publish a report listing the names of "identified distributors" of pornography—including stores that sell *Penthouse* or *Playboy*.

Now, what self-respecting store would want to see its name published by the Justice Department on such a porn-distributors blacklist? Nor does the letter indicate that there's any way to avoid this fate—other than to stop selling the offending items.

And so, not surprisingly, 7-Eleven capitulated to the government threat of blacklisting and decided to stop selling *Penthouse* and *Playboy*.

This has led to government-stimulated censorship of constitutionally protected speech. Appellate courts that have considered the issue have concluded that *Playboy* and *Penthouse* aren't obscene under the Supreme Court's current test. Even Falwell conceded as much in a recent television appearance. Accordingly, the government is constitutionally prohibited from interfering in any manner with the sale of these magazines to adults who want to read them.

But the threatened Meese Commission blacklist most certainly *does* constitute interference. It sends a chilling message to all stores that sell these magazines: stop selling them or risk being included on the attorney general's list.

When government agencies like the Meese Commission lend their support to "private" censorship efforts—such as those carried out by Falwell and his allies—these efforts no longer remain private. The heavy thumb of government is placed firmly on the censorship side of the scale. The threatened Meese Commission blacklist has become an indispensible tool of the Falwell boycott.

All of this is uncomfortably reminiscent of the bad old days of McCarthyism and the Hollywood-and-TV blacklists. In those days, the actual decisions to fire artists were made by private movie studios and TV stations. But the heavy thumb of government—the Senate's McCarthy Committee and its House counterpart—was palpable. Most thinking Americans now condemn the McCarthyite blacklists. The threatened Meese Commission blacklist is at least as dangerous.

If this deadly combination of private economic pressure and public blacklisting works, there will be few limits on zealots' ability to censor controversial literature. Falwell's hit list won't end with *Playboy* and *Penthouse*. Today it includes fashion magazines, movies, home videos, and books. Tomorrow it may cover literature advocating abortion, birth control, alternative lifestyles, and anything else that doesn't promote "traditional family values" as Falwell defines them.

As long as the Falwells of this country operate without government support, the matter remains a private one to be debated in the marketplace of ideas. But when the U.S. government comes to the assistance of censorship groups—as it has done with the Meese Commission blacklist—the issue becomes one of government censorship that must be resisted by all freedom-loving people, regardless of their personal feelings about *Playboy* and *Penthouse* magazines.

April 15, 1986

87
Porn, Whatever It Is, Shows No Link to Rape

The attorney general's Commission on Pornography is apparently about to misinform the American public about the "relationship" between what it calls "pornography" and violence. In its preliminary report it has concluded that most pornography—whatever that means—"bears some relationship to the level of sexual violence, sexual coercion or unwanted sexual aggression."

The commission cites no valid scientific support for what it calls its "tentative" evidence, but there is nothing tentative about its call for increased censorship of sexual material. Rarely has so dangerous a conclusion been based on such flimsy evidence.

In the first place, no one knows what "pornography" means. Even the late Supreme Court Justice Potter Stewart—who, along with his judicial colleagues, probably look at as much alleged pornography as any porno dealer—threw up his hands and admitted that he couldn't define pornography, but claimed to know it when he saw it.

Well, I used to think that I knew it when I saw it. However, recent muscle-flexings by the censorial coalition of religious fundamentalists and radical feminists have given new and broadened meaning to this old concept. Now "pornography" includes books that are degrading to women, phonograph records containing sexually suggestive lyrics, television programs and movies that undercut traditional family values, and mainstream magazines like *Playboy, Penthouse, Cosmopolitan*, and *Rolling Stone*.

Even if the commission were to limit its claims to "hard-core pornography"—explicit sexual depiction—the evidence points convincingly against any provable relationship to violence. Countries that tolerate the highest levels of hard-core pornography—the Scandinavian and Northern European countries—have far lower levels of sexual violence than many countries that censor such material. Censorship seems to provide a more fertile breeding ground for sexual violence than does freedom. Countries like Saudi Arabia, the Soviet Union, and Iran—which censor all sexually explicit material (and almost everything else)—have among the highest rates of rape and sexism in the world.

The commission simply has no scientific basis for its confident conclusion that "substantial exposure to materials of this type bear some causal relationship to the level of sexual violence." If such exposure really did cause sexual violence, I would worry about the commissioners and their staff, since they've spent much of the last year looking at dirty movies, books, and magazines. Perhaps they should be quarantined until the pernicious effects of their exposure have worn off.

On a more serious note, the commission's conclusion will inevitably lead to a new "Twinkie"-type defense. The killer of San Francisco Mayor George Moscone and city official Harvey Milk argued, with some success, that his crimes were caused by eating too many Twinkies. Now brutal rapists are sure to claim that it wasn't their fault: "The devil—porn—made me do it!"

The relationship between what we read, see, and hear and what we do is complex. Even the social scientists whose research is relied on by the porn commission dispute its simple-minded conclusions. "These conclusions seem bizarre to me," one of the leading researchers said. "It's the violence more than the sex, and negative messages about human relationships, that are the problem. And these messages are everywhere." Another expert on rape found 11 factors that were correlated with rape, but concluded that none of these factors—including pornography—"can be taken to be a cause of rape."

The commission acknowledges that it cannot rest its case on the scientific evidence. Its executive director, Allen Sears, who is widely regarded as a close ally of the religious right, has pronounced that "science does not give the complete answer."

But if science does not prove an empirical relationship between pornography and violence, what does? Herein lies the most dangerous aspect of the commissioners' approach. They seem prepared to substitute religious, moralistic, and polemical beliefs for science. They are attempting to smuggle their own values into what purports to be a factual inquiry into cause and effect. Several commissioners are onto their colleagues and may file dissenting reports, but the majority are still determined to issue an empirical edict that the world is indeed flat and that pornography is the cause of many of its evils.

Ideas may be dangerous, whether they are contained in gun magazines, Marxist literature, religious or atheist tracts, the Declaration of Independence, feminist writings or racial bigotry. But our Constitution prohibits government from protecting us from ideas, no matter how pernicious or offensive they may be. We must wait until ideas ripen into action. Such waiting may involve costs. Some crimes that might have been prevented by censoring ideas may be committed. However, all freedom involves costs. And the costs of allowing citizens to choose what they want to read or view are worth it. If you don't believe me, ask any citizen who lives under a regime of censorship. If the pornography commission's pseudo-science is taken to its illogical extreme, we may soon be able to ask ourselves about the evils of censorship.

May 23, 1986

88
Press Is Punished for Doing Its Job

The editor of a major U.S. newspaper, and the newspaper itself—the *Providence Journal*—were recently convicted of the crime of publishing an article they had a constitutional right to publish. The editor was given an eighteen-month suspended sentence and ordered to perform 200 hours of community service. The newspaper was fined $100,000.

How can anyone be criminally punished for printing something that he was constitutionally entitled to publish? The answer requires a brief description of the bizarre story behind this case, a story that goes back a generation and evokes images of *The Godfather*.

In the late 1960s, the FBI installed an electronic "bug" in the office of the alleged Godfather of the New England Mafia, Raymond Patriarca, Sr. The FBI overheard some juicy conversations about the "family business" between the senior Patriarca and his son Raymond Jr. The only problem was that the installation of the bug was illegal. Accordingly, the evidence gathered by the FBI couldn't be used against the Patriarcas in a criminal prosecution, since the "exclusionary rule" prohibits the government from introducing evidence against a defendant that was obtained in violation of his rights.

For several years, the secret tapes lay dormant in the FBI archives. Then, in 1985, following the senior Patriarca's death, the *Providence Journal* invoked the Freedom of Information Act to obtain copies of some of these tapes. Because of their obvious public interest, the newspaper wanted to publish excerpts in an article about organized crime.

Patriarca Jr. brought a lawsuit designed to stop the newspaper from printing the excerpts. In a remarkable decision, the federal judge, Francis J. Boyle, enjoined the *Providence Journal* from publishing the material. The judge reasoned that since the "exclusionary rule" forbids the *government* from *using* illegally obtained evidence against a defendant, it follows that *a private newspaper* can be enjoined from *publishing* such material.

The trouble with the judge's decision is that the exclusionary rule simply doesn't apply to private citizens—especially newspapers, which may not be enjoined from publishing news stories, regardless of the source. Boyle was flat-out wrong, as he was later big enough to admit.

But, meanwhile, the newspaper faced a dilemma. It could seek to over-rule the judge's erroneous decision on appeal—but if it did that, it would delay publication of what it regarded as a hot story. Or it could violate the judge's order on the grounds that it was confident of the order's unconstitutionality.

The *Providence Journal* chose the latter course: it simply ignored the court's order and went ahead and published the excerpts. Boyle, after acknowledging that he was wrong to issue his injunction, nevertheless held the newspaper in contempt and imposed the sentences. The *Providence Journal*, he said, had chosen to defy the court's order and "boldly communicate that defiance to hundreds of thousands of residents of this area." In other words, the newspaper had compounded its contempt by exercising its First Amendment right to "communicate" its position to the public.

All this must be quite baffling to nonlawyers. If the judge's original order was wrong, why should the newspaper have to follow it?

In most situations, a defendant will win if the order he violated was unconstitutional. Thus, if the legislature had enacted a statute forbidding newspapers from publishing certain material, the *Providence Journal* would have been free to take its chances and publish. If they were then prosecuted for such publication, they would be acquitted if the statute they violated was held unconstitutional.

But the *courts* have created an exception for disobeying orders of—you guessed it!—*the courts*. Even if a court order is unconstitutional, it must be obeyed. Refusal to obey it will be punished. The crime isn't the act of publishing the material: it's the act of defying the order of the court. The intended message is clear and reminiscent of the answer parents often give their children: "Because I'm your mother, that's why!"

However, what makes the orders of a court more sacrosanct than those of a legislator or a president? Part of the answer lies in the symbolism of the judiciary: judges consider themselves a secular priesthood. Their robes, the manner in which they are addressed ("May it please Your Honor"), their elevated benches—all convey a certain sanctity and absoluteness.

In reading about Boyle's somewhat paradoxical conclusion that the *Providence Journal* would be punished for disobeying his unconstitutional order, I was reminded of a wonderful cartoon that appeared in *The New Yorker* shortly after the Vatican eliminated a venerable dietary prohibition. The devil is asking his assistant: "Now what do we do with all the sinners who are here for having eaten meat on Friday?"

It may be proper for a church to damn sinners for defying its sacred authority, or for parents to discipline children for disobedience. But courts are neither churches nor parents, and citizens should be obliged to comply only with judges' lawful orders. The dignity of the First Amendment is at least as important as the authority of the courts.

April 22, 1986

UPDATE
This case is now before the Supreme Court.

89
Testing the Police for Drugs

Here's another answer to the old question: if a conservative is a liberal who's been mugged, then what's a liberal? The new answer: a liberal is a policeman who is being required to undergo random drug testing!

As more and more police departments are announcing new regulations regarding drug tests for officers, more and more policemen are becoming born-again believers in the Bill of Rights. For years, many police officers were among the most vocal deprecators of the Fourth Amendment's right to be free from unreasonable searches. "If the guy's got nothing to hide"—I've heard many cops argue—"then why does he have to hide behind the Constitution?" If the policeman isn't using drugs—some police chiefs are now asking—then why is he afraid to take the test?

Part of the answer to both questions is that occasionally the truly innocent are falsely incriminated by random searches or tests. The occasional rotten cop has been known to plant evidence or lie about what he saw. And the drug tests do sometimes turn up "false positives"—indications of illegal drug use when the person being tested took an over-the-counter medication. (Indeed an expert recently testified that people with dark skin pigmentation—blacks and Hispanics—may falsely test positive for marijuana in urine tests, which are highly sensitive to melanin, a substance with a chemical breakdown similar to marijuana that is more prevalent in dark-skinned people.)

But even more fundamental than the issue of accuracy is the issue of privacy. Neither the government nor management has any business randomly poking around into our pockets, our lockers, our bodily fluids, or our heads. The framers of our Constitution understood what a police-state felt like, even before the advent of urine tests, polygraphs, and wiretaps. They had endured the clumsy intrusiveness of the British colonial authorities: the general warrants, the writs of assistance, the random searches. As a group of Bostonians complained in 1772: "Our houses and even our bed chambers are exposed to be ransacked . . . by agents of the Crown."

The Bill of Rights was designed to prevent such abuses from reoccurring after the establishment of the new republic. But reoccur they have, under different and more sophisticated guises. As the director of Georgia Civil Liberties Union graphically asked: "Can you imagine the Founding Fathers saying that [employers] can make you drop your pants and urinate as a condition of getting or keeping a job?"

We often forget that in order to protect the rights of all Americans, the Fourth Amendment must be available to the innocent and guilty alike, to the cops as well as the robbers. As Justice William Brennan once put it: "Like most of the Bill of Rights, [the Fourth Amendment] was not designed as a shelter for criminals, but a basic protection for everyone; to be sure, it must be upheld when asserted by criminals, but it reaches us all alike. . . ."

Police officers are protected by the Bill of Rights, but in the past, their protections have been significantly curtailed by the public responsibilities they bear. Justice Oliver Wendell Holmes once quipped: "The petitioner may have a constitutional right to talk politics, but he has no constitutional right to be a policeman."

This attitude reflects the reality that the police are different: they are licensed to kill, maim, search, seize, and enforce order. A drugged-out janitor can only do so much damage with his broom. But a policeman high on cocaine may improperly fire a fatal bullet—or improperly fail to fire one. This increased public responsibility does not mean that police should have fewer rights than the rest of us, but only that their rights must depend on the realities of their job.

Before a police officer is subject to drug testing—or any other intrusive measure—there should have to be reasonable cause to suspect a violation of valid departmental rules. But reasonableness should vary with the type and degree of danger posed by the suspicion. Thus, a policeman with a gun— like an airplane pilot, a surgeon, or a government official empowered to make irreversible life and death decisions—should be subject to drug testing on the basis of a lower level of suspicion than an accountant, a salesperson, or even an athlete. (A policeman should not, on the other hand, be subject to political tests, loyalty oaths, or general lie detector intrusions which do not bear on his ability to handle deadly weapons.) The important point is that everyone has a right of privacy—though its content and level must depend on balancing the risks against the intrusions.

It warms my heart to see police officers quoting the Bill of Rights instead of Clint Eastwood. Perhaps some of them have now learned the lesson that whenever the rights of anyone—even accused criminals—are compromised, all of our rights are diminished.

Drug testing of police raises serious issues of civil liberties. These are issues around which rank-and-file police officers and card-carrying members of the American Civil Liberties Union can join forces. It will be interesting to see how well they get along together when the ACLU goes to court on behalf of the civil liberties of cops.

May 6, 1986

90
The Rise of the "Hanging Jury"

As the result of a recent Supreme Court decision, it will now be easier for prosecutors to convict innocent defendants in capital cases than in noncapital cases.

That is the inevitable consequence of Justice William Rehnquist's majority decision in *Lockhart* v. *McCree*. The issue in that case was whether potential jurors who strongly oppose capital punishment could be disqualified from deciding whether a defendant facing the death penalty was guilty or innocent of murder.

The background of this problem begins with a 1968 case in which the Supreme Court considered whether prospective jurors who opposed capital punishment could be disqualified from serving on juries in capital cases. The court decided that only those jurors whose opposition was so strong that they could not impose the death penalty under any circumstances could be excluded. But it left open the question of whether such jurors could be disqualified from deciding the guilt or innocence of capital defendants, as well as the penalty itself.

This problem arises in those states where one single jury decides both the guilt and the sentence in capital cases. In such states, any juror who is disqualified from ruling on the penalty is also automatically disqualified from ruling on guilt.

And therein lies the real dilemma. Every experienced trial lawyer knows that jurors who favor the death penalty are more likely to vote for conviction in close cases. This bit of commonsense/folk wisdom has been confirmed by studies that demonstrate that excluding jurors who could not impose the death penalty increases the likelihood of getting "conviction-prone" juries.

A recent editorial cartoon may have exaggerated this prospect, but it surely made the point. It pictured a jury shorn of all who oppose capital punishment as including a man sitting ready to pull the switch on an electric chair, a woman knitting a noose, and a couple of hooded executioners.

The reality is that people who are willing to impose the death penalty often don't believe as strongly in the presumption of innocence or the Bill of Rights as those who oppose the death penalty. Justice Thurgood Marshall pointed out in his dissenting opinion that opponents of the death penalty include a disproportionately large number of blacks and women. They also include more liberals, civil libertarians, and people distrustful of prosecutors.

It would be wrong, of course, for the entire jury to consist of that portion of the population that opposes the death penalty. But it is also wrong for it to consist entirely of those who favor it. Juries should reflect a cross-section of the community on this important issue.

Actually, there are three categories of death penalty opponents relevant to jury selection. There are those whose opposition to the death penalty: 1) would not preclude them from imposing it; 2) would preclude them from imposing it; or 3) would even preclude them from convicting a guilty murderer.

The recent Supreme Court case does not involve the first or third categories. Everyone seems to agree that moderates who are capable of imposing the death penalty should be allowed to serve as jurors, and that extremists who would acquit the guilty—"nullifiers"—should not be allowed to serve. The controversy is over the middle group: those who would not sentence a convicted murderer to death, but who would fairly decide whether the defendant was guilty or innocent.

In deciding that jurors who strongly oppose the death penalty could be excluded from the guilt phase of the trial, Justice Rehnquist was willing to assume that excluding this middle category of death penalty opponents will, in fact, produce juries that are "somewhat more conviction-prone" than juries that include a cross-section of Americans. He concluded "nonetheless" that the Constitution permits this kind of deck-stacking in favor of conviction.

His argument bears full quotation: "It is hard for us to understand the logic of the argument that a given jury is unconstitutionally partial when it results from a state-ordained process, yet impartial when exactly the same jury results from mere chance." Rehnquist seems to be saying that because chance could possibly produce a jury that favors the death penalty, it is illogical to fault a state rule that guarantees such a result. This is like saying that because chance could give your poker opponent a royal flush, you should not condemn him for producing the same winning hand by stacking the deck. Or to bring the analogy closer to the case at hand, it would make no difference—according to this twisted Rehnquistian logic—for a jury to turn out all white by chance or by "state-ordained process."

This ruling in favor of conviction-prone juries in capital cases raises at least two dangers: first, that more murder defendants will now be found guilty in close cases, because the juries will be stacked in favor of conviction; and second, that prosecutors will now seek the death penalty in more cases in order to secure a tactical advantage in obtaining guilty verdicts. The upshot will be not only more guilty defendants on death row, but more innocent ones as well.

May 13, 1986

91
Flying Past the Fourth Amendment

What would James Madison and Thomas Jefferson have thought if British redcoats had been able to peer around the walls of a private estate, without a warrant, to observe a private gathering of American patriots preparing to dump tea into Boston Harbor?

You can be sure that our Constitution's Founding Fathers would have been appalled at this breach of privacy. A person's home—whether it be a walled estate, a plantation, or a small cottage—was regarded as his castle, free from the intruding eye of government, without a warrant based on probable cause.

Now, 200 years after the adoption of our Constitution, the police have learned to use more sophisticated ways of peering around, over, and even through walls.

A recent Supreme Court decision involving a California man highlights the dangers of modern invasions of privacy. The local police reviewed an anonymous tip that a local homeowner was growing a few marijuana plants in his backyard. The police took a stroll to his house, but a tall fence obstructed their view.

Undaunted, the police chartered a small airplane and buzzed the backyard, flying low enough to get a good view of the yard. They saw—and photographed—a small swimming pool, a patio, and several marijuana plants. An arrest, felony trial, and conviction followed.

The California Court of Appeals reversed the conviction on the grounds that the homeowner's privacy was violated when the police flew over and photographed his fenced-in backyard without a warrant. The court reasoned that the existence of the high fence meant that the homeowner reasonably expected privacy from the intruding eye of the police.

The U.S. Supreme Court—which, in the past decade, has become a court of last resort for government, rather than for private citizens—reinstated the conviction. In doing so, it acknowledged that the homeowner did have "his own subjective intent and desire to maintain privacy as to his unlawful agricultural pursuits." But it concluded that even a ten-foot fence isn't high enough to keep out all intruding eyes. "Yet a ten-foot fence might not shield these plants from the eyes of a citizen or a policeman perched on the top of a tree or a two-level truck."

Or, one might add, what about a seven-foot-four basketball player—like Ralph Sampson—walking down the street practicing his rebounding technique? Or a kid on a pogo stick? Or a pigeon equipped with a miniaturized TV camera? Or a . . . well, you can fill in the endless list of imaginative variations.

The Supreme Court seems to be trying to show that if there's any possible way to thwart a subjective expectation of privacy, then the law will not recognize it as "objective" and therefore deserving of protection under the Fourth Amendment. Even a 100-foot concrete wall wouldn't have been enough, since—in the words of the court—the backyard could have been seen and photographed by "a passing aircraft, or by a power-company repair mechanic on a pole overlooking the yard." Or a partridge in a pear tree?

The court's decision isn't limited to marijuana growers. It authorized the police to fly over and photograph *anyone's* backyard without any cause whatever. They can photograph a homeowner skinny-dipping in the privacy of his enclosed pool, a group of people meeting secretly to discuss politics, a husband and wife making love in the bushes, or a group of Moonies gathering for a religious service.

The court ruled that it made absolutely no difference that the specific purpose of the police overflight was to photograph the suspected marijuana in the backyard and that the plane flew very low for this purpose. "We find difficulty understanding exactly how [the homeowner's] expectations of privacy from aerial observation might differ," said the court, "when two airplanes pass overhead at identical altitudes, simply for different purposes."

But what the justices have "difficulty understanding" is well understood by most Americans. There is an enormous difference between a "peeping Tom" and a person who inadvertently passes by a partially open windowshade. That difference is compounded when the deliberate intrusion into the privacy of one's home is committed systematically by the government rather than by a private citizen.

The four dissenting justices understood these differences. As Justice Lewis Powell put it: "Travelers on commercial flights, as well as private planes used for business or personal reasons, normally obtain, at most, a fleeting anonymous and nondiscriminating glimpse of the landscape and buildings over which they pass. The risk that a passenger on such a plane might observe private activities, and might connect those activities with particular people, is simply too trivial to protect against. It is no accident that, as a matter of common experience, many people build fences around their residential areas, but few build roofs over their backyards."

Our Founding Fathers also understood these differences even if Chief Justice Warren Burger—who wrote the majority opinion—does not. The hypocrisy of the Burger-Rehnquist-Meese-Reagan approach to constitutional construction is evident when they fail to mention the framers of our

Constitution if the framers' "original understanding" would not support the result in a particular case. They invoke the framers' intent when it supports a narrow reading of the Bill of Rights, but ignore it when it might support a broader reading.

May 27, 1986

92
The New High Court: Our Best Nineteenth-Century Minds

The resignation of Chief Justice Warren Burger and the promotions of Associate Justice William Rehnquist and Circuit Judge Antonin Scalia probably will have little short-term effect on the outcome of votes in most of the controversial issues now dividing the Supreme Court, but they will strengthen the right wing of the court in the long run.

Chief Justice Burger was a political and judicial conservative who occasionally compromised his views in the interests of harmony or future leverage. The newly designated chief justice, William Rehnquist, is a doctrinaire conservative who almost never compromises. During his fifteen years on the Supreme Court, he has rarely been outflanked on the right. But if there is any sitting federal judge who is capable of making Rehnquist appear more moderate, it is Antonin Scalia, who currently serves on the U.S. Court of Appeals for the District of Columbia Circuit.

The net result of the three-way switch will be for the conservative wing of the court as a whole to move toward a somewhat more doctrinaire position. The leadership of the court, both ceremonial and intellectual, will also become more ideological. Both Rehnquist and Scalia are intellectuals and scholars on a court dominated by practitioners. Their relative youth— Scalia is fifty and Rehnquist is sixty-one—and vigor will assure them disproportionate influence, both in the short and long runs. But the bottom-line numbers on most important votes will come out about the same, since one conservative has replaced another.

It is not as if Justice William Brennan or Justice Thurgood Marshall were leaving, which could have altered the current ideological balance of the court. That may, of course, happen in the not-too-distant future, but it has not happened yet.

Perhaps the least tangible, but most immediate, effect of the current change in personnel will come not from the elevations of Rehnquist and Scalia, but rather from the retirement of Burger. Chief Justice Burger has not served his own cause very well. He has been a divisive chief justice within the court, and not highly respected outside it for the quality of his legal work. His major contributions have been ceremonial and administrative, rather than substantive. His conservative opinions have been an easy target for liberal critics. Some civil libertarians have dreaded the day when he would leave and be replaced by a "better" conservative. That day has come.

One of the enduring legal legends of our age is that no president can really pick a justice to fit an ideology. Chief Justice–designate Rehnquist has himself perpetuated this view in a speech he made during the last presidential campaign. He argued that "there is no reason in the world" why a president should not try to "pack" the court with justices who agree with him, but cautioned that presidents don't always guess right. People change when elevated to the Supreme Court or to chief justice. Earl Warren, Felix Frankfurter, and Oliver Wendell Holmes all turned out quite different than expected by the presidents who appointed them.

But legends can be misleading when they are believed too literally. President Reagan has learned from the "mistakes" of his predecessors and is taking no chances with his appointments. Both Rehnquist and Scalia come with full warranties based on long track records. Neither will surprise President Reagan. They can be counted on to vote the president's way on most important issues.

Nor is the Senate likely to pose any barrier. Although some senators seem dissatisfied with the president's choices on ideological grounds, the excellent legal backgrounds of the nominees will make them difficult to oppose. Both have among the sharpest nineteenth-century legal minds in America. They will bring a new intellectual legitimacy to judicial conservatism. But they will make our rights—to expression, privacy, due process, and equality—a bit less secure.

Popular majoritarian views will go unchallenged more frequently, and there will be less sensitivity to the views of the politically disenfranchised and economically unempowered. This may translate into restrictions on abortions, affirmative action, voting rights, and safeguards for those accused of crimes, and into expansion of censorship, libel actions, and presidential power. It will also affect the tone and rhetoric of the justices, and may have a "trickle-down" effect on the lower federal, and even state, courts.

The battle for control of the Supreme Court into the next century is just beginning. Its outcome may well depend on timing. If the next vacancies—especially if they are left by liberals or moderates—occur while both the presidency and the Senate are under Republican control, we may well see a major change in our system of checks and balances. But if the Democrats gain control of the Senate or the presidency before the next vacancies, the changes are likely to be less dramatic.

As we approach the two hundredth anniversary of our Constitution, we may be about to experience some cataclysmic confrontations about the very meaning of that venerable—and vulnerable—document.

June 18, 1986

93
The Senate Should Not Rubber-Stamp Judges

With the recent nominations of a new chief justice, associate justice, and a particularly controversial circuit court judge, the question has once again been raised: what is the proper role of the U.S. Senate in approving judicial nominations made by the president?

The starting point must be the Constitution itself. Article II, Section 2 says that the president "shall nominate, and by and with the advice and consent of the Senate, shall appoint . . . judges of the Supreme Court." The Constitution goes on to give Congress the power to allocate to the president the power to appoint certain "inferior officers." But the power to appoint justices and judges is expressly divided between the president and the Senate.

Constitutional scholars have long debated the meaning of the Constitution's elliptical words. Professor Charles Black of Yale has argued that: "There is just no reason at all for a senator's not voting, in regard to confirmation of a Supreme Court nominee, on the basis of a full and unrestricted view, not embarrassed by any presumption, of the nominee's fitness for the office."

The history behind the adoption of Article II, Section 2, provides some support for this position. The original proposal was for the Senate alone to appoint justices. This idea received considerable endorsement at the Constitutional Convention, but the framers ultimately reached a compromise in which they unanimously decided to divide the appointing function.

The Federalist Papers proclaim the importance of the Senate's role, saying it should ensure that the president does not nominate justices and judges who are "in some way or other personally allied to him" or who show a kind of "pliancy" that might "render them the obsequious instruments of his pleasure."

And herein lies the enormous difference between the Senate's role in confirming *judicial* appointments and *Cabinet* appointments: Cabinet members are *supposed* to be the president's "obsequious instruments." They may be fired at his whim. They are his Cabinet, his aides, his party loyalists. Their job is to implement his political program, not to serve as a check and balance against him.

The courts—especially the Supreme Court—are supposed to be independent of the president. The justices and judges should not be the president's men and women. They should work neither for him nor with him. Presidents don't meet or speak privately with justices or judges. They don't have to get along with each other. The judiciary is the most important check and balance on presidential power. No president may fire a judge. Members of the judiciary are appointed for life.

In light of these constitutional and institutional considerations, it would be an abdication of responsibility for the Senate simply to rubber-stamp presidential nominations to the judiciary. Before making his recent nominations to the Supreme Court, President Reagan did not seek the "advice" of the Senate. He is merely seeking their after-the-fact "consent." It should be given only if it serves the national interest.

No one disputes the appropriateness of the Senate's refusing to consent to the nomination of an incompetent judicial appointment. Many senators regard Daniel Manion—nominated to become a federal appeals court judge—as incompetent to serve in that high judicial office, and they have voted against his appointment.

But virtually everybody acknowledges the competence of President Reagan's recent Supreme Court nominees. The question, as it relates to William Rehnquist and Antonin Scalia, is whether their elevation will strengthen or weaken our system of checks and balances. The primary role of the Supreme Court, under our Constitution, is to represent the disenfranchised, the unempowered, and those who have the least access to the popularly elected branches of government. The Supreme Court has experienced its finest hours when it has stood up to presidents and legislatures and has enforced unpopular mandates of the Constitution: desegregation in the South, reapportionment in rural areas, freedom of speech for the despised, basic rights for aliens, and due process for criminal defendants.

The Supreme Court is not supposed to win popularity contests; nor are its opinions supposed to get it high ratings in public opinion polls. Its job is to be a court of last resort for the citizens who can't afford to hire a lobbyist or make a fat political contribution, not a court of last resort for big government, big business, and big constituencies.

President Reagan's nominations to the Supreme Court are certainly popular. Why not? He is popular, and he has selected justices who promise to be "obsequious instruments of his pleasure." But the Federalist Papers—the bible of those who profess belief in interpreting the Constitution according to its original understanding—encouraged the Senate to serve as a "check upon the spirit of favoritism in the president" so as to prevent him from offering nominations "from a view to popularity."

President Reagan has performed his part of the constitutional process for appointing justices and judges. Now the Senate must perform its equally important role. Any senator who conscientiously believes that the national interest would be disserved by any of these appointments has a duty to vote against it.

July 1, 1986

For further discussion of the Supreme Court selection process, see columns 122–128.

94
Cigarette Pushers Have Rights, Too

Cigarettes kill, maim, and sicken. Anyone who doubts that truth should have his (and increasingly, her) head (and probably lungs) examined. There really is no longer any room for rational debate about the dangers of smoking, both to those who inhale and to those upon whom they exhale.

Yet, under our First Amendment, the cigarette industry has the right to argue its immoral position disputing the surgeon general and virtually every reputable scientist in the world. The cigarette pusher's argument falls in the category of quackery that includes astrology, alchemy, "the world is flat," and "you can get pregnant from kissing."

But our First Amendment prohibits both the establishment of any religion and the establishment of any official truth. Every citizen—whether a soapbox orator or a conglomerate owner—has the right to try to sell his ideas in the marketplace. "Eternal verities" have been proved wrong since the beginning of recorded history. Dissidents have been excommunicated—even killed—for arguing "absurdities"—for example, that the earth is round, that human beings evolved from apes, and that all persons are created equal.

As Woody Allen once quipped: "Everything our parents said was good for us has turned out to be bad for us: red meat, sunshine, milk, college!" The point is, we can never be sure enough to give the government the power to suppress deviant ideas, no matter how absurd they may sound to us now.

There is a movement currently afoot to ban cigarette smoking or to limit it to nonpublic places. The argument in favor of protecting nonsmokers from involuntarily ingesting the hazardous fumes of aggressive smokers is powerful. The old argument that your right to swing your fist ends at the tip of my nose also limits your right to puff your poison into my lungs. Extending that argument to purely private puffing raises troubling questions of paternalism when applied to adults (at least those who are not pregnant).*

An even further extension would be a prohibition on all cigarette advertising and even advocacy. Recently, an administrative law judge ruled that R. J. Reynolds—a company probably responsible for more deaths than Murder Incorporated—had an absolute right to publish an opinion article disputing the accepted wisdom that cigarettes kill.

The article was apparently deceptive and misleading in implying that the National Institutes of Health had questioned the link between cigarettes and certain diseases. The Federal Trade Commission claimed that it had the authority to review the article for false advertising.

The court rejected the FTC's jurisdiction over opinion articles of the kind published by R. J. Reynolds. It drew a distinction between advertising a specific product—"Smoke Winston"—and advocating a general point of view—"Cigarettes don't kill." The advertisement of a product is subject to review by the FTC. But the advocacy of a point of view—even the paid advocacy of a profitable point of view—is not subject to any government control.

The Supreme Court recently ruled that a state may ban all advertising of a product or activity when it has the power to ban the product or activity itself. In that case, Puerto Rico had banned local advertising of gambling casinos. (It apparently wanted tourists, but not locals, to lose their money.) It follows from this decision that a state could ban all advertising of liquor, since the Twenty-First Amendment expressly gives the states the power to ban liquor.

It is not clear whether a state could ban all cigarette smoking. But the Supreme Court's recent decision allowing Georgia to criminalize private homosexual conduct certainly suggests that it might uphold a ban on cigarettes.

But even if cigarettes could be banned, the tobacco industry would—and should—be allowed to fight against the ban by paid advocacy. Just as gay activists are entitled to advocate repeal of sodomy statutes, and marijuana activists are entitled to argue the virtues of grass, so too the cigarette industry must be permitted to promote its ideas, even if it is not permitted to push its pernicious product.

The line between advertising a product and advocating an idea is not always clear. The cigarette industry has mastered the art of sending the subliminal message to the susceptible consumer. If it gets the macho Marlboro man or the successful Virginia Slims woman to deliver its political message that nicotine is good for you, it may succeed in circumventing any ban on product advertisement. But that is the reality of contemporary communication. Even political candidates and office holders know how to use subtle symbols to get the voters to buy their product.

The answer to this kind of disinformation is true information. Both government and private sources must continue their campaign to educate the public—especially children and pregnant women—of the lethal dangers of smoking.

In the end, the cigarette industry's right to free speech may well cost lives. The First Amendment requires us all to tolerate views we find offensive as the price of being able to present views we deem essential. It's a good deal. Let's keep the marketplace of ideas open, even to bad ideas that may be harmful if accepted.

August 19, 1986

UPDATE
See column 96. Several months after I wrote this column, I wrote another which included the following:

Some well-known liberals, who ought to know better, are trying to have their constitutional cake and eat it, too. Out of one side of their mouths, they are demanding that the media—particularly television—accept condom advertisements. Out of the other side, they are urging Congress to prohibit all advertising of cigarettes in every medium, including newspapers and magazines.

Like these liberals, I personally approve of the widespread use of condoms as one means to help prevent AIDS, as well as unwanted pregnancies. I also despise cigarettes and have long advocated a ban on puffing smoke at innocent bystanders in public places. But I believe that there is one poison even more dangerous to the body politic than self-inflicted cigarette smoke, and that is government-imposed censorship.

If the government is allowed to ban all advertising of cigarettes, a contagious precedent will have been established. If Congress has the power to determine that cigarette smoking is so dangerous that even advertising it— speaking about it for profit—can be banned, it will be difficult to argue against congressional power to add all sorts of new items to its censorship list. Some do-gooder liberals will propose bans on advertising guns, alcohol, coffee, and boxing matches. Right wingers will suggest a congressional advertising "index" that might include such offending items as condoms, feminine hygiene products, sushi, and quiche. The censorship war would be on, and the American public would lose, because its right to choose from the marketplace of ideas—even commercial ideas—would be significantly curtailed.

95
Who Really Killed John Belushi?

The three-year prison sentence recently imposed on Cathy Smith for her role in John Belushi's drug overdose once again raises the complex question of who is responsible when one person supplies the drugs that cause another's death.

That issue seems to capture public attention primarily when famous people overdose. The tragic deaths of basketball player Len Bias and the late Robert Kennedy's son David generated demands for prosecution of the suppliers. The daily street deaths of dozens of faceless addicts rarely even provoke an investigation.

Cathy Smith's case was unusual in several respects. First, she seemed to bring it on herself. After Belushi's death in Hollywood on March 5, 1982, she was questioned by the police but released. It was only after she sold her story to the *National Enquirer* for $15,000 that she was prosecuted.

In that story, Smith told of her role in John Belushi's final fix, admitting that she had injected the comedian with heroin and cocaine at his request. Following three years of legal maneuvering, her excellent lawyer, Howard Weitzman, worked out the plea bargain that led to her sentence on charges of involuntary manslaughter and administering dangerous drugs.

In imposing the prison sentence, the judge said that Belushi, who had given Smith the money to buy the drugs, was "responsible for his own death." But he also ruled that the undisputed fact that Belushi had led a "drug-infested life" did not absolve Smith from some responsibility for supplying the fatal poison.

Members of John Belushi's family joined the prosecutors in urging a prison term. His widow's sister, Pamela Jacklin, said: "Because victims are willing does not mean you don't do something about it."

But who was the real "victim" and who the real perpetrator? If Cathy Smith—who knew Belushi for a week—was criminally responsible, what about the comedian's family and friends? What about the other suppliers and co-users—some celebrities themselves—who led Belushi down the inexorable road to his end? There is enough "responsibility" and "blame" for John Belushi's death—and those of the many other less famous druggies—to fill every seat in every courtroom in America.

Why, then, do we self-righteously use the pathetic Cathy Smiths of the world as scapegoats? Here is a woman—herself a helpless heroin addict—who was desperately seeking to introduce herself into the inner circle of celebrities in the only way she knew how: by getting drugs. The judge said: "You were brought into the action with Mr. Belushi's circle of friends because you were the connection, the source of the poison. . . . You knew how to use the needle."

Pamela Jacklin said that Cathy Smith's message to "the kids in our society" was: "If you want to be with celebrities, the way to do it is with drugs."

But was that Cathy Smith's message or John Belushi's? If a Cathy Smith does not come along, there will be some other drug gopher eager to satisfy the sick demands of the spoiled stars, pampered athletes, and selfish celebrities who use and abuse these sycophants.

There were a lot of fingers around the syringe that administered John

Belushi's final fix. Cathy Smith's were the easiest to spot because she foolishly—perhaps desperately—sold her story. She shouldn't be punished for telling that story, because it was a lot more honest than some of the others being told about the celebrity drug scene. But she was an easy target, and our legal system tends to focus on the most visible symptoms of pervasive diseases.

The search for the scapegoat—whether in the case of John Belushi, Len Bias, David Kennedy, or the faceless thousands of others—should not start and end with the naive friend who may have supplied the final fix. That will neither do justice to the dead, nor prevent future tragedies.

Cathy Smith was guilty of committing a crime like those committed every day by those who serve alcohol to teenage drivers, offer cigarettes to pregnant women, or sell Saturday night specials to obvious thugs. Such "facilitators" do bear a certain responsibility for how the customers abuse their products. But the primary responsibility lies squarely with the abusers themselves.

Defense attorney Howard Weitzman was almost certainly right when he opined that if John Belushi were standing in court on the day of sentencing, he might have said, "Wait a minute judge, I lived my life as I wanted to live it. Don't blame her." Or, at least, don't blame her alone. With those wonderfully expressive eyes, Belushi would have looked both inward and beyond the immediate source. Some of the accessories to John Belushi's death are still at large.

September 16, 1986

96
Should We Let Pregnant Women Smoke and Drink?

The medical evidence is now overwhelming that pregnant women who smoke too much, drink too much, or abuse drugs endanger the health of their babies. (So, by the way, do men who smoke in the presence of pregnant women.) No responsible person would want to bring a child into our already hazardous world with an extra preventable strike against him or her. Yet, many pregnant women and the men who live with them continue to indulge in practices that are not only self-destructive, but also baby-destructive.

A friend of mine just quit her job as a doctor in the obstetrics ward of an inner-city public hospital because she just couldn't bear another year of helping fourteen-year-old children (many who had themselves been born to fourteen-year-olds) give birth—prematurely—to drug-addicted or otherwise abnormal babies. She described the recurring scene of the pregnant child with fresh needle marks, or with a cigarette hanging from her lip, or with the smell of alcohol on her breath.

The boy-father—when he came along—was often the supplier of the sickening substance to his pregnant mate. My friend tried everything—from stern lectures to threats to warm, sisterly advice. But except for a few cases, nothing seemed to work. Baby after baby was born with handicaps that will be difficult, if not impossible, to overcome.

"Can't the law do anything to protect the babies?" my friend asked me.

Many people believe that you can just pass a law to solve nearly any problem. But the law is a blunderous instrument with little capacity to make refined distinctions. "What would you have the law do?" I responded rhetorically. "Would you want to make it a crime for a pregnant woman to smoke or drink alcohol?"

My friend, who is a committed feminist as well as a caring doctor, was torn. Her pro-choice position on abortion inclined her toward resisting any governmental intrusion into the decisions of a pregnant woman. "Keep your laws off our bodies" has become a rallying cry. Any compromise with that principle might lead down the slippery slope toward requiring all pregnant women to bear their children. After all—the argument would go—if you can legislate to prevent a pregnant woman from injuring her child, why can't you legislate to prevent her from killing it?

But the reality that my friend had confronted daily seemed equally persuasive. Here were pregnant women who had opted against abortion, who had decided to give birth. They all wanted healthy babies. They just needed help to keep them from hurting their own offspring through impulsive acts of self-gratification. And most of them were minors themselves. It was already illegal for them to be sold alcohol, cigarettes, and, certainly, drugs.

But what about adults who are pregnant? Should they be free to act irresponsibly toward the babies they have decided to bring into the world? Should Big Brother be empowered to watch over their every move?

There are many hard questions and few easy answers. The stakes on both sides are enormous; the implications of government-monitored pregnancies are frightening. But so are the implications of allowing a laissez-faire approach to the welfare of helpless babies.

In the end, the best approach probably lies somewhere between the extremes of enacting special criminal laws for pregnant women and allowing the present catastrophic situation to continue unabated. At the very least, more public education is necessary.

But that won't solve the problem. There will still be some pregnant women—children and adults—who are simply unwilling to look, or who are incapable of seeing, beyond their next drink, smoke, or fix. This leads to the most difficult question: should the law be given some limited power in extreme situations, where serious injury to the baby is a medical certainty?

In the end, both my feminist doctor friend and I remain adamantly pro-choice on the issue of abortion, and very torn on the desirability of some legislation designed to prevent abuses during pregnancy that virtually assure the birth of a handicapped baby.

The other day—as if to remind me that this was not exclusively a problem among inner-city kids—I was dining in a yuppie restaurant in Cambridge, Massachusetts. At the next table were a husband and wife. The wife was very pregnant. Both were chain-smoking, and they were on their second bottle of wine. I watched as she gulped down the Pouilly-Fuissé and lit her dozenth Virginia Slim. Finally, I turned and said: "You're blowing smoke on me and into your baby. Could you please stop?"

She did. He didn't. They both looked at me as if I were a meddling busybody. I felt like one.

I had done the right thing. But it wasn't enough. What else can be done on behalf of these helpless babies without unduly interfering in the lives of pregnant women?

September 16, 1986

97
Give Zakharov His Rights— Even If It's Not Fair

The deal between the United States and the Soviet Union, under which both Nicholas Daniloff and Gennadi Zakharov have been freed from prison—at least for now—raises some intriguing and ironic legal questions that have not been explored by the press.

The starting point of any rational discussion is, of course, that Americans who live in Moscow are subject to Soviet law and Russians who live in New York are subject to American law, and that the domestic laws of our two countries are radically different. In general, the American approach is that anything not specifically forbidden by statute is permitted. The Soviet approach, on the other hand, is that anything not specifically permitted is forbidden. We operate under a presumption of freedom, while they live under a presumption of regulation.

As it applies here, American law generally permits the gathering of information that the government would prefer to keep confidential, while Soviet law prohibits such collecting. American law generally frowns on "entrapment," while Soviet law encourages the tempting of people into criminality. American law insists on a presumption of innocence and generally favors pretrial release of arrested suspects, while Soviet law presumes the defendant guilty and demands his imprisonment pending trial.

Daniloff, an American citizen accustomed to the presumption of freedom, is now subject to the Soviet presumption of regulation. Zakharov, a Soviet citizen accustomed to regulation, is now entitled to many of the freedoms guaranteed by the U.S. Constitution.

It seems clear to me that Daniloff was almost certainly set up by the KGB, that he is not a spy for the U.S. government, and that he was arrested in retaliation for our arrest of Zakharov. But under Soviet law, that does not necessarily mean that Daniloff is completely innocent and not subject to detention, investigation, and trial. The Soviet law on spying includes collection of information for purposes of transfer to "a foreign organization" or for "use to the detriment of the interests of the USSR."

Any innovative and probing reporter may well run afoul of this outrageously broad—and, under American principles, unconstitutionally restrictive—language of the Soviet law, even if he has no malevolent intention beyond gathering information for a good story.

If Daniloff's actions were even arguably illegal under Soviet law, then the KGB is legally entitled to imprison him without a lawyer for nine months. This may sound incomprehensible to most Americans, but it is business as usual in the Soviet Union—at least for its own citizens. Under recognized principles of international law, every country is entitled to treat citizens of other countries who are physically within its jurisdiction exactly the way it treats its own citizens.

Zakharov is almost certainly a Soviet spy. But under American law, which governs his case, not only must he be presumed innocent, but he may legally be not guilty. Zakharov has many defenses available to him that would not be available to Daniloff. If he was illegally entrapped or illegally searched, his case may have to be thrown out. The prosecution may have difficulty overcoming the heavy burden of proving beyond a reasonable doubt that he had the requisite criminal intentions, or that he engaged in the narrow range of conduct specifically prohibited under our statutes.

While these issues are being decided, Zakharov may well be entitled to be free on bail. American bail law recently underwent considerable revision, making it easier to confine defendants before trial, and there are special considerations applicable to foreigners. But our Bill of Rights does provide that "excessive bail shall not be required," and it does not limit that right to American citizens. In any case, since Zakharov is now in the custody of the Soviet delegate to the United Nations, he is effectively out on bail. Some might argue that it is disturbing that it took a Soviet setup of an American to force us to comply with our own Constitution in this case.

It may be difficult for Americans to accept the ironic conclusion that flows from our presumption of freedom and the Soviet presumption of regulation: namely, that the Soviets are legally entitled to be far less fair to our citizens than we are entitled to be to theirs. That may not sound just, and indeed it is not. But would we really have it any other way?

Surely, we do not want to descend to their level of domestic tyranny, even in the way we treat citizens of other countries. Nor can we realistically expect the Soviet legal system—one of the most repressive in the world—to rise to our level, even in the treatment of our citizens. All we can realistically demand is that the Soviets not sink below the minimal level of human rights compliance expected of every civilized society. The tragedy is that the Soviet legal system flunks even that not-very-demanding test, both in regard to its own citizens and in regard to Nicholas Daniloff.

September 23, 1986

UPDATE
Both Daniloff and Zakharov were returned to their countries after relatively brief detentions.

98
Don't Look for Big Shifts at the High Court—Yet

The first Monday in October marks the beginning of the Supreme Court's new term. For the first time in eighteen years, the high court will be presided over by a new chief justice, William Rehnquist. It will also have a new associate justice, Antonin Scalia. Whether it will tilt in a new direction is the big question.

Don't look for dramatic changes too early in the term.

Among the most important decisions the justices make, before the term actually begins, is which cases they will hear and decide. They deny review to the vast majority of petitioners, limiting themselves to what they regard as the most significant.

On the first Monday, the Supreme Court clerk's office will announce which of the hundreds of cases accumulated over the summer recess the new court has accepted for argument. Court watchers will pore over these "grants" to see if a pattern is discernible, but I doubt that any obvious direction will emerge, since the new court is hardly in place yet. Moreover, it takes only a minority of four votes to decide to hear a case, and so these decisions can sometimes be misleading when attempting to chart a shift in majority thinking.

The next public hints may be observable during the oral arguments, which also begin in early October. (The cases that will be heard during the remainder of this calendar year were picked last term.) Seasoned practitioners realize that the questions asked by the justices don't necessarily give away their answers, but they do suggest the areas that are troubling those behind the mahogany bench.

Beyond specific questions by individual justices, we may also see a new tone set by the presiding chief. Warren Burger was something of a martinet who used the power of his gavel to cover his own intellectual and educational inadequacies. William Rehnquist is a supremely confident lawyer who enjoys the give and take of argument, and seems to care far less than his predecessor about appearances and traditions.

Media coverage of the court may reflect this change. Warren Burger sought to control his image and that of his court in several ways. He forbade television or radio coverage of arguments, either live or taped. He established a tightly controlled press office. He refused even to allow television coverage of his own public speeches, except under rigid conditions. This seemed to reflect not only his lack of self-confidence, but his preference for style (at which he was a master) over substance (at which he was mediocre at best).

Chief Justice Rehnquist is a far more open and relaxed person. I predict that during his tenure—though not at its very beginning—we will begin to see some television and radio coverage of the Supreme Court, and far more openness with the press and public.

Another difference between the old and new regimes—one that the public and press will not see directly—will be in the manner by which the chief justice presides over his "brethren" (and his one "sister"). The role of chief justice at the Supreme Court's super-secret conferences (no clerks or secretaries allowed!) is much discussed by court followers. But since the only sources of information about this important function are the justices themselves, it usually takes several years for an accurate picture to emerge.

It took less time in Burger's case because he was so bitterly despised by some of his judicial colleagues that they took to leaking Burger "horror" stories to the press. This process culminated in Bob Woodward and Scott Armstrong's best-selling exposé *The Brethren*, which shattered the secrecy of the Supreme Court conferences under Burger.

William Rehnquist is not likely to repeat his predecessor's mistakes by alienating colleagues with whom he has worked during part or all of his fifteen years on the high court. Moreover, he is personally quite popular with the other justices and has strong allies. Justice Sandra Day O'Connor is an old law school friend who may owe her own appointment, at least in part, to her new boss. And the newest justice, Antonin Scalia, is an ideological soulmate.

Even the liberals on the court seem personally relieved with the change at the helm and are looking forward to a more pleasant interaction among the justices.

The most enduring difference will be the most difficult to discern. The new chief justice and his new colleague are likely to become the intellectual leaders of the court. They both are young, vigorous, ideologically aggressive, intelligent, and well educated, and both are powerful writers. In close cases, the justices who comprise the ideological middle may well be nudged to the right by the sheer intellectual strength of the new chief and his newest ally.

It promises to be a fascinating term for Supreme Court watchers. It may also prove to be a watershed for the rights of all Americans. Watch closely.

September 30, 1986

99
The Price of a Life Depends on the Color of the Skin

Imagine a law that read: "The punishment for anyone who murders a white person is death; the punishment for anyone who murders a black person is life imprisonment." There were laws like that on the books in the days of slavery, except that the punishment for killing a black slave was far less than life imprisonment. But no civilized state would now enact a law that explicitly placed a higher value on a white life than on a black life.

Yet, throughout America, we see the implicit devaluation of black life. Medical and police services are better in white neighborhoods than in black ones. Fewer dollars are devoted to finding cures for diseases that strike primarily blacks. The media is more likely to play up the murder of a white victim—as, for example, in the front-page coverage devoted to a young white woman recently killed in New York's Central Park.* This happened in an area where several blacks have been killed; their stories were relegated to the back pages. Some of this difference may reflect social and economic class, rather than race alone, but it would be difficult to deny that race plays some role.

This double standard is also reflected in the process by which society determines who is to be executed and who spared. Despite the fact that we no longer have statutes explicitly punishing the murderers of whites more harshly than those of blacks, some of our states still have criminal justice systems under which the race of the victim has a considerable—if un-stated—impact on whether the murderer is sentenced to death.

Recently, the explosive issues of race, life, and death were argued before the U.S. Supreme Court. The case involves a black man named Warren McCleskey who was sentenced to die for killing a white policeman during an armed robbery in Georgia. His lawyers presented the high court with the results of the most thorough statistical analysis ever conducted on the role of the victim's race in death sentences.

To understand the significance of this study, done under the auspices of the NAACP Legal Defense Fund, some background is essential. First, the vast majority of murderers do not receive a sentence of death. In Georgia, for example, where the study was conducted, fewer than 10 percent of those convicted of deliberate homicide receive the death penalty.

This is because there is considerable discretion in the way a killing is treated—first by the police, then by the prosecutor, and eventually by the judge and jury. Each of these institutions is supposed to exercise its discretion in a nonracial manner, by considering aspects such as aggravating factors of the killing and the likelihood that the murderer may be reformed. But racial considerations seem to creep in.

The study found that killers in cases involving white victims were nearly eleven times more likely to receive a sentence of death than those in cases involving black victims. Now, this alone does not prove that the only reason for the enormous disparity is race. It may be that cases with white victims also involve nonracial factors that explain and justify the difference, though this would require incredible coincidences. In order to test for that possibility, those who conducted the study considered hundreds of other factors that could account for the difference, including the killer's prior record, his motivation, particularly vicious aspects of the murder, and whether it was committed along with other crimes. They still concluded that "race held as a predominate determiner of life or death."

The state of Georgia disagrees. I appeared with Georgia's attorney general, Michael Bowers, on ABC's "Nightline" the day after the Supreme Court argument, and Ted Koppel asked Bowers how he could explain these disparities on nonracial grounds. Bowers opined that the murders of white victims were, as a rule, more "aggravated" than the murders of black victims.

I pointed out that this sort of characterization by itself may implicitly reflect some racial perceptions: many white jurors—who identify with white victims—may view the very act of killing a white person as more aggravated than the killing of a black, even if the objective factors are similar.

The Georgia attorney general next argued that statistics alone mean nothing in a particular case, and that for McCleskey to prevail, he would have to show his own sentence of death was racially motivated. But since our legal system prohibits monitoring of jury deliberations, it will never be possible to discover what motivated a particular jury. Racism can be proved only through patterns of discrimination, established by careful statistical studies.

Whichever way the Supreme Court decides the case, the American public must still face up to the reality that Georgia and other states operate a two-tier system of imposing the death penalty: one for those who kill whites and another for those who kill blacks.

October 21, 1986

*The killing of Jenifer Levin by Robert Chambers.
See next column.*

100
Tortured Reasoning, Executed Prisoners

In two of its most significant and far-reaching decisions during this Supreme Court term, the court has invited the states to execute criminals who have neither killed nor intended to kill anyone, and to hasten the pace of executions that have been held up so far because of racial disparities in sentencing.

The first case, involving two teenage brothers who helped to break their father out of prison—but who killed no one—gave the pro-death penalty forces a weapon that will help them execute more people. I argued the case before the Supreme Court, and I know the two brothers. Now in their late twenties, they are decent young men. As children, they had been taught by their mother that their imprisoned father was a good man, despite his criminal record, which included a murder conviction. Disappointed that their father was not being paroled—he was an "honor" prisoner—the family concocted a plan to spring him from prison. The father promised his sons that no shots would be fired during the escape, and none were.

Several days after the escape, the getaway car broke down and the father ordered his sons to flag down a passing car. After placing the occupants of the flagged-down car into the broken-down one, the father sent his sons to get water, so that the occupants could survive the desert night. While the sons were getting the water, the father and his cellmate, who had escaped with him, killed the occupants. The sons stood by helplessly in shock.

Eventually the two sons were captured. A third son, also involved in the escape, was shot and killed by police. The father escaped, but was found dead of exposure several days later. The sons were offered a plea bargain under which their lives would be spared if they testified against their mother and other relatives who were believed to have participated in planning the escape. When the sons refused to testify against their own mother, they were placed on trial for their lives. Despite their age, the absence of any criminal record, and the undisputed fact that they neither fired the fatal shots nor specifically intended the victims to die, both brothers were sentenced to the gas chamber.

The Supreme Court, in a decision written by Justice Sandra Day O'Connor, agreed that they had not killed, nor had they intended to kill. Under existing Supreme Court precedents, these findings required the conclusion that they could not be executed. Just five years earlier, in a case involving the robbery of a home in which an elderly couple was murdered, the Supreme Court had ruled that it would be unconstitutional to execute the accomplice, a man named Earl Enmund, who was waiting in the getaway car.

O'Connor dissented from that five-to-four decision. Characterizing Earl Enmund as the "major" participant in the armed robbery—the man who "planned the capital felony"—she concluded that Enmund could be executed, despite the fact that he did not pull the trigger.

In the *Tison* case, O'Connor's dissenting view became the majority decision. But because she did not want to overrule the *Enmund* decision, she tried to distinguish Earl Enmund's role in the murders committed by his accomplices from the roles played by the Tison brothers. In order to do so, O'Connor simply rewrote history. She now characterizes Enmund as "the minor actor [who was] merely sitting in a car," rather than the "major participant [who had] planned the capital felony." Had a practicing lawyer so distorted the facts to serve his client's interest, he would have been subject to discipline.

In addition to minimizing Earl Enmund's role, O'Connor also exaggerated the Tisons' role and said they could be executed because they acted with "reckless disregard for human life"—an issue that was not considered by the state court. All in all, O'Connor's decision displayed an abysmal lack of judicial honesty.

Justice Lewis F. Powell's decision in the racial disparity case was more honest, but no less disturbing. The defendant, a black Georgia man named Warren McCleskey, was convicted of killing a white police officer during the holdup of a furniture store. McCleskey's lawyer introduced evidence indicating that defendants who kill white victims are far more likely to receive the death penalty than those who kill blacks. This is especially true of black defendants, the evidence showed.

Powell accepted the evidence—based on a study of more than 2,800 murder cases—as valid. But he concluded that such a "discrepancy that appears to correspond with race" does not necessarily establish deliberate racial discrimination in a particular case.

In reading Powell's decision, I was reminded of Al Campanis's answer to Ted Koppel's question about the statistical discrepancy between the number of black baseball players and the number of black managers. Both Powell and Campanis came up with explanations and rationalizations. But neither came up with a convincing argument that justified the disparities. Campanis, of course, lost his job with the Los Angeles Dodgers; Powell is still sitting on the Supreme Court.

Most likely, Campanis just came out looking bad when he made remarks that really were not racially motivated; he once roomed with Jackie Robinson. Powell, on the other hand, was once a member of a segregated country club.

Both Powell and O'Connor stretched the facts, the law, and common sense. Even those who favor capital punishment should be disturbed at the lengths to which some justices will go to continue killing people.

April 28, 1987

101
Supreme Court Is Not the "People's Court"

Attorney General Edwin Meese—in his latest attack on the judiciary—has compared the U.S. Supreme Court, in effect, to nine Judge Wapners whose job it is simply to resolve disputes between the particular parties to a litigation. If one accepts this "People's Court" approach to our third branch of government, it follows that—as Meese put it—a decision by our high court "binds the parties in the case," but does not "establish a 'supreme law of the land' that is binding on all persons and parts of government, henceforth and evermore."

In Judge Wapner's "People's Court," the decision is—to paraphrase a former justice of the Supreme Court—like a limited railroad ticket: "for this day and train only." Judge Wapner's job is simply to do justice between the particular disputants. (And a great job he does! I wish there were more Judge Wapners in the real courts of our nation.) Judge Wapner doesn't have to worry about the broad implication of his decisions since they do not establish any precedent, but merely settle past disputes.

The U.S. Supreme Court is very different from the "People's Court." First of all, it is not a people's court at all. No ordinary citizen has a right to bring his or her case before that august tribunal. The justices of the Supreme Court pick and choose those few cases they wish to hear. And mostly they pick cases brought to them by governments—federal and state—that are unhappy that citizens beat them in the lower courts.

Nor does the Supreme Court pick its cases in order to settle particular disputes or do simple justice between the parties. Those tasks are ordinarily left to the lower courts. When the U.S. Supreme Court takes a case, it generally does so in order to make broad judicial policy decisions that affect the entire nation. That is one of the reasons why we follow the Supreme Court so closely.

It is also one of the reasons why Edwin Meese cares so much about who gets appointed to the Supreme Court and what positions his Justice Department takes before that tribunal in controversial cases involving such issues as abortion, criminal procedure, and affirmative action.

Most important, the Supreme Court is perhaps the most important check on executive and legislative excesses under our constitutional system of checks and balances. It has the final word on the meaning of the Constitution, which all governmental officials are sworn to uphold. If it rules—at it did in 1954—that the "equal protection" clause of the Constitution means that no state may segregate black students by sending them to inferior public schools, then that interpretation becomes the law of the land.

Attorney General Meese dissents. Indeed, for some unfathomable reason, he picks desegregation as his primary example of a Supreme Court ruling that should not be regarded as "the supreme law of the land." Meese's selection of the Supreme Court's historic pronouncement in *Brown* v. *Board of Education* is especially troubling, since virtually no one today openly argues for a return to segregated public education. Nearly everyone outside of the lunatic fringe has accepted desegregation as the law of the land.

This was not always the case, as anyone over thirty-five surely remembers. In the decade following the Supreme Court's 1954 desegregation decision, several state governors—those in Alabama, Mississippi, and Arkansas come most vividly to mind—attempted to defy the decision. One of the arguments they used was precisely the one that Attorney General Meese is now making: that the Supreme Court's decision was binding only "on the parties in the case," namely young Miss Brown and the Topeka, Kansas school board.

Fortunately for America, that argument was rejected by the attorneys general who served under Presidents Eisenhower, Kennedy, and Johnson. It was also rejected—specifically, emphatically, and unanimously—by the Supreme Court itself, which in 1958 ruled that its interpretation of the Constitution as prohibiting state-upheld segregated education was indeed "the supreme law of the land," binding on all Americans.

If the Meese position had prevailed, anarchy and violence would have existed throughout the South. Every school board would have barricaded the doors of its white schools to black students until the court had decided that each particular student had a right to go to each particular school. Constitutional rights cannot thrive in that kind of atmosphere.

As usual, there is a kernel of truth to what Attorney General Meese says. Supreme Court decisions are not biblical pronouncements from Sinai chiseled into stone tablets. They are subject to reconsideration, overruling, and modification—by the Supreme Court itself, or by constitutional amendment. But until they are changed, they are binding on all Americans. That is why our Supreme Court is not just nine Judge Wapners deciding whether the local TV repairman has to return Ms. Jones's twelve dollars after not being able to fix her set.

The attorney general of the United States is not just like a police prosecutor in a small California town. And he should not treat the U.S. Supreme Court as if it were the police court in front of which he used to practice.

October 28, 1986

102
Judges Should Be a Breed Apart

The newest endangered species in our political bestiary is the courageous judge.

The black robe, the mahogany bench, and the marble pillars no longer provide sufficient protective coloration against the ravages of an impatient electorate. The people and politicians are coming to expect—indeed, demand—that judges follow their daily marching orders. The punishment for refusing to compete in popularity contests is the threat of electoral defeat— a threat that was recently carried out in California with the removal from office of Chief Justice Rose Bird and two of her colleagues; and in North Carolina, with the removal of three judges. In jurisdictions without popular election (or removal) of judges—most prominently the federal system, as well as some dozen states—the threat to lower-court judges is that they will not be promoted (or reappointed, where such a process governs).

The evolutionary response to this new threat is a growing timidity among many judges who are understandably concerned about their professional survival. The result may well change the nature of justice in America. Just as important changes in nature may produce a shift in the ecological balance, so, too, the political balance may be affected by a dramatic change in the nature of our judiciary.

The most important ecological process in our government is our unique system of checks and balances—the envy of the democratic world. U.S. sovereignty lies not with a single person, institution, or branch of government, but with a dynamic process of interaction among elected executives and legislators with staggered terms, and judges who are generally appointed or elected to much longer terms. Our system of checks and balances assumes that the judiciary will differ from the political branches— that it will respond to the sound of a different drummer, or at least to a somewhat different rhythm or beat.

The judiciary is supposed to be more sensitive to the needs of those who cannot demand immediate attention from elected representatives—racial, religious, ethnic, and other minorities, as well as the politically and economically disenfranchised.

The judiciary is not supposed to respond to every blip in the pollsters' most recent computerized attitude survey. It is supposed to reflect more pervasive values that often are not politically popular at any given moment.

The judiciary is the guardian of those measures in our federal and state bills of rights that protect the minority from the majority. It must do justice even when there are shrill cries for expediency. And doing justice requires attention to means as well as ends—to process as well as product.

This might be compared to an insurance policy. Paying the periodic premium is no fun; we get nothing material in return. But the theory is that these payments will protect us against grave dangers that we hope will never face us.

We pay a constitutional premium each time a judge frees a dangerous criminal because his constitutional rights were violated, each time a Nazi is permitted to march through Skokie, and each time a judge spends public funds to appoint a lawyer for an obviously guilty defendant.

In these cases, the process—the means—has required us to pay a costly premium. But that is the price of due process, choice, freedom, and privacy. The Bill of Rights is our insurance policy against government abuse. By building up capital over the years, we hope to empower our judiciary to serve as a bulwark against oppression, even—perhaps especially—when that oppression has popular backing.

Judges who respond to the election returns have no right to the honorable title of judge or to the enormous power that accompanies that high office. It was judges with an eye to election returns who ordered the deportation of thousands of immigrants during the nationalist hysteria of the 1920s; who closed their eyes to lynchings in the South during the 1930s; who sustained the detention in concentration camps of 110,000 U.S. citizens of Japanese descent in the 1940s; who caved in to McCarthyism in the 1950s; who tried to thwart the Supreme Court's desegregation orders in the 1960s; who regarded a woman's right to choose to terminate her pregnancy as a crime in the 1970s; and who treat gay men and women as criminals in the 1980s.

This is certainly *not* an honor roll of judicial courage. But it is an inevitable consequence when judges abdicate their function as a check on legislative, executive, and popular excesses and leap injudiciously onto the political bandwagon in a futile effort to keep up with ever-changing popular fashion.

The crowning irony is that the Reagan-Meese administration is demanding that judges must not become legislators: they must not make the law, simply *apply* it. But this simple-minded sophistry makes them more like legislators, responsive to the will of today's majority.

Fortunately, our system of checks and balances is ever-so-subtle. This year's Senate elections imposed a check on the power of the executive to control our judges. The Senate Judiciary Committee—through which all federal judicial nominations must pass—will now be controlled by a party that differs from the president's. This will, at least, soften the influence of one political party on the independence of the federal judiciary.

November 18, 1986

See columns 122-128.

103
Judge Was Pioneer, Conscience of the Nation

David Bazelon is certainly not a household name to most Americans. Yet Judge Bazelon—who just retired after thirty-six years of distinguished service on the U.S. Court of Appeals for the District of Columbia—has been your conscience in Washington since 1949.

No single judge—whether on the Supreme Court, the lower federal courts or the state courts—has had a more profound impact on the law's sensitivity to human needs. His resignation provides an appropriate occasion for some words of appreciation.

First, a word of personal devotion from one of his greatest fans. I was Bazelon's law clerk immediately upon my graduation from law school. He has been my mentor for two decades. But he has also been the mentor of hundreds of lawyers, professors, judges, legislators and ordinary, decent people. His contributions are so wide-ranging and enormous that they defy brief summary, but they affect our daily lives in many tangible ways.

Bazelon first came to public attention in 1954 when he wrote the Durham decision, which revolutionized the law of insanity in the United States. Prior to Bazelon's Durham decision, a defendant could successfully plead not guilty by reason of insanity only if he could demonstrate a clear psychotic break with reality. Bazelon opened up the insanity defense to the urban poor whose crimes were the product of their upbringing, social conditions and other deprivations. His Durham decision desegregated the mental hospitals, much like the Brown decision—rendered during the same month in 1954—desegregated schools.

Bazelon's Durham formulation has itself undergone many changes, rejections and attacks over the past thirty years. But no intelligent discussion of the important relationship between law and psychiatry can ever again be conducted without making reference to the ground-breaking Durham case.

Bazelon has also been a pioneer in bringing legal services to the poor and the disadvantaged. As a judge, he saw the enormous disparities between how the wealthy are treated in court and how the poor are mistreated. He wrote a series of decisions raising hard questions about this inequality. Although he provided few final answers, he pricked the conscience of a nation, and he goaded the U.S. Supreme Court into action in several cases.

Next he turned his attention to the ravages being inflicted upon our environment by nuclear wastes, pollution and other destructive forces. Although often rebuffed by the Supreme Court, he forcefully brought these issues into the forefront of the judicial imagination.

Nor was Bazelon simply a liberal fighting conservatives, a Democrat battling Republicans, an activist struggling against judicial restraint. He was truly a conscience of all people. I was his law clerk during the Kennedy administration, which is regarded as the golden age of American liberalism. Yet he was constantly battling with the Kennedy Justice Department, urging them to back up their rhetoric with reality. Despite his resignation, I am confident that he will continue to battle current and future administrations until his last breath.

One factor, however, may transcend all of his substantive contributions to jurisprudence—and that is the impact he has had on so many people in so many important positions of government and education today.

No student can go through a three-year course at any major law school without studying the life work of David Bazelon—and I predict that this will be true well into the next century. The reason for Bazelon's continuing impact is that his primary role—as he saw it—was to raise enduring questions, not to provide transient, trendy solutions. He saw the role of the courts—especially the intermediate appellate courts, such as the one he served on—as uniquely capable of raising questions and directing them at the Supreme Court, the lower District courts, the legislatures and the executives. Bazelon was at his finest when he threw the ball back at government officials, making them think hard, reconsider and question their own programs and political solutions.

He has been our voice in Washington, a voice of skepticism, yet a voice of realism. He persisted in raising old-fashioned questions of morality even while other judges were analyzing issues in terms of simplistic costs and benefits.

The best judges rarely seek or obtain public accolade. Judging is, at its best, a reclusive profession. That is why so few Americans know very much about this most important American hero.

I certainly am not known for effusively praising the judiciary. Indeed, part of the reason I have been so critical of so many judges is that I learned at the feet of one who set a tone and provided a model that few can meet. Perhaps in that respect Bazelon has made me too tough a critic of others. I know he would be proud of having provoked hard questions, even about the judiciary that he loves.

A heroic judge is finally hanging up his black robes. But it isn't the robes or the gavel that give a judge his or her authority and enduring power. It's what is underneath the robe, and how the gavel had been wielded. Underneath Bazelon's robe, there has always been a man of deep compassion and concern for the downtrodden—a man who used his gavel to teach, rather than to merely dictate. Many of his questions remain unanswered—but we are all the better for his persistence in asking them.

June 3, 1985

104
Impeachment:
For Emergency Use Only

The call for impeachment is being heard more frequently these days than at any time since Watergate. Following the Iranian arms-for-hostages "non-deal," President Reagan's credibility dipped to an all-time low and shrill demands for his impeachment have been heard from some radical quarters. You can "smell a whiff of Watergate in the air," commented newscaster Daniel Schorr.

In the past several years, Reagan's impeachment has been proposed by Ramsey Clark, Jesse Jackson, New York Representative Ted Weiss, actor

Ed Asner, and several hundred Brown University students. Even former first lady Rosalynn Carter was quoted as saying, "Jimmy would have been impeached if he had done some of the things that this administration has gotten away with."

One federal judge was recently impeached and removed from office, and two more are in the pipeline. There have been several failed attempts to impeach other judges—including a trio of federal appeals court judges who ordered a new trial for convicted murderers. However, the smell of judicial blood is in the air—especially after the electoral removal of California's Chief Justice Rose Bird and two of her liberal colleagues on the bench.

The other day I opened the mail to find a personalized, individually numbered, and official-looking document—a "Petition and Charges" against Attorney General Edwin Meese III, calling for his "removal from office." It specified six "counts," ranging from "undermining the integrity and independence of federal courts" to "violating the separation of church and state." It looked very official, except that it was directed to "the United States Court of Public Opinion" and had a fund-raising letter for the American Civil Liberties Union attached to it.

However, the accompanying letter adds that this is "very serious [and] cannot be taken lightly" and compares the ACLU's current effort to remove Meese from office to "our campaign in 1973 to impeach Richard Nixon."

Whether this latest ACLU gambit is really a serious removal effort, akin to the Nixon impeachment, or merely a fund-raising gimmick, it is certain to backfire. It trivializes and cheapens the Constitution's impeachment and removal process, which is to be used in specified instances of lawlessness. So, in the end, this ACLU campaign to remove Meese will weaken an important constitutional safeguard that may be needed in the future.

Whatever else one might say about Meese, it seems clear that he (unlike John Mitchell, his predecessor several times removed) is trying to undercut our civil liberties by working *within* the law. Indeed, the ACLU's principal criticism is precisely that he is *using* the law, especially the courts, to implement his reactionary agenda. He is pressing that agenda on receptive judges whom he has recommended for appointment after subjecting judicial candidates to political tests and virtual loyalty oaths. He may be violating the spirit of the Constitution, but he certainly is obeying its letter and playing by its rules.

Meese's opponents should do the same. The Constitution expressly provides that "the President, Vice President and all civil Officers of the United States, shall be removed from office on Impeachment for, and Conviction of, Treason, Bribery or other high Crimes and Misdemeanors." The radical surgery of impeachment was not intended to be a routine political remedy for dissatisfaction with performance in office, and it should be reserved for extraordinary cases of lawlessness, corruption, or tyranny.

I opposed Meese's appointment as attorney general and have criticized most of his policies. However, I strongly oppose any effort to remove him or his boss from office via impeachment or any other form of extraordinary proceeding, so long as they play by the rules of the Constitution.

Our Constitution provides for other political remedies proportional to the dangers posed by officials whose actions undercut our faith in their leadership. One such remedy is the midterm congressional election, mandated by the Constitution. This serves as an imprecise referendum on executive popularity—especially when the president campaigns vigorously on behalf of his party's candidates and programs.

This year—even before the Iranian fiasco—the voters returned control of the Senate to the Democrats. This means that it will be far more difficult for Reagan and his attorney general to shape the judiciary to their parochial political liking. The Senate Judiciary Committee in particular—and Congress in general—will now serve as a more effective check on executive excesses. Foreign policy decisions will be subject to more probing congressional oversight. And the presidential veto—itself a countercheck on legislative excess—will be more easily overridden.

All in all, the political medicines are working effectively to keep the body politic relatively stable. Radical surgery is not called for, especially against a lame-duck president during his last two years in office.

Now 1988 is just around the corner and the presidential campaign has already begun. Those who invoke the cumbersome and extraordinary process of impeachment and removal should, instead, focus their energies on the ordinary political process. It really does work.

Impeachment and removal are important parts of our constitutional self-defense system. However, they should generally remain behind a window with a sign that reads, "Break glass only in case of constitutional emergency."

November 25, 1986

105
The Fifth Amendment:
It's All the Rage This Year

Yet another answer to one of my favorite questions: If a conservative is a liberal who's been mugged, then what is a civil libertarian? The current answer is a conservative who's being investigated. The Iran-contra investigation is turning many Reagan conservatives into instant civil libertarians.

After six years of nearly constant condemnation of every amendment but the Second—the right to bear arms—suddenly Reaganites seem to be appreciating the Bill of Rights. Even President Reagan himself—who used to condemn "Fifth-Amendment Communists" when he was a Hollywood informant for the FBI—now understands and justifies the invocation of the privilege against self-incrimination by his friends and associates.

As the president put it when asked whether he was disappointed that two of his former aides—national security advisor John M. Poindexter and Lieutenant Colonel Oliver L. North, Jr.—had invoked the privilege: "I think it should be perfectly obvious. It's not new or unusual. It has happened many times before." What he failed to mention is that he has, in effect, now invited former and present high-ranking government officials to use the privilege to avoid answering important questions put to them by congressional committees.

The Fifth Amendment provides that "No person shall . . . be compelled in any criminal case to be a witness against himself." This protection applies in legislative hearings as well as at criminal trials. Any witness may invoke the Fifth Amendment, so long as there is a realistic possibility that a compelled answer could provide a link in the chain of evidence that might lead to his conviction in a criminal case. This formulation has led many conservative critics of the amendment to complain that it provides a protective shield only for the guilty. "If he has nothing to hide," goes the argument, "then why is he hiding behind the Fifth Amendment?"

That question deserves an answer. There are circumstances under which a truthful answer to a question can help to convict an innocent person. For example, an innocent man may have had a powerful motive to kill his pregnant mistress—although he, in fact, was not the killer. Admitting that motive—say, a demand for money by the victim shortly before the killing—could help convict him of a crime he did not commit. In the Iran-contra affair, an admission by a witness that he shredded documents (which is generally not a crime in itself) could be viewed as incriminating, even if the witness did not violate any substantive criminal laws.

Over the past century, law enforcement officials have figured out a way of getting around the apparently absolute strictures of the privilege against self-incrimination. The witness is given immunity from criminal prosecution. A witness who is given "transactional immunity" cannot be prosecuted at all for the crime—the "transaction"—about which he is compelled to testify. A narrower form is called "use immunity," which simply means that the government cannot use the testimony given by the witness (or any leads it develops from this testimony) against him in a criminal case.

Not surprisingly, both Poindexter and North are seeking the broadest possible immunity in exchange for any testimony they might give. This raises an interesting dilemma for the congressional investigating committees. If Poindexter and North are given immunity and testify that the buck stopped with them, there will be no criminal prosecution of anybody— except perhaps a few low-level operatives. If, on the other hand, Poindexter and North can provide incriminating evidence against even higher-ranking government officials, the trade-off might be worth the cost.

The problem is that until the special counsel who will investigate these goings-on really gets down to the nitty-gritty, any congressional committee that gives a high-ranking official immunity will be buying a pig in a poke.

What all this comes down to is that Poindexter and North, by invoking the Fifth Amendment now, may simply be trying to buy time in an effort to get the best deal. They may be doing what is best for them. But it is unseemly—to put it mildly—for the president of the United States to encourage any member of his administration to invoke the privilege against self-incrimination, especially since many Americans believe that full and truthful testimony may point to a somewhat different picture of the president's role in this entire mess.

Indeed, some courts have held that it is improper for anyone other than a witness's own lawyer to advise the witness to invoke the Fifth Amendment. This is especially so when the witness could provide testimony contrary to the interests of the person urging him to remain silent. Some courts have regarded such advice as obstruction of justice.

And so, the Fifth Amendment is in the news once again. But oh, how different it seems to those who are now justifying its invocation! What it all goes to show is that the Bill of Rights really was designed to protect all of the people all of the time.

December 9, 1986

106
Insiders and the Evil Intentions of the Small Investor

Although the Iran-contra scandal has pushed the insider trading scandal off the front pages, Ivan Boesky and his friends are still sending shockwaves through the securities industry. The recent publicity given to the notion that insider trading is actually illegal has raised some eyebrows among the small customers of stockbrokers.

"I certainly assumed my broker *had* insider information," is a common reaction these days. Many average investors—housewives, doctors, store owners, working people—believe that their fast-talking brokers really do have access to sources of information that they could not tap.

You know the pitch: your broker's voice turns to a kind of stage-whisper as he tells you about the Arizona bank that is rumored to be a target of a takeover. How does he know? "The word is out on The Street." He can "get you" a couple of hundred shares, but you have to move quickly. You take the bait and buy. The stock sits there for a while and then begins to drift downward.

You call your trusted broker to complain. He's not worried. (They never seem to be worried about *your* money!) He aggressively advises you that this is the time to "double up"—to increase your investment while the stock is down, so that you can make your money back more quickly when it rebounds, as it surely will. Again you bite. The stock plummets. The broker stops returning your calls. He is busy baiting his line for new fish.

There are, of course, enormous differences in degree—indeed in kind—among "insider information," as that term is used by lay people. At one extreme is the kind of information bought by people like Ivan Boesky for enormous sums of money: specific facts—numbers, dates, amounts, names—that are, by law, required to be kept from risk arbitrageurs. At the other extreme is the entirely lawful (indeed commendable) research that brokerage firms are supposed to do before they recommend a stock to their customers.

Between these extremes are a wide variety of sources, techniques, and gambits that give certain traders an edge in the competitive game of prediction and timing that may make the difference between bonanza and bankruptcy. Some are entirely legal, while others more questionable. The line is far from clear.

But aside from the legalities are the moralities. Many brokerage firms—including some of the most prestigious—practice their trade in a highly dubious manner. Lehman Brothers, for example, has its secretaries imitate the voices of telephone operators saying, "Person-to-person call to Mr. Jones from vice president Brown of Lehman Brothers." It sounds so important and personal. I have received several such calls—even after complaining about the practice. I took the first one, thinking it might be someone other than an aggressive stock salesman seeking to hawk his wares. Now my secretary is under instructions never to take any calls from Lehman Brothers even if it's from Lehman himself.

Another deceptive technique—which exploits the common appetite for the insider insight—is for a broker to call and tell you that he's not trying to sell you stocks, but rather that he has information about a particular company that he wants to share with you so that he can inspire your confidence in him.

I'm reminded of the scam widely practiced a few miles uptown from Wall Street, in front of Grand Central Station. A hustler comes up to an out-of-towner and offers to sell him an expensive brand-name watch for a fraction of its cost. The out-of-towner, believing that the watch is a valuable stolen item, buys it. He later learns that it was not stolen at all, nor is it valuable; instead it is a cheap imitation, worth considerably less than he paid for it. A buyer has been cheated by a seller who knows how to exploit his customer's evil intention.

The stock transaction is, of course, different in many ways. The laws on insider trading are far less clear than the laws on buying stolen property. But the atmosphere of multiple deception and subtle manipulation is similar.

In a recent "60 Minutes" exposé, Mike Wallace interviewed several investors who had lost money after being pressured to buy stocks from First Jersey Securities. A number of former brokers for the company confirmed that it was First Jersey's technique to buy penny stocks in marginal companies and then push them on small investors at enormous profits to First Jersey, but with undisclosed risks to the investors.

The Boesky affair and its variants are symptoms of more pervasive problems on Wall Street. This would be a good time to look more probingly into the ethics of stock trading. The Supreme Court may well have an opportunity to take such a look, because it just agreed to review the insider trader conviction of former *Wall Street Journal* reporter R. Foster Winans.

December 16, 1986

UPDATE
*The Supreme Court affirmed Winans's conviction without providing much
clarity to the definition of insider trading.*

107
Smoking at Someone Else
Should Be a Crime

Cigarette smoking in public places can no longer be considered merely a
"victimless" act of self-destruction. A new report to Congress by the surgeon general cites scientific evidence that "environmental tobacco
smoke"—the carcinogen that smokers puff into your face—causes un-
counted cases of lung cancer and other deadly diseases among nonsmokers.

This is how the surgeon general put it: It is now clear that disease risk
due to inhalation of tobacco smoke is not limited to the individual who is
smoking, but can extend to those who inhale tobacco smoke emitted into
the air. The report relies on "an abundance of evidence" that "a substantial
proportion of the lung cancer deaths that occur among nonsmokers can be
attributed to involuntary smoking."

In light of the enormous number of people suffering from lung cancer, it
is likely that nearly everyone will have friend, relative, or loved one who is
victimized by other people's smoke. I myself have an aunt and a dear
friend—both nonsmokers—who are suffering from lung cancer. Both may
be victims of involuntary "smoking."

There's an old adage that says, "Your right to swing your fist ends at the
tip of my nose." That can now be amended to read, "Your right to puff
carcinogenic smoke ends at the tip of my nose." Every adult smoker has the
right to decide whether to contaminate his or her own lungs, but not the
right to decide to contaminate my lungs or the lungs of any other nonsmoker or private smoker. To put it clinically: a public smoker may have the
right to inhale, but not the right to exhale.

It is quite remarkable that a society that devotes so much time, money,
and energy to criminalizing purely victimless crimes done in private—
homosexuality and recreational drug use, to cite a couple—cannot seem to
get behind the surgeon general's proposal to ban smoking in public. And

those people who always seem to advocate prohibitions against adults reading or viewing pornography on the grounds that it could hurt children seem to forget about the children who are literally sickened by thoughtless parents who smoke on them. The surgeon general's report concludes that children under the age of two have a far greater chance of developing serious bronchitis or pneumonia if they live with parents who smoke in their presence.

It would be entirely constitutional, and indeed highly desirable, for every jurisdiction to outlaw smoking in public places. Perhaps there should be designated smoking areas—much like there should be designated nudist beaches in out-of-the-way places—but only if there is enough room for the nonsmoking majority to engage in its own activities without coming into contact with the offending minority. In other words, exceptions to the presumption against smoking in public should be permitted only when it is clear that the paramount rights of nonsmokers will not be hindered.

A ban on private smoking in homes with young children would make theoretical sense but would be far more difficult to enforce than a public ban. It also would raise privacy issues that would not arise from a ban limited to public areas.

In the absence of criminal statutes or regulations prohibiting public smoking, nonsmokers could resort to private lawsuits. Blowing carcinogenic smoke onto an unwilling recipient might well be an assault, analogous to unwanted touching. But individuals can't spend their lives in court bringing individual suits against every offending smoker. On the other hand, class actions by nonsmoking employees, airline passengers, or shoppers could produce court injunctions requiring employers, airlines, or stores to prohibit airborne assaults on nonsmokers.

None of this will happen, of course, unless there is a public outcry demanding change. The multi-billion-dollar cigarette industry will fight against any proposal that may reduce the number of cigarettes consumed. It will denounce the surgeon general's report as unscientific and will continue to advertise its deadly product in the contexts of athletic events, healthy outdoor scenes, macho men, and sexy women. The cigarette industry has a constitutional right to push its poison, but the citizens have no obligation to consume it.

Eventually, the war against smoking in public will be won not by laws alone, but by a combination of public education and public regulation. People, especially young people, will continue to smoke in public as long as such conduct is regarded as acceptable—even sexy or cool. Peer pressure will be required to end public smoking, because we certainly don't want to station "cigarette cops" on every street corner.

Smokers must simply learn that it is not only impolite to smoke at people, but it is also hazardous to the health of others. Compulsive smokers who can't help puffing in public must be treated as the public menaces they really are. If they can't stop themselves, they must be stopped by the law.

December 23, 1986

For a discussion of banning cigarette advertising see Column 94.

108
Defending a Terrorist:
More than Just a Bad Dream

The night after the West German government announced the capture of the alleged TWA hijacker, Mohammed Ali Hamadei, I had the defense lawyer's recurring nightmare. I dreamt that I was asked to defend Hamadei. It's a nightmare lawyers have all the time: that they will be asked to defend unpopular and sometimes despicable clients.

I vividly recall my first such dream. It was shortly after Adolf Eichmann—the Nazi who supervised the Holocaust—was apprehended in South America and brought to Israel for trial. Following Eichmann's execution, Dr. Joseph Mengele became the focus of the dream. Then it was Ted Bundy, the convicted murderer believed to be responsible for the brutal killing of dozens of women. Now, it was Hamadei, a Lebanese accused of taking part in the 1985 hijacking of a TWA jet, in which an American navy man was beaten, shot to death, and dumped on an airport runway.

Several times, this dream actually has come true. Most recently, I was asked—and I agreed—to help represent Wayne Williams, who is thought to be "the Atlanta child killer," on a motion for a new trial. (The evidence against him, by the way, turns out to be extremely weak.)

For some lawyers, the prospect of working to free someone like Hamadei probably does not bring sleepless nights. Many would simply refuse to defend that kind of person. A few radicals would welcome the opportunity for political reasons.

The difficult dilemma would be faced by the kind of lawyer who believes that every defendant is entitled to the best defense—no matter how heinous his crime or apparent his guilt—but who also despises terrorism to the depths of his soul. Since I fit into this category, I spend many nights dreading the morning phone call to my office from the judge or family member asking me to defend my enemies.

I doubt that I will receive a call from Hamadei. But if I did, not only would I probably agree to represent a man like him; I would also try my best to get him off. I would try to free him even if I knew for a certainty that he was guilty and that he would engage in terrorism again.

I would not, of course, cheat or lie for him, just as I would not cheat or lie for an innocent and sympathetic defendant. That is not part of my job. My job is to use all available legal tactics to my client's advantage. If we ever begin to compromise or create exceptions to the principle that everyone is entitled to a defense, we endanger our system of justice for all.

How would I approach the Hamadei case? First, I would fight the U.S. extradition request to the West German government, whose extradition treaty with us precludes it from turning over any accused criminal who might be sentenced to death. U.S. law permits the execution of an air pirate who murdered, while West German law does not. (Most Western European democracies have abolished the death penalty altogether.)

The U.S. Justice Department has agreed not to ask for the death penalty. But under our system of separation of powers, it is difficult for the United States to guarantee that it will not execute Hamadei. A grand jury will decide which crimes to charge him with; a regular jury will decide on his guilt or innocence; the possible sentences are authorized by the legislature and imposed by the judge. President Reagan can, of course, promise to commute any death sentence to life imprisonment, but what if his successor reneges?

The next line of defense would be to argue that Hamadei's crimes were of a "political character." An American court recently refused to extradite to Great Britain a member of the Irish Republican Army who killed a British soldier and then broke out of prison. The court found these acts to be political and ruled that extradition is not permitted for such crimes.

Finally, if extradition were granted, the defense lawyer would have to defend Hamadei on the merits before an American court. The defendant himself would decide the nature of his defense. Would it be political? Would it challenge the jurisdiction of American courts to try foreigners for crimes committed abroad? Would Hamadei deny he was one of the hi-

jackers? Would he simply stand mute? Whatever he chose to do—within
the limits of law and professional ethics—would determine how his defense
attorney would handle the case.

In the end, Hamadei would almost certainly lose, if he is guilty. The
American legal system provides important safeguards against convicting
the innocent—especially the right to counsel—but it works pretty well in
that the guilty are generally convicted at a trial, even with the best defense.

Whatever the outcome of a case like this, the nightmarish fact is that, in
order to defend our precious heritage of liberty, even terrorists who would
take away our rights must be given theirs.

January 20, 1987

UPDATE
Hamadei did not call me, but a television producer did. He was contem-
plating a TV drama based loosely on the above scenario. I was the legal
consultant, and the drama, titled, "Terrorist on Trial: The United States v.
Salim Ajami" aired nationally on January 10, 1988.

109
Of Meese and *Miranda*

A staff report to Attorney General Edwin Meese argues that overturning
the Supreme Court's 1966 decision in *Miranda* v. *Arizona* would "be
among the most important achievements of this administration—indeed of
any administration—in restoring the power of self-government to the people of the United States in the repression of crime."

The *Miranda* decision, which the report characterizes as the "epitome of
Warren Court activism," is well known to most American movie and
television viewers. As anyone who watches "Hill Street Blues" or "Cagney
and Lacey" knows, it requires the police to give criminal suspects a warning before subjecting them to custodial questioning. The warning, which is
often read from a *"Miranda* card," varies slightly from state to state, but the
following is fairly typical:

> You have the right to remain silent. Anything you do or say
> may be used against you in a court of law. You have the right to

consult an attorney. If you cannot afford an attorney, one will be provided for you without cost. Now that I have advised you of your rights, are you willing to answer questions?

Failure by the police to give the warning—to *"Mirandize"* the suspect—may result in the exclusion from evidence of any resulting confession or admission. Many Americans believe that such exclusion results in guilty defendants going free.

But the *Miranda* rule does not require the freeing of criminal defendants, even if their constitutional rights have been violated. It merely prohibits the prosecution from using non-*Mirandized* statements in its case against the defendant. If the prosecution has other independent evidence sufficient to convict the defendant, it may use it, and the guilty person will go to jail.

If the defendant takes the witness stand on his own behalf, the prosecution may then use statements obtained in violation of *Miranda* to cross-examine him. There are numerous other exceptions to, and limitations on, the *Miranda* rule.

But despite these exceptions and limitations, there are some cases in which the failure of the police, whether deliberate or inadvertent, to give a proper *Miranda* warning will result in the freeing of a guilty defendant. (A common example of an inadvertent violation is when a subject who—unbeknownst to the police—does not understand English is not given a *Miranda* warning in a language he understands.) Although cases in which guilty defendants actually go free because of the *Miranda* rule are statistically few, there is understandable concern—and inevitable media coverage—any time a horrible criminal goes free because "the constable bungled," as one Supreme Court justice said.

Despite the small number of criminals who are freed as a result of *Miranda* violations, that decision has assumed—in the words of the Justice Department report—a "symbolic status." That symbolism appears to transcend its actual impact on law enforcement. Indeed, few police chiefs, FBI officials, or other law enforcement spokespersons are pushing for an abrogation of *Miranda,* now that the cop on the beat has learned to live with it.

As Gerald Arenberg, executive director of the National Association of Chiefs of Police, put it: *"Miranda* isn't the problem with crime. The problem is we don't have enough jails and . . . we're not targeting career criminals." He believes that Meese's attempt to overturn the ruling "just seems to be an exercise in futility."

A careful reading of the Justice Department report suggests that its criticism is not limited to the *Miranda* decision itself but extends to the

Fifth Amendment, on which it is based. In lieu of the current *Miranda* warning, the Justice Department has proposed the following:

> You do not have to make a statement or answer questions. However, if you have anything to say in your defense, we advise you to tell us now. Your failure to talk at this interview could make it harder for a judge or jury to believe any story you give later on.

Such a warning would change the substance of the Fifth Amendment's privilege against self-incrimination, and not just the procedures for implementing it. The privilege against self-incrimination gives a criminal suspect the absolute right to remain silent in the face of police interrogation. If "failure to talk" can later be used against the suspect in front of a judge or jury, the right to remain silent would become a hollow mockery. How can a citizen have a right, and at the same time be "advised" that if he invokes that right, it will be made "harder" for him?

The *Miranda* decision is indeed a symbol. It stands for every citizen's right to know about his or her rights and to be free to exercise them without fear of reprisal. Oliver North and John Poindexter knew about their right not to incriminate themselves before a congressional committee. Ernesto Miranda did not know about his right not to incriminate himself in an Arizona police station. It would be a sad day if America went back to the time when the exercise of one's constitutional rights depended on the level of one's education and the ability to hire a sophisticated lawyer.

January 27, 1987

See columns 3, 4, 43, 50, 89, 91, 105, and 140.

110
Fans Scream for Blood but Shouldn't Get It

Imagine the following hypothetical scene. It's next year's Super Bowl. The Giants and the Broncos are battling in a rematch for the biggest prize in football. Thousands of fans are in the stadium. Millions more are watching at home. It's the fourth quarter. The tension is mounting. The quarterback fades back and throws a touchdown pass. In frustration, the defensive lineman who almost sacked him gives him a late hit. The quarterback retaliates with a blind side punch. Players from both sides begin to push and shove. The officials blow their whistles, but the fight continues.

Suddenly, a group of policemen on horseback appear and break up the fight. The officials express gratitude and the players begin to line up to continue the game. But the police captain arrests the lineman and the quarterback, puts them in handcuffs, and takes them away. The charge: assault and battery. The punishment: up to a year in jail.

Could it happen? It could and it has—in other sports. Several hockey players have been criminally charged with felonious assault over the years. And now the mayor of Boston, Raymond Flynn, has called for police action in aggravated cases of sports violence, especially if the leagues themselves fail to control the fighting. A Boston city councilor recently introduced an ordinance that would require Boston's Finest to arrest professional athletes who commit violent acts on the ice or the parquet basketball floor of Boston Garden. The ordinance exempts boxing, but for all other sports it mandates prosecution for any violent act forbidden by law.

There is little chance that so vague an ordinance could be enacted or enforced. If taken literally, it would require the police to arrest Larry Bird every time he committed a foul or Wayne Gretzky every time he came to town and aimed a slap shot at a goalie or a hard body check at a defenseman. But somewhere along the line, someone has to take some responsibility for unneeded violence in sports.

Off the court and outside the rink, it is a crime to slap another person's arm, direct a hard rubber object at his head, or bang him into a wall. But these "assaults" are part of sports. The sponsor of the Boston law was quick to explain that he did not intend his ordinance to apply to such "normal" sports moves or even to "quick fights," but only to "melees and mayhem," as if those terms were clear and self-defining.

What is needed are specific guidelines and penalties for each sport. Initially, they should, of course, come from the sports leagues themselves. But what if the leagues refuse to control violence, as many believe is the case with the National Hockey League?

The fact is that violence is rampant in professional hockey. Players have been seriously injured by hard wooden weapons called hockey sticks. There is so much fighting during hockey games that Rodney Dangerfield tells a joke about the time he "went to the fights and a hockey game broke out." A National Hockey League game without at least one "good fight" is regarded by many fans as an incomplete experience. The fans demand fights and the officials do little to discourage them. The penalties and fines are generally trivial and are regarded as a cost of doing business as usual.

If the National Hockey League really wanted to stem violence on the ice, it could do so by making it clear that the league simply will not tolerate fighting. The National Basketball Association has certainly succeeded in sending out a message that it will not tolerate drug use. Although the recent lifetime suspensions (subject to reconsideration after two years) of two Houston Rockets may not end secret drug use by every player, they will certainly reduce its incidence by increasing the price of getting caught. And fighting on the ice is far easier to detect than snorting in the bathroom.

If the National Hockey League does not begin to get serious about violence, we may well see the enactment of ordinances in Boston and other cities. It would be too bad if it came to that, but a city does have the right to regulate violence within its jurisdiction.

Regulating sports violence by criminal laws is certainly a last resort. But if any criminal ordinance is eventually enacted, it should be very specific and limited to assaultive behavior that risks grave injury and that is not part of the game. Assaults with a hockey stick—especially after the whistle has blown—are primary candidates for criminalization. Punches to the head are a close second.

Somewhat more questionable are deliberate fouls and penalties that go well beyond accepted norms, such as those that have caused serious— sometimes career-ending—injuries to several football players.

One major problem with criminal legislation would be the possibility of selective enforcement against visiting team players. The leagues may be able to apply sanctions far more equitably than local police, prosecutors, or juries.

Let us hope that the leagues themselves—especially the National Hockey League—make criminal legislation unnecessary. But if they don't begin to take sports violence seriously, the politicians will.

February 3, 1987

111
Step Right Up and Get Your Clean Urine Here

You're sitting at your desk, daydreaming. The weekend is at hand: T.G.I.F.

Suddenly, the serenity is broken. Your boss walks in. "Charlie, it's your turn," he says. You fear that a last-minute rush of orders may deprive you of your weekend rest; but it's worse that you expected.

"You've got to drop your pants and leave us a little sample before you go home today—the random drug testing mandated by the home office. Don't worry. It's for the potheads and snorters, not for guys like you and me."

But you are worried. Last night at a party, you took a few puffs of a joint. The previous weekend you snorted a line of cocaine. You don't think of yourself as a druggie. You indulge maybe two or three times a month. Your performance at work is never affected. But you can't decline; that would mean your job.

You turn to an office mate for advice. He smiles and tells you that American initiative has come to the rescue. He pulls a small packet of powder out of his pocket. It looks like a drug, but he explains to you that it is actually the antidote: clean urine powder. Just add warm water and turn it in at the company lab.

This is not just a fantasy: several firms are, in fact, marketing various kinds of "clean" urine samples. "You can actually *study* for a urine test," boasts one ad for a company that instructs you how to fool the machine. Another company guarantees that its urine comes from members of a Bible-study group right from the buckle of the Bible Belt. You can't get much cleaner than that!

Not that this is a completely new idea; paroled drug addicts, who are often required to take regular urine tests, have been borrowing or buying fresh urine from friends, relatives, and associates for a long time. However, so many people are now subjected to drug tests that selling the stuff in packages has become a viable business. Necessity is certainly the mother of this illegitimate child of the 1980s.

But is all this really legal? Law enforcement authorities want to close down these companies, claiming that they will destroy legitimate drug testing. The innovative business people marketing the products argue that it is perfectly reasonable to fight fire with fire, and technology with counter-technology.

A few analogies come to mind. Term-paper factories, "head shops," and stores that sell radar detectors all cater to customers who probably are committing criminal or, at least, fraudulent acts. Some states have enacted laws to criminalize such businesses, and it probably will be made a crime to defraud urine testers, especially when the tests are mandated by law. Those who sell the cheating devices probably will be regarded as accessories to fraud.

This entire process of action and counteraction is quintessentially American. The government starts the game by overreacting to the real problem of heavy drug use among employees in drug-sensitive jobs—transportation workers, police, and the members of the military—by trying to catch even moderate users in nonsensitive jobs. The free market responds with a shield that is also far too wide. It threatens to neutralize even the most limited testing narrowly focused on sensitive employees.

A balance must be struck. It is unlikely that the government will strike the appropriate balance, since getting soft on drug use is almost always bad politics. Nor are the increasingly pro-government federal courts likely to intervene on behalf of employees, except perhaps in egregious cases. But the free market may well succeed where the law fails.

It turns out that these new-fangled cheating devices are not absolutely foolproof. They can be detected, but only at considerable expense. A rational market probably will limit the expensive counter-detection to the most drug-sensitive jobs. Thus, the federal aviation authorities will probably decide that it is worth the extra money to make sure that pilots and air traffic controllers are not cheating the drug tests, but they will hesitate to spend the additional money on flight attendants or ticket agents. The effect of all these spy vs. spy machinations may well be a relatively rational limitation on effective drug testing.

The moral costs of this back-and-forth process are, however, considerable. The current overly broad testing may breed a distrust of government, which will lead to a cynical acceptance of cheating. Any acceptance of cheating, even one limited to overly broad drug testing, cannot help but spread to other areas. In the end, it would be far better to strike the proper balance directly, rather than through this twisted free-market mechanism.

In other words, the Bible Belt Urine Kit is no answer to the overkill of drug testing, but rather a symptom of it. Drug abuse is a problem that must be addressed sensibly—not sensationally or surreptitiously.

February 10, 1987

112
Homicide and the Seat-Belt Defense

And now a new wrinkle in the seat-belt controversy. As states continue to debate the merits of mandatory seat-belt laws, an innovative criminal defense lawyer has made use of such a law in defending a negligent homicide case.

The facts themselves make a strong argument for wearing seat belts. Defendant Jeffrey Smith and a passenger were driving in one car. Smith was wearing a seat belt; his passenger was not. Smith tried to pass another car in a dangerous maneuver. His car collided head on with a third car. The driver of the third car was not wearing a seat belt; his passenger was. Not surprisingly, the two persons who wore seat belts lived. The ones who did not, died. Smith was charged with negligent homicide.

His lawyer introduced an affidavit by an expert from the Transportation Research Institute who concluded that: "The people who died had a very high probability of living, had they been following [the] seat-belt law."

The lawyer argued, in effect, that although his client may have caused the crash, he did not cause the deaths. At the very least, the victims themselves contributed to their own deaths by failing to comply with the mandatory seat-belt law. This novel defense apparently worked, and the jury acquitted the defendant. The jury foreman acknowledged that the victim's failure to wear seat belts was the "significant factor" in the acquittal.

Under the American system of justice, individual jury verdicts do not carry any precedential weight. Future juries will not be told what the *Smith* jury did and will be free to render contrary verdicts. But jury verdicts like this one do have significance. They send a message to prosecutors. They alert defense attorneys to the possibility of making similar arguments in future cases. They can have a contagious effect on other juries through the media and word of mouth. And, perhaps, they can have some impact on suicidal drivers and passengers who still believe it is safe to drive unbuckled. (I recently rented a Hertz car in St. Martin, which came without seat belts. The local Hertz manager actually tried to convince me that seat belts weren't necessary on that island's many windy roads.)

Eventually, the appellate courts will have to confront the question of whether the failure of the victims to wear seat belts should be a defense or a mitigation in cases where a driver is charged with vehicular homicide.

Similar questions will be posed in civil cases, in which the drivers are sued for the tort of wrongful death.

There are cogent arguments on both sides of this intriguing issue. In general, the law requires an assailant to "take his victim as he finds him." For example, if an assailant punches someone in the mouth with force insufficient to kill a normal person, but unbeknownst to the assailant, his victim is a hemophiliac who then bleeds to death, the assailant is generally guilty of homicide (though not of first-degree murder). Or as Professor Yale Kamisar of Michigan Law School recently put it: "If I rob a bank and knock a customer over the head, and the guy is too fat for his own good, can I say he wouldn't have died if he had been in better shape?"

But it is not against the law to be "out of shape" or to be a hemophiliac. It *is* against the law in Michigan for people in the front seats of cars not to wear their seat belts. If it is true that the victims would not have died but for their own voluntary violation of law, there is a compelling argument that the defendant should be held criminally responsible for their injuries, but not for their deaths.

Several years ago a man was shot in the head and mortally wounded. But his heart continued to beat and might have kept him "alive"—though he was "brain dead"—for a considerable period of time. His family agreed to donate his heart for an organ transplant, and he "died" as a result of the removal of his heart. The question was then raised as to whether the person who shot him could be charged with murder under a statute that required the deaths to follow the shooting within "a year and a day." The defense argued that but for the organ removal, the victim might have lived for more than a year and a day. The issue was never clearly resolved in that instance and remains a law professor's hypothetical case.

The seat-belt defense will also confound and divide the courts until it is authoritatively resolved by legislatures or appellate decisions. My prediction is that the victim's failure to wear a legally mandated seat belt will continue to influence jurors in both civil tort cases and criminal homicide cases, but that the legislatures and appellate courts will be reluctant to create a formal seat-belt defense.

The best way to avoid these problems is for all drivers and passengers to buckle up. In that way the number of automobile deaths will decrease dramatically and no one will be able to raise a seat-belt defense.

February 17, 1987

See columns 6, 12, 49, and 79.

113
The Buying of a Witness

When I read that John Gotti—who the government says is the boss of the Mafia's first family—was acquitted by a jury, my reactions were mixed. On one hand, I am no fan of organized crime. I always root for Eliot Ness's men when I watch reruns of "The Untouchables." On the other hand, our present-day Eliot Nesses often use techniques that might be more appropriately employed by criminals than by authorities attempting to enforce the law.

The government's primary weapon in its war against organized crime is the bought witness. (Its other is the wiretap.) In order to buy a witness (or, more realistically, to rent one, since they don't always stay bought)* the government is prepared to pay enormous sums of money.

Even more important, it can offer considerations far more valuable than cash. Not only can it spare the witness imprisonment, but it can also provide him with a new identity, start-up funds for a new business, a phony credit history, and, in some instances, a promise to close its eyes to continuing or further crimes. (In the *Gotti* case, a witness testified that government agents had offered him drugs if he would testify.)

Why does the government go to such extraordinary lengths? The answer, according to government sources, is that unless they make it worthwhile for associates of criminals to risk their lives by testifying, witnesses simply will not come forward. Without such witnesses, it would be difficult, sometimes impossible, to make cases against those who commit either "victimless" crimes or crimes in which the victims cannot or do not complain—such as in organized crime, political corruption, insider trading, and the like.

Prosecutors who use these witnesses claim to do so reluctantly. They realize that some jurors will be uncomfortable when asked to convict a defendant on the word of someone who has sold out to the highest bidder. They argue to the jury that the government didn't choose this witness; the defendant chose him as an associate.

"When you prosecute the devil, you have to go to hell for eyewitnesses, and you get the devil's associates, not a bunch of angels." That line of argument generally works, as evidenced by the recent string of successful prosecutions against alleged organized crime capos. But in the *Gotti* case, the string ran out; the jury simply refused to send Gotti and several others to prison on the basis of bought testimony.

Just before the jurors rendered their surprising acquittal, they requested that the judge send into the jury room a chart prepared by the defense listing the crimes committed by the seven major government witnesses who had made deals to testify. The chart showed nearly seventy crimes, involving murder, drugs, kidnapping, and perjury. The witnesses had admitted under cross-examination that lying was a way of life for them and that they had, in the past, lied repeatedly when it served their interests.

The government's argument—that these chronic liars had suddenly gotten religion, now that they had switched from the Mafia's payroll to the government's—apparently fell on deaf ears in this case. But there are thousands of convicted criminals now serving long sentences on the basis of similar arguments and similarly bought testimony. Many of them, undoubtedly, are guilty, but some of them are most certainly innocent—or, at the very least, victims of perjured testimony given by people who were hired by government lawyers.

The risks of perjury in such cases is considerable. Every bought witness realizes that the government will pay only for testimony that helps it win its case. The great temptation, therefore, is for the witness to tailor his testimony to fit that end. Generally, there is a perfect fit, requiring no tailoring at all. Sometimes, a few minor alterations are required for cosmetic purposes. In some cases, the entire suit has to be redone to fit the prosecution's design.

These witnesses-for-hire know better than to tell honest prosecutors about the tailoring. Some highly ethical prosecutors—who place the integrity of the system above their own records of wins and losses—have a keen eye for tailored merchandise. Others—who want to hear what they are being told—are easily taken in by clever stitching designed to cover up major changes.

In prosecuting criminals, even organized criminals, the noble end of putting them out of business does not justify the ignoble means of buying witnesses. Prosecutors, like everyone else, get what they pay for. A bought witness may tell the truth—but only if it suits his interest to do so. The *Gotti* jury apparently believed that the government either did not get its money's worth—or got more than its money's worth—from the witnesses that it rented to testify. In rendering a verdict of acquittal, the jury sent a message. I hope government prosecutors pay attention.

March 17, 1987

*See columns 45 and 46 on recanted testimony.

114
Joke Law Is Nothing to Laugh At

At Harvard Law School, where I teach, a well-intentioned student, writing in the school newspaper, has urged all members of the university community "to make a personal decision neither to tell nor listen to racist or sexist jokes." The city of Long Branch, New Jersey, doesn't just urge this as a personal decision; it has actually prohibited municipal employees from telling "jokes or stories based on ethnic or racial types or sex." I knew it would come to this.

The student's argument about the evils of such jokes deserves to be heard. He believes that "racist and sexist jokes contribute to prejudice and stereotypes and the overall dehumanization of [those] joked about." He acknowledges that "jokes don't rise to the level of overt vicious behavior," but he insists that they "cultivate a social context of . . . willed ignorance" and "reflect a callous indifference that tacitly invites the more overt actions of others."

I have little doubt that some of these observations are somewhat true for some people. They are probably also applicable, more or less, to a wide range of public and private expression, including such popular media as television, magazines, songs, films, and advertising. We are, after all, what we read, learn, see, and otherwise experience. What makes jokes any different?

Before trying to answer that, I must disclose my own strong bias. I love jokes of all kinds—good ones, bad ones, silly ones, clever ones, puns, dialect jokes, dirty jokes, clean jokes, even "shaggy-dog" and "no-soap-radio" jokes. (If those references escape you, you are not a real joke aficionado.) I admit that I am offended by certain genres of cruel, malicious, and gross jokes, but I regard that purely as a matter of taste. I tell jokes—endlessly, repeatedly, and inappropriately, as my friends, family, and students will gladly attest. My idea of eternal damnation would be a humorless hell—or heaven.

Indeed, I've visited such places. In the Soviet Union, people are put in prison for telling anti-Soviet jokes. (Not surprisingly, some of the best anti-Soviet jokes come from the gulags: for example, a guard asks a prisoner serving a ten-year sentence what he's in for. The prisoner says, "Nothing at all." To which the guard replies, "I don't believe you—for nothing at all they give you just five years, not ten.")

Jokes, by their very nature, are necessarily provocative, upsetting, and stereotypical—at least to some. Humor, like offensiveness, is in the eye, ear, and psyche of the beholder. Ethnic humor, especially, is often a double-edged sword. For example, the best collections of Jewish jokes—originated mostly by the subjects themselves—contain negative stereotypes that may offend at the same time that they convey a poignantly positive message. Some other jokes have no such redeeming value.

Who should be the arbiter? At what point on the continuum from good-humored to grossly offensive should self-censorship be imposed? When, if ever, should the governmental gag be placed over the mouth of the joke teller? Which evil is worse: censorship or incivility? And what about spontaneity? Don't we give up too much when we demand that everyone carefully consider whether his or her words will break the law—even among friends—before he blurts out a funny remark that might offend someone? These are the kinds of questions we must ask before we too easily succumb to the temptation of submitting to any regime of censorship—self-imposed or otherwise.

Self-imposed censorship has the virtue, at least, of being self-regulating. Thus, uniform standards of offensiveness need not be articulated and enforced, the way they must be if the government becomes involved, as it has in Long Branch. Imagine the inevitable disputes that will arise if the joke police begin enforcing the ban against jokes "based on ethnic or racial types or sex." Joke judges (or joke juries) will have to sit in judgment to determine whether to sentence the offending joker to jail or to some other appropriate punishment. (Gilbert and Sullivan's *Mikado* would be able to figure out how "to let the punishment fit the crime"—perhaps a few weeks of mandatory exposure to Don Rickles's humor.)

As soon as the Long Branch edict goes into effect, a new genre of jokes will surely emerge—one always does. It could be "neuter" jokes: "Did you hear the one about the nondescript person . . . ?" Every listener will fill in his or her own blanks and imagine the ethnicity and gender of the joke's subject. I guess that will be progress.

As with all speech, the best answers to bad jokes are good jokes, not no jokes. Let those who would ban sexist and racist jokes spend their energies coming up with better and funnier anti-sexist and anti-racist jokes. Jokes are a laughing matter, and there should be only one criterion for judging them: whether or not they are funny.

March 24, 1987

115
Junkies' Needles May Kill Us All

For years, some criminologists have been urging a sensible approach to the terrible problem of intravenous heroin use. Under this approach, medically certified "mainline" adults would receive direct injections of heroin supplied by the government. Such a proposal would not solve the intractable problem of heroin addiction, but it would at least reduce the amount of crime that heroin addicts commit in their desperate search for a way to pay for drugs.

The growing AIDS epidemic now makes such an approach to intravenous drug use an absolute public health necessity. At the moment, about 90 percent of the more than 32,000 Americans who have been diagnosed as having AIDS fall into the "high-risk" groups of male homosexuals and intravenous drug users. A recent *New York Times* study has made it abundantly clear that intravenous heroin users are the most probable "bridge" for the transmission of AIDS to the population at large.

The homosexual community is undertaking extraordinary educational efforts to convey the importance of "safe sex" and other measures required to stem the spread of the deadly disease. These steps seem to be working, at least to some degree. There are also some programs to educate drug users about the dangers of AIDS. But most intravenous heroin addicts simply are not educable. They have passed the point of control. They are desperate slaves to their addiction.

AIDS is spread among heroin addicts when they share hypodermic needles. Needles are inexpensive, but they are available only by medical prescription, which means that addicts use scarce needles repeatedly. Usually they don't have much regard for sterile conditions.

Addicts then transfer the disease to nonaddicts during sex. Many male addicts live with women, upon whom they depend for support. Some of these women are prostitutes—as are many female heroin addicts. Surprisingly, in this age of concern over the spread of AIDS, a considerable number of men of all ages and backgrounds still frequent prostitutes. Not all of them use condoms. It is only a matter of time until this transmission mechanism brings AIDS into the mainstream American family—unless the transmission is cut off at its source.

Since the source is the shared hypodermic needle, that should be the focus of the public health concern. The shared needle must become a relic of the past, if not for the benefit of the addicts themselves, then in order to save the lives of their innocent victims who will contract AIDS because an addict shared a needle years earlier at a shooting gallery in a distant neighborhood.

Simply passing out clean needles to addicts—which some people recently have advocated—will not address the problem. Addicts will sell anything for the quick fix, even their own health, and eventually their lives. The desperate addict will sell his clean needle to a somewhat less desperate addict and continue to share dirty needles with other desperate addicts.

One might also argue that some addicts will prefer the camaraderie of the shooting gallery to the antiseptic atmosphere of a state-run heroin clinic. But many addicts are extraordinarily docile and enervated. They will drift toward the easiest lifestyle consistent with their addiction. And it will be easier for an addict to find his way to a free clinic than to hold up a grocery store, run from the police, and then locate a drug source. Eventually, the official fix would replace the pattern of robbery, shared needles, and shooting galleries for many, perhaps most, addicts.

It's not a pretty picture, the government becoming a dispenser of heroin. But it's a lot prettier than the picture, now projected by public health officials, of hundreds of thousands, perhaps millions, of American men, women, and children dying from a disease over which they have no control.

The public policy choice is not whether addicts should get drugs; they will, whether we like it or not, by any means possible. The choice is, rather, how they will get the drugs. It's time to stop moralizing over the evils of heroin addiction, because there is little we can do about that problem. We must turn our attention to the far more pressing problem of AIDS transmission.

March 31, 1987

116
Freedom of Speech for the CIA

Recently, a jury acquitted Amy Carter, Abbie Hoffman, and others after they broke the trespassing law during a protest against CIA recruiting at the

University of Massachusetts. But it seems that some of those who support such protests don't think that the CIA has reciprocal rights of free speech. Among them are some members of the American Civil Liberties Union.

Radical groups throughout the country are trying to bar CIA recruiters from college and university campuses. They argue that the CIA has engaged in unlawful conduct and has thus forfeited its claim to legitimacy. Pointing to the formal policy guidelines at the University of Massachusetts and other schools that limit recruiting privileges to "law abiding" and "legitimate" organizations, these groups are demanding that such policies be interpreted to exclude the CIA.

At the Carter-Hoffman trial, the defense presented the testimony of Morton Halperin, director of the ACLU legislative office. Halperin said, in essence, that the CIA is not only a violator of the law, but a recidivist. This defense obviously impressed the jury, which acquitted all the defendants despite the undisputed evidence that they had engaged in trespassing.

The fact that one jury in western Massachusetts accepted a defense of "necessity"—that it was necessary for Amy Carter and Abbie Hoffman to violate the law a little bit to prevent far greater violations of law by the CIA—does not mean, of course, that other juries will do the same. Nor does it mean that the CIA should be banned from further recruiting at the University of Massachusetts or elsewhere. Indeed, banning the CIA from university campuses would establish a dangerous precedent and would be inconsistent with civil liberties principles that mandate freedom of speech for all points of view.

Supporters of the CIA should be allowed a forum to present their views at any university that considers itself bound by either the letter or spirit of the First Amendment. Even if no one wants to listen, it would be wrong to try to prevent advocates of an unpopular viewpoint from trying to persuade a hostile audience. In any event, there are students who do want to listen, and their rights would be curtailed by a ban.

Thomas Lesser, one of the lawyers who represented Carter and Hoffman, agrees that the CIA and its supporters should not be prevented from speaking on university campuses. "They have the right to conduct informational meetings or participate in debates," he acknowledges. But he and many others draw the line at recruiting. He argues that a government agency has no right to recruit students into engaging in unlawful conduct. His attempt to draw the line at recruitment, however, does not withstand principled analysis.

Imagine how differently those who advocate a ban on CIA recruiting would feel—and act—if the shoe were on the other foot. What if the Civil Rights Division of the Justice Department had been banned from recruiting on the University of Mississippi campus in the 1960s? Many at that university honestly felt that the Justice Department was acting illegally in forcing schools to desegregate. Or what if a group of radical anti-CIA activists were banned from recruiting participants for its next sit-in demonstration? Or what if the African National Congress were prohibited in the United States—as it is in South Africa—from recruiting, on the ground that some of its activities are admittedly illegal? I doubt we would see Amy Carter or Abbie Hoffman leading demonstrations in favor of such bans.

The CIA's attempt to recruit on university campuses is a political act of speech. It should be answered in kind, with protests, debates, teach-ins, and pickets—but not with a ban. Students have the right—indeed the need—to hear all sides of issues. This is especially so when it comes to issues as important as the CIA's role in formulating and implementing our government's policies at home and abroad. Those who believe that the CIA is engaging in unlawful conduct have an obligation to persuade their listeners to try to change those policies by democratic means. But they should not try to shut down those who disagree.

If some students are persuaded to work for the CIA, fine. If others are not, that is fine, as well. In a democratic society committed to freedom of speech, the appropriate balance should be struck in the marketplace of ideas—not forced upon the population by the government, the university, or a particular political group.

For the ACLU, this should be a simple issue. But because that organization has become, unfortunately, a convenient coalition of principled civil libertarians (who favor maximum freedom of speech) and political leftists (many of whom oppose the CIA), we are likely to see a divisive battle over whether the CIA should be banned from recruiting on campuses.

Unless principle prevails over politics, the credibility of the ACLU—as a neutral advocate of all free speech—will suffer. More importantly, a ban on the CIA will be another step on the road to erosion of the very rights that the ACLU was founded to protect.

May 19, 1987

117
A Judicial Cover-Up?

Iranscam notwithstanding, Washington is not the only place in the country where government officials prefer not to notice evidence of possible wrong-doing in their midst. I think that something similar is happening in Rhode Island—a state that has been wracked recently by accusations of corruption in its legal system.

Our story begins with a drug indictment against two young men. The defendants were represented by four of the best lawyers in Boston, men and women with excellent reputations. During preparations for the trial, a Rhode Island lawyer who was representing the government's main witness "actively sought a private meeting" between his client and a defendant, according to court affidavits.

This was unusual, since lawyers for government witnesses almost never allow their clients to meet privately with defendants in criminal cases. According to the affidavits, filed by the defense lawyers in conjunction with pretrial motions, the Rhode Island lawyer indicated in "numerous different ways" that his client could be "tremendously helpful" to the defendants or that he could be "a good government witness."

One of the Boston lawyers recalled that, in his discussions with them, the Rhode Island lawyer added that he didn't know what his client would ask for at the private meeting and that he "did not want to know."

The defense lawyers suspected that a bribery attempt might be afoot, and so they informed the U.S. attorney in Boston, where the meeting was to take place. The U.S. attorney's office there arranged for the FBI to secretly record the meeting by "wiring" the defendant. On a tape, later presented in court, the witness told the defendant that "I can do great harm to you," and demanded that the defendant pay him more than $250,000, claiming that the defendant owed him that amount from previous drug transactions. The implication was clear: unless the defendant paid him, the witness would do him harm at the trial.

The defense lawyers brought this conversation to the attention of Ronald Lagueux, the federal district judge to whom the drug case had been as-signed. Lagueux conducted a hearing on their allegation that the witness had solicited a bribe. The judge's reaction, after hearing witnesses, was to attack the defense lawyers. He called one of them, Andrew Good, a "clever manipulator who cannot be completely trusted," another "a name-dropping . . . self-proclaimed expert on greed." He staunchly defended the witness's lawyer, who he said had been "bushwacked."

Judge Lagueux acknowledged that the witness had "demanded $250,000." But he said he believed that the witness was merely trying to collect a drug debt "which in his mind was due him," rather than "extorting money from [the defendant] in exchange for altering his testimony." (As if a demand by a witness for payment of a quarter of a million dollar illegal "debt" in order not to "do great harm to you," could be anything other than a bribe solicitation.)

One of the Boston lawyers, Norman Zalkind, then filed a motion seeking the disqualification of Judge Lagueux on the ground that he was biased against the Boston attorneys and favored the Rhode Island lawyer. The judge responded to this entirely proper legal motion by declaring that Zalkind should be disciplined for his "gratuitous, scurrilous, scandalous personal attack on me and on my integrity."

After denying the motion, the judge suggested that Zalkind should be barred from his courtroom and perhaps even indicted. Judge Lagueux has scheduled a disciplinary hearing for September, in which he will seek to bar Zalkind from participating further in the case. The judge plans to conduct this hearing himself, thus serving as both prosecutor and judge.

This kind of behavior was familiar to me. Although we have never met, Judge Lagueux issued a similar threat against me last year after I had written a book about the Claus von Bulow case, in which I criticized several Rhode Island judges and lawyers (not including him). Without having read my book, Lagueux declared in a statement to the press that I had "no credibility" because of what I had said about Rhode Island and that I would never be allowed to practice in his courtroom.

What explanation could there be for such conduct? One possible explanation is that Judge Lagueux does not want the Rhode Island legal community exposed to charges of corruption or other irregularities beyond those it has already suffered.

In one recent illustration of how the Rhode Island "justice" system works, the chief justice of the state supreme court, Joseph Bevilacqua, was suspended and later retired amid allegations that he had associated with members of organized crime. Around the same time, the state's attorney general, Arlene Violet, charged that judicial corruption was widespread in Rhode Island.

(Violet lost a reelection bid after her opponents generated an investigation of her on charges that she had overzealously prosecuted some defendants. That investigation, being conducted by the new attorney general, is still continuing.)

Judge Lagueux, let me make clear, has never been implicated in any of these charges. However, Judge Lagueux apparently sees his role as defender of the Rhode Island system against all who would criticize it. (In his attack last year, he charged me with not understanding "how law is practiced in Rhode Island." I proudly plead guilty to that compliment.) It seems to me that if proper criticism is discouraged in this way, we will never see an end to corruption in Rhode Island or elsewhere.

Although "cover-ups" are generally orchestrated by those involved in crimes, when a judge actively attacks those who bring to light a suspicious event, the term "cover-up" seems appropriate. (There is nothing to suggest that Judge Lagueux was himself involved in a bribery attempt.)

Some of the defense lawyers involved in this case are considering asking the House Judiciary Committee to investigate whether the judge's actions constitute an impeachable offense. If the committee wants to look into this affair, its inquiry will, of course, be overshadowed by other congressional committees' investigations of the Iran-contra affair. But even if it doesn't create big headlines, our legislators in Washington certainly ought to look at what's going on in Rhode Island in general and in Judge Lagueux's courtroom in particular.

May 26, 1987

For later developments, see column 137.

118
Alice in Wonderland Replaces the Constitution

The Supreme Court seems to be relying these days more on *Alice in Wonderland* than on the Bill of Rights as precedent for criminal justice decisions. In its most recent trashing of constitutional protections, a majority of the high court ruled that an arrested defendant—even one without a record of violence—can be sent to jail *before* he is even tried. This reversal of our presumption of innocence is reminiscent of a dialogue between Lewis Carroll's Alice and the Queen:

> "There's the King's Messenger, he's in prison now, being punished; and the trial doesn't even begin till next Wednesday; and of course the crime comes last of all."
> "Suppose he never commits the crime?" asked Alice.
> "That would be all the better, wouldn't it?" the Queen responded. . . .
> Alice felt there was no denying that. "Of course it would be all the better," she said; "but it wouldn't be all the better his being punished."
> "You're wrong . . ." said the Queen. "Were you ever punished?"
> "Only for faults," said Alice.
> "And you were all the better for it, I know!" the Queen said triumphantly.
> "Yes, but then I had done the things I was punished for," said Alice. "That makes all the difference."
> "But if you hadn't done them," the Queen said, "that would have been better still; better, and better, and better!" Her voice went higher with each "better," till it got quite to a squeak. . . .
> Alice thought, "There's a mistake here somewhere. . . ."

There are several mistakes in the Queen's logic and in the Supreme Court's decision. The first lies in the belief that judges are capable of predicting which arrested suspects are likely to commit future crimes.

Chief Justice William Rehnquist glibly assumes that judges are capable of glimpsing the future through their judicial crystal balls, but evidence strongly suggests that if judges are given the power of preventive detention they will tend to confine too many people. The reason is simple: if the judge makes the mistake of jailing a defendant who does not commit a crime, no one will ever learn of the error. But if the judge makes the mistake of releasing a defendant who then commits a crime, that error will become front-page news. And judges—especially elected judges—will generally seek to avoid negative headlines holding them responsible for crimes. This means that judges will follow the dictum, "When in doubt don't let him out."

Moreover, if Rehnquist is correct in assuring us that judges can predict who will be dangerous, then what is to prevent the enactment of legislation authorizing preventive detention of "dangerous" people who have not yet been accused of any crime. I can hear the law-and-order demagogues invoking the old proverbs about "A stitch in time" and "An ounce of prevention." Years ago cartoonist Walt Kelly had a hound dog sheriff who would shout "Quick, put 'em in jail *before* they do something!" Rehnquist seems to invite such an expansion of preventive detention by declaring that imprisonment before trial is not really punishment at all. He should visit some of the "nonpunishment" jails around the country before trying to sell us that bill of goods.

Despite its *Alice in Wonderland* quality, the Supreme Court's decision will probably prove quite popular with a public that is frightened of crime and impatient with constitutional safeguards. The public identifies far more closely with the potential victims of crime than with the potential victims of injustice. But the Bill of Rights was not intended to produce popular results. It was intended to limit government power. Its provisions reflect the view that it is far better for ten guilty to go free than for even a single innocent to be wrongly imprisoned. Hence our strong presumption of innocence, our requirement of proof beyond a reasonable doubt, and our other guarantees of a fair and effective defense.

Putting a defendant behind bars before the trial will affect his ability to gather evidence of innocence or mitigating factors. It will also give the prosecutor an enormous advantage in plea bargaining.

Most important, however, it empowers the police, the prosecutor, and the judge to imprison, without any judgment by a jury of ordinary citizens. In practice the grand jury tends to be a rubber stamp for prosecutors. Only the petit jury—the trial jury—hears both sides of the case before rendering a verdict.

And therein lies the crux of the problem. Confining a defendant before he has had an opportunity to gather his evidence and present his case is simply not the American way. As Justice Thurgood Marshall said in his dissenting opinion, preventive detention is more "consistent with the usages of tyranny and the excesses of what bitter experience teaches us to call the police state." In fact, the Soviet Union employs preventive detention widely against dissidents, especially when visiting dignitaries arrive. And other police states have used preventive detention as a substitute for trial.

No single Supreme Court decision can create a police state in America. But if the current trend continues, we will have taken a dangerous step in the direction of *Alice in Wonderland* justice, where the sentence comes first and trial—if it is held at all—is an afterthought.

June 2, 1987

119
Freedom of Religion Means
the Freedom to Be Mean

Most organized religions have a process for ostracizing, excommunicating, or otherwise ridding themselves of sinners. The Jehovah's Witnesses call theirs "shunning," and it is ostracism with a vengeance. No member of the church—even close friends and family—may have any contact with a shunned former member. If they breach this wall, they too will be shunned.

Perhaps the most famous shunned person in recent history has been superstar Michael Jackson, who left the Jehovah's Witnesses. But their response to him was, in effect, "You can't quit; you're fired." And being fired meant being shunned by all members who wanted to remain in the church. Even Jackson's own mother is reportedly under the shunning order.

In a church as close-knit as the Jehovah's Witnesses—as with the Amish or Mennonites, who have similar rules—a shunning order can be a sentence of emotional solitary confinement. For a person whose whole life has been within the church and whose friends and family are all members, there is no place to go for solace. No place, except the courts!

In a recent case, a shunned Alaskan woman named Janet Paul brought suit against the governing body of the Jehovah's Witnesses, claiming that the actions of the church caused her extreme emotional harm. The church responded by arguing that shunning is a religious practice required by the Bible, which calls for apostates to be cast out. Thus, since shunning is part of their religion—the argument goes—no court may interfere with its exercise regardless of how much harm it may cause.

The U.S. Court of Appeals for the Ninth Circuit, which covers the far western portions of the country, agreed with the Jehovah's Witnesses. It ruled that even severe emotional harm to a shunned person must be tolerated "as a price well worth paying to safeguard the right of religious difference that all citizens enjoy."

If courts were free to inquire into alleged harms caused by various sects, virtually every religion—mainstream or marginal—would have its tenets challenged by disgruntled members. Religion wields a powerful influence over the lives of many. Inevitably, it disappoints and frustrates some.

Imagine the lawsuits that would follow from a legal rule allowing dissatisfied customers of religions to sue. Jewish male dropouts might seek legal redress for their circumcisions. Former Catholic priests might complain of having missed out on years of marriage. Protesting Protestants could allege that their religions had been placed in a bad light by TV evangelists.

The courts must stay out of religious squabbles, even when religions act irresponsibly, hurtfully, or unfairly. Recently, the Supreme Court ruled that churches have the right to hire and fire all employees—even those performing secular functions—on the basis of religion.

Religion is—or at least should be—a matter of choice, certainly when it comes to adults. If someone does not like or believe in their religion, the option is to leave and find another religion—or nonreligion. It is often painful to make important transitions, especially transitions involving faith, practice, and community. That is why—as a matter of simple decency— church leaders should make leaving as guilt-free and nonrecriminatory as possible. And most do. But the remedy against those churches that are insensitive to the human needs of their former members must be within the church organization—not within the realms of government regimentation or entanglement.

As a nation, we are already paying far too much attention to the inner workings of churches. The media fascination—indeed voyeurism—with PTL and television evangelism is regrettable, even if it is understandable. The implications of a government probe into whether contributors to Jim and Tammy Bakker were cheated when their money went into expensive homes and cars is frightening. Who is to say that a biblical theme park is a less authentic religious edifice than a lavish church, a gaudy synagogue, or an ornate mosque? What is the constitutionally correct salary and expense account for a minister, priest, or rabbi?

The law has generally drawn the line at fraud. If the alleged religious leader really does not believe what he is preaching and is intending to bilk his parishioners, the law is prepared to step in. But the line separating fraud from fanaticism is not a sharp one, and there is a danger that dissident prophets may be seen as falling on the fraud side more often than the mainstream preachers are.

The court of appeals was correct in recognizing that we "pay a price" for our religious freedoms—as we do for our other freedoms. It is probably little comfort to Janet Paul, whose friends and family refuse to speak to her, to know that her sacrifice is made in the interest of religious freedom for all of us. But that is true. If she had won her case, no religion would be free to practice any tenets of its faith, except those that were completely without risk of harm. And we would need a governmental agency to guarantee that every religion—like every can of food or every drug—was properly packaged, fairly labeled, and free of negative side effects.

June 30, 1987

120
His (Version of the) Truth
Is Marching On

I was sitting around with a group of criminal lawyers the night before Oliver North testified. We were speculating about what he would say. Surprisingly, for a group of contentious advocates, we all agreed. Even more surprising, we turned out to be right on the mark.

We didn't have a crystal ball or a direct line into North's conversations with his lawyers. We just had a lot of collective experience with "preparing" witnesses to testify. Although the very concept of "preparing" a witness sounds vaguely suspect—why, after all, does anyone have to be "prepared" to tell the truth—all lawyers are required to go through that exercise. Its principal purpose is to make certain that the witness is not surprised by hostile or trick questions from the cross-examining attorney on the other side.

Another important purpose—somewhat more suspect—is to help "shape" the witness's testimony into the most exculpatory, or least incriminatory, form. Lawyers who employ this technique justify it by pointing out that objective facts are subject to varying interpretations, and that the witness has a right to present the facts so as to encourage the interpretation most favorable to his position.

With this in mind, the first step in preparing your witness's testimony is to set out the hard evidence against him that no one could possibly dispute; for example, tape recordings, documents signed by him, or the testimony of disinterested observers. The second step is to fit your witness's testimony around this hard evidence.

Thus, if a criminal defendant were caught by the police—or even worse on videotape—with a smoking gun in his hand and a dead body on the floor, his testimonial options would be severely constrained. He could hardly deny that it was he who was caught or that the body was dead. He could, however, claim self-defense, insanity, or even—though this would be stretching it—that he came into the room after the shooting and innocently picked up the gun. (I once actually had a client who tried to make such a preposterous claim, but I talked him out of taking the witness stand.)

In the context of the North testimony, the hard evidence included the facts that: 1) arms were sent to Iran and profits diverted to the contras in possible violation of law; 2) North had told various people that he had the president's approval for such actions; 3) North had told the Iranians—in a conversation that was taped—that if the truth came out, the president would be impeached; 4) North shredded numerous documents relating to his activities.

As these hard facts are set out, it becomes fairly obvious how North's testimony can be shaped around them to serve his goals, which are to avoid incriminating himself or blaming the president. North should testify that at the time he acted, he assumed that the president had authorized his actions, but that it now turns out that his assumption was wrong. So far as his statements to others that the president had in fact authorized the actions and would be impeached if the truth were disclosed, North should testify that he was deliberately dissembling as part of his job, but that he is now telling the truth.

This, of course, is pretty much what North told the committees. He also followed several other standard rules of testimony: Attribute as many conversations to the dead man (in this case William Casey); use the fact that documents were admittedly shredded as a sword, rather than just a shield (in this case by testifying that he kept detailed ledgers of every penny of cash and travelers checks, but then destroyed the ledgers at Casey's insistence); and admit, indeed proclaim, that, when there is no possible excuse or justification for what you did (phonying up the documents on the security fence at his home), you were just plain wrong.

The fact that North's testimony coincided almost exactly with what experienced criminal lawyers predicted he would say does not prove that he was lying or even stretching the truth. It does suggest, however, that his testimony should be scrutinized quite carefully by the investigating committees.

Nor does North's testimony in any way impugn the integrity of his very able lawyers. Even if it were to turn out that North's account was not the unvarnished truth, that would not necessarily mean that his lawyers participated in the varnishing process. North is obviously smart enough to figure out how to fit his testimony around the facts.

By his own account, North is a practiced fabricator. Dissembling to our enemies was part of his job description. He was the designated liar in dealing with the Iranians. He has admitted—indeed boasted—that he would have done anything to serve his country's interests and to protect his president.

The question that Congress, the special prosecutor, and the American people will have to answer is: would Oliver North stretch the truth in his testimony before the congressional committees if he believed that by doing so he was serving the national interest and protecting the president?

A man who has spent so much of his recent life deceiving so many people may not himself realize when he is stretching the truth. As Sir Walter Scott put it, "Oh, what tangled web we weave/When once we practice to deceive!" Few witnesses have ever been so practiced at the art of deception.

July 10, 1987

121
Liberal: A Conservative Whose Friends Are in Trouble

There's nothing quite like listening to a law-and-order conservative self-righteously extol the virtues of the Bill of Rights. Senator Orrin Hatch of Utah—a committed and vociferous opponent of individual rights in most contexts—waxed eloquent in defense of Admiral John Poindexer's individual rights during the Iran-contra hearings recently. Hatch's statement could be embossed on the membership cards of the American Civil Liberties Union.

I tried to copy down every word he spoke, but I was so shocked by the fact that these words were coming out of Hatch's mouth that I might have missed an adjective here and there. But this is the thrust: "Sometimes we spend a great deal of time on defending national security. Sometimes we don't spend an equivalent amount of time on protecting individual rights."

Hatch then went on to tick off a list of constitutional violations to which he thought Poindexter was being subjected by the congressional hearings. It was a list that would have made any civil libertarian proud. He complained, as civil libertarians often do, about the "catchall conspiracy laws" that are capable of accordionlike expansion to cover all manner of conduct. He objected to the nebulousness of the "obstruction of justice" statute. He even invoked the claim of double jeopardy—only half in jest—in support of Poindexter's motion that Congress withdraw its subpoena for his appearance, on the grounds that he is a target of possible criminal charges.

Although Hatch eventually voted against Poindexter's motions, he went out of his way to legitimate the admiral's legal arguments and to urge his lawyer to raise them again in any criminal proceeding.

It is ironic to note that Poindexter's objections—which Hatch characterized as "good legal points"—are precisely the kinds of claims that Hatch and others of his ilk, like Attorney General Edwin Meese, call "technicalities" when they are raised by others, of whose politics and actions they disapprove. What is sauce for the conservative goose is apparently not sauce for the liberal gander on Hatch's menu.

Nor are liberals immune from this kind of double-standard hypocrisy. Many radicals on the left applauded a Massachusetts jury's recent acquittal of Amy Carter and Abbie Hoffman. They were charged with trespassing at the University of Massachusetts in protest of CIA recruitment on that campus. Their defense—not unlike Oliver North's—was necessity. They argued that the law should not be strictly interpreted in their case, because they acted as they did in order to prevent a greater evil. But when North argues the necessity of fibbing to Congress on the same grounds, these same radicals demand several pounds of his flesh and insist on using a strict interpretation of the law to do the cutting.

There are few really principled civil libertarians in public life. Most of those who claim to invoke the principle of the Bill of Rights do so selectively, only when it serves their political interests. Many feminists, for example, eloquently invoke freedom of choice when it comes to abortion, birth control, and gay rights. But some of the most vocal—for example, Gloria Steinem—conveniently forget about choice when an adult claims the right to choose to read or watch pornography in private. They are doing precisely what Hatch did in defense of Poindexter's "individual rights." (Hatch, by the way, has no problem of inconsistency on abortion, homosexuality, gay rights, or pornography; he is opposed to the individual's right to choose to engage in any of these activities.)

At a recent meeting of the Civil Liberties Union of Massachusetts, the issue was whether the First Amendment permits a university to ban CIA recruiting on its campus. The hypocrisy was so thick you could cut it with one of the hardbound copies of the Constitution recently issued by Warren Burger's bicentennial commission.

Radical opponents of the CIA made an argument in favor of censorship that would have made Joe McCarthy proud. Eventually, a majority supported the CIA's right to recruit on campus, but not until after a bruising political battle about the virtues and vices (mainly vices) of that organization.

Perhaps some good will come from this latest selected invocation of the Bill of Rights by Hatch. Maybe the Iran-contra hearings have truly sensitized him to the dangers of overly broad criminal statutes and to the virtues of constitutional safeguards for all those facing possible criminal charges. Only time will tell whether he is prepared to generalize his eloquent statements about individual rights and apply them to all citizens in jeopardy of governmental overreaching, rather than limiting them only to his friends and fellow conservatives.

Whenever I debate law-and-order conservatives, I am greeted with the observation that "A conservative is a liberal who's been mugged." I can attest to the truth of that quip, having become a sort of temporary conservative several years ago, when my son was mugged while working as a newspaper boy. I was prepared to see the perpetrators hang from the highest tree. Fortunately, my irrational views were ignored by the sentencing judge, as well they should have been, because I was too personally involved to offer any objective input.

But if a conservative is a liberal whose son has been mugged, then it is equally true that a civil libertarian is often a conservative whose friends are being investigated. These current investigations have turned a considerable number of law-and-order conservatives into selective civil libertarians. Now that they've joined the club, I urge them to remain, and recognize that the protections of the Bill of Rights are for everybody.

July 16, 1987

122
The Supreme Court
May Swing Right

The unexpected resignation of Supreme Court Justice Lewis Powell poses an intriguing challenge to President Reagan. Potentially, the vacancy could precipitate the most significant shift of personnel and ideology on the

Supreme Court since Justice Arthur Goldberg replaced Justice Felix Frankfurter in 1962. That replacement gave then-Chief Justice Earl Warren the solid fifth vote necessary to create the "Warren Court" and to implement its revolution in rights. The person eventually selected to replace Powell could have a similar impact in the opposite political direction.

Justice Lewis Powell has often stood as a formidable barrier against Chief Justice William Rehnquist's desire to move the court quickly and firmly to the right. Powell, a Virginia Democrat whose pragmatism served him well as a corporate lawyer and president of the American Bar Association, started his tenure as a justice without a fixed ideology. He marked out a series of conservative positions that generally stopped short of pressing to the outer limits of their logical and ideological reach. Powell saw his role as cautioning the majority when it was simply going too far. Two recent cases illustrate the moderating role he has played.

He joined the five-four majority in upholding a Georgia statute criminalizing consensual homosexuality, but he wrote a separate opinion warning that "a prison sentence for such conduct—certainly a sentence of long duration—would create a serious" constitutional issue. His message seemed clear: don't go too far or you'll have me to reckon with, and I'm the swing vote.

He wrote the Supreme Court's five-four decision upholding the death penalty, despite statistical evidence showing that killers whose victims are white are more likely to be sentenced to death than killers whose victims are black. But then—just months later—he wrote the court's five-four decision striking down a Maryland law that allowed the jury to consider a "victim impact statement" in deciding whether to impose the death penalty.

Perhaps the most influential opinion written by Justice Powell in his sixteen terms on the court was in the *Bakke* case, which upheld affirmative action programs in higher education. That, too, was a compromise, in which Powell approved efforts to achieve diversity but disapproved simple racial quotas. This time, he cautioned the liberals against going too far.

In selecting a replacement for this bellwether of caution, President Reagan will not have a totally free hand. He is a lame-duck office-holder embroiled in controversy over the Iran arms sales. The Justice Department—which traditionally plays an important role in proposing and screening nominees—is at the center of the storm. Ultimately, some important facets of this still unfolding scandal may end up before the high court, as the issue of the Nixon tapes did back in the days of Watergate. For example, the constitutionality of the legislation providing for a special prosecutor as well as the legal scope of the Boland Amendment may be decided by a closely divided Supreme Court.

The Senate is certain to be wary of any nomination that is seen as an attempt to affect the vote on such issues. This probably excludes from consideration any Justice Department lawyers who have taken positions on these and other matters relating to the Iran-contra investigation. It may also lower the stock of Robert Bork, currently a judge of the Court of Appeals in the District of Columbia. Although Bork has the right credentials and ideologies, his role as the hatchet man in the Saturday Night Massacre—he was the only high-ranking Justice Department official willing to obey President Nixon's order to fire special prosecutor Archibald Cox—may make him seem all too willing to take political marching orders. President Reagan may not be anxious to give his Senate opponents an opportunity to rehash Watergate and suggest comparisons to current events.

Nor are we likely to see this president repeat the blunder made by the last lame-duck president who had an opportunity to fill an important Supreme Court vacancy. President Lyndon Johnson nominated his confidante Abe Fortas, then a sitting justice, to replace Earl Warren, who had announced his intention to resign as chief justice. But the move backfired when questions were raised about Fortas's character and the role he had played in advising the president over Vietnam. The upshot was that the Fortas nomination had to be withdrawn and Johnson never got to make another. The vacancy was filled by President Nixon's nomination of Warren Burger.

If President Reagan were to nominate a close confidante or an ideological extremist, he might well run into problems similar to those experienced by Johnson. One way around these problems might be to follow President Franklin Roosevelt's example: select a member of the very body that must confirm the nomination. Republican Senator Orrin Hatch of Utah would satisfy the president's ideological litmus test, but it seems doubtful that he will be eligible. Congress voted pay raises for justices recently, and the Constitution prohibits the appointment of a member of Congress to an office for which the pay has been raised during the member's congressional term.

Were Bork or Hatch to replace Powell, the Reagan-Rehnquist court would be complete, and a precipitous move to the right could be anticipated.

June 29, 1987

UPDATE
For an update, see columns 123-128.

123
Robert Bork:
Hatchet Man at a Massacre

Elliot Richardson—the man who resigned as U.S. attorney general rather than fire Watergate special prosecutor Archibald Cox back in 1973—has praised President Reagan's Supreme Court nominee, Robert Bork, for the role he played in Cox's firing. Bork, you will recall, was solicitor general at the time, which made him the third highest Justice Department official. President Nixon, fearful that Cox was hot on his trail, was determined to get rid of the meddlesome investigator.

He ordered Richardson to dismiss him, but the attorney general refused and resigned. Nixon then gave the order to the number two man, William Ruckelshaus, but he, too, refused and was fired. Finally, Nixon asked Bork to do the dirty deed. Bork unceremoniously gave Cox his walking papers.

These were bad times for good government and dangerous times for the Constitution. President Nixon's firing of Cox was, perhaps, the lowest point in the Watergate era. It showed the embattled president at his most cynical: exercising constitutional power, not for the benefit of the nation, but rather to preserve his own personal position. It was the most flagrant conflict of interest in many a decade.

Robert Bork believed that the president was acting within his constitutional authority in dismissing the special prosecutor. Bork may even have been correct, as a pure matter of law. But what Nixon was doing was wrong; he was invoking the constitutional doctrine of separation of powers in a self-serving effort to abort an investigation that he knew would point the finger at him.

If a president were to exercise his constitutional power to terminate an investigation of a corporation in which he held large amounts of stock, everyone would agree that his actions were unconscionable. Constitutional power should never be exercised by a president for the purpose of personal enrichment. But what President Nixon did by ordering the firing of Cox was far worse, because more than mere money was involved. Nixon's career and reputation, and perhaps even his freedom, were on the line.

No self-respecting Justice Department official—regardless of how he felt about the legality of President Nixon's order—should have been willing to implement it. It is not enough that a presidential order be technically legal. It should not be fundamentally unconscionable, as this one was.

But Bork went along with Nixon's naked exercise of power and became the hatchet man at the "Saturday Night Massacre," as it quickly became known. He was simply following orders—legal ones in his view. But that is no excuse when the orders were as profoundly wrong and self-serving as Nixon's were.

Now comes Elliot Richardson to assure us that he urged Bork to stay on and obey the president's order. If this is true, it certainly puts Richardson in a different light. If Richardson resigned only because he had made a pledge to Congress not to fire Cox, rather than because he believed that the firing of Cox by Nixon was fundamentally wrong, he was acting more out of personal obligation than principle. If Richardson, behind the scenes, was urging Bork to do what he himself was refusing to do publicly, then it is difficult to see the heroism in his actions.

My mother always taught me that if you make a promise, you keep it, both in the letter and in the spirit. Urging someone else to violate your promise is not keeping that promise. If someone tells me and a friend a secret on the condition that it not be revealed, I would not be keeping that promise if I publicly refused to disclose it, but privately urged my friend to do the dirty work.

Richardson makes a further argument in defense of his former subordinate. He credits Bork with having maintained continuity at the Justice Department and having successfully urged President Nixon to appoint another special prosecutor, Leon Jaworski, to replace Cox.

I would have loved to have been a fly on the wall at the conversation between Nixon and Bork. If Bork told the president the unvarnished truth—namely that any honest special prosecutor would almost certainly find a smoking gun—I doubt that Nixon would have been willing to sign his own arrest or impeachment warrant. We don't know what Bork said in any private conversation. Maybe we will learn at the confirmation hearing.

What we do know from Bork's action in firing Cox is something about his concept of how government officials should act during times of crisis. We know that he is willing to obey orders when he accepts their legality, but without questioning their morality, motivation, or basic decency.

Bork's character was tested deeply during Watergate, in a way that the characters of most people are never tested. In my view, he failed the test. Nothing Elliot Richardson says can change history.

For the senators who must consider his nomination to the Supreme

Court, this should raise troubling questions. The nomination comes at a time when the Supreme Court may well be asked to resolve controversial constitutional questions about the legislation authorizing a special prosecutor, the Boland Amendment, and other conflicts between presidential and congressional powers.

These questions, reminiscent of Watergate, must have been on Senator Edward Kennedy's mind when he said of the Bork nomination: "[President Reagan] should not be able to reach out from the muck of Irangate, reach into the muck of Watergate, and impose his reactionary vision of the Constitution on the Supreme Court and on the next generation of Americans."

July 2, 1987

124
Bork and North as Mirror Images

The two Reagan men on whom Congress will be focusing this summer—Lieutenant Colonel Oliver North and Supreme Court nominee Robert Bork—do not seem to have very much in common. But together they reflect the two sides of President Reagan's approach to government, most particularly to legislation.

Robert Bork claims to believe in legislative supremacy: when the legislature—federal or state—passes a law, it is not the role of the courts to second-guess its wisdom, or to try to stretch it to fit the judge's own personal views of what the law ought to be. Both in letter and in spirit, the legislatively enacted rules must govern. This approach—simplistically called "judicial restraint"—is what the president and the attorney general said they were looking for in a Supreme Court nominee.

Yet at the same time, the president is said to admire Oliver North's very different approach to legislation: if you don't like it, circumvent it, even if you have to lie to Congress and deceive the ultimate policy makers, the American people.

These two approaches reflected by two of the president's men may sound paradoxical, but they are not. They simply demonstrate the hypocrisy behind the label "judicial restraint," as it is used by President Reagan and

Attorney General Edwin Meese. They support judicial restraint, because they believe that it will advance their political goals: a rollback of abortion rights, racial integration, the rights of criminal defendants, and other "minority" interests. When "restraint" does not serve their political interests, they are prepared to appoint an activist like Colonel North to subvert the law.

During his testimony before the joint congressional committee investigating the Iran-contra affair, North repeatedly swore his allegiance to the rule of law. Although he admitted lying to friend and foe alike—including to Congress and to the attorney general—he believed that he was not breaking the law. (He was, since lying to a law enforcement official is a federal crime.) Although he plainly intended an end run around the constraints of the Boland amendment and other congressional restrictions on his actions, he believed that he never once violated the letter of that amendment or of any other law.

But the law is always written in terms capable of multiple constructions. This is especially true of the language of the Constitution and its amendments. Words written in 1787 or 1791 or 1868 do not speak with clarity and certainty to 1987 listeners. They require interpretation, construction, and exposition, which are not simply semantic tasks capable of being performed neutrally and scientifically. Meaning is in the mind—and the politics—of the beholder and interpreter.

When far-right politicians call for compliance with the "original intent" of the Constitution's framers, they are seeking a judicial outcome consistent with their politics.

There are many federal judges—liberal, conservative, and reactionary—who behave on the bench the way Ollie North behaved in the White House. They "use" the law to promote their own views of justice and politics. They stretch, pull, tug, avoid, and evade the letter and spirit of the law in the name of what they believe to be a "higher" good. Consider, for example, Robert Bork's flip-flop on the right to privacy. The Fourth Amendment commands that "the right of the people to be secure in their persons, houses, papers and effects" shall not be abridged except under specified circumstances. The word "secure" had a meaning in 1791 roughly comparable to the word "privacy" today.

Back in 1963, Bork wrote in an article that the legislatively enacted integration of restaurants and hotels would be an unconstitutional violation of the privacy rights—he called them "personal liberty rights"—of restaurant and hotel owners. This view is bizarre in light of the fact that restaurants and hotels are "public houses," which have been regulated by law since well before enactment of the Constitution.

But Bork now insists that there is no right to privacy, even in the most intimate personal relationships in nonpublic places. He told us this in a 1984 opinion justifying the dismissal of a member of the Navy on the sole grounds that he practiced homosexuality. Under this equally bizarre view, married couples may have no right to practice birth control or experiment with nontraditional sex positions in their bedrooms. Indeed Bork said as much, in an article criticizing the Supreme Court's decision protecting the rights of married couples to secure birth control advice.

These preposterous interpretations of the Constitution—that the owners of public houses have a greater right to privacy than do people in their bedrooms—are not unlike some offered by Oliver North in his testimony.

Both Robert Bork and Oliver North are part of the Reagan legacy. Bork serves Reagan's interests by acting with restraint to uphold legislation that the administration supports. North serves his commander in chief's interests by actively sabotaging legislation that the administration opposes. Together, they constitute two heads of a hypocritical Hydra that speaks the language of principle, but acts duplicitously in the interest of politics.

August 3, 1987

125
Bork: A Closet Judicial Activist

Finally Robert Bork's dark secret is beginning to surface.

President Reagan's nominee to the swing seat on the Supreme Court is a closet judicial activist—at least when it comes to vindicating the rights of big business. He believes in exercising judicial restraint only when asked to vindicate the rights of the poor, the disenfranchised, and the ordinary citizen—the underdog.

A systematic study of every decision in which Judge Bork has participated since ascending the federal bench in 1982, demonstrates convincingly that Bork is willing—indeed eager—to substitute his own personal, political, and economic judgments for those of elected officials when it serves the right-wing agenda.

This is what the 149 page report compiled by the Public Citizens Litigation group found:

> Where anybody but a business interest challenged executive action, Judge Bork exercised judicial restraint. . . . However, when business interests challenged executive action . . . Judge Bork was a judicial activist, favoring the business interest in every split decision in which he participated.

The group, headed by respected Supreme Court litigator and law professor Alan B. Morrison, concluded that in forty-eight out of fifty cases where Bork was the swing vote he cast that vote "against the underdog."

Although the Justice Department sought to dismiss the study as the "mathematical acrobatics" of a liberal group, Judge Bork's votes speak for themselves. They suggest that working men and women, consumers, minorities—ordinary Americans—will have a proven enemy on the High Court if Judge Bork is confirmed.

In 1963, he characterized civil rights acts which would desegregate public hotels and restaurants as laws of "unsurpassed ugliness." He argued that the majority of decent people who enacted the civil rights laws had no right to restrict the liberty—the privacy—of the bigoted minority that persisted in its desire to discriminate. This perverse view of "minority rights"—directed against blacks and other racial minorities—was treated with ridicule by the legal profession.

During his confirmation hearing to be solicitor general—an office which he abused by firing Special Prosecutor Archibald Cox during the Watergate investigation—Bork claimed to have changed his mind about civil rights laws. But views so deeply held do not so easily change on principle alone.

In 1984, Judge Bork embraced the very views which he had characterized as "unsurpassed ugliness"—that a majority should be able to impose its moral views on a minority. But this time the minority consisted of homosexuals, and Bork held that "legislation may implement morality," even if that "morality" is based on prejudice against homosexuals.

This flip-flop on majority and minority rights has led Ronald Dworkin, a distinguished professor of jurisprudence at Oxford, to suggest that Bork did not change his mind over principle. "It is hard to resist a less attractive conclusion: that his principles adjust themselves to the prejudices of the right, however inconsistent these might be," Dworkin wrote.

That unattractive conclusion seems best to fit the data. The report of the Public Citizens Litigation Group concludes:

> Judge Bork's performance on the D.C. Circuit is not explained by the consistent application of judicial restraint or any other judicial philosophy. . . . Instead, in split cases, one can predict his vote with almost complete accuracy simply by identifying the parties in the case.

Professor Dworkin's analysis of Bork's decisions and writings, made without benefit of the statistical report of the Litigation Group, brings him to a similar conclusion—that Bork has no coherent judicial philosophy; that his claim to judicial restraint, to abiding by the original intent of the Framers, is a flimsy facade behind which sits a right-wing Wizard of Oz.

As Dworkin puts it, "He uses original intention as alchemists once used phlogiston, to hide the fact that he has no theory at all, no conservative jurisprudence, but only right-wing dogma to guide his decisions."

President Reagan, who seems to know nothing about Bork's judicial philosophy, has called him a detached moderate, who exercises judicial restraint in the spirit of Justice Felix Frankfurter. Frankfurter, who had been a political liberal before his appointment to the Supreme Court, often voted against his own personal and political views, in the interests of judicial restraint.

For example, Frankfurter cast the deciding vote in a 1947 case, in which a black teenager was sentenced to death by electrocution, but the electric chair had broken down as the switch was pulled. Frankfurter's personal views against the death penalty were well known—as a law professor, he had worked tirelessly to try to save Sacco and Vanzetti from execution—but despite being "strongly drawn" to the views of those who would have spared the young man's life, he could find nothing in the Constitution which justified "enforcing my private view" rather than that of the elected officials.

I have yet to find one case—a single significant instance—in which Bork's political right-wing views clashed with judicial restraint and where he opted for the latter. Robert Bork is no Felix Frankfurter. He is far closer to Edwin Meese.

The question now, as Ronald Dworkin has aptly put it, is: "Will the Senate allow the Supreme Court to become the fortress of a reactionary anti-legal ideology with so meager and shabby an intellectual base?"

September 10, 1987

126
White House Plays
Bait and Switch on Bork

Americans watching the Bork hearings are making a shocking discovery: the Robert Bork nominated to serve as the potential swing justice by President Reagan is a different person from the Robert Bork that the Senate is being asked to confirm. As in a zany plot from a Gilbert and Sullivan operetta, some diabolical prankster must have switched the two Borks while our attention was diverted by the Iran-contra hearings.

The Robert Bork who was nominated by the president—we'll call him "White House Bork"—is, in the words of a senior White House aide, anything but a moderate. "It's a mistake," the aide said, "to try to make him into something he isn't. The truth is that he is a right-wing zealot."

A confidante of the administration recently boasted that Bork's vote on issues like abortion, free speech, and religion is expected to make a difference. "This is exactly the reason the Justice Department selected him," he said.

White House Bork—the activist who is expected to outlaw abortions, limit our freedom of speech, and lower the wall of separation between church and state—is the man that White House ideologues want to serve on our highest court. That is certainly what they are whispering to their reactionary constituents on the far right.

But in order to get him confirmed, they have to pretend—at least for now—that he is someone else.

So they took him to a public relations plastic surgeon and had him repackaged as a moderate. The new, if temporary, Robert Bork—we'll call him "Confirmable Bork"—is an altogether different person. He is not the same man who once looked at the principle underlying the federal public accommodations law of 1964, outlawing Jim Crow segregation in hotels and restaurants, and called that principle one of "unsurpassed ugliness."

Confirmable Bork will not dare repeat the insulting analogy he has used so often in the past, comparing a married couple's right to practice birth control with a corporation's right to generate "smoke pollution." The new Bork will play down the fact that he has condemned courts that refused to enforce the kind of racial and religious restrictions that Chief Justice William Rehnquist had in deeds to his homes.

Those of us who have known White House Bork for twenty-five years, through his academic writing and judicial opinions, will not be able to recognize Confirmable Bork.

I'm reminded of the old joke about the eighty-year-old Californian named Irving who is visited by the Angel of Death. Irving, who had been a faithful widower for ten years, pleads for an additional six months to satisfy his one fantasy of dating a young, beautiful Malibu woman. The Angel consents and Irving spends thousands of dollars remaking himself into a young man: tummy tuck, face-lift, toupee, etc. Finally he meets the woman of his dreams, who invites him to her pad for a soak in the hot tub and a drink. On the way to her house, Irving is struck by lightning and killed. At the Pearly Gates, he complains that the Angel of Death broke his promise. The Angel looks at Irving and says apologetically: "Irving, I'm really sorry, but I didn't recognize you." That is exactly what the Senate should say to Confirmable Bork.

He should not be judged on the basis of his carefully prepared answers to the senators' questions. He should be judged on his record. And his record is that of a man who speaks out of both sides of his mouth.

When he was running for nomination by the president, he tried to portray himself as the zealot the White House wanted on the court. He used to write what some Washington observers call "Ed opinions"—judicial decisions directed to Edwin Meese, who he knew would be instrumental in selecting the next Supreme Court nominee. He also made "Ed speeches," about how important it was to overrule unjustified Supreme Court precedents by appointing the right justices.

Now that he is running for confirmation, his constituency has changed from the extreme right to the center. And he has tailored his rhetoric to fit his new constituency. Because both Robert Borks are charming, witty, and persuasive, there is a real danger that his "bait and switch" tactic may work on several of the swing senators he has been lobbying.

For our system of checks and balances to work, the Senate—and their constituents, the American people—must know the product they are being asked to approve. Truth in advertising demands as much even of a used car. Phillip Kurland, a conservative law professor at the University of Chicago, has made the request: "Will the real Robert Bork please stand up?" The Senate, he correctly points out, "should not be asked to consent to the appointment of both Dr. Jekyll and Mr. Hyde."

September 21, 1987

127
When the Bench Becomes Soapbox

President Reagan recently characterized the Senate's consideration of Robert Bork as "a political joke," and vowed to exact revenge on Bork opponents by trying to find a new nominee "they'll object to as much as they did this one." In a prepared campaign speech on behalf of the Bork nomination, the president presented his candidate as a champion of law and order who does not "confuse the criminals with the victims."

Republican presidential candidate Jack Kemp has bought time to present TV ads on behalf of Judge Bork, a man of "law and order" who would "uphold traditional conservative values."

While no one can dispute the White House claim that the debate over the future of the Supreme Court has become highly political, two important questions remain: who is primarily to blame for politicizing the judiciary, and can the process of politicization be reversed?

An answer to the first question requires a longer view that goes back to a time well before the Bork debacle. Throughout our history, the Supreme Court appointment process was relatively nonpolitical, in the sense that presidents did not select nominees primarily on the basis of their expected votes on particular issues. (The process has always been partisan in the sense that nominees are generally selected from the president's party.)

But there have been a few crucial periods during which nominations were made with an eye toward ensuring that the president's politics were served by the Supreme Court. These included the early conflict between Federalists and Republicans, and the pre–Civil War years, and most recently during the New Deal. Franklin Roosevelt, after failing in his attempt to pack the court in order to make sure that his New Deal was not judicially dismantled, clearly selected his nominees in the expectation that they would vote to uphold New Deal legislation. But on other issues, the justices he selected were as diverse a group as any that has graced the marble temple.

In recent decades, however, the process has been largely depoliticized. For example, President Gerald Ford's selection of Judge John Paul Stevens had nothing to do with how that little-known jurist would likely vote on any specific issues. The same was true of President Kennedy's nominations of Byron White and Arthur Goldberg.

Even President Lyndon Johnson's choices of Abe Fortas and Thurgood Marshall cannot be explained on the basis of their anticipated votes. Johnson picked Fortas because he was a close personal friend—a criterion perhaps even worse than politics. He picked Marshall primarily because he correctly regarded it as important for a distinguished black finally to sit on the high court.

Neither Presidents Eisenhower nor Truman had political litmus tests for their nominees.

The recent pattern of depoliticization was first broken by Richard Nixon's nomination of former Chief Justice Warren Burger, who, as a circuit judge, had actively campaigned for the job by sending the White House copies of his tough law-and-order speeches and opinions. Nixon's next two nominees were seen as so political that they were rejected by the Senate. Apparently chastened by this experience, his next three nominees reflected greater balance.

Jimmy Carter was the only president in recent memory not to fill any Supreme Court vacancies, and it is impossible to know for certain who he would have selected or why. But it is fair to speculate from his lower court nominations that Carter would have looked more to the nominee's gender, ethnicity, or race than to his or her politics.

During President Reagan's nearly seven years in office, he has politicized the process for selecting all federal judges more than any president in recent history. The White House established a judicial screening procedure that included ideological litmus tests for every candidate.

The Bork nomination is thus only the latest manifestation of President Reagan's attempt to politicize the judiciary. And the Senate is acting well within this historic function to check and balance the executive branch. As an early commentator on the Constitution put it: "A party nomination may be justly met by party opposition."

It is difficult to know what the future holds. Already, bitter conservative supporters of the Bork nomination are vowing revenge against the nominees of a Democratic president. But it will be difficult to exact that revenge if the next president once again depoliticizes the selection process by nominating judges without regard to their anticipated votes on specific issues.

October 19, 1987

UPDATE
On October 23, 1987, the Senate voted fifty-eight to forty-two against the confirmation of Judge Bork. Next, President Reagan proposed Douglas H.

Ginsburg. Ginsberg asked that his name be withdrawn after disclosures that he had used marijuana. On November 11, 1987, he nominated Anthony Kennedy who was unanimously confirmed and appointed on February 3, 1988.

128
High Court Meets Without Magic Nine

The Supreme Court began its 1987 term without its ninth member. There is, of course, nothing unconstitutional about deciding cases with fewer than nine justices. The Constitution does not specify any particular number of justices or even that the total be an odd number, to avoid ties.

It is Congress that has determined the current numerical composition of the high court: one chief justice and eight associate justices. Although Congress could not eliminate any current seats without impeaching their incumbents, it could decide either to increase or decrease the number of associate justices in the future.

In the 1930s, President Franklin Delano Roosevelt tried to add several associate justices for political reasons. His court-packing plan, which had the support of future nominee Felix Frankfurter, was rebuffed. As a nation, we seem to have become comfortable with the number nine, and suspicious that any attempt to change it might be politically motivated.

The temporary absence of a ninth justice—and in this instance a potential swing vote—should not trouble us greatly. The vast majority of important cases decided by the Supreme Court require only four votes, not five. Of the thousands of cases submitted annually, only a relative handful are actually heard by the justices.

Thus, the decisions not to hear the cases—not to grant certiorari, to use the legal jargon—are often the most significant ones made, since they leave undisturbed the lower court decisions and generally put an end to the litigation. Under the Supreme Court's own rules, it takes but four votes to grant review. Even if five justices are opposed, the minority of four prevails on the issue of review.

Of the cases actually heard, relatively few are decided by a five-to-four

292————————————————————————————————*Alan M. Dershowitz*

vote. With only eight members, either the court will decide by a tie vote, or it can await its full complement before rendering its judgment. If the vote is a tie, the lower-court decision remains in effect, which is similar to a decision to decline review in the first place. Of course, the few five-to-four cases are the ones that make the most headlines and are most controversial. It is those that are likely to be held in limbo pending the confirmation of a ninth justice.

It now looks like the court may remain shorthanded for some time. The Senate Judiciary Committee's nine-to-five disapproval of Judge Robert Bork's nomination not only doomed him, it also sent a message of caution to the White House about subsequent nominees. The message is that the American public is not ready to accept a justice who wants to roll back fundamental constitutional rights.

Nor should those who will recommend nominees assume that a Senate that has rejected one nominee will somehow be forced to accept his successor. President Richard Nixon made that mistake in nominating G. Harold Carswell following the defeat of Clement Haynsworth. Now that a coalition of concerned Americans has managed to persuade nearly 60 percent of those polled that Judge Bork should be defeated, there is every reason to believe that this coalition will remain together to monitor the next nominee.

In order to avoid a repetition of the Bork disaster, the president should nominate a true moderate who will have approval from American men and women of every social, ethnic, economic, and religious background. This should be a time of healing and consensus rather than of further divisiveness. Although the Supreme Court could survive with eight justices for several months, it would be preferable to have the vacancy filled before very long. This will not happen if a Bork clone—or someone even more divisive—is nominated.

If President Reagan and his advisers make the mistake of nominating another reactionary, and if that nominee is also defeated, this lame-duck president may lose the power to fill the current vacancy, as President Lyndon Johnson did in 1968 following his abortive attempt to promote his buddy Abe Fortas to chief justice.

The Constitution provides that a presidential appointment must be made with the "advice and consent" of the Senate. This would be a good time for the president to seek the advice of the Senate—including its Democratic majority—before he requests its consent. And the Senate leadership should not be content to play a passive role.

The Senate is a full partner in the Supreme Court appointment process. The 1986 election, which turned the Senate over to the Democrats, was as relevant a mandate as the prior presidential election. Lest there be any doubt about that, the recent public opinion polls—even with their margins of error—confirm the fact that President Reagan and Attorney General Edwin Meese have lost touch with the pulse of mainstream America, at least when it comes to the Supreme Court. Perhaps it has something to do with the bicentennial, but for whatever reason, it seems clear that most Americans do not want to cash in their constitutional insurance policy of liberty. The Bill of Rights is alive and well. Let's keep it that way.

October 12, 1987

129
Stallonography

The other night I went to the movies on business. I certainly wouldn't go to see *Cobra*—Sylvester Stallone's newest shoot'em upper—for pleasure. But several movie buff friends urged me to see the film that was going to make my job harder. As a criminal defense lawyer, I have to know what the jurors and judges are thinking, and many people think along the lines of the latest popular movies and TV shows. So off I went to a neighborhood cinema in Somerville, Massachusetts, to watch *Cobra* and to watch those watching it.

What I saw was horrifying. The hero of the movie is a police officer from the so-called "zombie squad"—the unit assigned to deal with psychotic killers in whatever manner the unit's members deem fit. His name is Marion Cobretti, but everyone calls him Cobra. His creed is simple: The only answer to violence is more violence. He is contemptuous, to the point of physical assaults, of journalists or police who believe that even criminals deserve constitutional rights: "The courts are civilized. I'm not civilized. This is where the law stops and I begin," he says. He mocks those who try to understand criminal behavior: "Crime is a disease, and I'm the cure," he hisses at a criminal whose head he is about to blow away in the name of therapy. "You have the right to remain silent," he solemnly intones as he prepares to silence a gasoline-soaked criminal by dropping a match on him.

As I watched the movie and those watching it, I thought of the recent social science research designed to show the impact of pornography on attitudes and actions. Though partisans on all sides of the censorship issue seem to delight in misreading and misapplying these studies, one conclusion does seem clear: Watching lots of films that portray women as enjoying being raped may affect the attitudes of some viewers toward that despicable crime. Should this shock anyone?

It certainly shouldn't surprise any civil libertarian defender of free speech. Those of us who spend our lives defending freedom of expression do so—at least in part—because we firmly believe that speech does matter, that ideas do have an impact on conduct. We acknowledge the power of government to punish unlawful actions, but we resist the power of government to act preventively by punishing the expression of ideas—even bad ideas.

The ideas contained in the film *Cobra* are, in my view, bad ones. They mock our constitutional heritage. They glorify "vigilante justice" (which is an oxymoron in any society committed to the rule of law). They encourage a simpleminded view of crime as a product of inherent evil. They frighten people into trusting only greater violence as the response to crime. And in the end they may even stimulate additional violence among some already inclined toward physical responses to any provocation, no matter how slight. (In one scene, our hero slugs the driver of a car who would not move to make room for him.)

I'm sure that Stallone would argue that his message is antiviolent, but that showing violence is necessary to convey that message. Similarly, the Commission on Pornography has decided to include graphic descriptions of pornography in its report, to illustrate its evil. Whatever the purpose, it will assure more readers, just as Stallone's violence assures more viewers.

Stallone's other films may be even more dangerous. Our president is a self-proclaimed admirer of the Rambo school of foreign policy, and the machine gun made famous by Rambo has been a hot-selling toy among our nation's youngsters.

Yet there is no call for an attorney general's commission to study the effects of "violentography" on our nation's attitudes and actions. The moral majority is not conducting boycotts of theaters that show such movies. Supermarkets and convenience stores have not stopped selling violent books, magazines and videos on "moral" grounds. (Nor, by the way, have they stopped selling cigarettes or alcoholic beverages, which kill more people in a day than pornography has ever killed.)

Nor should there be any censorship—public or private—of Stallonography. There should be competition against the dangerous ideas reflected in these movies. Let other moviemakers make better movies glorifying nonviolence and the rule of law. This will not be an easy task, any more than it has been easy to answer the negative messages of pornography by making nonsexist, nonexploitative erotic films.

But nobody ever said that the way of the First Amendment—the marketplace of ideas, rather than a government monopoly on speech—is the easy road. Tyrants take the easy road. Free people choose the way that affords each citizen the right to arrive at his or her truth by going in any direction, and even by stepping off the main highway in search of the untrodden path.

I'm glad I went to see *Cobra*. I hope the millions of others who go to see it will reject its ideas, but I'm happy that they have the freedom to choose whether to accept or reject ideas that I find pernicious.

June 9, 1986

130
Attorney General Must Be Free of Political Ties

Most Americans probably believed that presidents who were elected after the disgraced President Nixon would have learned at least one important lesson from Watergate: do not follow the tradition of appointing cronies, political operatives, or close relatives as attorney general. The tradition, of course, has a venerable lineage, and has not been limited to Republicans. Franklin D. Roosevelt and John F. Kennedy followed it.

But Watergate devastatingly showed the dangers of an attorney general who placed personal loyalty to the individual in the Oval Office above his obligation as chief law enforcement officer. Nixon's attorney general, John Mitchell, was—to put it bluntly—a crook. He was eventually convicted of obstructing justice, rather than furthering it, and he went off to prison along with other White House lawyers.

Following that debacle, it appeared as if a new tradition might be started. President Ford appointed a man he didn't even know, and a Democrat to boot. Edward Levi was no friend, political operative, or relative. He had nothing going for him other than his reputation as a fair-minded legal scholar who had served as president of the University of Chicago and as dean of its law school. He performed with distinction and helped to restore the luster of the Justice Department, which had become badly tarnished under his immediate predecessors.

When President Jimmy Carter was elected in 1976, I was a member of one of his transition panels. I wrote the president-elect urging him to continue the recent tradition of appointing the attorney general from outside his political family. I urged him to retain Attorney General Levi as a symbol of his commitment to bipartisanship. He ignored the advice and appointed a Georgia friend, Griffin Bell. (Carter's distrust of non-Georgians was a major reason for some of the failures in his presidency.)

Then came Ronald Reagan, who proceeded to make two of the worst appointments imaginable. First he picked his own personal lawyer, William French Smith, a somewhat somnambulistic socialite who seemed to spend most of his time at Washington parties, leaving the running of the department to young, ambitious professionals.

Had there been any crisis during Smith's tenure, it would have been interesting to see whether he placed loyalty to his client over his obligation to the Constitution. Indeed, if an issue arose that required the attorney general to disclose conversations between him and his client, a classic conflict of interest might have been presented. But there were no real testing episodes during Reagan's first term. And when Smith left office, hardly anyone noticed.

But everyone noticed who his replacement was. President Reagan nominated one of his closest political cronies, Edwin Meese III, who had already demonstrated an insensitivity to the ethics of government employment by accepting "loans" from people who were seeking appointments from the administration.

Following his confirmation, things got worse. The whole story of his involvement in the selling of arms to Iran and the diverting of the profits to the Contras—at best legally questionable, at worst in direct violation of law—has yet to be told. Oliver North's testimony, if it is to be believed, certainly provides cause for believing that Meese did not behave in the highest traditions of law enforcement.

His "investigation" was a Keystone Kop parody of Dragnet. ("Just give us the facts, sir—in a couple of days, unless you need more time to destroy the evidence.") The image of Oliver North shredding documents while

Justice Department officials sat nearby reading other documents is one that will remain frozen in the American mind for years to come.

Nor do we know the whole story of Meese's role in the Wedtech scandal. What we do know is that with all of the ongoing investigations of his conduct, he hardly has any time to do the work of attorney general. But maybe that's a blessing in disguise, considering what he did when he did have time on his hands.

Whether Meese will survive these investigations and complete his term is an open question. What seems clear is that the person who is elected our next president must learn the combined lessons of Watergate and Iran-scam—of Mitchell and Meese. The American people are entitled to a real attorney general, who is willing to and capable of enforcing the law in the interest of the people, rather than evading it in his own self interest, or in that of his friend in the Oval office.

With these considerations in mind, I call on every presidential candidate to announce—now—that he (or she, if Pat Schroeder decides to announce) will make a firm commitment to appoint as attorney general a distinguished lawyer who is not a crony, political operative, or relative. The candidates need not announce the specific nominees in advance, but it is important that they commit themselves to the appropriate criteria for selecting this most important Cabinet member.

The American people can ill afford yet another repetition of Watergate or the Iran-contra lawlessness. No single Cabinet appointment can assure that scandals will not recur, but an independent attorney general can play an important role in keeping a president and his administration within the bounds of the law.

August 10, 1987

131
Charge and Acquittal
Warrant Equal Time

Recent newspaper headlines have announced the acquittals of several well-known criminal defendants following long trials, and even longer investigations. Former Secretary of Labor Raymond Donovan and film director John Landis were the most recent victor-victims in endurance trials. Previous unsuccessful marathon prosecutions involved car maker John DeLorean and Governor Edwin Edwards of Louisiana.

These men—all of whom were made to endure months of negative newspaper publicity, pretrial proceedings, and trials—were among the wealthiest and most powerful defendants ever dragged through our legal system. Their ultimate acquittals by unanimous juries did not restore the status quo for them and their families. They lost millions of dollars in legal expenses and foregone earnings, thousands of days of their lives, and other irretrievable intangibles that cannot be counted or measured. But because of who they are, they will almost certainly bounce back.

What happens to those caught up in the criminal justice system who are not as fortunate? A recent case in point involved a respected Catholic priest from North Providence, Rhode Island.

While I was representing Claus von Bulow in his appeal from his conviction for attempted murder, a young man named David Marriott came forward and volunteered some information that—if true—would have helped us prove von Bulow's innocence. In support of his evidence, he told us that he had told the story to a Catholic priest several years earlier.

We interviewed the priest—Father Philip Magaldi—and he corroborated Marriott's story. We then submitted their affidavits as part of a new trial motion. Ultimately, we won the appeal; however, von Bulow was granted a new trial on issues unrelated to the affidavits, so the evidence they provided was never brought before any court.

At the very end of von Bulow's second trial—while the jury was deliberating—someone leaked to the press that Father Magaldi had been secretly indicted for committing perjury in his affidavit. Though his parishioners and friends never doubted his innocence, the priest was devastated. The evidence against him consisted of the testimony of David Marriott and a tape recording that Marriott had allegedly made of a conversation between them in which the priest "admitted" that certain statements made in the affidavits were untrue. Marriott was given immunity from prosecution in exchange for his agreement to testify against the priest.

For two years this indictment hung over Father Magaldi's head, as he continued to serve his parishioners. Finally, in late June of this year, as he was about to go to trial, James O'Neil, the newly elected attorney general of Rhode Island dropped a bombshell: he announced that all charges against Father Magaldi had to be dismissed.

It turned out that three months before the indictment had been issued, the incriminating tape had been submitted to an independent laboratory for testing. The lab had told the former attorney general, Arlene Violet, that "the tape had been altered (in a significant manner) and the voice could not be positively identified as that of Father Magaldi."

The suppressed lab report, according to the new attorney general, "negates any evidentiary value of this tape." It also renders the only witness against the priest—David Marriott—"unreliable." O'Neil concluded that the case "probably should not have been the subject of an indictment" in the first place. (The word "probably" was surely a charitable gesture toward his predecessor, since it is absolutely clear that no indictment should ever be brought on the basis of a tape with no "evidentiary value" and a witness who is "unreliable.")

Father Magaldi was obviously relieved by the decision, as were his loyal parishioners. But he can never be made whole for the damage done to his rights and reputation.

Either the original prosecutor or the grand jury that indicted Father Magaldi failed to perform their duty. If the prosecutor did not tell the grand jurors that the lab had found the tape to be "altered in a significant manner," then the prosecutor was at fault. If the prosecutor did advise the grand jury of this important fact and it indicted Father Magaldi nonetheless, then it fell down on its job.

Among the worst offenders were the members of the press. Father Magaldi's original indictment was headline news around the country. For example, the *Boston Globe* ran a front-page story headlined "Rhode Island Priest Indicted on Perjury Charge," with a picture of Father Magaldi. But when the prosecutor dropped the charges and announced that they probably should not have been brought in the first place, there was virtually no coverage outside Rhode Island. I combed the *Boston Globe* for even a brief mention of Father Magaldi's vindication and found nothing.

At least when a defendant is acquitted, there is generally a story. It never quite counteracts the original headlines announcing the indictment. But it provides a record for history. A historian reading newspapers outside of Rhode Island will learn of Father Magaldi's indictment, but not of his vindication. This just isn't fair. Dropped charges apparently sell fewer newspapers than trumped-up charges.

August 17, 1987

132
What Bush and Others
Miss at Auschwitz

Vice President George Bush recently ended his four-day trip to Poland with a visit to the Nazi extermination camps of Birkenau and Auschwitz. The Polish government has turned Auschwitz into a museum of martyrology and requires Polish schoolchildren to tour it.

Vice President Bush and his wife Barbara were obviously moved by the striking contrast between the beauty of the surrounding Polish landscape and the horrors of the genocidal machine within the barbed wire. Like many other official visitors, he laid a wreath at the Wall of Death, where 2,000 people were executed by Nazi firing squads.

But even more important than what the vice president was shown by his Polish hosts was what he was not shown. My son and I visited Auschwitz several weeks before the vice president. Quite deliberately we decided not to go on an "American" or "Jewish" tour. We followed a group of Polish schoolchildren in order to find out what they are told about this museum and what it represents. It was a shocking and infuriating experience.

The children—indeed typical East European visitors—are not told, as Bush was, that nearly all of the 4 million people murdered in the camps were Jews who were gassed solely because they were Jews. The Polish visitor is told that the victims were Polish citizens. Indeed, in one room in the Polish pavilion—each country occupied by the Nazis has a pavilion—there are hundreds of pictures of the dead martyrs.

My son and I gasped in shock as we passed the photographs and read the names under each of them: there was not a single Jewish name; every one was Polish. (The Jewish names are included in the archives, but the visitor has to wait in line and ask to see the alphabetical list.) In the adjoining room, there is a display of photographs of babies and children gassed in the camps. Beneath their pictures there are no names—only numbers. The reason is clear: Polish babies and children were not murdered at Auschwitz; only Jewish (and Gypsy) babies and children were gassed as part of the Nazi genocide.

Each of the Eastern European national pavilions goes out of its way to downplay the uniquely Jewish nature of the Holocaust. None mentions the fact that Jews were transported to Auschwitz from the far-flung corners of the Nazi empire. From points as distant as Corfu, Norway, and France, entire Jewish populations were transported to Auschwitz for systematic execution. Even some American Jews, trapped in Europe during the war, were gassed. The Nazi goal was not simply to get rid of Jews who were in the way or who were partisans or communists—as it was with other groups. The goal, which came precariously close to becoming achieved, was to rid the world of every Jewish man, woman, and child—finally and systematically.

Not all the intended victims were Jews. But all the Jews were intended victims. This point, made so eloquently by Nobel laureate Elie Wiesel, is lost on the typical visitor to Auschwitz.

Indeed the opposite point is sometimes made, quite explicitly. In the Hungarian pavilion, the following caveat appears in bold print: "The theme of this exhibition is not the fate of the Jewish people. What it wants to narrate is Hungarian history." At the entrance to the Czechoslovakian Pavilion, there is a beautiful marble memorial to the victims of the extermination camps. Each of the names of the camps is etched into marble: "Treblinka, Mauthausen, Oswicim (Auschwitz), Bergen-Belsen, Dachau." Surrounding these names are hundreds of Christian crosses—but not a single star of David. (There is a small Jewish pavilion, but it is not part of the usual tour.)

The message to the Eastern European tourist is clear and deliberate: the Nazis randomly killed the occupied population until the Red Army defeated them and rescued the survivors. Because it omits the special nature of the "final solution" against the Jews, the message is false and pernicious.

Also omitted is the tragic story of what happened to the Jewish remnants who survived the Nazi genocide. Of the 3.5 million Jews who lived in prewar Poland, only a few thousand survivors decided to remain there. They came back to their homes, only to find many of them looted and occupied by locals, some of whom were angry at their return and disappointed that the Nazis had not completed their work.

In the town of Kielce, more than a year after the Germans had withdrawn, local Poles systematically murdered forty-two Jewish survivors. Then in the 1950s and again in the 1960s, government-sponsored campaigns of anti-Semitism frightened the remaining Jewish population— except for a handful of assimilated intellectuals and a few people too old to leave—into emigrating to the United States and Israel. What the Nazi army failed to do—make Poland completely "Judenrein" (free of Jews)—the

Poles themselves managed to complete. Vice President Bush was not told of the complicity of many—though certainly not all—Poles in the extermination of European Jewry.

The next time a high American official visits Poland, he should insist on seeing what the Polish people are shown. The picture of pervasive Polish anti-Semitism at Auschwitz and elsewhere is not a pretty one—even forty-five years after the Nazi retreat.

October 5, 1987

UPDATE
This column generated more hate mail—including a demand to Harvard that I be fired—than any other.

133
Crime and the Stuff of Life

The days of the "perfect crime" are numbered. New technological, biological, and genetic breakthroughs in crime detection may soon render current police methods obsolete. A careful criminal can cover up obvious clues by wiping away his fingerprints or wearing shoes that make no distinctive marks. But nearly everyone leaves a small—perhaps microscopic—part of themselves behind, especially following a crime of violence. And crime-solving techniques now on the drawing board or in the experimental phase hold great promise of turning these subtle clues into proof positive against dangerous criminals who are currently evading apprehension.

One futuristic technique, called "genetic fingerprinting," can now turn the tiniest fragment of a person's body—a bit of hair, a speck of skin, a droplet of blood or semen or saliva—into conclusive evidence of a suspect's presence at the scene of the crime. And since it is far more difficult to avoid leaving "genetic fingerprints" than ordinary fingerprints, this new technique is being greeted enthusiastically by law enforcement officials.

A "genetic fingerprint" is a readout of a radioactive probe of certain regions of the DNA. (The DNA, or deoxyribonucleic acid, is the basic building block of life.) The readout takes the form of a series of parallel bars in an X-ray film. It looks something like the black and white lines of the universal price code that appears on grocery products, magazines, and other consumer items. The likelihood that the DNA of any two people will produce identical readouts is on the order of millions, or even billions, to one. There is one small hitch: identical twins, who have different finger-prints, may produce the same genetic readouts. This quirk will surely be grist for the mystery novelists' mills, but it is unlikely to create real compli-cations for the police in day-to-day criminal investigations.

Already, this revolutionary technique has contributed to a rape convic-tion in a British court. The defendant was accused of assaulting a handi-capped woman. Several months after the brutal rape, a semen stain found on the victim's clothes was matched with the genetic pattern of the sus-pect's blood. This match provided the crucial evidentiary link necessary to convict.

Genetic fingerprinting has also been used to absolve at least one suspect of guilt. A 17-year-old hospital worker, charged with the murder-rapes of two 15-year-old girls, was freed when his genetic prints did not match evidence found at the crime scenes.

One important advantage that this new technology has over some more traditional crime-lab tests is that genetic material remains testable even after the passage of years. Thus, old stains and particles that could not be tested by conventional means may still yield probative genetic clues. Another advantage is that the genetic test is far more discerning than other tests, which can merely rule out suspects, but cannot positively establish a match. Finally, the printout is not very expensive, averaging $200 to $300 a test.

The principal disadvantage is that American crime labs are not currently geared up to make maximum use of genetic testing. It requires an enor-mous memory bank of prints in order to use a specific print to discover the individual who may have left it. The FBI has long maintained a storehouse of conventional fingerprints from around the country—indeed the world. It also has a computerized retrieval system that speeds up the process of identification. Thus, if a fingerprint is found at the scene of a crime and the police have no idea to whom it belongs, they can match it with the millions of prints in the FBI's memory bank. But the FBI has no comparable collec-tion of genetic prints, nor is it likely to be able to gather such a collection in the foreseeable future.

For that reason, genetic prints, despite their precision, will not soon replace the ordinary fingerprint as the primary means of identification and discovery of suspected criminals. It may, however, supplement the finger-print and other conventional laboratory tests, particularly in matching clues with individuals who are already suspects.

Nor is the genetic fingerprint likely to be the final breakthrough in the never-ending war against crime. The possibilities boggle the mind, ranging from neuropsychological techniques for probing the human mind to psychosurgery capable of altering behavior.

The important point is that just because a technique is new and efficient does not mean that it is necessarily desirable—or undesirable. Each innovation must be judged on its merits and demerits—on the balance it strikes in preventing crime without compromising the most basic rights of privacy and autonomy.

The virtue of genetic fingerprinting is that it does not threaten fundamental values any more than traditional crime-lab tests. But it does improve on the accuracy of such tests. All persons interested in improving the accuracy of criminal justice—both by convicting more guilty persons and clearing more innocent ones—should welcome genetic fingerprinting and other new techniques that do not encroach on civil liberties.

December 4, 1987

134
The Future of Our Constitution

We, the people, are now celebrating the two hundredth anniversary of our Constitution. At this historic time it is necessary to set a course for the future that will continue to uphold the basic premise of our Constitution—liberty and justice for all.

Many naysayers throughout history have attempted to sabotage the future of our great nation by warning against and exploiting the fragility of her basic doctrine. The Constitution, however, has successfully survived these false predictions of doom.

Our Constitution has also met strong opposition from a number of more realistic assaults. These attacks threatened our ability to hold to the fundamental design established by our Founding Fathers. For instance, during the Civil War President Lincoln tried to suspend the writ of habeas corpus—the primary legal vehicle for enforcing many of the protections contained in the body of the Constitution. During World War II, 110,000 Japanese Americans were stripped of their most basic right of freedom when they were rounded up and confined in concentration camps. McCarthyism, which savaged our freedoms of speech and association for nearly a decade, was yet another danger to our constitutional liberties.

But I'm afraid that the Constitution will face some of its most bitter tests in the years to come. Even though the body of our Constitution is celebrating its bicentennial, I'm skeptical it will survive these challenges wholly intact to celebrate the two hundredth anniversary of the Bill of Rights—the first ten amendments to the Constitution, enacted in 1791. Although they are called amendments, the Bill of Rights is an organic part of the original document. Without them the Constitution would not have been ratified. By itself the Constitution created a structure for centralized power without sufficient assurances of liberty. The Bill of Rights gave us a strong government without the power to censor newspapers or otherwise curtail the rights of its citizens.

This very moment our Constitution and its Bill of Rights may be threatened by the most serious danger they have ever confronted. The menace is not religious zealots or repressive politicians. It is not a human being or a group of human beings. It is the AIDS virus and the fear it has generated. The perils posed against our liberty are much greater than they were during some of our past crises, which were generated by fear alone and whipped up by opportunistic politicians. In the case of AIDS, however, both the virus and the fear are real, and fears based upon legitimate threats are a far greater risk to our survival.

The fear of AIDS contains all the elements necessary for a genuine civil-liberties disaster. At present the perceived "culprits" are gay men and intravenous drug users. And the bridge between the homosexual and heterosexual communities is prostitutes, particularly those from minority backgrounds who are I.V. drug users. When these elements are combined, we have a prescription for political scapegoating of the worst kind.

I have little confidence in most of our leaders when it comes to depoliticizing an issue as emotionally laden as AIDS. I have somewhat more confidence in the decency of the American public. But their decency will be sorely tested if AIDS spreads more pervasively through the heterosexual, non-drug-using communities. AIDS will test the coverage of the insurance policy we call our Constitution (as well as most conventional insurance policies).

I also suspect that in the next decade we will encounter other technological, biological, and ecological dilemmas that the framers of our Constitution could never have anticipated. Consider, for instance, governmental intrusion on the privacy of individuals. The framers were deeply concerned about this issue and manifested that concern in the Fourth Amendment which guarantees that the "right of the people to be secure in their persons, houses, papers, and effects" shall not be unreasonably restricted. They had experienced intrusive governmental searches, eavesdropping, and spying; so they wrote a constitutional amendment capable of dealing not only with these specific evils but also with as-yet-unanticipated violations of the right to privacy. Although the framers could not imagine the current state-of-the-art intrusions—wiretapping, miniaturized bugs, satellite interceptions, and computerized files—it is clear that they did not intend the Constitution to become obsolete with every change in technology. They endowed us with constitutional policies and language sufficient to adapt to the inevitable changes of the future.

Even today we cannot begin to predict each of the scientific discoveries that await us in the third century of our constitutional history. The ever-changing lines between the human and the nonhuman, and even the possibility of alien life, will pose inescapable challenges to our Constitution. The world we live in barely resembles the one in which our Founding Fathers resided, and the world (or worlds) our grandchildren will inhabit may bear little resemblance to our own. Yet our Constitution must be capable of adapting to and governing all these worlds.

It will take a broad-based commitment to liberty to weather the approaching constitutional storms. We will survive these challenges only if we remain together as a nation proud of our legacy of freedom and refuse to succumb to the seductive temptations of the quick fix. If we make it to 1991 with our Constitution intact, we will truly have something to celebrate.

December 11, 1987

135
A Daughter's Death,
a Mother's Responsibility

In one of the most controversial criminal trials in recent history, a mother stands convicted of driving her 17-year-old daughter to suicide. The issue was whether the mother's attitude toward, and demands on, her teenage daughter "created an environment so deleterious to Tina's mental health that it proved to be a substantial and contributory cause to her suicide," according to the charge.

Even the undisputed background facts presented an ugly picture of a family out of control. The authorities charged 40-year-old Theresa Jackson with compelling her daughter Tina to work as a nude dancer in a strip joint. Tina's older brother Rico also was a nude dancer. Their mother helped young Tina to get the job, according to authorities, by doctoring her birth certificate. She also failed to seek treatment for her daughter following an earlier suicide attempt.

The mother faces 25 years in prison at her scheduled December 3 sentencing following her conviction for aggravated child abuse, procuring a sexual performance by a child, and forgery. Her defense was that Tina was a schizophrenic exhibitionist with a "depraved mind," and that there was nothing she could do to prevent her suicide. One of the witnesses against the mother was her stripper son.

But the state's star witness was a man who never met Tina and did not interview the mother. Dr. Douglas Jacobs, a psychiatrist and the director of the Suicide Education Institute of Boston performed a "psychological autopsy" of the suicide. He concluded from Tina's school and hospital records, as well as depositions of her friends and family, that "had it not been for this young girl being the victim of an exploitative relationship with her mother—feeling powerless and hopeless—she would not have suicided."

Not surprisingly, the mother's defense attorney vigorously objected to this Monday morning psychologizing. He warned that if this kind of testimony were allowed, "every parent whose child commits suicide will be second-guessed in every case from this point on." The defense lawyer also challenged the basis for the psychiatrist's conclusions: "He is hypothesizing about the state of mind of someone who he never met."

The judge obviously was intrigued by the issue: "It's novel, it's fascinating, it's a first." In ruling to allow the jury to hear the results of Jacobs' psychological autopsy, the judge concluded that he believed "the jury is astute enough to determine if this man knows what he's talking about." That, of course, is less than certain. Juries often are over-impressed by experts with fancy degrees and a smooth, avuncular style.

The real issue, however, was not Tina's state of mind when she killed herself, since Tina was not on trial for suicide (though suicide—really "attempted suicide"—is still a crime in some states). The only defendant was Tina's mother, and it was her state of mind that was at issue.

There is evidence that Tina's mother was at least as emotionally disturbed as the daughter, and that the entire family situation was grossly pathological. Had the jury believed that the mother was mentally ill, it might have been reluctant to hold her criminally responsible for her failures as a parent. Even the most "normal" and best-educated parents have great difficulty dealing with disturbed children. Obviously the difficulty is exacerbated when a parent, too, is mentally ill.

Although teen suicide is a big problem, it is still true that only a tiny percentage of teenagers—even abused teenagers—resort to the desperate measure of taking their own lives. The most qualified experts have been unable to come up with accurate predictive criteria for determining which young people will or will not try to end their lives. There are guidelines, to be sure, but there are no crystal balls.

Had Jacobs interviewed Tina before her suicide, I wonder if he would have predicted her self-destructive act. We must never forget that some abused children break out of their victimization and become productive members of society. Autopsy is always more certain than diagnosis.

There can be little doubt, at least in retrospect, that Theresa Jackson was not a good mother. She seems at least partially responsible for her daughter's death—both morally and psychologically. The difficult question is whether she ought to be held legally responsible under the vague and general statutory rubric of "child abuse."

The jury made its decision, but the legal issue will almost certainly go up on an appeal. And an appellate court might well conclude that it is inappropriate to prosecute a mother on such vague and general charges. The criminal law must give fair warning of precisely which kinds of immoral and dangerous conduct are covered by criminal statutes.

Eventually, the issue probably will have to be confronted by legislators who will decide whether to enact new criminal statutes specifically punishing abuse that drives a child to suicide. If legislatures decide to enact such statutes, they will have to strike a thoughtful balance between protecting children from preventable abuses and scapegoating parents for tragedies that are beyond their control. It will not be an easy job.

November 3, 1987

136
Assault With a Deadly Virus

Pfc. Adrian Morris Jr., a 27-year-old Army clerk at Fort Huachuca, Arizona, has become the first person ever prosecuted for having sex after being told that he carried the AIDS virus, and not warning his sex partners or using protection. This type of prosecution was inevitable, as are the complex legal problems that necessarily accompany it.

The initial question is whether this highly anti-social and immoral conduct is a crime at all, and, if so, what crime it is. Legislatures, which have the responsibility for creating and defining criminal violations, rarely keep the penal code abreast of changing threats. For example, people had been cheating credit card companies for several years before the penal code specifically made credit card fraud a felony. Before the statute books were brought up-to-date, prosecutors prosecuted credit-card cheats using the laws criminalizing fraud or other illegal commercial transactions. Some crooks got away with their cheating because the available statutes simply could not be stretched to cover their misconduct.

Similarly with AIDS, there are currently no laws on the books specifically barring someone who knows he's afflicted with the AIDS virus from having unprotected sex with an unsuspecting partner. Accordingly, Morris is being prosecuted for "aggravated assault." But the crime of aggravated assault conjures up the image of violent beatings, rather than consensual lovemaking. Of course, the "consent" given by Morris' sex partners was based on a false—if unstated—premise. Namely that Morris was not afflicted with a deadly contagious virus. In that sense the crime seems more like fraud than assault. The "aggravated" aspect certainly fits, however, since the potential outcome is lethal.

The time has come for legislators to enact specific statutes criminalizing the kind of conduct with which Morris has been charged.

One of the elements in any such crime must, of course, be the defendant's actual knowledge that he (or she) is infected with the AIDS virus (or, perhaps, is in such a high-risk category—like intravenous drug users—that he must presume he may be infected). The best evidence of actual knowledge would be proof that the defendant was told he had tested positive for the presence of the HIV antibodies. But here is the rub: The results of AIDS tests are supposed to be confidential.

This tricky issue was recently addressed by the Army Court of Military Review in the Morris case. The prosecuting attorney had tried to introduce into evidence the test results which had showed the presence of the AIDS virus, but the judge excluded the results on the ground that they were confidential under the Army regulations. Had this ruling stood, it would have been virtually impossible to prove that Morris knew he was infected before he had sex with his unsuspecting partners.

But the reviewing court overruled the trial judge and held that the test results could be introduced against Morris. It ruled that the test results could not be used as evidence of "past misconduct," such as homosexual acts or intravenous drug use. But it concluded that despite the absolute language that promised confidentiality, the regulation "does not prohibit use of test results where they directly relate to future misconduct."

The distinction is well taken for several reasons. First, there is a difference between using the test to uncover past acts which may violate Army rules (such as homosexual encounters or drug injections) and using it to help prevent future misconduct (such as the acts charged against Morris).

Second, the nature of the past "misconduct" is not nearly as serious as the nature of the future misconduct. Many people believe that homosexual sex is not misconduct at all, and that intravenous drug use is primarily self-destructive. But no reasonable person can minimize the severity—indeed barbarity—of having unprotected sex with an unsuspecting partner after learning that you have the AIDS virus.

Under the reviewing court's decision, the prosecution, in this and other cases, will be able to use test results to show that the defendant knew he was infected. This, in turn, may encourage infected soldiers to refrain from engaging in unprotected sex with unsuspecting partners.

If the court-martial concludes that Pfc. Morris did, in fact, have unprotected sex with three different people after learning that he was infected, there can be little doubt that he would deserve punishment. But there are grave dangers in stretching existing laws—whether they be laws which define the crime or laws which promise blanket confidentiality—to achieve this desirable end. The laws must be changed now to provide precise, predictable and proportionate legal responses to the culpable and dangerous conduct with which Pfc. Morris has been charged.

October 27, 1987

137
A Judicial Double Standard on Free Speech

Imagine your reaction if you were to open the pages of a nationally circulated magazine to find yourself portrayed as a drunk having incestuous sex with your mother in an outhouse. It is not surprising that the Reverend Jerry Falwell was outraged when he saw *Hustler* magazine's parody of the popular Campari ad in which he described "his first time." Nor is it surprising that a Virginia jury awarded Falwell $200,000 for the "emotional distress" he suffered.

What is surprising is that a unanimous Supreme Court—in an opinion written by its most conservative member, Chief Justice William Rehnquist—ruled that the First Amendment fully protects *Hustler*'s gross and offensive parody, irrespective of how much intentional distress its publisher intended or caused. Chief Justice Rehnquist candidly acknowledged that he would have preferred to find a rule that protected only the sort of reasonable political cartoons that appear in our daily newspapers, while condemning the kind of gross distortions of the type *Hustler* publishes. But he doubted there is any standard or rule that a court could devise for distinguishing the reasonable from the gross.

Even more surprising than the result is the broad interpretation Rehnquist gives to the constitutional right of free speech. He declared that "the First Amendment recognizes no such thing as a 'false' idea." Nor must the criticism of public people be limited to "reasoned or moderate" attack; it may include "vehement, caustic, and sometimes unpleasantly sharp attacks." It may also include caricature, satire, exaggeration, hyperbole, mockery, and ridicule. And finally, the publisher may even be motivated more by "hatred or ill-will" than by a genuine wish to improve or reform.

This broad interpretation gives any citizen the right to criticize presidents, governors, and senators. Indeed, Chief Justice Rehnquist cites examples from our history of caustic caricatures of some of our most beloved presidents, including George Washington, Abraham Lincoln, Teddy and Franklin Roosevelt. It also gives any citizen the right to ridicule public figures, such as the Reverend Falwell, who do not hold elective office but who "by reason of their fame, shape events in areas of concern to society at large."

The irony is that there are some judges who seem to believe that the only public officials who are exempt from criticisms are—you guessed it—*judges*. In a decision rendered on the same day as the *Falwell* case, a federal district judge in Rhode Island named Francis J. Boyle punished a lawyer for having the audacity to show "disrespect for the Court"—in reality for accusing an individual judge of bias. Judge Boyle's opinion reads as if it were written in an entirely different country than the one whose Supreme Court rendered the *Falwell* decision. "There is no right to advocate untruth," writes the man in robes who apparently believes his gavel gives him the power to divine truth.

The story underlying this attempt to suppress criticism of the judiciary is simple. A Massachusetts lawyer in a criminal case filed a motion to disqualify another Rhode Island federal judge named Ronald Lagueux. The lawyer claimed that Judge Lagueux was biased against the Massachusetts lawyer in that case because of a prior confrontation between one of the lawyers and Judge Lagueux. (That prior confrontation involved a book I had written about the Claus von Bulow case, which was critical of certain members of the Rhode Island judiciary; without even reading the book, Judge Lagueux informed the press that because of what I said in the book I would never be allowed to practice in his courtroom; one of the lawyers in the unrelated criminal case had written to Judge Lagueux on my behalf complaining about his actions.)

Judge Lagueux became so angry at the lawyer in the criminal case for filing the entirely proper motion that he referred the matter to his colleague, Judge Boyle, for the possible imposition of sanctions.

Judge Boyle had no difficulty ruling that the First Amendment does not protect a lawyer who expresses an "opinion" or a "conjecture" critical of a judge's impartiality. Nor will the lawyer be excused even if he did not know that his assertions of bias were "false," so long as he "did not know that his accusations were true." In other words, unless a lawyer is certain that his assertions against a judge are entirely true—and that a fellow judge will so find them—he must keep his mouth shut at the risk of professional discipline.

It cannot be the law, as Chief Justice Rehnquist ruled, that disrespect for—even ridicule of—the president and the public preacher will be tolerated under the First Amendment, but, as Judge Boyle ruled, that "disrespect for the Court" will not be tolerated. Nor can it be the law, as Chief Justice Rehnquist held, that the "First Amendment recognizes no such thing as a 'false' idea," but, as Judge Boyle held, that "there is no right to advocate untruth." There cannot be different laws for citizens who criticize presidents than for lawyers who challenge judges. Judges are neither above the First Amendment nor above criticism.

The one thing Judge Boyle need not worry about is that his opinion in this case will be caricatured. It stands by itself as a gross caricature of justice.

March 3, 1988

For some background on this case, see column 117.

138
Censorship Has No Place on Campus

Some of a college student's most important learning experiences take place outside the formal classroom setting. Political rallies, guest lectures, campus movies, and dormitory "bull sessions" all supplement what the professors teach in class. Some colleges and universities seem to understand this better than others.

Throughout the country, efforts are underway to prevent college students from being exposed to certain "controversial" points of view, "offensive" forms of expression, and "dangerous" people. University administrators justify such censorship by invoking their paternalistic role as protectors of the students. But often, they are simply capitulating to pressure from alumni, parents, politicians, faculty and even students.

A few recent cases in point:

The faculty of at least one college, Colby in Maine, recently voted to ban the CIA from recruiting on campus. The reason offered was that the CIA was engaged in illegal activities in Central America. But that surely was not the real basis for the vote. Martin Luther King had also been engaged in illegal activity during the 1960s, and this "liberal" college would have welcomed him with open arms to recruit for his noble cause. It is the political nature of the allegedly illegal activity that distinguishes the cases.

A majority of the faculty at Colby College approve of King and disapprove of the CIA. That is an entirely plausible personal view. But it is not the basis for denying students who disagree with it the right to hear from, or be recruited by, the CIA. Indeed, a majority of the Colby students apparently do not want to ban CIA recruiters—not that majority should rule in freedom of speech contexts. The college administration has yet to resolve the deadlock. If the faculty view prevails, the Colby students will be denied the very academic freedom faculty members insist on for themselves.

At Boston University last year, the administration tried to ban dormitory window banners that proclaimed opposition to the university's policy regarding divestment from South Africa. The students took the university to court and won. A Massachusetts law prevents private colleges, as well as government agencies, from denying citizens their civil rights and liberties.

The faculty at Colby should read the judge's opinion, which includes the following observations: "Indeed nowhere in our society is the protection of the free flow of ideas more important than in the university community, the quintessential marketplace of ideas. . . . Within the university, student dormitories play an important role for students' exercise of their freedom of expression, providing students with the only area reserved exclusively for their personal use. Such use, of course, includes the student's right of free speech. . . . Students at learning institutions have a right to engage in symbolic protest."

The Committee of Discipline at Massachusetts Institute of Technology did read the Boston University decision and acted consistently with it in a recent case. MIT has a policy on "sexually explicit" films that requires a committee to pass on whether the movie to be shown portrays sexuality "positively," "normally" and in a nonsexist manner.

My nephew, Adam, who is a junior at MIT, regarded the policy as objectionable; indeed, as objectionable as many people, including him, regard sexist films. He tried unsuccessfully to have it changed. Then he decided—on his own—to engage in an act of civil disobedience and show the controversial film *Deep Throat* on a video machine in his own dormitory lounge. Although that film had been declared constitutionally protected by a Cambridge court in a case involving Harvard students who showed it, it clearly was sexually explicit and probably in violation of the MIT policy. About 80 students—men and women—watched the film without incident.

The dean filed a formal complaint before the Committee on Discipline, and Adam defended himself by attacking the film policy as a violation of his constitutional rights and his academic freedom, as well as those of the viewers. After a long hearing, the committee agreed and dismissed all charges on the ground of academic freedom, in effect rendering the film policy inoperative. Now any student at MIT can decide for himself or herself which constitutionally protected films to show or watch on campus.

At Syracuse University, as well, students have a right to watch or listen to anyone they please, including obnoxious racists like Louis Farrakhan. Efforts to revoke a student government grant to bring Farrakhan to the campus were properly rebuffed—just as efforts to prevent a South African apologist for apartheid from speaking at Harvard were defeated. Both universities survived the controversy, and the students were the better educated for it. The irony is that some who supported freedom of speech for one racist opposed it for the other—and vice versa.

At my own law school, Harvard, a single student caused the cancellation of a scheduled speech by Adolfo Calero, the leader of the Nicaraguan Contras. Despite security precautions, he simply jumped on the podium in a threatening manner, and the proceedings stopped.

A committee has now been established to take steps to assure freedom of expression for all students, including those who wish to peacefully picket, heckle or otherwise protest the speakers, films, or other forms of expression. That is both good educational policy and good constitutional law.

November 24, 1987

139
A Double Standard
for Husband Killers

On a recent Oprah Winfrey show, the topic was "Is it open season for wives to kill their husbands?" Among the questions posed was whether a new double standard now exists: Can wives more easily claim "self-defense" when they kill abusive husbands than when the roles are reversed?

The impetus for this debate was a number of wives who have killed their husbands and then successfully defended themselves by putting their dead victims on trial. Most of the women in the studio audience, at least those who spoke up, were cheering for the female vigilantes. To those watching the show, the operative rule would now seem to be: If your husband has beaten you, don't leave him or call the police. Get a gun and blow him away!

Popular culture—TV, movies, newspapers and magazines—often has a greater impact on people's behavior than the law itself. Indeed, most Americans learn their law not from dusty statute books, but from the manner in which cases are treated in the media. (Even my students sometimes confuse Judge Wapner and the verdicts reached by juries in "L.A. Law" with the precedents of real courts.)

Following "The Burning Bed," a TV movie in which an abused wife set fire to her sleeping husband's mattress, there were several real life bed-burnings and similar examples of "self-help." Can we now anticipate a slew of Bernadine Goetzes and Clintene Eastwoods pointing loaded magnums at their abusive husbands and snarling "C'mon, make my marriage?"

The most extreme case, of course, was the recent acquittal of a Queens, New York woman, Stella Valenza, who had paid three assassins to murder her abusive husband. Valenza and her hit men tried three times, succeeding only in wounding her husband. Although not a single state would authorize self-defense on these facts—the defendant must be in imminent danger and have no recourse to the police—a jury of Bernhard Goetz think-alikes unanimously acquitted Valenza of all fourteen counts of attempted murder, conspiracy to murder, and weapons charges. (It will be interesting to see what happens to the three male assassins when they are tried separately for attempted murder.) The Queens jurors obviously intended to send a message to abusive husbands: In our neighborhoods, the punishment for abusing a wife is death, or at least the risk of death, by hired assassin.

Several women on the Oprah Winfrey show bragged that they, too, had shot, knifed, scalded, or otherwise maimed their abusive husbands. The audience cheered as one woman explained why scalding a man with boiling grits was better than using plain old water: "Grits stick longer and leave more permanent scars." They listened attentively as a caller justified her decision not to leave her husband: "That would be too good for him. I want to live with him and make his life hell until the day he dies." That is a perfect prescription for madness—or homicide.

The problem of physically abusive husbands is a serious and widespread one. Police in many cities do not respond adequately to what they regard as "domestic quarrels." Many men believe that a marriage ceremony gives the husband a license to beat, rape, and maim their wives. The apparent increase in self-help violence by wives is obviously a symptom of this deep societal problem and of the law's inability—or unwillingness—to take spouse abuse seriously and offer real protection to battered women. But vigilantism is not the answer for several reasons.

First of all, it won't work. Men also have guns and knives. An escalation of domestic violence will cause more deaths and injuries among wives. The fact that more husbands will also be killed may satisfy the lust for vengeance among some, but it will not bring back to life the dead mothers, daughters, and wives who also will be killed in the increasing exchange of violence.

Second, although some women—like Valenza—may be able to talk their way out of jail by putting their husbands on trial, most juries will continue to follow the law and convict the guilty wives. These verdicts do not make the same kinds of headlines that acquittals do.

Finally, it is simply wrong for anyone to kill when there is a lawful alternative that can save lives. Abusive husbands should be separated from their wives and made to bear the appropriate punishment—including imprisonment and payment for relocation and support.

The law cannot be different for men and for women. There cannot be a double standard for self-defense based on gender. To be sure, the size and strength of the combatants should be taken into account when a genuine case of self-defense is presented. But when the defendant has carefully planned the assassination of an abusive spouse, the rules must be the same for an abused wife as for an abused husband. No one is empowered by the law to become judge, jury, and executioner, exacting revenge after the fact. That is the role of the law alone.

January 5, 1988

140
No More Perry Mason Surprise Witnesses

Remember the old Perry Mason ploy? The defendant is about to be convicted of murder. The evidence against him seems overwhelming. Suddenly, the great defense attorney snatches victory from the jaws of defeat by dramatically summoning to the stand his surprise witness.

The hapless prosecutor expresses shock as the witness points the finger of guilt at no one else but the prosecutor's own star witness—the one who had falsely accused Mason's client of the crime. The exposed perpetrator confesses. Perry Mason is embraced by his grateful client. Justice is done.

You may still be able to see "surprise witnesses" in old reruns of courtroom dramas, but from now on the script will have to be rewritten. The Supreme Court recently ruled that a judge may refuse to allow a defense attorney to call a surprise witness. Of course, it's a bit more complicated than that, but at the bottom, that is the message of *Taylor* v. *Illinois*.

Ray Taylor was charged with attempting to murder Jack Bridges in a street fight involving several people. There was a conflict in the testimony. Prosecution witnesses said they saw Taylor shoot Bridges. But defense witnesses testified that Bridges was accidentally shot by his own brother, who was trying to protect him during the encounter. It was a classic case of which witnesses the jury would believe.

Along comes the surprise witness. On the second day of trial, the defendant's lawyer tried to call a witness who was prepared to testify that he had seen the Bridges brothers with guns before the shooting. This would have lent some support to the defense claim that one of the Bridges brothers had shot the other.

The problem was that Illinois, like other states, has a rule requiring the defense attorney to notify the prosecution in advance of the entire witness list, except in extraordinary circumstances. Taylor's defense attorney had violated that rule.

There are many possible reasons why a defense lawyer would not include a witness on a pretrial list: The witness may have come forward—or been discovered—only after the trial began; the witness may be afraid of harassment from the person he intends to finger; the lawyer may simply have been lazy, forgetful, or negligent; or the lawyer may be trying to make it more difficult for the prosecution, caught unaware, to impeach or contradict the surprise witness.

In the Taylor case, the trial judge apparently believed that the defense attorney had made a deliberate tactical decision to catch the prosecution off guard. The judge also thought that the testimony of the surprise witness was "suspect."

The issue of whether the testimony was suspect should, of course, have been left to the jury.

The trial judge could have called a recess and permitted the prosecution a day or two to prepare its rebuttal. The defense attorney could also have been disciplined for violating the Illinois rule. But instead of taking these simple steps—steps that would have preserved the rights of both the defendant and the prosecution—the judge decided to "punish" the defendant for the conduct of his lawyer by totally excluding the testimony. The jury never heard this important witness and those who might have contradicted him.

Without this witness—and the evidence that the Bridges brothers were armed—the jury had little choice but to convict.

The Supreme Court affirmed the conviction as well as the notion that it is proper to punish a defendant for the misconduct of his lawyer. Although, as the dissenting justices pointed out, "there was no evidence that the defendant played any role" in his lawyer's decision, the majority justices ruled that barring the witness was an appropriate "penalty" for the defense attorney's violation of the rule.

The dissent argued that this amounts to visiting "the sins of the lawyer on the innocent client." It also potentially distorts "the truth-seeking process by excluding material evidence of innocence in a criminal case." It is ironic that most of the majority justices oppose the so-called "exclusionary rule," which keeps evidence of guilt from the jury when a police officer or prosecutor violate the Constitution. They argue that victims and other citizens should not be punished because the constable blundered. But they seem eager to impose a similar "exclusionary rule" on the defendant's ability to give evidence of his innocence when his lawyer has violated a nonconstitutional rule.

The prospect of an innocent defendant spending years in prison, or even being executed, because his lawyer failed to notify the prosecution of a surprise witness simply is not fair.

February 9, 1988

141
Students Can Fight Censors

Dear High School Editor, I know how disappointed you must be in the U.S. Supreme Court's recent decision authorizing school principals to censor your school newspaper. Many concerned citizens are upset at the negative message this sends to high school students about freedom of speech and journalistic responsibility. We are also concerned about the message it sends to high school principals: that they are relatively free to impose their own views about controversial subjects—such as divorce, birth control, and sex—on a captive audience of public school students.

We should all be proud of the student editors of the Hazelwood, Missouri, *Spectrum*, who took their censorship complaint all the way to the nation's highest court. If ever student journalists proved they could act responsibly, Cathy Kuhlmeier and her fellow editors certainly did by the manner in which they responded to their principal's heavy-handed censorship. Even though they lost, it was a good civics lesson.

The Supreme Court's decision does not mark the last word about the freedom of high school students to publish uncensored newspapers. This open letter is intended to encourage you to take a somewhat different path from the one taken by most high school papers today. Do what real newspapers do: Become independent! Form a journalism club outside the formal structure of the school. Start small—perhaps a one-page typed and photocopied newsletter. Try to get a few local merchants to place small ads. Charge a nickel a copy. Compete with the school's "official" paper. That's how Thomas Paine and John Peter Zenger began.

The school cannot censor outside newspapers—it would be good journalism and good education. It will teach you about the real world of newspaper. You must sell your product, cultivate readers, find advertisers. You must compete in the open marketplace of ideas. If you are to succeed, your paper must be better than the principal's paper.

There has always been something anomalous about officially sponsored school newspapers. It is difficult to expect those who pay the piper not to try to call the tune. This is especially true when the official newspaper is a monopoly.

Even independent newspapers have piper-players who try to call tunes: large advertisers, subscribers, conglomerate owners. But at least they are not government officials. And let there be no mistake: School principals are government officials, answerable to school boards and other politicians.

My advice is to try to capitalize on the widespread outrage of many educators, journalists, and civil libertarians over the Supreme Court's decision. Try to get some seed money—a few hundred dollars for start-up costs—from those who believe in freedom of the press. Approach local newspapers, television stations, and magazines with a proposal and a modest request.

I hereby offer $500 of my own to any group of responsible students at the Hazelwood East High School who are prepared to continue in the tradition of Cathy Kuhlmeier and her fellow editors who challenged censorship. If you want to start an independent newspaper reporting on matters of interest to the students, my small contribution will probably cover the printing cost for two or three issues. Then you're on your own. I will not demand the right to see copy in advance. I am confident that you will exercise your freedom responsibly.

There is no assurance that the principal will approve. Few of those in power like to be criticized by those whom they cannot control. He many even try to stop you from distributing it on the campus. And the law is unclear about whether he can. The Supreme Court, in the Hazelwood case, went out of its way to leave that issue open. Test the issue: Try to distribute your independent newspaper within the school grounds. If the principal tries to stop you, sue him. Or distribute the paper outside the school gates.

There is no doubt that the current Supreme Court majority is seeking to cut back on the rights of high school students. The majority of justices seem to have more faith in the exercise of power by the authorities than in the exercise of rights by students. The American way is to fight back when your rights are being curtailed—even against school principals, and even against the Supreme Court.

The independent school newspaper is one way to do it in a civilized, mature, and constructive manner. The eyes of the nation will be upon you. Show the American people that high school students can exercise their First Amendment rights responsibly, in good taste, and with journalistic integrity. Show the world that censorship—of a high school newspaper in Hazelwood, Missouri, or anywhere else—is not the American way.

January 26, 1988

142
Murder by Magazine

The case is a civil libertarian's nightmare. A murder victim's family is suing *Soldier of Fortune* magazine, claiming that an advertisement it ran led directly to the killing of Sandra Black. That macho journal of guns, guts, and gore used to run classified ads such as the following one, which is the subject of the lawsuit:

> "Ex-Marines. 67–69 Nam Vets. EX-DI, weapons specialist—jungle warfare. Pilot. M.E. High Risk Assignments. US or overseas."

When Robert Black read that ad, he wrote to John Wayne (what else?) Hearn, its author, and inquired about seeing his gun collection. One thing led to another and soon the two gun fanciers were talking business: Black would pay Hearn $10,000 to murder Black's wife. (Black was having an affair with another woman.) This was nothing new for killer Hearn. It would be his third murder for hire in nineteen days. The assassination business, it appears, was thriving, now that there was a place to advertise one's lethal talents.

The crime was quickly solved. The husband who contracted the killing was sentenced to death and is awaiting execution, while the actual trigger-man is serving a life sentence. Suing either of them would do the victim's family little good, since neither has any money. But *Soldier of Fortune* magazine, and its parent company, Omega Group Ltd., have—what lawyers aptly call—"deep pockets."

The magazine is defending on First Amendment grounds. It claims that the ad was constitutionally protected free speech, which does not specifically mention any illegal activities: "The ad is a very plain vanilla ad, the kind you would expect to find in a magazine of that type," says that magazine's lawyer, apparently missing the irony of his own admission.

Au contraire, responds the family's lawyer: It was "an unequivocal offer to commit domestic criminal services." Indeed, he says he will prove that the magazine was aware of the ad's implications, and that "over twenty felonies in a two month period" can be connected to classified ads run by *Soldier of Fortune*.

The reason this case keeps civil libertarians awake at night is that the lawsuit is over words that are claimed to have caused violence—a concept that has broad implications beyond this lawsuit. Not all words in all contexts are, of course, constitutionally protected: a Mafia boss who orders one of his soldiers to "fire" at a rival gangster is no more protected than a hooligan who falsely and maliciously shouts "fire"—or sets off a fire alarm—in a crowded theater. The reason their words are not protected in these contexts is that they are stimuli to immediate—almost automatic— actions that the government may lawfully seek to prevent.

An ad in a magazine is quite different, especially when it is the magazine and publisher that are being sued, rather than the author of the pregnantly ambiguous ad.

To illustrate the problem imagine the following sitution: Husband hires killer to murder his wife; they agree that the murder is to take place when husband is in Europe with an alibi; killer will be informed of the day by a coded ad in the local newspaper that says "Happy Birthday Gwendolyn;" the day after that ad appears, killer murders Gwendolyn. Surely the newspaper is not responsible for the murder, even though its ad led directly to it. A newspaper or magazine cannot be held responsible for unanticipated misuses of its advertising columns.

But the issue in the *Soldier of Fortune* case is precisely whether the magazine should have anticipated that its not-so-vanilla ads would be used by professional assassins and criminal clients who would make use of such ignoble *and illegal* services. If the victim's family can prove that the magazine was, in fact, on notice that these ambiguous "high-risk assignment" ads were invitations to assassinations, they may very well be able to collect from the magazine.

If *Soldier of Fortune* is held responsible for the Black murder, the implications—both civil and criminal—for other magazines could be staggering. Will magazines that run "personal" ads be held responsible for rapes committed—or for venereal disease contracted—during dates arranged as a result of the ads? Will magazines which run ordinary gun advertisements be responsible for death or injuries resulting from weapons sold to criminals or crazies?

The courts have already struck down as unconstitutional several attempts to hold publishers of alleged pornography responsible for assaults purportedly committed by those who have been exposed to offending smut. The fear is that if porn publishers can be sued by rape victims today, will publishers of revolutionary tracts be responsible tomorrow for violence caused by those who read—and act on—the writings of Lenin, Hitler,

Moses, Jesus, Malcolm X, and Meyer Kahane? And if publishers are responsible, why not booksellers, libraries, and universities?

Unless it can be shown that *Soldier of Fortune* magazine was aware that the ad in question was a coded invitation to assassination, the safer course for the First Amendment would be to limit responsibility to the killers themselves, and let the magazine—which is no longer running these ads— off the hook.

February 1988

The jury found the magazine liable and awarded plantiffs $9 million in damages. An appeal is being taken.

143
There's More to Law Than Helping the Rich Get Richer

As 40,000 new law students begin classes, the question is again being raised: What does the future hold for the American legal profession?

We are already the most overlawyered country in history. There are nearly 700,000 practicing lawyers in a population of 237 million—a ratio of one for every 339 citizens. At the current rate of growth we may have a million lawyers before the end of the century.

Despite these numbers, most people who need an attorney can't get one. In that sense we have too few lawyers—or at least too few who are willing to represent clients who cannot pay megabuck fees. The vast majority of private lawyers' time is devoted to helping a small minority of wealthy people preserve or enhance their wealth. Working-class Americans, not to mention the poor, simply can't afford the three-figure hourly fees that many lawyers now charge. And so these citizens often fail to take advantage of their rights. The upshot is that they lose material benefits to which they are entitled—and worse.

The most striking example of the failure of the Bar to service public needs can be seen on the death rows of several states. It may be hard to believe, but nearly one-third of the more than 1,600 inmates awaiting execution do not have access to one of our 700,000 practicing lawyers.

Each of them did, of course, have a lawyer—not always one of the highest quality—during the trial itself and on the first appeal. But many states refuse to pay for a lawyer to continue representing the condemned inmate after this. And many death-penalty cases are won only afterward— on writs of habeas corpus or on review by the Supreme Court. Though some courts and anti-death-penalty organizations do provide lawyers at the last stages of some cases, a large number of death row inmates remain unrepresented at crucial points. Without the assistance of a lawyer, the death row inmate has no real access to the courts as he confronts the law's most extreme penalty.

This is a scandal; it is as if all the medical doctors in America were performing elective cosmetic surgery while the emergency wards of our hospitals had no doctors. Now we are seeing many of our most talented young lawyers getting out of law altogether. Realizing that the practice of corporate law is just another business, they are looking to the bottom line, which says that there is more money to be made in investment banking.

But what about the real lawyers—the Clarence Darrow and Ralph Nader types who care about the quality of justice, the protection of consumers, the defense of underdogs? There is a great need, and indeed market, for more lawyers of this kind. They may never make the millions of dollars to which bankers and corporate lawyers aspire. But they can do good—and also do pretty well at the same time.

The good that they can do is virtually unlimited. There are frontiers of the law that have barely been explored and that certainly need all the legal talent that they can attract. These include the rights of the homeless, the handicapped, and the illiterate; international human rights of dissidents; consumer and employee rights in relation to large corporations; access to medical care by the aged and infirm, and the rights of victims and witnesses.

But few lawyers seem to be thinking in these terms today. The lure of the big buck is too strong. How much more civilized it seems to sip cognac in the penthouse of a skyscraper discussing a merger than to drink coffee out of paper cups in the basement of a rundown tenement planning a rent strike. How much more pleasant it must be to sit across the conference table from a corporate president than across the bars from a mugger.

But the legal profession has the responsibility to help those who most need it, not only those who can best afford it. "How much justice can you afford?" reads the sign atop many a lawyer's desk.

When I begin teaching my first-year criminal-law class I hurl a challenge at the statistics showing that nearly all of them will end up representing the superrich, and I dare them to defy the odds by devoting at least some of their professional lives to representing the needy. I shock them by predicting that more of them may end up as criminal defendants than as criminal lawyers. Many of them respond by sincerely insisting that they will work for the downtrodden. But every year the trend continues: More and more of our best and brightest sail off into the corporate horizon, leaving behind their roots and responsibilities.

Maybe this year will be different. Maybe more of the 40,000 new law students will understand that there is more to the noble profession of law than helping the superrich get even richer. Maybe the organized Bar will finally get around to recognizing its responsibility to the vast majority of our citizens. Maybe.

September 4, 1986

Thematic Overview

Although the columns are arranged in roughly chronological order, they can easily be read—or assigned—by subject matter. A breakdown by the major subjects follows:

Freedom of speech censorship, and the First Amendment: Columns 16, 17, 18, 23, 24, 25, 26, 39, 40, 58, 63, 72, 83, 88, 94, 114, 116, 127, 138, 141.

Pornography, obscenity, censorship, and the First Amendment: Columns 30, 52, 57, 62, 71, 72, 78, 86, 87.

The Fourth and Fifth Amendments and the Exclusionary Rules: Columns 3, 4, 7, 8, 43, 50, 89, 91, 105, 109, 140.

The death penalty: Columns 27, 47, 90, 99, 100.

Church and state: Columns 13, 48, 53, 72, 119.

The Supreme Court, justices and judges: Columns 92, 93, 98, 101, 102, 103, 117, 122, 123, 124, 125, 126, 127, 128, 137.

Terrorism: Columns 32, 33, 70, 108.

Iran-contra: Columns 105, 120, 121, 124.

White collar crime: Columns 29, 56, 106.

AIDS: Columns 64, 65, 66, 115, 136.

Rape: Columns 20, 34, 45, 54, 56.

Seat belts and car crimes: Columns 6, 12, 49, 79, 112.

Vigilantism and self defense: Columns 35, 36, 39

Science and technology: Columns 5, 22.

Lawyers and law firms: Columns 1, 2.

Conservative and liberal hypocrisy: Columns 34, 38, 39, 40, 60, 61, 67, 73, 79, 89, 94, 104, 105, 116, 121, 138, 140.

Index of Cases

Case Citation and Subsequent History

29   *In re Union Carbide Corp. Gas Plant Disaster at Bhopal*, 809 F.2d 195, *cert. denied, Executive Committee Members* v. *Union of India*, __ U.S. __ 98 L.Ed.2d 150, 108 S.Ct. 199 (1987)

31   *Falwell* v. *Flynt*, see column 137.

32, 33   *In re Doherty*, 599 F. Supp. 270 (S.D. N.Y.) *dismissed*, 615 F. Supp. 755 (S.D. N.Y. 1985), *later proceeding, Doherty* v. *United States Dept. of Justice*, 775 F.2d 49 (2d Cir. 1985).

34   *People* v. *Liberta*, 64 N.Y.2d 152, 485 N.Y.S.2d 207, 474 N.E.2d 567 (1984).

34   *Columbia* v. *Bouie*, 239 S.C. 570, 124 S.E.2d 332, *rev'd*, 378 U.S. 347 (1964).

35–37   *People* v. *Goetz*, 68 N.Y.2d 96, 497 N.E.2d 41, 506, N.Y.S.2d 18 (1986).

41   *R* v. *Zundel*, 56 C.R. (3d) 1 (Ont. Ca. 1987).

42   *Ake* v. *Oklahoma*, 470 U.S. 68 (1985).

42   *Gideon* v. *Wainwright*, 372 U.S. 335 (1963).

43   *Oregon* v. *Eistad*, 470 U.S. 298 (1985).

44   *Shepard* v. *Maxwell*, 384 U.S. 333 (1966).

45, 46   *People* v. *Dotson*, 99 Ill. App.3d 117, 54 Ill. Dec. 416, 424 N.E.2d 1319 (1st Dist. 1981), *post conviction proceeding*, 163 Ill. App. 3d 419, 114 Ill. Dec. 563, 516 N.E.2d 718 (1st Dist. 1987).

47   *Tennessee* v. *Garner*, 471 U.S. 1 (1985).

48   *Nally* v. *Grace Community Church*, 157 Cal. App.2d 912, 204 Cal.Rptr. 303 (2d Dist. 1984), *later proceedings*, 194 Cal. App.3d 1147, 240 Cal. Rptr. 215 (2d Dist. 1987), *rev. granted*, 243 Cal. Rptr. 86, 747 P.2d 527 (1987).

50   *People* v. *Carney*, 34 Cal.3d 597, 194 Cal. Rptr. 500, 668 P.2d 807 (1983), *rev'd, California* v. *Carney*, 471 U.S. 386 (1985).

51   *Commonwealth* v. *Stowell*, 389 Mass. 171, 449 N.E.2d 357 (1983).

52   *Jaffree* v. *James*, 544 F. Supp. 727 (S.D. Ala. 1982).

53   *Wallace* v. *Jaffree*, 472 U.S. 38 (1985).

53   *Lynch* v. *Donnelly*, 465 U.S. 668 (1984).

55   *State* v. *von Bulow*, 475 A.2d 995 (R.I. 1984), *cert. denied*, 469 U.S. 875 (1984).

56   *People* v. *MacKay*, 490 N.E.2d 74 (Ill. App. 1st 1986).

57   *J-R Distributors, Inc.* v. *Eikenberry*, 725 F.2d 482 (9th Cir. 1984), *rev'd, Brockett* v. *Spokane Arcades, Inc.*, 472 U.S. 491 (1985).

58   *In re Snyder*, 734 F.2d 334 (8th Cir. 1984), *rev'd*, 472 U.S. 634 (1985).

60–61   *Polovchak* v. *Meese*, 774 F.2d 731 (7th Cir. 1985).

63   *Spiritual Psychic Science Church of Truth, Inc.*, v. *City of Azusa*, 39 Cal. 3d 501, 703 P.2d 1119, 217 Cal. Rptr. 225 (1985).

68   *Interstate Circuit, Inc.* v. *City of Dallas*, 390 U.S. 676 (1968).

69   *Kelley* v. *R.G. Industries*, 304 Md. 124, 497 A.2d 1143 (1985).

70   *Robinson* v. *California*, 370 U.S. 660 (1962); *In re Doherty*, 599 F. Supp. 270 (S.D. N.Y.) *dismissed*, 615 F. Supp. 755 (S.D. N.Y. 1985).

71   *American Booksellers Assoc.* v. *Hudnut*, 771 F.2d 323 (7th Cir. 1985), *aff'd*, 475 U.S. 1001 (1986).

76   *Nix* v. *Whiteside*, 106 S.Ct. 1328 (1986).

77   *Carter* v. *Rafferty*, 621 F. Supp. 533 (1985).

78   *Roe* v. *Wade*, 410 U.S. 113 (1973). *Kingsley International Pictures Corp.* v. *Regents of the University of the State of New York*, 360 U.S. 684 (1959).

81   *United Steelworkers of America* v. *Weber*, 443 U.S. 193 (1979.) *Local Number 93, International Association of Firefighters* v. *City of Cleveland*, 478 U.S. 501 (1986). *Local 28 of the Sheet Metal Workers' International Association* v. *Equal Employment Opportunity Commission*, 478 U.S. 421 (1986).

82   *Nix* v. *Whiteside*, 106 S.Ct. 1328 (1986).

83   *Bethel School District No. 403* v. *Fraser*, 478 U.S. 675 (1986). *Tinker* v. *Des Moines Independent School District*, 393 U.S. 503 (1969). *Tinker* v. *Des Moines Independent School District*, 393 U.S. 503 (1969).

84–85   *Bowers* v. *Hardwick*, 478 U.S. 186 (1986).

86   *Playboy Enterprises* v. *Meese*, No. 86-1346 (D. D.C. July 3, 1986).

88   *Providence Journal Co.* v. *Federal Bureau of Investigation*, 602 F.2d 1010 (1979) *cert. denied*, 444 U.S. 1071 (1980).

90   *Lockhart* v. *McCree*, 476 U.S. 162 (1986).

91   *California* v. *Ciraolo*, 476 U.S. 207 (1986).

99   *McCleskey* v. *Kemp*, 107 S.Ct. 1756 (1987).

100   *Tison* v. *Arizona*, 107 S.Ct. 1676 (1987). *Enmund* v. *Florida*, 458 U.S. 782 (1982). *McClesky* v. *Kemp*, 107 S.Ct. 1756 (1987).

101   *Brown* v. *Board of Education*, 347 U.S. 483 (1954).

103   *Durham* v. *United States*, 214 F.2d 862 (D.C. Cir. 1954).

106   *Carpenter [w/Winans]* v. *United States*, 108 S.Ct. 316 (1987).

109   *Miranda* v. *Arizona*, 384 U.S. 436 (1966).

117   *In re Cooper*, 821 F.2nd 833 (1st Cir. 1987).

118   *United States* v. *Salerno*, 107 S.Ct. 2095 (1987).

119   *Paul* v. *Watchtower Bible and Tract Soc. of New York, Inc.*, 819 F.2d 875 (1987).

122   *University of California Regents* v. *Bakke*, 438 U.S. 265 (1978). *Bowers* v. *Hardwick*, 478 U.S. 186 (1986). *McClesky* v. *Kemp*, 107 S.Ct. 1756 (1987). *Booth* v. *Maryland*, 107 S.Ct. 2529 (1987).

140   *Taylor* v. *Illinois*, 108 S.Ct. 646 (1988).

141   *Hazelwood School District* v. *Kuhlmeier*, 108 S.Ct. 562 (1988).